Backcountry Skiing

California's Eastern Sierra 2nd Edition

200+ Ski Descents Covering the Entire Eastern Sierra from Mount Whitney to Matterhorn Peak.

By Dan Mingori & Nate Greenberg

Dedication

This book is dedicated to all the snow-loving dogs out there. The true powder hounds. We know you love the snow even more than we do, and we hope this book inspires and motivates your owners to get you out there a little more often.

Acknowledgements

This book, and the effort required to research, compile, and design it has been a labor of love. Though Dan and I are the authors, we could not have completed it without the help of many of our good friends.

In particular, we would like to thank our designer, McKenzie Long, who not only put up with us through the process, but helped refresh the layout and make the book more user friendly. Dave Pegg at Wolverine Publishing has been incredibly supportive from the very first edition. Ali Feinberg put an incredible amount of time into proofreading content, providing feedback and guidance, putting up with Nate, while also serving as a great backcountry partner. Tony Dublino and John Ellsworth provided some much needed input and beta on terrain and approaches.

But the creation of a guidebook goes far beyond the tasks of writing and editing, and this book would not have been possible without a group of dedicated and reliable partners, joining in on the "research." Compiling a list of names isn't easy for fear of forgetting someone, but our hats are off to: Jim Barnes, Kevin Smith, Jason Templeton, Brian Robinette, Jon Crowley, Brett Lotz, Frank Fazzino, Dan Molnar, Christian Pondella, and countless others. Yee ha!

— Nate Greenberg & Dan Mingori

BACKCOUNTRY SKIING CALIFORNIA'S EASTERN SIERRA: SECOND EDITION
Authors: Dan Mingori and Nate Greenberg.
Maps: Nate Greenberg.
Photographs: All photographs by Dan Mingori, unless otherwise credited.
Design: Wolverine Publishing, LLC and McKenzie Long at Cardinal Innovative.
Published and distributed by Wolverine Publishing, LLC.

Cover photo:
Jon Crowley beneath Mt. Dade (page 239). *Photo: Dan Mingori.*

Opening page photo:
Chelsea Morgan skiing Mt. Tinemaha (page 316). *Photo: Dan Mingori.*

International Standard Book Number:
978-193839317-4

Wolverine Publishing is continually expanding its range of guidebooks. If you have a manuscript or idea for a book, or would like to find out more about our company and publications, contact:
Dave Pegg
Wolverine Publishing
PO Box 195
New Castle, CO 81647
970-876-0269
dave@wolverinepublishing.com
www.wolverinepublishing.com

Printed in China.

Brian Outhwaite dropping into the Mammoth Crest.

WARNING!

Skiing and snowboarding are dangerous sports that can result in death, paralysis or serious injury. Read and understand this warning before using this book.

This book is intended as a reference tool for advanced/expert skiers and snowboarders. The terrain it describes can be or is extremely dangerous and requires a high degree of ability and experience to negotiate. This book is not intended for inexperienced/novice skiers and snowboarders. Nor is it intended as an instructional manual. If you are unsure of your ability to handle any circumstances that may arise, employ the services of a professional instructor or guide.

The information in this book is unverified, and the authors and publisher cannot guarantee its accuracy. Assessments of the difficulty of and risks associated with the terrain are based on opinions and are entirely subjective. They depend to a large extent on the experience of the rider and the conditions on the mountain, which can change from hour to hour, day to day. Snow depths can play a large part in the relative difficulty and danger of the terrain described herein. Numerous hazards exist that are not described and which are not marked on the mountains. Skiing or snowboarding any terrain in this book, regardless of its description or rating, may cause death, paralysis or injury.

Please take all precautions and use your own ability, evaluation, and judgment to assess the risks of your terrain choice on a particular day, rather than relying on the information in this book.

The easiest runs in this book would be considered black diamond terrain at virtually any ski resort in the US — the majority of them would be double black diamond, or harder. In the backcountry, you will encounter danger, hazards, and conditions that you won't find at any ski resort in the US. In addition to expert skiing ability, you must also possess at least a basic level of mountaineering and route finding skills. The ability to use a map and compass are essential.

It is imperative that you own, carry, and know how to use an avalanche beacon, shovel, and probe when skiing the terrain described in this book. More important is an understanding of avalanche assessment and safety procedures. Know what to look for, know the signs, and know when to turn around. Your cell phone will most likely not work in the mountains, and help is usually very far away.

The authors and publisher make no representations or warranties, expressed or implied, of any kind regarding the contents of this book, and expressly disclaim any representation or warranty regarding the accuracy or reliability of information contained herein. There are no warranties of fitness for a particular purpose or that this book or the information in it are merchantable.

The user assumes all risk associated with the use of this book and with the activities of skiing and snowboarding.

OR OUTDOOR RESEARCH
DESIGNED BY ADVENTURE

Contents

37

70

75

235

299

339

Advertisers

Now it's your turn...
Sierra Mountain Guides
Experience the World Class skiing of the Eastern Sierra with an AMGA certified ski guide.
www.sierramtnguides.com | (760) 648-1122

Introduction

Ben Kahn skiing Birch Mountain.

The Eastern Sierra

Located far away from the cities and beaches to the south and the hustle and bustle of the Tahoe Basin to the north, the Eastern Sierra is an oasis for mountain enthusiasts. The "Eastside" is the heart of the Sierra Nevada, comprised of the highest peaks in the range and characterized by open mountain vistas, vast amounts of public land, and pristine Wilderness areas. With canyons that cut west from Highway 395 in the valley below, the 150 mile stretch of mountains that spans the distance between Lone Pine and Bridgeport is truly a backcountry skier's paradise.

The Eastern Sierra, also known as the High Sierra, offers something for everyone—from the novice backcountry user to extreme skiers alike. For those with the time and energy to devote to earning their turns, there is a lifetime of possibilities here. Within this portion of the range, you will find incredible geologic and topographic diversity—which translates into incredible skiing diversity. Each region has its own unique character, and the ski tours and descents described on the pages that follow will take you into some of the most amazing public land this country has to offer. From broad, high elevation plateaus, to exposed knife-edge ridges, the Eastern Sierra will not disappoint. The skiing here is arguably some of the best in world, and with the high peaks, deep snowpack, and pleasant weather, you can enjoy skiing from late fall into June or later.

The majority of the ski descents in the range are found on the north and east aspects of the mountains. As winter storms come in from the coast, they are typically accompanied by high winds blowing from the south and/or west. The snow is subsequently deposited on the leeward slopes. Coincidentally, these are also the aspects that are most visible from the towns and roads that sit at the base of the range. From the valley floor, the chutes, bowls, and peaks tower above, and beg to be skied.

Highway 395 is one of the most scenic drives in the country. The Mono County section is a California Scenic Byway, and was recently recognized as one of the five most beautiful highways in America. The highway

Overview Map

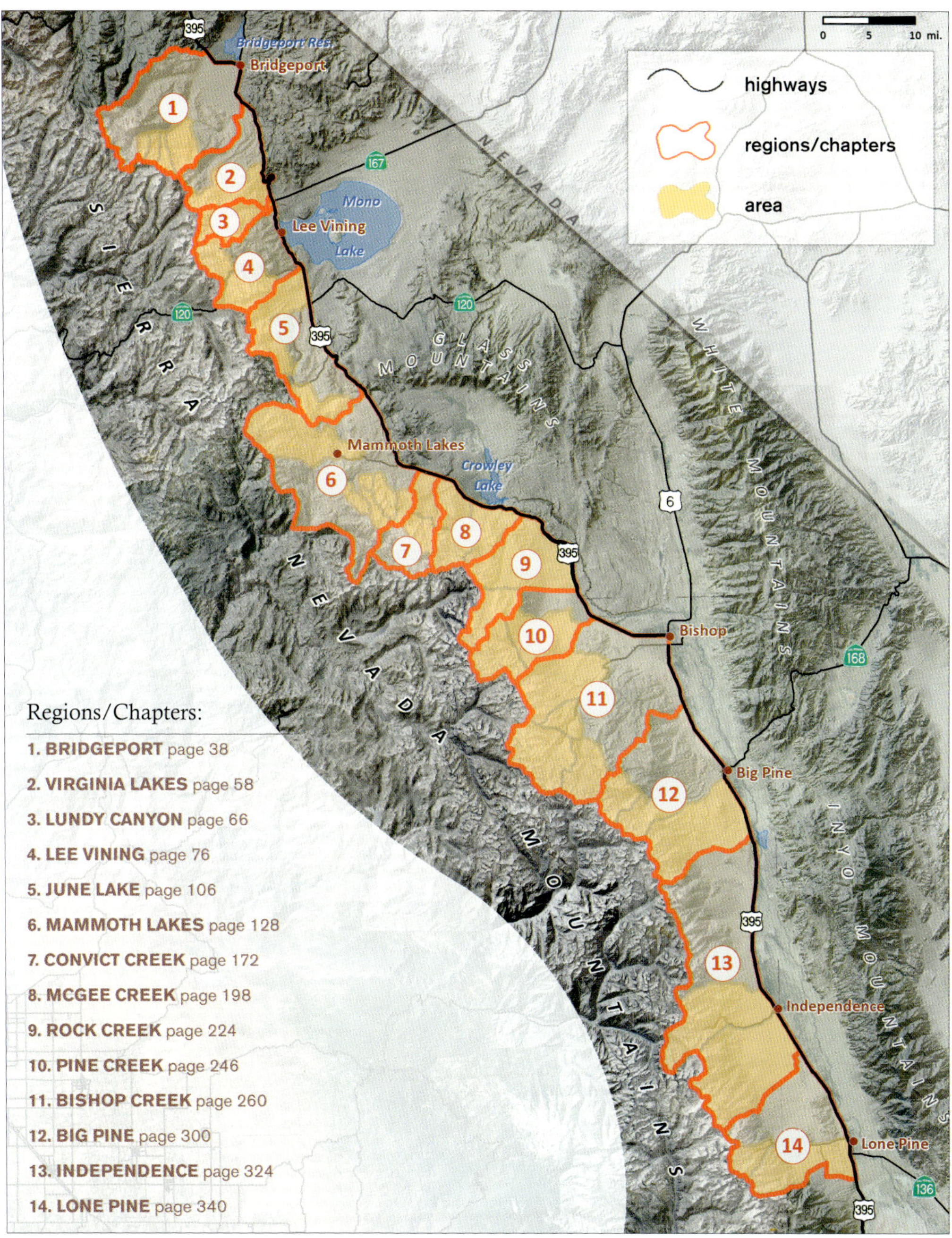

is the primary transportation corridor along the east side of the range, and as you travel along it, you are treated to stellar view of this endless playground.

The terrain and relief of the Eastside is often overwhelming for people who have never been here before. Foothills are virtually non-existent. Instead, a high desert valley immediately abuts the steep peaks to the west, which in places rise nearly 10,000' above you. Though countless people gaze upon this terrain, the majority of it is untouched during the winter months. The major population centers of the state are several hours away from this remote part of California, and with less than

A storm breaks over Mt. Tom.

50,000 people living in the immediate area, it is easy to find yourself all alone as you journey into the hills.

Much of the terrain covered in this book can be characterized by deep valleys with chutes, couloirs, and rocky faces cutting through the steep canyon walls. Near the head of the valleys and canyons, bowls and snowfields abound, creating a mix of practically every type of terrain imaginable.

A unique characteristic of the Eastside are the large drainages which cut west, deep into the primarily north-south trending crestline. In almost every one of these drainages is a summer road, meaning that during the shoulder season access to the high country is relatively direct and easy. That said, fairly long approaches are common, particularly during the months of January and February when the snowline can reach the valley floor and make these roads impassable. As you drive along Highway 395, the peaks seem close and easily accessible, but as you start skiing towards your destination, this perspective quickly changes. Skiing away from the parking lot, you'll notice your car getting smaller and smaller without the mountains seeming to get any closer!

Most of the high country is accessed via drainages that lead from the base of the peaks to the valley floor below. Some are easily navigable; others choked with brush or lined with steep canyon walls. Some peaks are accessed via prominent ridge lines or open faces; others require scrambling through 3rd Class terrain.

Snow conditions vary drastically here, and you must be able to handle anything that Jack Frost and Mother Nature can dish out. While we all dream of finding bottomless powder, the reality is often very different. With a huge range of elevation and terrain, it's possible to find nearly every type of snow on any given day in the High Sierra.

The wind is the number one enemy of skiers in the range, and the sun can either work in your favor, or turn perfect snow into mashed potatoes. Many people think that only wet-and-heavy snow falls in California, with the term "Sierra Cement" often thrown around. But don't let the myths discourage you: the east side of the range receives much drier snow than the west, and what does fall here allows for skiing on very steep slopes with relatively stable conditions. While Utah and Wyoming may boast lighter fluff, we in the Sierra can ski the lines that our brethren in the Rockies can only stare at in wistful wonder.

We've done our best to provide you with the basic information you need to find success, while leaving enough out to allow for adventure. Flip through the book, find something that strikes you, and have at it.

Welcome to the Eastside and some of the greatest skiing in the Lower 48!

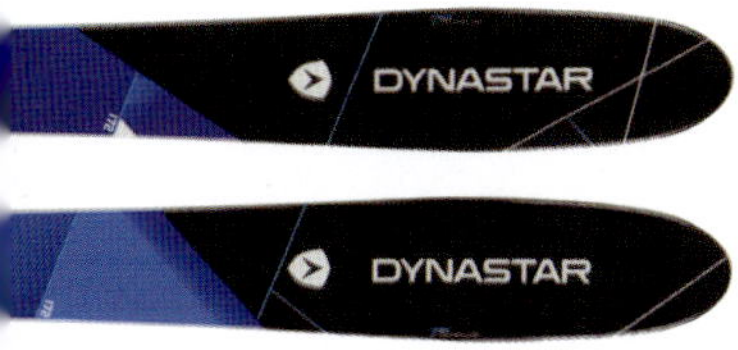

ARMADA
ARMADA
JP
AUCLAIR
PHOTO: DANIEL RÖNNBÄCK

Seasons

WINTER

The arrival of snow in the high-country transforms the range overnight. Since much of the landscape is comprised of rock and talus slopes, snow brings a welcome respite from the knee-jarring summer mountain routes and provides definition to the complex terrain. However, early season storms often do not bring enough snow to ski on, with most descents requiring a few feet of good, dense snow.

November and December can be frustrating, with just enough snow to prevent you from hiking the alpine terrain, but not enough for you to ski it.

The midwinter months typically bring heavy snowfall along with short days. Due to the long approaches that characterize much of the Eastside, most people stick to the smaller stuff during this time of year. In between storms, the sun will shine, and at times it can feel downright hot in the towns of Mammoth Lakes and Bishop – even in January. Luckily you can almost always find winter snow on protected north- and east- facing slopes, despite what your thermometer says.

Depending on the season, some of the descents in this book may not even fill in until February or March, if at all. March is typically considered a transitional month, bridging the gap between winter and spring and marking the beginning of longer days. As the sun climbs higher into the sky, the shadowed slopes we turned to in January and February start to see sunlight, and in between storms east and south faces begin to develop corn snow. Fret not, however, as March is historically one of the snowiest months each year, making it prime time for picking off big mountain lines in the high country.

SPRING

For many locals, the backcountry season doesn't even start until mid-March. With longer days, more consistent conditions, and (often) easier travel, the spring is when the Sierra seems to come alive. The warmer temps and higher sun help the snowline to rise—making the higher elevations more accessible, and lower elevations less desirable. Though most of the "front-country" peaks begin to melt out (giving the illusion that the season is quickly coming to an end), deep within the mountains the snowpack remains skiable well into the summer.

March and April are possibly the two best months for touring in the Sierra. After a few days of warm weather, the snow on lower-elevation, sun-exposed terrain begins to turn to corn. A deep snowpack and refrozen corn makes for incredibly easy access in the mornings, and delightful skiing later in the day (assuming you don't miss the window).

Though the big storms seem to slow down in April, we almost always get a few good late season dumps. Spring snowstorms can complicate things, making for sticky, gloppy snow and difficult travel. But these conditions usually don't last long, as the powerful California sun makes short work of the fluffy stuff, transforming it back to corn within a few days.

As the spring progresses, the approach roads begin to melt out, shortening the approach to the mountains, though often requiring some technical driving through 4WD terrain. Fishing is one of the major contributors to the local economy of the Eastern Sierra. Season opener (referred to as Fishmas) is the last weekend in April, and fisherman flock to the region for opening weekend the same way skiers flock here for Mammoth's first chair in November. This boost to the economy is what motivates CalTrans, Mono, and Inyo Counies to remove snow from most of the roads that access the canyons, lakes, and summer trailheads. It's an equally exciting time for fishermen and skiers, with Rock Creek, Onion Valley, South Lake, Tioga Pass and many other highly popular drainages opening up for the first time in six months.

Weather & Conditions

Without living in the Eastern Sierra, it is hard to fathom how much it can snow here in such a short amount of time. Storms frequently drop over a foot of snow at a time, and it isn't uncommon for four to six feet to accumulate over a couple of days. Between the periods of intense weather are clear blue skies, and with over 300 days of sunshine a year, the climate makes you quickly forget what the terms "overcast" and "flurries" even mean.

As with any mountain range, the High Sierra has weather that changes by the minute, and planning a trip more than 48 hours in advance is never a good idea. Be prepared to alter your plan, and always have a backup (or at least a sturdy, spacious tent and a deck of cards). Past April, things calm down quite a bit. The occasional storm/wind event is always a possibility, but the threat lessens as the season winds down.

The best resource for detailed weather is NOAA's website (www.noaa.gov) which provides the ability to get a pin-point forecast by clicking on a small Google map for the location in question. This is strongly advised over just reading the forecast for Mammoth, Bishop, or any of the other towns along Highway 395.

WIND

The Eastern Sierra is known for having high winds. As storms roll in and blow out, they are almost always accompanied by a lot of wind. It is not uncommon to see ridgetop winds of 100mph + during the brunt of the storm, and it is rare that a storm will settle in without any hint of wind.

High winds create very large cornices and serious wind-loading during storm cycles. Storms typically track from the southwest, loading up the leeward north and east slopes—and as luck would have it, these are also our favorite aspects to ski. Be very wary of any slopes during and immediately after a storm, as they often hold pockets of deposition that can be easily triggered by a human.

High winds can also create extremely challenging ski conditions, particularly on wide-open slopes. The north wind is the scourge of the Eastern Sierra and the phrase "north wind" is often accompanied by a string of obscenities. It pounds our favorite slopes and turns our powder into wind-board.

The wind can also have its advantages, buffing out some aspects with silky smooth snow, and forming windboard on others. Though not as fun as powder, consistent windboard makes for good predictable skiing in the steeps, along with easy travelling conditions to reach them.

Take advantage of the firm snow and bag a more remote peak, and instead of focusing on finding powder, focus on the mountaineering aspect of the sport. There is an old saying in mountain towns that there is no bad snow, just bad skiers. While that may be debatable, one thing is for sure: bad conditions in the backcountry are still better than good conditions at the resort.

SUN

Often referred to as "The Range of Light," the Sierra regularly has long stretches of sunny, bluebird days in between its vicious winter storms. As the season progresses, the sun's rays become more intense and impact the snowpack quickly and dramatically.

On the warm days of spring, the snowpack can soften up by mid morning, creating problems for skinning, skiing, and snow stability. Trying to climb peaks in the blazing sun can also be unpleasant, with the snow acting as a mirror, reflecting the suns rays back up at you. Don't forget to put sunscreen on the bottom of your nose and chin. Bottom line—in the spring, it's a good idea to get up very early in order to avoid some of these unpleasant, and potentially deadly things.

Avalanche Danger

Avalanche safety and evaluation are beyond the scope of this book. You should seek out professional instruction to be properly prepared to travel and ski in the backcountry in the winter. Do not be lulled by the false sense that the Sierra snowpack is "bomber." Catastrophic avalanches can and do occur and multiple avalanche fatalities have occurred in the Sierra in recent years. If you are new to winter backcountry travel or want to increase your skills, take an avalanche course from a reputable instructor – before you head out into the backcountry. A list of avalanche courses and education opportunities can be found on the **Eastern Sierra Avalanche Center** website (www.esavalanche.org).

Having said this, the Sierra snowpack is generally more stable and consistent than most other intermountain and continental snowpacks in the Lower 48. Despite common belief, the Sierra is really not a maritime snowpack, and there are a wide variety of microclimates throughout the regions mentioned in this book. During major storms, it's not uncommon to see ridgetop winds in excess of 100mph in the Tioga Pass or Mammoth Lakes Regions, accompanied with several feet of snow. The same storm cycle could deposit less than a third of the amount of snow in canyons like Rock Creek or Pine Creek, with far calmer winds.

Most of the avalanche cycles in the Sierra happen during or immediately after major storm cycles.

It is not uncommon for lower density snow (6-9% water by volume) to fall during the middle and end of storm cycles in the Sierra, but since most of the storms come from the west, they typically start out wet. This generally lends to good stratigraphy in the snowpack and allows for bonding to take place between new and old snow relatively quickly. Coupled with 300+ days of sunshine a year, most of the nasty, deep instability conditions like depth-hoar or buried surface facets don't occur frequently. Instead, clean, easy shear planes form along ice lenses and stiff or firm wind layers.

The Sierra snowpack is by no means magical, and varies as much year to year as it does from one location to another. Complacency kills, as does being lulled into a sense of safety due to lack of natural slides. That said, skiing steep terrain in the middle of winter is not a death wish, as long as you time it right and are smart about how you do it.

Moment
TC
TRIPLE CAMBER

UNDER

WORLD

Jason Templeton peers into the North Couloir of Mt. Lamarck

Josh Ellis and company climbing the Coke Chute.

Terrain Considerations

CHUTES AND GULLIES

The one thing that the Eastside is blessed with is an abundance of chutes and gullies. What makes this range even more unique is how skiable most of this terrain is, even in the heart of winter. Unlike the Rockies, the Sierra snowpack tends to be much more stable, and if you choose terrain carefully and time things properly, it is possible to find great conditions in some gorgeous lines.

LAKES, STREAMS & RIVERS

Many approaches described in this book involve following and crossing over streams and lakes. In the middle of winter, most of these water bodies are frozen solid, and crossing poses little challenge or safety concern. It is wise to be suspect of ice during early and late season, however. Always check conditions before venturing out across seemingly frozen water. If in doubt, it is better to go around than to fall into a lake.

CORNICES

The high winds that plague the Eastside translate to a lot of snow being transported across ridgelines and deposited rapidly on lee slopes. In addition to the wind-loaded pockets that are found farther down these slopes it is common to find large cornices atop them.

Cornices pose a major threat to backcountry travel—both during the ascent, and descent. If you are climbing a slope with a cornice above, be mindful of the size and likelihood of the cornice breaking naturally due to increased warming or loading. If you are travelling along the top of terrain, be extra cautious and stay well back from the edge of the ridge. More than one competent skier has fallen prey to a cornice breaking out from under them unexpectedly.

BERGSCHRUNDS

With an abundance of steep terrain that drops onto glaciers or valley bottoms below, bergshrunds can become unusually large in this range. While this phenomenon certainly isn't unique to the Sierra, we feel it is worth mentioning since glacier travel is a foreign concept to many Californians.

A bergshrund is a crack or crevasse that forms between rock and snow, found at the base of a rock wall or steep chute. As the season progresses, the snow settles under its own weight and begins to recede from the rocks. Even moving as little as an inch a day, this distance can add up by the middle of April. As the entire snowpack slowly slides downhill these cracks will get wider, creating a sort of moat that can be 50 feet deep in places.

On the descent, bergshrunds can be easier to navigate, as we have speed on our side and our skis/boards are often bigger than the span we have to cross. The ascent is a different story, however, as bergshrunds generally form at the point where it is too steep to skin, and we start booting. If in steep glaciated terrain beneath rock walls, be sure to test each step before committing to it, and it is worth checking the depth with a pole, axe, or probe.

Equipment

As backcountry skiing has grown in popularity, more and more equipment has been added to the market. Gear has evolved and improved, becoming more high tech and much more accessible. Unfortunately, this also comes with the tendency for people to place more emphasis on the equipment, and less emphasis on learning how to use it.

If you spend more time talking to shop employees than you do skiing, then even the lightest, most expensive gear isn't going to make a difference. Conversely, if you have spent thousands of days skiing in jeans on your wooden skis, then you already know that equipment is irrelevant. The fact is, you can get away with using whatever gear you want, as long as you know how to use it. Equipment is highly personalized and your choice in gear is entirely up to you. We're not interested in telling you what to do, what to wear, or what to ride. But we are going to make some recommendations.

These recommendations are not meant to be a comprehensive list, and you should already have a good idea of what is necessary to bring along for a ski trip. The things listed here are those that apply specifically to the Sierra. That is, these things are important for this particular area, and may or may not be necessary elsewhere.

It goes without saying that you should always carry an avalanche beacon, shovel, and probe. Unfortunately, we have to say it anyway: Always carry a beacon, shovel, and probe. And learn how to use them first.

SKIS & SPLIT BOARDS

Modern alpine touring (AT), telemark, or splitboard equipment is the preferred method of winter transportation. While snowshoes may work for some of the closer stuff, they are not recommended for anything that is far from the road. Many of the approaches in the area are long and go through rolling terrain. Having a free heel with the ability to kick and glide is essential. Using snowshoes will slow you down considerably and can turn a few hour trip into a two day nightmare.

ICE AXE / CRAMPONS

The combination of sun and wind can create variable conditions throughout the year, and we can get more than our fair share of bulletproof wind-board. If you are heading out to do something steep, we recommend bringing along an ice axe and a lightweight pair of general mountaineering crampons.

SKIN WAX

The importance of skin wax can only truly be appreciated by those who have needed it, but not had it. Here in the "Range of Light," only those with a propensity towards masochism head out on a backcountry tour without a purple bar of Black Diamond® Glop Stopper© or its liquid counterpart. With the amount of sunlight in the Sierra, encountering gloppy snow can happen any time of year. When glopping (the technical term for snow sticking to your skins) occurs, it is hard to reverse. Your skins will get wet, which attracts more snow, and the snow that sticks underfoot picks up even more snow, until you are essentially skinning on snowballs. A few preventative swipes with skin wax can make the difference between a pleasant tour in the hills and a grueling uphill battle.

VERTS

Verts are silly looking, simple plastic snowshoes that are essentially lunch trays with basic bindings. The hard plastic frame straps to your boot, giving it more surface area, just as a snowshoe would. The main difference is that they do not hinge at your toe, meaning that you can dig it into the slope without the heel falling out from under you.

Verts aren't used often, but they can be extremely useful on the Eastside when climbing steep couloirs in unconsolidated snow. The extra surface area can make the difference between wallowing around up to your waist, or saving your energy for the awesome ride down.

ROPES

This is a ski book. If you're using a rope, you aren't skiing. Ropes are generally reserved for those who lack skill, patience, or both. With millions of skiable couloirs in the range, it's hard to imagine why anyone would want to rappel. That said, there are a handful of peaks and lines referenced that simply beckon to be skied, but require rappels, or where having the added element of safety is welcomed.

GOGGLES

For December and January, it is extremely rare to ski anything that is in the direct sunlight. While you may ascend a sunny ridge or catch a few rays on the canyon floors, all of the chutes will be in the shade at this time of year. Because of this, you may want to consider getting some low light lenses for your goggles for descents during these months. Flat light becomes a way of life, particularly on the wide open slopes.

GLOVES & EXTRA LAYERS

While the Sierra may be known for its moderate temps, bear in mind that it is a major mountain range. The weather changes quickly, and if you are climbing a north- or east-facing aspect, you may not be able to see the storms coming. While you may be sweltering in the sunlight, you can be freezing as soon as you duck into the shadows. Extra layers are essential in the Sierra and a warm pair of mitts can make or break your day – even during the warmth of spring. In fact, emphasizing the spring is important. Most people carry extra layers in the midwinter, but leave those things at home once the spring hits. The air temps might not be all that cold and a light windbreaker might be all you'll need to keep your body warm while moving. However, a surprise wind will quickly render your fingers useless if you're just wearing lightweight spring gloves. As a rule of thumb, if there is any wind at all forecasted for the Town of Mammoth Lakes, then it will most likely be fairly windy in the upper elevations. As spring hits, there may not be large snowstorms, but the wind will still be blowing. As a photographer, 90% of the weight in my pack is camera equipment. Since that stuff never gets left behind, I have to find other ways of lightening my load. I can't tell you how many times I've left the mitts behind in an attempt to shave weight. I don't know how many of those days have been spent with numb fingers atop a rocky ridge. It's funny, the camera equipment doesn't do me much good if my fingers are too numb and swollen to use it. Ironic, huh?

SHELLS

Everyone has their own opinion on this, so we're not sure if adding ours is going to help any. Given that most of the weather is sunny and clear, hard shelled jackets are typically overkill, unless you are heading out in the storm. Having a hard shell pant is often nice, especially if you expect to be booting or spending a lot of time wallowing around. No matter what—have something that can block the wind.

First Aid, Emergency Supplies, & Wilderness Medicine

Most of the terrain presented in this guide is within a day's approach from the road, but that's only when everything is going right. Even the smallest injury could drastically affect your ability to get back to the road, or to get help to you. As a result, carrying a well stocked and balanced first aid kit and having some wilderness medicine knowledge is highly recommended. Help can be very far away. In addition to medical supplies, leave a Mylar sleeping bag (emergency blanket) and a micro-puff jacket at the bottom of your ski pack all season long, winter or spring, regardless of where you're headed. You never know when something is going to go wrong, and having just that little bit of extra equipment for shelter if you are forced to spend the night out could make all the difference in the world.

Cell phones have limited use in much of the range, and once in a canyon or beyond the Highway 395 corridor it is unlikely you will get a signal. Still, it is possible to send and receive calls in the oddest of locations, so carrying a phone can be a good idea. Just don't rely on it. Keep in mind that cell phones can interfere with avalanche transcievers so it is best to keep them switched off and packed away unless you absolutely need it.

Winter Camping

Depending on conditions (your own and those of the snow and weather), you may choose or need to camp out for some of the descents described in this book. Winter camping adds yet another dimension to backcountry skiing. Though the finer points are too in-depth for this book, there are a few factors specific to the Sierra that are worth noting.

Generally speaking, you can expect moderate temps during the late spring and early summer months. However, temperatures can frequently reach -20°F above 10,000', and the wind can make things just plain miserable. Keep this in mind when picking a camp spot.

Winter camping is allowed in the Sierra so long as you have a Wilderness Permit. Permits are required for camping 365 days a year, and can be picked up free of charge at the nearest Ranger Station.

Water

Water treatment is a tough subject to cover. Many longtime locals have hiked in the summer and winter without ever treating the water. But, that doesn't necessarily mean it is safe to do so.

Nearly all of the canyons referenced in the book are popular in the summertime. Pack trains travel throughout the region, heavily polluting the trails and subsequently the creeks and lakes. Except in the more remote, higher elevation locations, be sure to treat any water, even if after a long day in the hot spring sun it becomes very tempting to just fill your water bottle from a river.

While you may not see many signs of humans during

Basecamp below Bear Creek Spire.

your ski day, all of these areas see a huge amount of human traffic during the summer months. The lower elevation rivers and streams should be considered the most "polluted" of the Sierra. As you get higher in elevation, the threat diminishes, but it should always be a concern.

The spring sun is incredibly powerful, so you should plan on drinking quite a bit of water throughout your day. If you are unsure of how much you'll need, it is a good idea to bring a water filter or a small stove to melt snow.

Touring

The Sierra is prime for long ski tours, with many classic routes and loops pioneered decades ago. Though touring is still alive and well today, the primary focus of this book is on peaks and descents that are accessible within a day from the car. That said, there are plenty of objectives listed in this book that make for excellent overnight trips, and whenever possible we have provided information on how to link lines up with neighboring peaks and descents.

The Skiing

The popularity of backcountry skiing is rapidly rising, and with so many different ways to enjoy the backcountry, the sport is now appealing to a broader audience. Ski mountaineering is also becoming less of a fringe sport, with more people realizing the appeal of the adventure up, just as much as the run down.

One reason for the increase in popularity is that the level of skiing has been pushed beyond the limits of what most resorts can offer. What was once considered "cutting edge" is now commonplace.

A combination of technology, popularity, and motivated athletes has pushed skiers to find new challenges in every aspect of the sport. The jumps and halfpipes have gotten bigger, but resorts can do very little to appeal to the skiers looking for steeps, exposure, and other excitement.

MEADOW SKIPPING, PEAK BAGGING, & SKI MOUNTAINEERING

Some of the descents listed in this book may not appeal to you. Some terrain is too short and flat. Some aspects have too many trees to make for good skiing, or require too much bushwhacking on the skin up. Some peaks have long, rolling approaches with very little fall-line skiing, and others seem contrived with difficult lines through rocky faces.

At either end of the spectrum, you will find those seeking the backcountry for their own version of excitement. Some folks are looking to get away from the hustle and bustle of the resorts, and have no desire for the adrenaline of skiing a steep line. Others are constantly seeking the next big thing. Luckily, the Eastside is an equal opportunity mountain range, with just as much moderate terrain as there is extreme.

Though there is plenty of low angle terrain referenced in this guide, much of what is covered could be classified as peak bagging, adventure skiing, or ski mountaineering. Most backcountry skiers enjoy the way up just as much as the way down—though some are looking for a little more adventure while doing so. Regardless, the allure of backcountry skiing is simply being out in the mountains. Skiing into a drainage you've never seen before, attaining a new summit, and soaking in a different view are all part of the experience.

ALPINE STARTS

Getting going early is the key to success in the Sierra. While it may sometimes seem overkill to see the sunrise on your drive to the trailhead, it's always better than seeing the sun set before you have made it home.

Ethics & Etiquette

We are lucky to have such a wild, untamed, and largely unpopulated range. Crowds are virtually nonexistent here. There are no heli-ski operations, no Snowcat-tours, and the Wilderness boundaries and topography keep the snowmobiles to just a few select areas.

The horror stories from other ranges make the Eastern Sierra all that more appealing. We don't have to fight for parking spots at the "one" backcountry trailhead, nor worry about a helicopter load of skiers getting dropped in from above. Other than the occasional snowmobiler, the only other people out there will be like-minded backcountry skiers, doing the same thing you are doing. That is, if you even see anyone at all.

SNOWMOBILES

There are very few spots in the Eastern Sierra where one can access skiing entirely by snowmobile, and since the focus of this book is on human powered skiing, we will let you obtain that info on your own. That said, snowmobiles do have a place in accessing some of the backcountry. The approaches to many of the peaks involve long distances of flat terrain, and the use of a snowmobile can make short work of those approaches.

Jason Templeton atop Alpine Col.

This is particularly true for those areas with summer roads that access them. If taking a snowmobile into the mountains, you should always carry a map and a GPS and be aware of your exact location, as the Wilderness boundaries are easy to cross if you are not paying attention. Study the map before you go—that extra quarter mile really isn't worth the penalty.

SKIN TRACKS

If you are traveling on snowshoes, please be respectful and stay out of the skin track. If following a hiking trail or in dense forest, this may not be possible, but for the most part, the terrain around here is wide open and there is no reason to ruin the track for other users.

For those on skis: Don't be rude to the snowshoers. The fact is, they are simply unaware of what they are doing. The only thing worse than a person snowshoeing a skintrack is the self righteous skier that yells at him.

ENCOUNTERING NON-SKIERS

The Eastern Sierra is an incredible range to get out and do all kinds of activities. After only seeing skiers for months on end, it's easy to forget that there are other users out there, doing things other than skiing.

While the majority of the peak-baggers wait until summer to get into the mountains, you will occasionally encounter climbers and mountaineers that are on foot during the winter months. Mt. Whitney and the U/V Notches are the two places that this is almost guaranteed, but any one of the other steep couloirs can be an attraction.

For the most part, these encounters do not create problems. Problems do, however, arise in (steep) close quarters, with two different user groups and two different mentalities trying to mix. As skiers, we are constantly dealing with sluff, and therefore know where the safe spots are in the couloirs, and we have learned to stop there when people are skiing above us. Those on foot may not be able to move out of the way as quickly, and may not realize the importance of getting out of the way. Even when the avalanche danger is low, you will be sending down snow and ice chunks as you ski. This can be bothersome and even dangerous to those below you. Try to be courteous to the other users, and give them plenty of time to find a safe spot.

History

There is a long history of ski touring and ski mountaineering in the Eastern Sierra. The stage was set with Snowshoe Thompson's crossing of the Sierra in the 1800's, and built upon by Orland Bartholomew's winter descent of Mt. Whitney in 1929, and the pioneering of Norman Clyde and cohorts through the '30s. During

the '40s, '50s, and '60s the Los Angeles Chapter of the Sierra Club Ski Mountaineers regularly ventured into the Rock Creek and Big Pine Creek drainages. The first real guidebook for the range was written in the early '70s by H.J. Burhenne, and by the end of the decade many of the big lines were getting skied. The adventures and expeditions continued throughout the '80s, with a common cast of characters who were as talented on the stone as they were on the snow. By the '90s most of the obvious lines had first descents, though a few intrepid souls continued to find wrinkles and stake their claim.

The truth is we are not historians, nor amazing researchers. Despite our interest in ski history and desire to know who skied each line first, we decided to stick to what we know and leave the real story telling to someone better equipped to tell it. Instead, this book is focused on the beautiful peaks and descents that we all enjoy today—with a respectful nod to those who pioneered these same lines decades ago.

Using This Guide

ORGANIZATION

This book covers fourteen major watersheds. We use these as natural breaks in the book, assigning a separate chapter to each of these "Regions." Within each of the chapters/regions are a series of "Areas" (designated with ▣), which focus more on specific terrain features: mountains, canyons, drainages, or clusters of peaks. Every descent (↘) is tied to a peak (△), and each has a reference map, picture, approach/descent description, and basic statistics about the line in an easy to read chart.

Some of the peaks described in this book border drainages, with approaches and descents of opposing aspects. In these cases, the peaks are covered in more than one Region or Area, with the corresponding aspect in the appropriate section to maintain consistency and reduce confusion. The maps provided at the beginning of each chapter and Area section help define what is included, and identify where surrounding terrain is referenced.

In this edition of the guide, we made an effort to provide the high level details of each line in a basic table. Atop each table, simple icons represent the three most important factors in line choice: aspect, difficult, and slope angle.

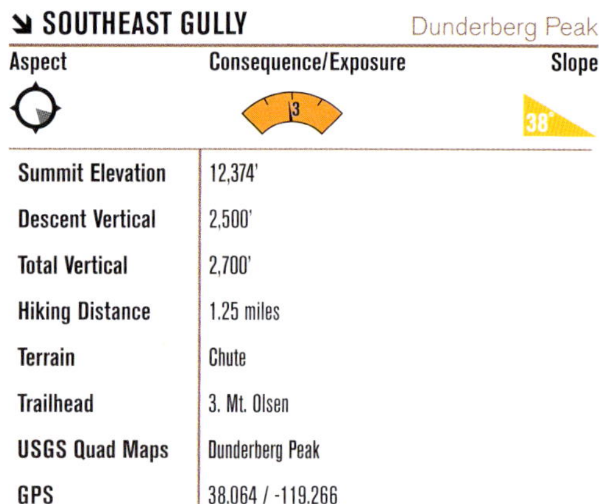
SOUTHEAST GULLY — Dunderberg Peak

Aspect	Consequence/Exposure	Slope
	3	38°

Summit Elevation	12,374'
Descent Vertical	2,500'
Total Vertical	2,700'
Hiking Distance	1.25 miles
Terrain	Chute
Trailhead	3. Mt. Olsen
USGS Quad Maps	Dunderberg Peak
GPS	38.064 / -119.266

ASPECTS

The aspect provided refers to the dominant direction each descent faces.

SLOPE ANGLE

The slope angle refers to the steepness of the run, and is based on typical conditions during an average snow year. Providing an accurate measurement is difficult, as slope angle can change dramatically based on the amount of snow. In general we try to describe the steepest part of the run, recognizing that in some cases there may be a short steep section with the rest of the line being much lower angle, and the opposite in other situations.

DIFFICULTY RATINGS

During the creation of this book, we struggled with figuring out how to assign a level of difficulty to each descent. Over the years, a handful of different rating systems have come and gone. These ratings were an attempt to standardize ski descents in the same way that the Yosemite Decimal System standardized rock climbing. Fortunately, snow and rock are two very different elements, and a precise way of rating ski runs simply doesn't work. The biggest factor that affects difficulty is snow depth. If the snowpack is thin, even the easiest of slopes can seem intimidating and challenging. If the snowpack is deep, things become much easier. These discrepancies become more prominent as the difficulty (and pitch) increases. The difficulty of a slope can change greatly, as rocks get scoured or become covered, or snow conditions change from soft and smooth to bulletproof wind board. Combine all of these factors and you have inconsistencies that are nearly impossible to rate.

That said, we have made an attempt to rate the Consequences & Exposure (C/E) associated with each of the descents in an attempt to give you a more complete picture of the descent itself. While this is a relatively subjective method of assessing risk, when coupled with the other information, it should help you get a better understanding of the descent. The ratings are as follows:

C/E: 1 Falling is generally OK, as you will likely be able to stop yourself should you fall while skiing. In addition, there is low probability for injury associated with hitting terrain features such as rocks, trees, cliffs, etc. Examples of descents in this category include Red Cone Bowl (Mammoth Lakes Region) and the Main Avy. Path (Mammoth Lakes Region).

C/E: 2 Consequences of falling on these descents are higher based on more complex terrain features. Potential for injury associated with hitting terrain features is higher, though it is still likely that you will be able to arrest during a fall. Examples of descents in this category include The Fingers (Mammoth Lakes Region) and The Bardini Chutes (Mammoth Lakes Region).

C/E: 3 Potential for injury during a fall on these descents is higher based on more complex terrain features including rocks, trees, narrower chutes, and small cliff-bands. In good conditions it may be possible to arrest during a fall and there is generally a moderate amount of space to do so before encountering any major terrain features. Examples of descents in this category include Bloody Couloir (Mammoth Lakes Region) and Esha Peak (McGee Creek Drainage).

C/E: 4 If you fall on one of these descents, you will most likely be injured and could potentially be killed. More complex terrain features exist, including large rocks and cliffbands, as well as steeper chutes. There is less room to arrest yourself if you were to fall. Examples of descents in this category include Third Pillar Chute (Tioga Pass Region) and the Y-Chutes (Mammoth Lakes Region).

C/E: 5 Falling on one of these descents will most certainly be fatal. Large, complex terrain features are abundant and the room for arresting a fall is minimal or nonexistent. Examples of descents in this category include the summit entrance of The North Couloir on Red Slate (Convict Creek Region) and Gutter Chute (Tioga Pass Region).

Alpenglow Sports™
A California Backcountry Shop
Photo: Josh Hejl

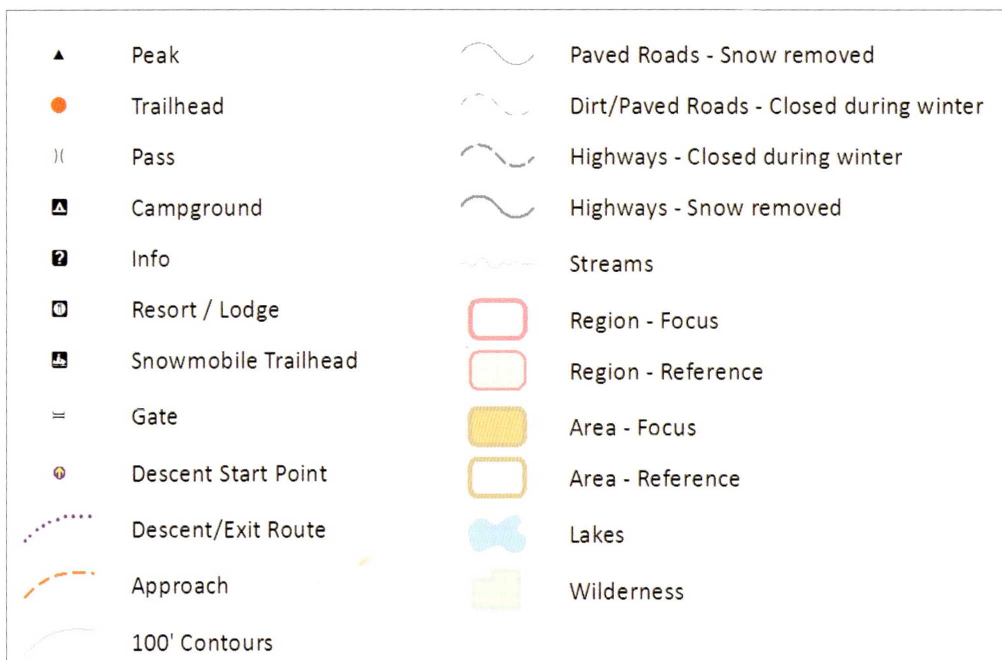

ELEVATIONS

Elevations are referenced four different ways throughout the book, as described below:

Trailhead Elevation: Trailheads are referenced in the introduction of each chapter. An elevation is provided for this location, along with seasonal access constraints and driving directions.

Summit Elevation: Refers to the maximum elevation of the line, or summit of the associated peak.

Descent Vertical: Refers to the elevation lost on the main part of the line. This could be referred to as "fall line skiing." Since most of the descents in this book require long approaches on rolling terrain, this number will almost always be shorter than the Total Vertical.

Total Vertical: The difference between the summit and trailhead elevation

HIKING DISTANCE

Hiking distances have been calculated for each of the approaches based on the approach lines drawn on the maps. Please note that these numbers are estimates only. Depending on the actual route chosen, terrain, or unexpected obstacles, they can vary.

We have purposefully omitted specific time estimates for approaches or "length of day," and have instead listed distances and elevations gained during approaches. The amount of time required for a trip greatly depends on a number of factors, the largest being the conditions of the snow and the fitness of the group. What may take 20-30 minutes on spring corn can take 2-3 hours after a heavy snowfall. Obviously, the information provided in this book is no substitute for backcountry travel experience, including safe route selection, and proper use of equipment. If you doubt your ability to move quickly, start with a relatively short approach and use that as a gauge for objectives that are a little farther away.

TRAILHEAD

At the beginning of each chapter, we have listed all of the trailheads contained within. Please be aware that a number of these "trailheads" are undeveloped and in many cases may consist only of a small plowed parking area at the end of a road. Please be respectful of other users and park in such a way as to not obstruct local traffic or others needing to get in and out. The directions contained in the Trailheads section will get you to the parking lot, which is referenced as the starting location for the approach described with each descent.

USGS QUAD MAPS

Each descent references the USGS 7.5' (1:24,000 scale) topographic quadrangle maps that cover that area. The maps included in this book were created for reference purposes only and are in no way intended for navigation. They are meant to simply show you where one peak or descent is relative to another. If you are unfamiliar with the area, we strongly recommend that you pick up the quad map(s).

GPS

Every descent listed in this book has a set of Latitude and Longitude coordinates expressed in Decimal Minutes. These have been provided to assist you in mapping these locations on top of USGS maps or on personal GPS units. Please be aware that these are not extremely accurate measurements and were calculated based on the general area of the descent, not necessarily the exact entrance to a chute.

MAPS

There are two different types of maps throughout the book, both of which use the same set of symbology which is referenced above. Each chapter opens with a Regional Overview map, showing the breakdown of the Areas within relative to the terrain in that section. An Area Detail map is provided at the beginning of each Area which shows the peaks, approaches, and descents. Please keep in mind that these maps are at different scales and are for reference purposes only.

Notes on Using This Book

Being a good skier is only part of the equation. Knowledge of mountains and snow is equally important. As you begin to challenge your skiing abilities, mountain knowledge becomes essential, no matter what that ability level is.

It is essential to read the descriptions for each descent. Don't just look at the slope angle and terrain, particularly for those descents that may be pushing your ability level. We have tried to provide as much information as possible, but when working with a medium that changes from day to day, it is impossible to be perfectly accurate. Backcountry skiing is an adventure, and under certain conditions, any one of these runs could be potentially fatal.

SAFETY CONCERNS

In a few instances we have listed some approaches that do not directly follow the intended descents. We have listed these alternatives for your information, and are in no way recommending them. While it is generally best to first climb your intended descent, for one reason or another, you may choose not to do that. Many people fear for their lives while booting up a steep couloir, only to breath a huge sigh of relief as soon as they put their skis on to go down the same couloir. Others are the exact opposite, and may choose an easier descent after climbing the steeps. Because of this, we have provided as much information as possible, listing alternate ascent/descent routes. Ultimately the decision will be yours.

SUMMITS

Whenever possible (and where applicable) you will find information on how to attain the summit of a mountain. This is an often overlooked aspect to backcountry ski days, but summits are important.

Bear in mind that most summits and ridges are exposed to harsh and varying weather every day. Conditions change, and the often used "3rd Class" can be very serious in ski boots and potentially fatal when mixed with a bit of snow or ice.

The definition of 3rd Class is somewhat open for interpretation. 4th Class is even more nebulous, and you won't find any instances of it being used in this book. Once the climbing becomes even moderately technical, we call it 5th Class for simplicity and severity sake.

If you're into bagging summits, allow for a lot of extra time to get to/from the top of your ski descent. Many of these summit ridges are comprised of big blocks. Learning to read this terrain and move quickly and efficiently across it is yet another skill that takes time to learn. Going up usually isn't too bad. But coming back down is much more difficult, scary, and tiring. Thankfully, the High Sierra is mostly granite, which generally translates to large talus blocks and relatively solid terrain.

Transportation, Logistics, & Emergency Information

MAMMOTH HOSPITAL

Located on Sierra Park Road in Mammoth Lakes – 24 hour emergency services, as well as a world-class orthopedic department.

www.mammothhospital.com | (760) 934-3311

NORTHERN INYO HOSPITAL

Located at 150 Pioneer Lane in Bishop, off of West Line Street. (760) 873-5811

EASTERN SIERRA AVALANCHE CENTER

The Eastern Sierra Avalanche Center (ESAC) is a grassroots based, community driven effort with a mission of providing backcountry enthusiasts with the information they need to make smart decisions. The Center has been in operation since 2006 and relies heavily on its member base and the community-at-large to stay operational. In partnership with Inyo National Forest, ESAC is the place for avalanche conditions and information for the terrain between Tioga Pass and Bishop Creek. Visit the website for the latest forecasts, conditions, and news. Become a member to support the center and receive the avalanche forecasts emailed directly to you. A list of avalanche courses for the season and other educational events are also on the website.

www.esavalanche.org | Avalanche Hotline: (760) 924-5510

MAMMOTH MOUNTAINEERING

Located on Main Street in Mammoth Lakes, Mammoth Mountaineering Supply offers everything you need for an adventure. They have a full fleet of splitboard, telemark, AT, and cross-country demo skis, boots, and skins for rent, as well as the latest and greatest backcountry gear for sale. Their knowledgeable staff can help you get outfitted and also help point you in the right direction. You will also find a similar selection of equipment at their Gear Exchange location in Bishop.

www.mammothgear.com | (760) 934-4191

CALTRANS

Winter storms can close roads throughout the Eastern Sierra or cause roads to have chain restrictions. Caltrans provides current road conditions throughout the state of California on its website and on its automated phone line.

www.caltrans.gov | (800) 427-7623/(800) GAS-ROAD

Jon Crowley and Jason Templeton atop Point Powell.

Relevant highway numbers are:

- 395 (main highway that parallels the mountains)
- 203 (Main Street in Mammoth Lakes, becomes Minaret Road on the way to the Main Lodge)
- 120 (Tioga Pass – closed for the winter until late May or June)
- 158 (June Lake Loop)
- 168 (West Line Street in Bishop)

The status of some trailhead roads (such as Whitney Portal or Rock Creek) is not available through Caltrans. For more information on these roads, read the corresponding chapters and inquire locally.

FRONT-COUNTRY CAMPING

There are a number of designated campgrounds administered by the Forest Service scattered throughout the Eastern Sierra. These sites are typically closed during the skiing months, but depending on the time of year they may be accessible for your trip. With the exception of trailheads and "concentrated recreation sites" like the June Lake Loop, Lee Vining Canyon, and Mammoth Lakes Basin, free camping in undeveloped sites is available on most National Forest land. Check in with Inyo National Forest for information.
www.fs.fed.us/r5/inyo/ | (760) 873-2400

WILDERNESS PERMITS

Wilderness permits are required for overnight travel on public land, both on National Forest and National Park land. Consult with the respective agency when planning your trip. Generally these permits are free, but some specific regulations or fees may apply.

LOCAL ESTABLISHMENTS & EATERIES

We encourage you to check out some of the smaller, local eateries along the Highway 395 corridor. Each town has its own unique character, and we think you may be pleasantly surprised by some of the fine establishments hidden away here. For many of these small towns, winter is the slow season. At the beginning of each chapter we have recommended a handful or our favorites.

WINTER CLIMBING

Sitting at 5,000', Bishop is more of a climbing community than a skiing community. Except during the heaviest of winter storms, most of the boulders and crags around Bishop are climbable year round (and some are more 'in-season' during the winter months). When it's dumping snow in Mammoth, it is possible to find sunny skies at the Happy Boulders. See the Bishop Bouldering guidebook by Wills Young and Mick Ryan, available from www.wolverinepublishing.com.

GUIDING SERVICES

The following guides offer winter and spring guiding and avalanche courses. For more information visit their websites.

Sierra Mountain Center
174 West Line Street, Bishop
(760) 873-8526
www.sierramountaincenter.com

Sierra Mountain Guides
312 North Main St, Bishop
(877) 423-2546
www.sierramtnguides.com

Sierra Mountaineering International
236 North Main Street, Bishop
(760) 872-4929
www.sierramountaineering.com

Alpine Skills International
11400 Donner Pass Rd #200, Truckee
(530) 582-9170

Random Notes

SKIING VERSUS BOARDING

Throughout this book, we use the terms "ski," "skiing," and so on. We are in no way trying to exclude the snowboarders, mono skiers, or anyone else out there enjoying the winter wonderland. Continually writing "ski/snowboard" or "skiing/snowboarding" becomes tedious. The term "skiing" is meant to refer to any and all forms of snow sliding, so please, take no offense to our terminology.

NAMES

Without any sort of official way of keeping track of the named ski runs, we're sure we have inadvertently made mistakes on our labels. You may notice that the names of some runs differ from what you have been calling them for years, and in some instances, we have assigned names to things that we couldn't find any history on. We are in no way trying to imply first descents or naming rights on these lines. We are simply trying to help this book make sense. If you find any errors, or want to add input, please let us know. You can send a message to our Facebook page: www.facebook.com/Backcountryskieasternsierra.

The Checklist

THE CLASSICS

Over the years, certain peaks and descents have attained a sort of "classic" status. These are the highly coveted lines that stand out in the minds of backcountry skiers. The classic descents are the runs that appeal to visitors and locals alike and are those you want to return to, regardless of how many times you've skied them. The Eastern Sierra has a lot of skiable terrain, and as you drive along Highway 395 the number of options can seem overwhelming. If you are new to the area, or are only visiting for a few days, the the list of classics on the following page is a great place to start. It provides an introduction to each of the regions in this book, and gives you a glimpse at the endless terrain at your fingertips.

There are many factors that contribute to the making of a classic ski descent, and it's difficult to define exactly how a mountain earns its classic status. Everyone has their own opinion on what makes for good skiing, but for some reason, we all seem to agree that certain mountains stand out above the rest.

The number one factor is the aesthetics of the peak. Yes—even mountains get judged on their appearance. The classic peaks stand aloof from their neighbors. They are distinct and tower over the others in the area. When it comes to the skiing, these peaks have an equally distinct skiable slope – big couloirs splitting rocky faces catch the eye of any backcountry skier. Being able to ski directly from the summit of a mountain is a major bonus. Any peak that consistently has a skiable line from its summit is more appealing. Unique location is another factor that contributes to classic status. Excellent views are offered just about anywhere in the mountains, but the classic peaks have views and scenery that are exceptional. Put all of these things together, and you have the Eastern Sierra's "Best of the Best" list.

The Checklist

THE CLASSICS

Bridgeport Region:
- ❑ East Couloir, Matterhorn Peak (page 52)
- ❑ Ski Dreams (page 52)

Virginia Lakes Region:
- ❑ South Peak (page 62)

Lee Vining Region:
- ❑ The Dana Couloir, Mt. Dana (page 91)
- ❑ East Face, False White (page 85)

June Lake Region:
- ❑ Mt. Wood (page 115)
- ❑ Mt. Gibbs (page 109)

Mammoth Lakes Region:
- ❑ Mt. Ritter (page 131)
- ❑ Bloody Mountain (page 164)
- ❑ The Sherwins (page 135)

Convict Creek Region:
- ❑ Red Slate (page 193)

McGee Creek Region:
- ❑ Esha Peak (page 215)

Rock Creek Region:
- ❑ Pipsqueak Spire (page 241)
- ❑ Mt. Abbot (page 236)

Pine Creek Region:
- ❑ Feather Peak (page 258)
- ❑ Mt. Tom (page 249)

Bishop Region:
- ❑ Basin Mountain (page 265)
- ❑ Mt. Emerson (page 272)
- ❑ Mt. Lamarck (page 283)
- ❑ Mt. Darwin (page 287)
- ❑ Mt. Thompson (page 292)

Big Pine Region:
- ❑ The U and V Notch Couloirs (page 304)

Independence Region:
- ❑ Mt. Williamson (page 337)

Lone Pine Region:
- ❑ Mt. Whitney (page 343)
- ❑ Mt. Langley (page 352)

ROADSIDE ATTRACTIONS

These runs are very close to the road, and can typically be completed in just a few hours or less. If you are looking for an easy day, are just getting into backcountry skiing, or want to get in some turns before work, try one of these:

Bridgeport Region:
- ❑ Crater Crest (page 56)

Virginia Lakes Region (spring only):
- ❑ Dunderberg Peak (page 60)
- ❑ South Peak (page 62)

Lee Vining Region (spring only):
- ❑ Ellery Bowl (page 88)
- ❑ False White (page 84)

June Lake Region:
- ❑ Carson Peak (page 120)

Mammoth Lakes Region:
- ❑ The Sherwins (page 135)
- ❑ Punta Bardini (page 154)

Convict Creek Region:
- ❑ Batch Plant Bowls (page 175)
- ❑ Mini Morrison (page 180)

McGee Creek Region:
- ❑ McGee Mountain (page 202)
- ❑ Red Mountain (page 221)

Pine Creek Region:
- ❑ Tungstar Bowls (page 254)

Bishop Region:
- ❑ Table Mountain (page 277)

Big Pine Region:
- ❑ Kidd Mountain (page 308)

Independence Region:
- ❑ Independence Peak (page 332)
- ❑ Kearsarge Peak (page 327)

Lone Pine Region (spring only):
- ❑ Thor Peak (page 342)

1 Bridgeport

Jon Crowley drops in beneath The Doodad.

1. Bridgeport

BRIDGEPORT REGION:

- Little Slide Canyon:
  - Δ KETTLE PEAK
  - Δ INCREDIBLE HULK
- Blacksmith Creek:
  - Δ MT. WALT
- Horse Creek/Matterhorn:
  - Δ THE DOODAD
  - Δ MATTERHORN PEAK
  - Δ HORSE CREEK PEAK
  - Δ TWIN PEAKS
- Twin Lakes Area:
  - Δ CRATER CREST

Region Trailheads

1. Twin Lakes
2. Mono Village

The historic small town of Bridgeport was once a haven for miners and ranchers—sitting just a short distance from the Nevada border, and the gold mines of the Bodie. Today, Bridgeport is the seat of Mono County, and is known primarily as a summer recreation destination (with fishing and climbing its major attractions). Though the town is cold and sleepy in the winter, the mountains above this quiet community provide the terrain for some of the finest backcountry skiing in the range.

The backdrop for Bridgeport is the Sawtooth Ridge, which is a sub-range of peaks that forms the northeastern boundary of Yosemite National Park. It seems appropriate to start this book with the Sawtooth Ridge as it is the Sierra at its finest, and home to some of the most aesthetic, clean, and unique rock spires in the range.

This long, jagged ridge spans a handful of small drainages and marks the unofficial beginning to what is known as the High Sierra. To the north, the peaks are less dramatic, and the canyons less defined. As soon as you hit the Bridgeport Region, the rolling foothills are almost instantly replaced by the more dramatic landscape that defines the Eastside.

The sights in this region are enough to make any climber or skier drool. There are a handful of ultra-classic alpine rock climbs here, with Matterhorn Peak and the Incredible Hulk being the most popular. In between all of these granite walls and spires are countless steep, north-facing chutes.

Getting There & Getting Going

The skiing in the Bridgeport Region is accessed from Twin Lakes, which lies roughly 12 miles southwest of town. The road to the trailhead is plowed year-round, providing access to a handful of residences back in the canyon, and backcountry enthusiasts reap the benefit. Despite the

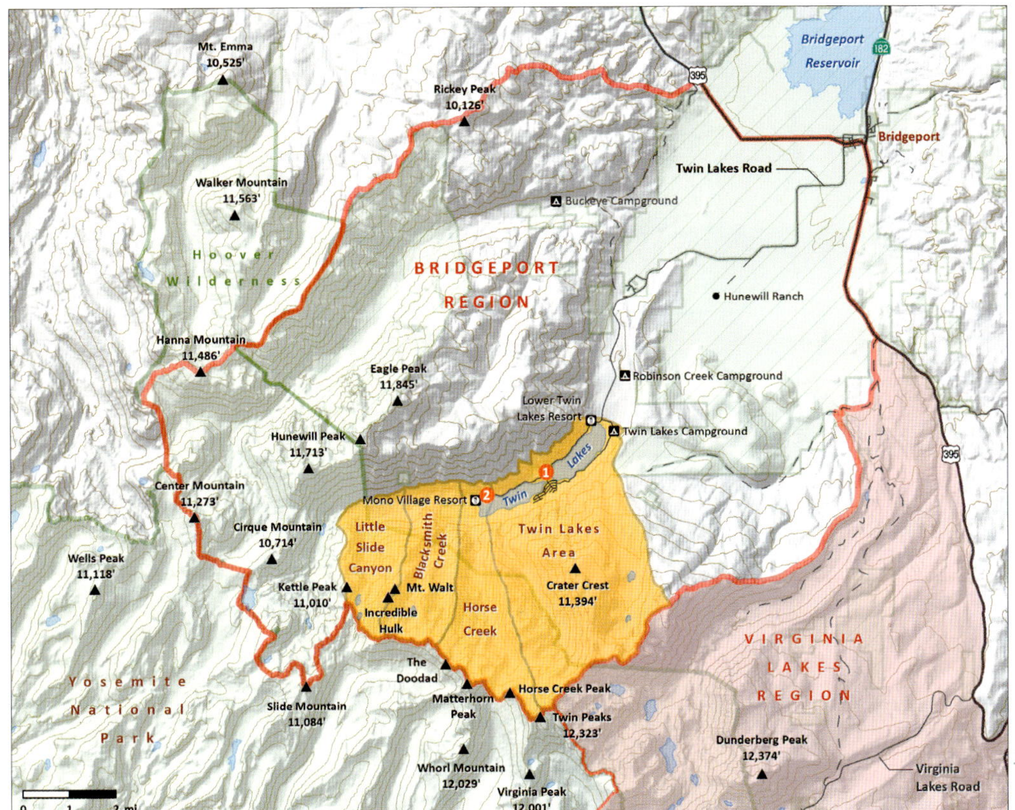

easy access to incredible terrain, skier traffic remains relatively calm until the spring. As the lower elevations around Lake Tahoe begin to melt out, however, many diehards look to extend their season by heading south on Highway 395, and this is the closest destination with higher-elevation skiing.

The town of Bridgeport sits about an hour north of Mammoth (55 miles), and about two hours south of Reno (110 miles), on Highway 395. To reach Twin Lakes, turn south onto Twin Lakes Road, located at the west end of town next to the Shell Station, and follow it to the trailheads listed below.

The Matterhorn Drainage is by far the most popular in the region, primarily because it is the only one with a major summer trail going into it, and is the closest to the trailhead. The added benefit of the trail is realized in the early and late season, where access to this canyon via the trail is easier than its trail-less counterparts. The bottoms of all the Bridgeport Region canyons are fairly low in elevation and filled with dense standing and downed trees, boulders, and vegetation, so with a thin snowpack, getting into and out of these areas can be a bit of a chore.

1. Twin Lakes Trailhead (Year-Round) *7,150'*

Follow Highway 395 to the north end of town and turn south onto Twin Lakes Road. Follow this for approximately 12 miles to its intersection with Patterson Road (which crosses the creek dividing Upper and Lower Twin Lakes), at the housing area called Twin Lakes Estates. Find a spot to park off Twin Lakes Road (dig yourself one if none are available) and begin your journey south along Patterson Road until you hit snow. Do not drive down or obstruct Patterson Road, as people get towed for this offense.

Please understand that Twin Lakes Estates is a private subdivision. Although the great majority of residents are gone in winter, there are full-time residents who deserve the utmost respect. Please keep loud voices, wandering dogs, and any lavatory needs to the public lands beyond.

2. Mono Village (Year-Round) *7,150'*

From the town of Bridgeport, travel approximately 13 miles along Twin Lakes Road until the road ends beside Upper Twin Lake just before Annett's Mono Village. Parking is limited, but is available on the lakeside road shoulder about 100 yards from the entrance into Mono

Village. If no shoulders have been plowed, or the existing plowed area is full of cars, you are well advised to dig yourself a space completely off the road instead of risking the possibility of emerging from a blissful tour to find your car towed. DO NOT park in the snowplow turnaround at the end of the road, obstruct the entrance to Mono Village, or drive into Mono Village. People regularly get towed for these offenses.

Please understand that Mono Village (pretty much the entire valley floor) is private property. Although the resort is shut down in winter, there are full-time residents who live in the cabins and deserve the utmost respect. Please keep loud voices, wandering dogs, and any lavatory needs to the public lands beyond.

Eats, Digs, Services, & Supplies

Like many of the other small towns along the Highway 395 corridor, Bridgeport is more of a summertime destination. Locals refer to summer as "Fishing Season" and winter as "Freezing Season." Since most people traveling Highway 395 during this time of year are just passing through, many of the businesses are closed during the winter, and don't reopen until April.

That said, there are some basic amenities in the winter. J's on the Corner, Rhino's, and Hays Street Cafe are open year-round, and typically serve three meals a day. In the spring more restaurants open up, such as The Barn. Between the gas stations and Bridgeport General Store you should be able to find most of the basic necessities. Wilderness permits can be obtained at the USFS ranger station located on Highway 395, just south of town.

Joe Stewart climbing Kettle Peak.

Looking west at Kettle Peak from The Incredible Hulk.

▣ Little Slide Canyon

Little Slide Canyon is best known for the popular back-country "crag" The Incredible Hulk, and sees a tremendous amount of summer traffic. The winter is a totally different story. Since it is smaller, farther away, and lacking in 'big' lines compared to Matterhorn and Blacksmith drainages, the canyon is relatively quiet when there is snow on the ground.

This canyon is notorious for the swamp that lies at its base. During the winter, the swamp freezes over and is relatively easy to cross. As spring arrives and the lower elevations melt out, the swamp comes back to life and can be the crux of the day.

Little Slide Canyon Access: From the entrance gate for Mono Village (Trailhead #2), head west through the RV park along the main road. Pass the store and entrance kiosk, then veer right. Continue almost due west, staying to the north of the creek. As you near the western edge of Mono Village, you should encounter a Do Not Enter sign and a chain across the road. Continue west along the road, which eventually turns to a trail that weaves its way along the canyon floor.

After about 2½ miles, and long after passing the entrance to Blacksmith Canyon, the entrance to Little Slide will come into view. There is a large swamp surrounded by a good-sized forest that opens up as you near the mouth of the canyon.

The eastern side of the canyon mouth is protected by a large rocky outcrop. In the summer, the trail crosses the creek on a large log just east of this feature then heads steeply up and over it and into the canyon. In the winter, it is best to generally follow the same approach, staying away from the mouth of the canyon and the dense forest that protects it.

△ KETTLE PEAK *11,010'*

Kettle Peak is a jagged series of gendarmes separated by many short chutes. The character of the peak changes dramatically as you climb into the canyon. From below, the craggy spires are prominent, but the chutes between them are hidden. When looking down on Kettle Peak from higher in the canyon, the East Face looks smaller and flatter, but the chutes are obvious.

Unlike most chutes in the Sierra, which drop from the summit onto an open slope below, the East Couloir on Kettle Peak is wedged between an upper and lower face.

There is another chute on Kettle that is a little farther up the canyon. This one is arguably even more aesthetic, but it does not go to the summit. To reach it, simply continue skiing up the canyon a short distance and around the corner. It is also possible to ski up/down the large ramp on the east side of the peak.

↘ EAST COULOIR
Kettle Peak

Aspect | Consequence/Exposure 2 | Slope 30°

Summit Elevation	11,010'
Descent Vertical	1,300'
Total Vertical	3,000'
Approach Distance	7 miles
Terrain	Chute
Trailhead	2. Mono Village
USGS Quad Maps	Buckeye Ridge, Matterhorn Peak
GPS	38.134 / -119.373

Approach: Follow the Little Slide Canyon Access description provided at the beginning of this section into Little Slide Canyon.

Once in the canyon, stay on the east side of the creek, crossing the large, open slope toward a cliff band near the base of Mt. Walt. Pass the cliff band on the uphill (east) side, below Mt. Walt, and then contour into the canyon proper. At this point, the East Face of Kettle Peak will be directly above you on the west side of the canyon.

To reach the base of the couloir, continue up-canyon toward the south side of Kettle Peak, where the chute will come into view. Climb the chute to the more moderate slopes above, and continue on to the summit.

Exit: Reverse your approach.

Δ INCREDIBLE HULK *11,520'*

The Incredible Hulk is one of the most prominent and eye-catching features of the Sierra. While climbers ogle over the clean lines and corners on its pyramidal face, skiers are drawn to the equally distinct couloirs that frame it.

Technically speaking, The Hulk is really just a subpeak of Mt. Walt, sitting just below the rocky ridge that separates Little Slide and Blacksmith Canyons. But, as one of the finest alpine climbing venues in the US (and possibly the world), don't even think about considering this one a "sub" peak.

The right couloir is the tamer of the two couloirs on the Hulk, and is the summer descent from the summit. Most people ski the lower portion of the couloir, below the dogleg that climbs the final several hundred feet to the summit ridge.

↘ HULK COULOIR–RIGHT
Incredible Hulk

Aspect | Consequence/Exposure 3 | Slope 38°

Summit Elevation	11,000'
Descent Vertical	1,300'
Total Vertical	3,000'
Approach Distance	7 miles
Terrain	Chute
Trailhead	2. Mono Village
USGS Quad Maps	Buckeye Ridge, Matterhorn Peak
GPS	38.119 / -119.413

Approach: Follow the approach description for Kettle Peak into Little Slide Canyon. As you climb higher into the canyon, the Hulk looms above you. Continue to its base—trending upward toward the right (west) side. Skin and boot the couloir to your desired high point.

↘ HULK COULOIR–LEFT
Incredible Hulk

Aspect | Consequence/Exposure 3 | Slope 40°

Summit Elevation	11,000'
Descent Vertical	1,300'
Total Vertical	3,000'
Approach Distance	7 miles
Terrain	Chute
Trailhead	2. Mono Village
USGS Quad Maps	Buckeye Ridge, Matterhorn Peak
GPS	38.121 / -119.412

The left is the steeper and wilder of the two Hulk Couloirs, and much larger than it appears from below. As you climb higher into the line, its true character is revealed. What appeared from below to be a narrow slot, is actually plenty wide for multiple people. This couloir tops out on the ridge, providing excellent views of the upper sections of Blacksmith Canyon.

Approach: Follow the approach description for Kettle Peak into Little Slide Canyon. As you climb higher into the canyon, the Hulk looms above you. Continue to its base—trending upward toward the left (east) side. Skin and boot the couloir to your desired high point.

Looking south at Mt. Walt from Mono Village.

▣ Blacksmith Creek

Blacksmith Creek is one of the more attractive drainages in the region—home to numerous chutes and technical faces. Unfortunately, it can also be one of the more difficult and unpleasant to access, especially during periods of low snow. The best way to avoid bushwacking is to stay out of the canyon bottom and away from the creek, sticking instead to the canyon walls and traversing.

While Mt. Walt may be the most popular ski descent in this canyon, do not overlook the countless smaller options that are tucked away in its granite walls. At the head of the canyon you will find many short chutes, as well as the large open slopes of Eocene Peak. Blacksmith Creek is an excellent spot to avoid the crowds for a weekend basecamp.

△ MT. WALT *11,581'*

From the parking areas at Twin Lakes, most of the peaks in the area are obscured from view—the exception being Mt. Walt. From this perspective, Mt. Walt is the most prominent peak of the Sawtooth Ridge—looming over Blacksmith Creek and dividing it from Little Slide Canyon. Catching morning sun, its Northeast face is a striking feature.

↘ NORTHEAST/BURHENNE COULOIR — Mt. Walt

Aspect | Consequence/Exposure: 3 | Slope: 35°

Summit Elevation	11,581'
Descent Vertical	3,500'
Total Vertical	4,000'
Approach Distance	7 ½ miles
Terrain	Face, Chute
Trailhead	2. Mono Village
USGS Quad Maps	Buckeye Ridge, Matterhorn Peak
GPS	38.123 / -119.41

This is the obvious gully splitting the Northeast Face of Mt. Walt. Though what can be seen from the trailhead is impressive, the majority of the route to the summit is hidden from view, as it wraps around the corner and climbs behind the rocky face above.

Approach: There are two ways to access the summit of Mt. Walt. The common route climbs directly up the gully from the Blacksmith Creek side. Though this route is more direct, it is very exposed and prone to avalanche—it was the site of a 2006 slide that killed a local ski patroller. The longer route is safer and comes in from Little Slide Canyon.

Incredible Hulk
Left Couloir

Looking south into the upper portion of Horse Creek.

For this route, refer to the Little Slide Canyon Access description provided at the beginning of the Little Slide Canyon area earlier in this chapter.

Once in the canyon, stay on the east side of the creek, crossing the large, open slope toward a cliff band near the base of Mt. Walt. Pass the cliff band on the uphill (east) side, below Mt. Walt, then continue up the west face to the ridgeline. From here it is possible to gain the summit.

For the Blacksmith Canyon approach, head south through Mono Village and cross the river on a large bridge. Once across, head west for approximately ½ mile and begin climbing into the canyon. A short, steeper treed slope gives way to the main canyon above. As you enter the main canyon you will reach a bench where the terrain changes dramatically. There are a handful of sections of aspens that must be negotiated, but that clears up quickly.

From here, the rocky ridge of Mt. Walt will be directly above you. Climb a short, steep face through a gully and onto the next bench above. The top of this steep section has a large, moderate slope above it that contributes to very serious wind-loading at the rollover. This was the avalanche location triggered by a skier skinning the slope. Extreme caution should be taken, as there is very little cover.

Above the steep section, a gentle bowl climbs to another bench below the summit. Follow this up the gradually steepening slope as far as the snow will allow. The uppermost sections of this peak are rocky and very exposed to the wind, so they may not hold snow at certain times. As you climb to the summit, you will pass two north-facing couloirs that run down to Little Slide Canyon. These are great options for those looking to do a loop through two canyons.

Exit: Descend into Blacksmith Creek and follow your track back to the car.

▣ Horse Creek/Matterhorn

This is, by far, the most popular drainage in the Bridgeport Region—partially due to the draw of Matterhorn Peak, and partially due to the fact that it is the closest and easiest to access. As you enter Horse Creek Canyon, an abundance of skiable terrain surrounds you. Though all of it seems tempting, it is best to set your sights on the lines higher in the canyon, as the lower lines pale in comparison.

Horse Creek Access: From Mono Village (Trailhead #2), head south through the RV park and cross the creek on a large bridge at the southern edge of the resort. Continue along the east side of Horse Creek, climbing into the lower reaches of the drainage to a small bench. Just past this point the canyon branches, with the right (west) arm leading toward Matterhorn Peak, and the left (east) the upper portions of the canyon.

Darren Weimeyer in the Hulk's Left Couloir.

Jon Crowley climbs beneath The Doodad.

△ THE DOODAD *11,680'*

The Doodad is not a peak or even a high point on the ridge, but as you enter the Matterhorn cirque, you will realize why it has acquired its own name. Along the fairly uniform ridge above you sits a large, random block. This oddity is affectionately known as the Doodad, and is one of the many unique and interesting features tucked away in the Sawtooth Ridge.

The bowls and gullies below this section of the ridge offer many good opportunities for skiing, but great care must be taken to identify and navigate to one of the few passable lines that cut through the slabs and cliffs that make up the lowest 500' of the descent.

Below the Doodad is a large rock face, with two similar chutes on either side. The left one is a bit wider and more moderate. The right one twists at the top and becomes a little steeper. Hidden at the top of this couloir you will find the Doodad's little brother (Choc-col-lot): a chockstone the size of a bus, lodged at the top of this chute, creating a tunnel entrance to/from the ridge.

↘ NORTH COULOIRS

The Doodad

Aspect	Consequence/Exposure	Slope
	3	35°

Summit Elevation	11,500'
Descent Vertical	1,500'
Total Vertical	4,500'
Approach Distance	4 ½ miles
Terrain	Chute
Trailhead	2. Mono Village
USGS Quad Maps	Buckeye Ridge, Matterhorn Peak
GPS	38.099 / -119.39

Approach: Follow the Horse Creek Access description provided on page 46 into the Horse Creek drainage. As the drainage splits near the North Ridge of Matterhorn Peak, bear right and climb a small drainage which leads toward the base of the peak. As the drainage benches out, break out to the right (west) and continue up to another bench which provides access to the glacier below the Doodad. From here, boot the couloir of choice.

Looking southwest from Horse Creek.

Exit: Reverse your route, taking care around the creek. The terrain will naturally funnel you toward the open water, so be sure to follow the location of the summer trail. This will involve a bit of traversing at the end of your day, but will ultimately save you time and energy.

△ MATTERHORN PEAK *12,264'*

Matterhorn Peak is one of the more aesthetic, picturesque peaks in the range. It is bordered by couloirs, on its east and west flanks. There are also a few other chutes on its east shoulder, with the most prominent being Ski Dreams.

Matterhorn Approaches: Follow the Horse Creek Access description provided on page 46 into the lower portion of the drainage. As Horse Creek narrows near the North Ridge of Matterhorn Peak, cross the creek and head southwest up a small drainage that eventually reaches the base of the North Face.

From here, the Matterhorn couloirs loom above your head, with the West Couloir to the looker's right. Skin to the base of your line, then climb to the top.

Matterhorn Exits: Reverse your route, taking care around the creek. The terrain will naturally funnel you toward the open water, so be sure to follow the location of the summer trail. This will involve a bit of traversing at the end of your day, but will ultimately save you time and energy.

↘ WEST COULOIR — Mattherhorn Peak

Aspect	Consequence/Exposure	Slope
	3	35°

Summit Elevation	11,600'
Descent Vertical	1,600'
Total Vertical	4,500'
Approach Distance	4 ½ miles
Terrain	Chute
Trailhead	2. Mono Village
USGS Quad Maps	Buckeye Ridge, Matterhorn Peak
GPS	38.095 / -119.383

As you approach the base of the Matterhorn's impressive North Face, two obvious couloirs clearly flank the main summit. The West Couloir is the wider (and tamer) descent to the looker's right of the peak, descending from a spire-guarded notch through a nice wide offset couloir.

Approach: Follow the Matterhorn Approach description referenced on this page. Once beneath the North

Chris Gallardo beneath Matterhorn Peak.

Juan Gelpi nearing the top of Mt Walt.

Face of Matterhorn Peak, the West Couloir is the dominant line to the looker's right.

↘ EAST COULOIR

Mattherhorn Peak

Aspect | Consequence/Exposure 3 | Slope 40°

Summit Elevation	11,900'
Descent Vertical	1,900'
Total Vertical	4,800'
Approach Distance	4 ½ miles
Terrain	Chute
Trailhead	2. Mono Village
USGS Quad Maps	Buckeye Ridge, Matterhorn Peak
GPS	38.093 / -119.381

The East Couloir is directly to the looker's left of the main summit of Matterhorn Peak, and is actually comprised of a left and right branch, separated by a rocky outcrop. Unfortunately, these lines have a tendency to get scoured by the wind, making the upper portions a bit more technical and requiring navigation through some shallow, rocky terrain. As a result, many will set their sights on the East Couloir, only to opt for Ski Dreams as they grow closer. But this line does bring you the closest to the summit of Matterhorn, and if that is your objective, this is the preferred option. And, if you are lucky enough to find it in good condition, this is one of the ultra-classics of the range, with a long skiing history.

Approach: Follow the Matterhorn Approach description on page 50. As you near the base of Matterhorn Peak, you will be directly beneath the East Couloir. Follow that to the top.

↘ SKI DREAMS

Mattherhorn Peak

Aspect | Consequence/Exposure 3 | Slope 35°

Summit Elevation	11,800'
Descent Vertical	1,800'
Total Vertical	4,700'
Approach Distance	4 ½ miles
Terrain	Chute
Trailhead	2. Mono Village
USGS Quad Maps	Buckeye Ridge, Matterhorn Peak
GPS	38.094 / -119.378

Ski Dreams is the prominent line that seems to collect snow no matter which way the wind has been blowing. This is also the most popular ski descent in the canyon, due to its visibility from lower in the canyon and trail-

Toby and Buddy Schwindt climbing Ski Dreams.

head. There is an additional narrow chute just east of Ski Dreams that can be reached by walking just a few hundred feet along the ridge. Note that this line descends into a slightly different drainage higher in Horse Creek.

Approach: Follow the Matterhorn Approach directions on page 50. From here, the couloirs loom above. Ski Dreams is the wider couloir to the looker's left of the rocky ridge that separates it from the East Couloir. Skin up the apron, then boot to the ridgeline.

HORSE CREEK PEAK 11,332'

Along the ridgeline between Matterhorn Peak and Twin Peaks is Horse Creek Pass, a low spot just southeast of Matterhorn Peak and Ski Dreams. Just beyond the pass is a peaklet known as Horse Creek Peak, which is a striking rocky feature with beautiful couloirs on either side.

NORTH COULOIRS — Horse Creek Peak

Aspect	Consequence/Exposure	Slope
	3	40°

Summit Elevation	11,000' (west), 11,500' (east)
Descent Vertical	1,300' (west), 1,500' (east)
Total Vertical	3,800' (west), 4,300' (east)
Approach Distance	4 ½ miles
Terrain	Chute
Trailhead	2. Mono Village
USGS Quad Maps	Buckeye Ridge, Matterhorn Peak
GPS	38.09 / -119.364

These are the couloirs that flank either side of the rocky, spire-laden ridgeline that is Horse Creek Peak. The right-hand line is closer to Horse Creek Pass, and the left-hand closer to Twin Peaks.

Approach: Follow the Horse Creek Access description provided on page 46 into Horse Creek. As the canyon narrows near the North Ridge of Matterhorn Peak, continue up the drainage following the path of least resistance, typically on the east side of the drainage. After passing the East Ridge of Matterhorn Peak (just up from Ski Dreams), you will see Horse Creek Pass and the first of the North Couloirs on Horse Creek Peak. Continue to the base of the couloir of choice and skin and boot your way to the top.

Exit: Reverse your route, taking care around the creek. The terrain will naturally funnel you toward the open water, so be sure to follow the location of the summer trail. This will involve a bit of traversing at the end of your day, but will ultimately save you time and energy.

TWIN PEAKS 12,323'

Twin Peaks dominates the skyline at the head of the Horse Creek drainage. The North Face is an impressive feature with some great ski terrain, which is hidden from view until you are directly beneath it.

NORTH FACE — Twin Peaks

Aspect	Consequence/Exposure	Slope
	3	38°

Summit Elevation	12,323'
Descent Vertical	1,800'
Total Vertical	5,200'
Approach Distance	5 ¼ miles
Terrain	Chute
Trailhead	2. Mono Village
USGS Quad Maps	Buckeye Ridge, Matterhorn Peak, Dunderberg Peak
GPS	38.084 / -119.354

This is the bowl between the two peaks and the easiest way to their summits, should that be your objective. The west summit can hold snow most of the way to the top, and on big snow years, there are be a handful of steep chutes/faces that fill in here.

The east summit also has a number of chutes that descend from the shoulder into the Cattle Creek Drainage. From the bottom of these, it is easy to simply traverse back over into Horse Creek.

Approach: Follow the approach for Horse Creek Peak into the head of the drainage.

From here, the world is your oyster, with numerous options laid out in front of you off either summit and the ridgeline in between. Continue to the base of the couloir of choice and skin and boot your way to the top.

Exit: Reverse your route, taking care around the creek. The terrain will naturally funnel you toward the open water, so be sure to follow the location of the summer trail. This will involve a bit of traversing at the end of your day, but will ultimately save you time and energy.

Looking south at the North Face of Horse Creek Peak.

Looking south along the Matterhorn-Horse Creek ridgeline.

Twin Peaks East Summit

Horse Creek Peak

▣ Twin Lakes Area

△ CRATER CREST *11,394'*

Located at the outer elbow of the Twin Lakes drainage, the North Face of Crater Crest is extremely exposed to the wind and rarely holds snow. When it is filled in though, it offers easy access to some great terrain.

The North Face of Crater Crest is riddled with chutes, faces, and steep glades that drop thousands of feet to Twin Lakes. This is a skier's paradise, where options and opportunity are tied only to how creative you can be with your line.

↘ NORTH FACE — Crater Crest

Aspect	Consequence/Exposure	Slope
N	3	38°

Summit Elevation	11,394'
Descent Vertical	4,000'
Total Vertical	4,000'
Approach Distance	2 ½ miles
Terrain	Chute
Trailhead	1. Twin Lakes
USGS Quad Maps	Twin Lakes
GPS	38.129 / -119.339

Approach: From Twin Lakes (Trailhead #1), continue south along Patterson Road across the creek connecting the two Twin Lakes. Once on the snow, skin south and slightly east into a small drainage that is located just east of the last major ridgeline of Crater Crest's North Face. Continue up this feature to the summit ridge, then on to the peak's summit and the top of your chosen line.

Exit: You can generally ski your line right back to the south side of the Twin Lakes Estates development and Patterson Road.

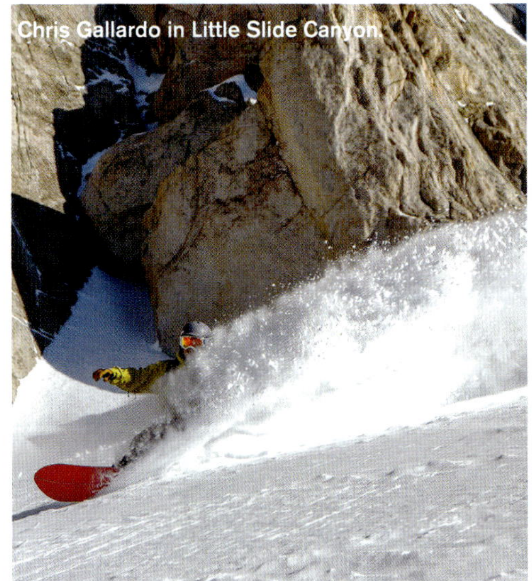
Chris Gallardo in Little Slide Canyon.

2 Virginia Lakes

Jason Templeton enjoying early season coverage on South Peak.

2. Virginia Lakes

VIRGINIA LAKES REGION:

- Virginia Lakes Area:
  - Δ **DUNDERBERG PEAK**
  - Δ **MT. OLSEN**
  - Δ **SOUTH PEAK**
  - Δ **BLACK MOUNTAIN**

Region Trailheads

3. Mt. Olsen Parking/Staging
4. Virginia Lakes Trailhead

Next to Tioga Pass and the Bishop Creek areas, Virginia Creek is one of the most popular and heavily accessed spring skiing destinations on the Eastside. Winter use of the area is also not uncommon, as it is an easy snowmobile ride (snowmobiling is fairly popular in this area) or skin from the point of winter closure to the trailhead along Virginia Lakes Road.

Virginia Lakes is also a popular fishing destination, and like most other canyon roads on the Eastside, fishing is the justification for the road getting plowed in the spring. In low snow years, however, Mono County has been known to plow the road to the pack station, which provides even easier access to the variety of terrain this region offers.

Though there isn't a ton of vertical to be found here, the Virginia Lakes region is a great place to have a leisurely day in the backcountry. With the exception of the north-facing lines off Black Mountain, most of the terrain in this drainage is immediately visible from the road as you are driving in to the lakes.

Getting There & Getting Going

The Virginia Lakes road turns off of Highway 395 at the top of Conway Summit, just across from the Caltrans Maintenance Station, and adjacent to an old restaurant and residence. This is approximately 13 miles south of Bridgeport and 12 miles north of Lee Vining. At the top of Conway Summit, turn west onto Virginia Lakes Road. Note that the trailheads described below are accessible only in the spring when the road is plowed, via snowmobile, or skinning. The point of winter closure is about ¼ mile from the Highway 395 intersection.

3. Mt. Olsen Parking/Staging (Spring Only) — *9,675'*

From Highway 395, travel up Virginia Lakes Road for approximately five miles, where the road levels out as it enters the main portion of the canyon. By this point you will have passed Dunderberg Meadow Road and the Virginia Lakes Pack Station on your right. As you begin to pass the last small subdivision on your right-hand side, keep an eye out for a small road and parking area on the south side of the road. It is fairly typical to see people parked along the road here.

4. Virginia Lakes Trailhead (Spring Only) — *9,850'*

A half mile or so beyond the Mt. Olsen staging area, the Virginia Lakes Road comes to an end in a looped parking area. There are restrooms here, and typically a lot of fishermen getting ready to venture out onto the lakes.

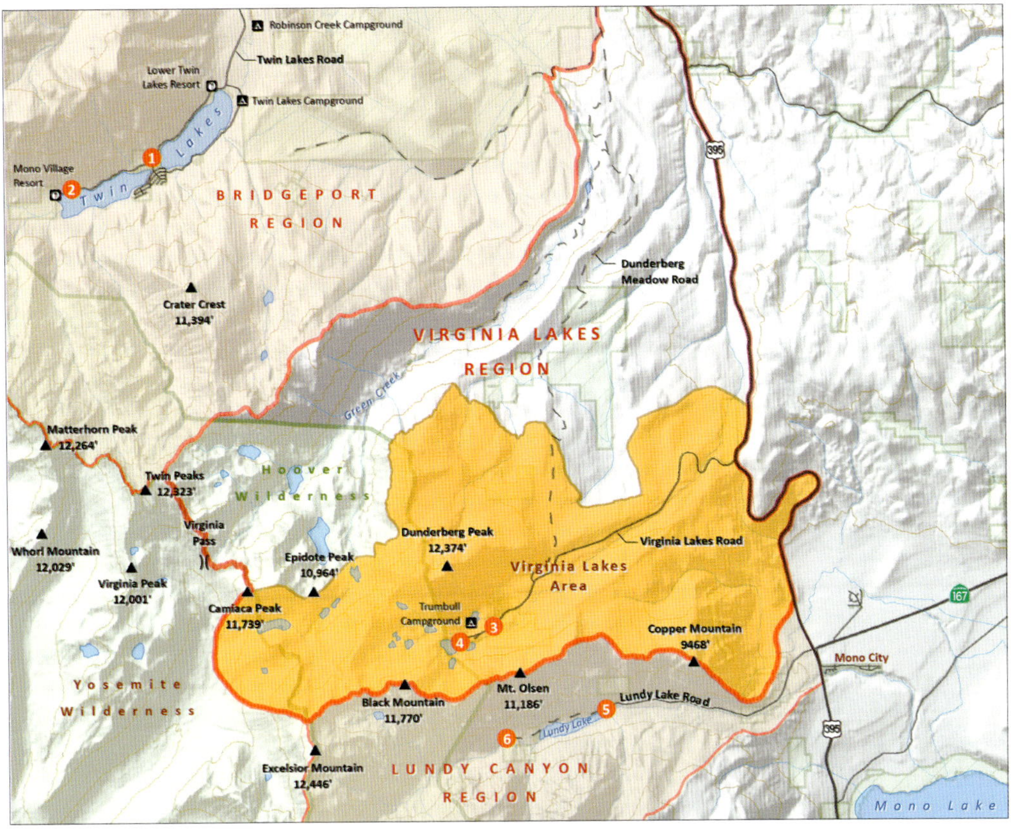

Robinson Creek Campground
Twin Lakes Road
Lower Twin Lakes Resort
Twin Lakes Campground
Twin Lakes
Mono Village Resort
BRIDGEPORT REGION
Dunderberg Meadow Road
Crater Crest 11,394'
VIRGINIA LAKES REGION
Green Creek
Matterhorn Peak 12,264'
Hoover Wilderness
Twin Peaks 12,323'
Virginia Pass
Whorl Mountain 12,029'
Virginia Peak 12,001'
Epidote Peak 10,964'
Dunderberg Peak 12,374'
Virginia Lakes Road
Virginia Lakes Area
Camiaca Peak 11,739'
Trumbull Campground
Copper Mountain 9468'
Mono City
167
395
Yosemite Wilderness
Black Mountain 11,770'
Mt. Olsen 11,186'
Lundy Lake Road
Lundy Lake
Excelsior Mountain 12,446'
LUNDY CANYON REGION
Mono Lake

Eats, Digs, Services, & Supplies

There are no services to speak of in the Virgina Lakes Area. The closest services can be found in either Bridgeport to the north or Lee Vining to the south. These towns are roughly the same distance in opposite directions.

Jason Templeton riding Black Mountain.

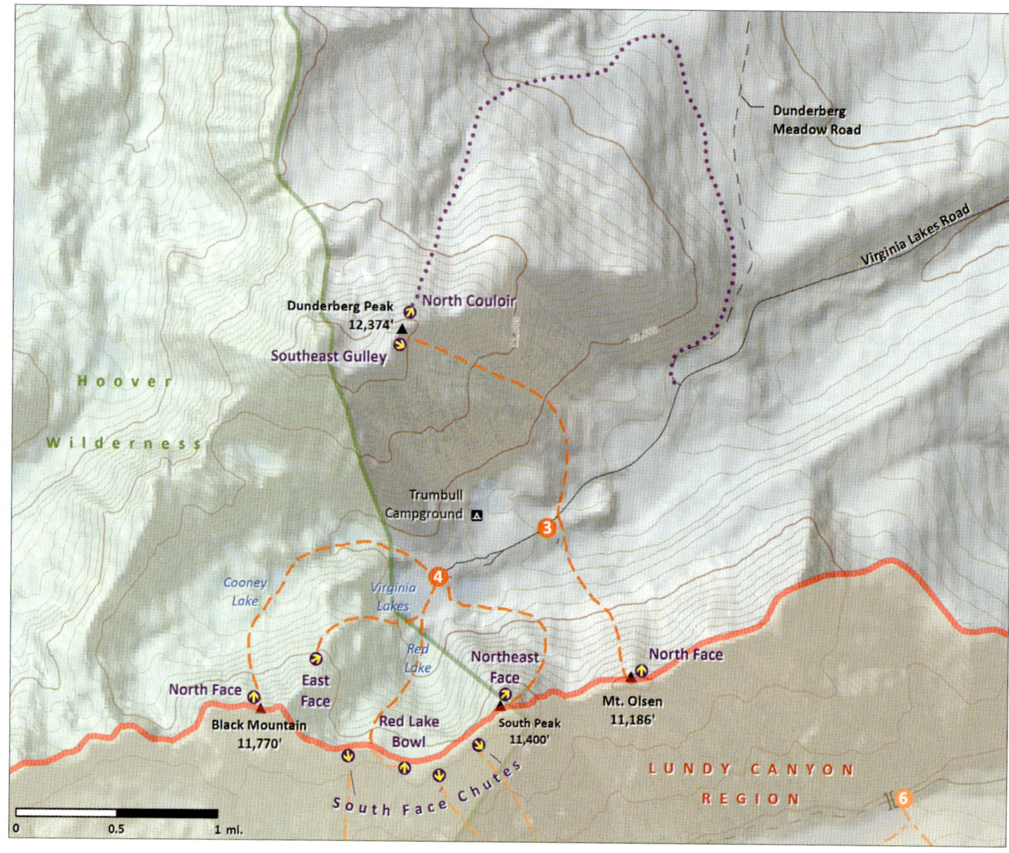

Virginia Lakes Area

△ DUNDERBERG PEAK *12,374'*

Dunderberg Peak is the most prominent summit in the Virginia Lakes Area, and also one of the more classic spring skiing lines in the Easten Sierra.

↘ SOUTHEAST GULLY — Dunderberg Peak

Aspect	Consequence/Exposure	Slope
	3	38°

Summit Elevation	12,374'
Descent Vertical	2,500'
Total Vertical	2,700'
Hiking Distance	¼ mile
Terrain	Chute
Trailhead	3. Mt. Olsen
USGS Quad Maps	Dunderberg Peak
GPS	38.064 / -119.266

This is a very popular spring destination, and one of the classics that you should be sure to tick off in the area. There are a few minor gullies that hold snow and feed into the main gully, all of which can be easily accessed from the trailhead and provide easy access to great corn skiing. But don't let the easy access fool you into thinking you can sleep late! This face heats up very quickly, and on most spring days you will want to be descending well before noon.

In recent years these gullies have been the site of a few close calls. Both natural and human-triggered avalanches are frequent here, as this zone heats up very quickly in the spring. These gullies rarely hold a deep snowpack, and the sun will permeate to the ground by midmorning.

Approach: From the Mt. Olsen Trailhead (#3), walk north onto the flank of Dunderberg, then ascend the gully. You'll likely be booting before you know it, and because of the freeze-thaw nature of this feature, crampons are recommended.

Exit: Follow your upwards track back to the car.

Looking south at the North Face of Dunderberg Peak.
Dunderberg Peak
North Couloir

↘ NORTH COULOIR

Dunderberg Peak

Aspect	Consequence/Exposure	Slope
	3	40°

Summit Elevation	12,374'
Descent Vertical	2,000'
Total Vertical	2,700'
Hiking Distance	¼ mile
Terrain	Chute
Trailhead	3. Mt. Olsen
USGS Quad Maps	Dunderberg Peak
GPS	38.066 / -119.265

In an area like Virginia Lakes where everything is visible from the parking lot, the North Couloir of Dunderberg is one of the more elusive lines. Though hidden from view from the Virginia Lakes drainage, the line is clearly visible as you travel south on Highway 395 from Bridgeport toward Conway Summit.

Be aware that this run drops into a separate drainage, and requires a little bit of work after your ski to get back to the Virginia Lakes Road and your car. From the summit there is a large ridge that separates the northwest and northeast faces, with the North Couloir dropping into the Dunderberg Meadow area. These two faces take you to very different locations, so if doing a loop or car shuttle, study the map and terrain before descending.

Approach: From the Mt. Olsen Trailhead (#3), walk north onto the flank of Dunderberg, then ascend the gully. You'll likely be booting before you know it, and because of the freeze-thaw nature of this feature, crampons are recommended.

Depending on the time of year and amount of snow on the road, it is also possible to access this side of the peak and the couloirs off Dunderberg Meadow Road from either Virginia Lakes Road or Green Creek Road. Snowmobiles also frequent this area from either starting point.

Exit: The exit varies depending on the time of year, the snowpack, and snowline, and whether you are interested in running a car shuttle or not. In general, the route out follows the Dunderberg Meadow Road back to Virginia Lakes Road. When both roads are clear, it is possible to do a car shuttle on this run. Otherwise, traverse to the east and ski along the roads until you reach your car.

Looking southwest from Virginia Lakes Road.

△ MT. OLSEN *11,186'*

As you get into the upper portion of the Virginia Creek Drainage, Mt. Olsen is the first prominent peak you see on the left-hand side. Mt. Olsen and Black Mountain form the southern ridgeline of the Virginia Lakes basin, and both offer great skiing right from the car

There are a variety of lines that can be skied off the north/northeast face of Mt. Olsen, all of which are visible from the car.

↘ NORTH FACE — Mt. Olsen

Aspect	Consequence/Exposure	Slope
	3	35°

Summit Elevation	11,186'
Descent Vertical	1,500'
Total Vertical	1,500'
Approach Distance	1 mile
Terrain	Face
Trailhead	3. Mt. Olsen
USGS Quad Maps	Lundy
GPS	38.041 / -119.245

Approach: From the Mt. Olsen Trailhead (#3), walk south along the dirt road, downhill and toward the creek and willow thicket. Find a spot to cross (there are many), and wind your way through the willow and onto the north flank of Mt. Olsen. A fairly direct and easy skin leads to the summit, though the uppermost part often requires some booting.

Exit: Follow your skin track back to the car—it doesn't get much easier than this!

△ SOUTH PEAK *11,400'*

Lying just west of Mt. Olsen, South Peak provides a similar set of experiences to its brother, with easy access to good skiing right from the car on South Peak's North and Northeast faces. While we only provide information on the Northeast Face, the North Face of South Peak can be accessed via the same approach, and offers a variety of moderately steep chutes and faces through cliff bands and relatively complex terrain.

↘ NORTHEAST FACE — South Peak

Aspect	Consequence/Exposure	Slope
	2	35°

Summit Elevation	11,400'
Descent Vertical	1,500'
Total Vertical	1,500'
Hiking Distance	1 mile
Terrain	Face
Trailhead	4. Virginia Lakes
USGS Quad Maps	Dunderberg Peak
GPS	38.04 / -119.257

This descent is a very popular spring destination in Virginia Lakes, as it is easy to access right from the car, typically offers great spring corn, and can often be summited without taking your skis off.

Approach: From Virginia Lakes Trailhead (#4), head south and around the west shore of a small lake before traversing under the North Face. Continue east and onto the flank of the Northeast Face, then to the summit.

Looking south at Black Mountain from Dunderberg Peak.

↘ RED LAKE BOWL

South Peak

Aspect	Consequence/Exposure	Slope
	2	35°

Summit Elevation	11,065'
Descent Vertical	1,200'
Total Vertical	1,200'
Hiking Distance	1 mile
Terrain	Bowl
Trailhead	4. Virginia Lakes
USGS Quad Maps	Dunderberg Peak
GPS	38.035 / -119.266

As the west ridge of South Peak wraps around and eventually connects to the summit of Black Mountain, it forms a relatively large bowl that lies directly above Red Lake. This is a very popular spring locale for folks looking to turn quick laps, or perhaps even ski some more challenging terrain in the headwall above the bowl itself.

Approach: From Virginia Lakes Trailhead (#4), head west along the south shore of Big Virginia Lake, then up a small rise into Red Lake basin. From here, you can either skin directly up the bowl or proceed to the west flank of the bowl and ascend a broad ridge feature to the South Peak/Black Mountain ridgeline.

Exits: Follow your upwards track back to the car.

△ BLACK MOUNTAIN *11,770'*

As the ridgeline extends west beyond Red Lake Bowl, it undulates before eventually reaching the summit of Black Mountain, the westernmost and largest of the peaks immediately surrounding Virginia Lakes. Black Mountain is a rather large, broad peak that affords a variety of terrain to ski on all of its aspects.

Though we only highlight the East and North faces in this chapter (and the South Face Gullies in the Lundy Chapter), there is also a good bit of terrain in the northeast bowl that sits just above Red Lake Bowl.

↘ EAST FACE

Black Mountain

Aspect	Consequence/Exposure	Slope
	3	35°

Summit Elevation	11,175'
Descent Vertical	1,200'
Total Vertical	1,300'
Hiking Distance	1 mile
Terrain	Face
Trailhead	4. Virginia Lakes
USGS Quad Maps	Dunderberg Peak
GPS	38.042 / -119.274

This descent is characterized by a small hanging snowfield/face that feeds into a several-hundred-foot gully

Brett Lotz on the North Face of Black Mountain. *Photo Nate Greenberg.*

off the more northeast summit of Black Mountain. The gully is a fairly prominent feature and can be clearly made out from the Virginia Lakes parking lot.

Approach: From the Virginia Lakes Trailhead (#4), head west and along the south shore of Big Virginia Lake to the base of the East Face. Skin and boot to the summit. Alternatively, skin through Red Lake Bowl to the west flank, then climb to the top of these lines from the back (south) side.

↘ NORTH FACE

Black Mountain

Aspect	Consequence/Exposure	Slope
	3	35°

Summit Elevation	11,770'
Descent Vertical	1,200'
Total Vertical	1,500'
Hiking Distance	1 ½ miles
Terrain	Face
Trailhead	4. Virginia Lakes
USGS Quad Maps	Dunderberg Peak
GPS	38.04 / -119.279K

The North Face of Black Mountain offers a wide range of options to skiers with intermediate–advanced skills who are competent and confident skiing in exposed and sometimes complex terrain. The North Face is lined with a number of gullies, chutes, and faces, divided by rocky ridges and spires. It's a beautiful location, often overlooked, with great views of Virginia Pass and the terrain that surrounds it.

Approach: From the Virginia Lakes Trailhead (#4), head northwest below the south flank of Dunderberg Peak and up a small draw that leads to Blue Lake. Continue around Blue Lake via its south shore, then up the drainage to the Cooney/Frog Lakes area. At this point you will start to see the varied terrain that comprises Black Mountain's North Face.

Exit: Follow your upwards track back to the car.

3 Lundy Canyon

Nate Greenberg dropping into the South Face Chutes in Lundy Canyon. *Photo: Josh Feinberg.*

3. Lundy Canyon

LUNDY CANYON REGION:

- Upper Canyon Area:
  - △ MT. SCOWDEN
- Lundy Lake Area:
  - △ GILCREST PEAK
  - △ MT. WARREN
  - △ DEER CREEK SHOULDER

Region Trailheads

5. Lundy Lake Dam
6. Lundy Canyon Trailhead

The Lundy Canyon Region houses some remarkable peaks and skiing opportunities, but is overshadowed by the larger neighboring regions of Virginia Lakes (to the north) and Lee Vining (to the south). The canyon is easily accessible all year long, and a great place to visit for those looking for a little solitude.

Getting There & Getting Going

The Lundy Lakes Road heads west off Highway 395 about seven miles north of Lee Vining, and 18 miles south of Bridgeport. The road climbs 1,300' into the small canyon as it leaves Highway 395, directly across from Highway 167 (Pole Line Road) just north of the small community of Mono City.

In winter months or during snowy periods, the road is gated and closed 3½ miles from the junction at Highway 395 at the east-outlet end of Lundy Lake. In the spring, the road is plowed another 1½ miles around the lake to provide access to Lundy Lake Resort and the Lundy Canyon trailhead. If the road is dry but still closed, cycling is a nice way to access the canyon.

5. Lundy Lake Dam (Year-Round) — 7,900'

From the junction of Highway 395, head west on Lundy Lake Road. Past a small subdivision of homes and a BLM fire station at the mouth of the canyon, the road climbs into the canyon. After about 3½ miles the road levels out as it approaches the outlet of Lundy Lake where there is an SCE-operated dam. There is a large dirt parking area on the south side of the road, and typically ample parking along the road itself at the gate.

6. Lundy Canyon Trailhead (Spring Only) — 8,050'

From the junction of Highway 395, head west on Lundy Lake Road. Past a small subdivision of homes and a BLM fire station at the mouth of the canyon, the road climbs into the canyon. After about 3½ miles the road levels out as it approaches the outlet of Lundy Lake where there is an SCE-operated dam and the winter-closure gate. Beyond this point, on the west side of Lundy Lake, is Lundy Lake Resort, which consists of a handful of cabins and a small store. Beyond the resort the road parallels the creek and some beaver ponds before reaching the trailhead.

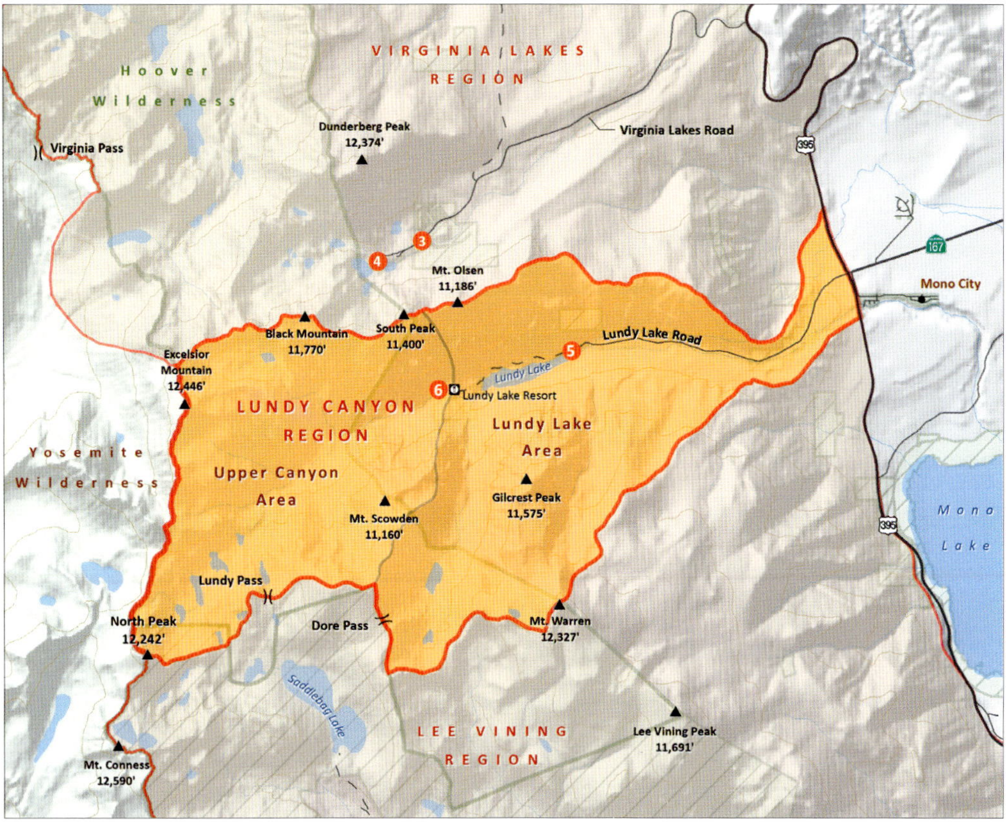

Looking south at the Lake Helen Chutes.

Eats, Digs, Services, & Supplies

Other than the modest store at Lundy Lake Resort, there are no services in this canyon. The closest services can be found in either Bridgeport (18 miles to the north), or Lee Vining (seven miles to the south).

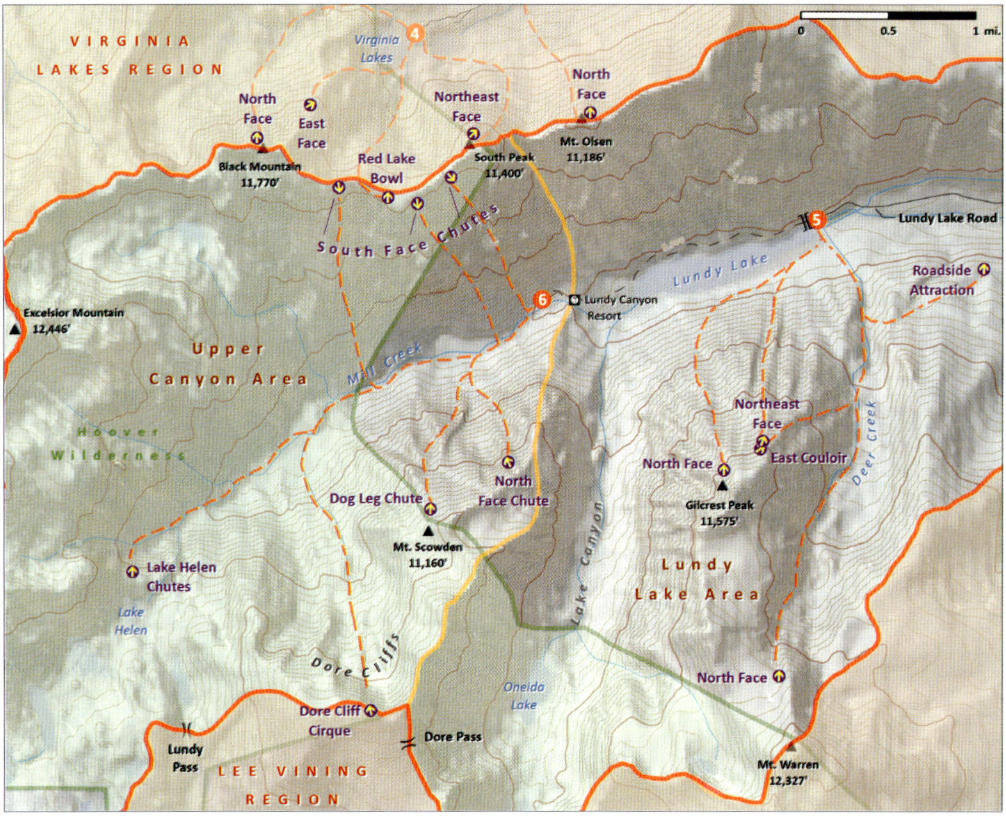

VIRGINIA LAKES REGION
Virginia Lakes
4
North Face
East Face
Black Mountain 11,770'
Northeast Face
North Face
Mt. Olsen 11,186'
South Peak 11,400'
Red Lake Bowl
South Face Chutes
5
Lundy Lake Road
Lundy Lake
Roadside Attraction
6
Lundy Canyon Resort
Excelsior Mountain 12,446'
Upper Canyon Area
Mill Creek
Hoover Wilderness
Northeast Face
East Couloir
North Face
Gilcrest Peak 11,575'
Deer Creek
North Face Chute
Dog Leg Chute
Mt. Scowden 11,160'
Lake Canyon
Lundy Lake Area
Lake Helen Chutes
Lake Helen
Dore Cliffs
Oneida Lake
North Face
Dore Cliff Cirque
Lundy Pass
Dore Pass
LEE VINING REGION
Mt. Warren 12,327'
0 0.5 1 mi.

Josh Feinberg dropping into the Dore Cliff Cirque. *Photo: Nate Greenberg.*

▣ Upper Canyon Area

Unlike many of the other Eastern Sierra drainages, the upper portions of Lundy Canyon are less steep and dramatic than the mouth, and offer a variety of smaller and more moderate terrain features. Though it takes a little longer to tour back into the depths of this drainage, the travel is relatively easy. If you are looking for a nice, quiet, and relatively remote zone to spend the day lapping terrain, this is a good spot to check out.

↘ LAKE HELEN CHUTES

Upper Canyon

Aspect | Consequence/Exposure 2 to 3 | Slope 30° to 40°

Summit Elevation	10,250'
Descent Vertical	1,200'
Total Vertical	2,250'
Hiking Distance	3 ½ miles
Terrain	Faces, chutes
Trailhead	6. Lundy Canyon Trailhead
USGS Quad Maps	Dunderberg Peak
GPS	38.005 / -119.293

Looking south across Lundy Canyon at the Dore Cliffs.

The Lake Helen Chutes lie at the head of Lundy Canyon in the vicinity of Lake Helen proper. There are a variety of options in this zone, consisting mostly of lower-angle east-facing terrain that drops from the lake back to the canyon floor. Just north of the Mill Creek drainage, which leads up to Lake Helen and Lundy Pass, is a moderately sized cirque that has steeper north- and south-facing terrain, and more moderate east-facing terrain.

Approach: From Lundy Canyon Trailhead (#6), travel up the Lundy Canyon drainage, roughly following the summer trail, for approximately 3½ miles. As you climb gradually higher in the canyon, you will encounter a couple of obstacles—the first being a dense stand of aspens, which eventually opens up at obstacle two, a beaver pond below a steep north-facing cliff. Traveling directly across the pond is typically not possible, so hugging the left (south) side of the drainage and side-hilling is usually the best option. The crux comes when it is necessary to cross over a steep wind lip that often forms on the ridge.

Beyond this point, travel eases again. As you reach the upper portion of the drainage, the creek splits, with the main branch leading to the terrain directly in front of you: the Lake Helen Chutes. Find your line of choice and skin or boot to the top

Exit: Follow your up track back to the car.

DORE CLIFFS CIRQUE

Upper Canyon

Aspect	Consequence/Exposure	Slope
	3	35° to 40°

Summit Elevation	11,750'
Descent Vertical	1,750'
Total Vertical	3,200'
Hiking Distance	3 miles
Terrain	Chute
Trailhead	6. Lundy Canyon Trailhead
USGS Quad Maps	Dunderberg Peak, Tioga Pass
GPS	37.993 / -119.268

The Dore Cliffs zone consists of a moderately sized hanging cirque with predominately north-facing terrain, flanked by eastern and western faces. Like the Lake Helen zone, the terrain here is slightly shorter, and offers a variety of options from lower-angle and moderate to steeper and more exposed. It's a great place to put in a boot pack and spin a few laps. It is also relatively easy to connect a line in this zone with something off Mt. Scowden on your way back to the canyon floor.

Approach: From Lundy Canyon Trailhead (#6), travel up the Lundy Canyon drainage, roughly following the summer trail, for approximately three miles. As you climb gradually higher in the canyon, you will encounter a couple of obstacles—the first being a dense stand

Danny Ranson and Sara Vigilante climbing Gilcrest Peak.

of aspens, which eventually opens up at obstacle two, a beaver pond below a steep north-facing cliff. Traveling directly across the pond is typically not possible, so hugging the left (south) side of the drainage and side-hilling is usually the best option. The crux comes when it is necessary to cross over a steep wind lip that usually forms on the ridge.

Beyond this point, travel eases again. As you reach the upper portion of the drainage, the creek splits. The main branch heads due west toward Lake Helen, and the southern branch into the Dore Cliffs Cirque. Head south up a moderate slope into the cirque, then pick your poison.

As you leave Lundy Lake Trailhead (#6) and travel up-canyon, it is hard to miss the large south-facing wall that looms over your right shoulder. The ridgeline of this face is the divider between Lundy Canyon and Virginia Creek, and spans the distance between Black Mountain and South Peak. Cutting through this mile-long face are a series of south-facing chutes that are longer than they seem, range in steepness from 35–40°, and have myriad interesting terrain features in their upper reaches.

↘ SOUTH FACE CHUTES

Upper Canyon

Aspect	Consequence/Exposure	Slope
	3	40°

Summit Elevation	11,245'
Descent Vertical	2,900'
Total Vertical	3,000'
Hiking Distance	2 miles
Terrain	Chute
Trailhead	6. Lundy Canyon Trailhead
USGS Quad Maps	Dunderberg Peak
GPS	38.036 / -119.271

Approach: From Lundy Lake Trailhead (#6), travel up the Lundy Canyon drainage, keeping to the bottom of the drainage until you reach the base of the chute you're interested in. Once located, cross onto the south slope, skin as high as you can, then boot to the summit. Given the aspect of these chutes, crampons can be useful (especially in spring).

Exit: Follow your up track back to the car.

△ MT. SCOWDEN 11,160'

Mt. Scowden is a seemingly innocuous peak, especially as you gaze at it from the trailhead. But looks can be deceiving, and as you approach the base of the north face and begin to look up it, you'll see why. The peak rises nearly 3,000' from the canyon floor and is riddled with complex and interesting terrain features that will make any backcountry skier drool.

↘ DOG LEG CHUTE

Mt. Scowden

Aspect	Consequence/Exposure	Slope
	3	38°

Summit Elevation	11,160'
Descent Vertical	2,800'
Total Vertical	3,100'
Hiking Distance	1 ¼ miles
Terrain	Chute
Trailhead	6. Lundy Canyon Trailhead
USGS Quad Maps	Dunderberg Peak
GPS	38.014 / -119.261

As you stare up the large north face of Mt. Scowden, Dog Leg Chute is the obvious aesthetic line that cuts through a large band of rock on the looker's right-hand side.

Looking west at Mt. Scowden's Northeast Face.

Approach: From Lundy Lake Trailhead (#6), travel up the Lundy Canyon drainage, roughly following the summer trail, for approximately one mile to the base of the north face of Mt. Scowden. From here, the Dog Leg Chute will clearly appear on the up-canyon (west) side of the north face as the lower reach of it dives through a rocky outcrop onto the slope before you. Skin to the base of the chute, then boot your way through the lower diagonal and continue uphill to the summit.

↘ NORTH FACE CHUTE

Mt. Scowden

Aspect	Consequence/Exposure	Slope
	3	38°

Summit Elevation	10,750'
Descent Vertical	2,500'
Total Vertical	2,700'
Hiking Distance	1 mile
Terrain	Chute
Trailhead	6. Lundy Canyon Trailhead
USGS Quad Maps	Dunderberg Peak
GPS	38.013 / -119.253

Slicing through the left-hand side of Mt. Scowden's north race is the stunning North Face Chute. Rising 2,700' from the canyon floor to the summit ridgeline, this chute has a nice little choke in the middle of otherwise open and moderate terrain.

Approach: From Lundy Lake Trailhead (#6), travel up the Lundy Canyon drainage, roughly following the summer trail, for approximately one mile to the base of the north face of Mt. Scowden. From here, the North Face Chute will appear to the right of the large buttress of rock that forms the left side of the north face. Skin to the base of the chute, then boot your way through the lower diagonal and continue uphill to the summit.

▣ Lundy Lake Area

△ GILCREST PEAK *11,575'*

Gilcrest Peak is clearly visible from Highway 395 as you travel through the Mono Basin and over Conway Summit. It is the guardian to Lundy Canyon, and offers quick access to some great terrain rising directly from the trailhead at Lundy Lake Dam.

Looking southwest at Gilcrest Peak from the Lundy Lake dam.

Kevin Smith riding Gilcrest Peak.

NORTH FACE

Gilcrest Peak

Aspect	Consequence/Exposure	Slope
N	3	38°

Summit Elevation	11,575'
Descent Vertical	3,500'
Total Vertical	3,700'
Hiking Distance	2 miles
Terrain	Face
Trailhead	5. Lundy Lake Dam
USGS Quad Maps	Lundy
GPS	38.012 / -119.231

The actual North Face of Gilcrest Peak isn't immediately obvious from the trailhead, as it is blocked slightly from view by a series of rocky ridges. There are actually a variety of options for skiing the North Face, all of which dive off the north–south-trending summit ridge. The most obvious line descends directly from the summit through some open faces and a small choke before reaching the apron below.

Approach: From Lundy Lake Dam (Trailhead #5), cross the outlet of Lundy Lake and head west along the south shore. There is an old mining road that traverses the North Face as it heads into the canyon between Scowden and Gilcrest. This often provides easier travel to the base of the North Face.

Once below your line of choice, skin as high as you can up the slope, then boot your way to the summit.

NORTHEAST FACE

Gilcrest Peak

Aspect	Consequence/Exposure	Slope
NE	4	40°

Summit Elevation	11,000'
Descent Vertical	3,000'
Total Vertical	3,100'
Hiking Distance	2 miles
Terrain	Face
Trailhead	5. Lundy Lake Dam
USGS Quad Maps	Lundy
GPS	38.018 / -119.227

Clearly visible from the Lundy Lake Trailhead, the Northeast Face of Gilcrest Peak is comprised of two main gullies separated by prominent rocky ridges and outcrops. The right-hand gully leads directly to the summit, while the slightly shorter left-hand one leads to the eastern summit ridge.

Looking south, up Deer Creek at Mt. Warren.
Mt. Warren
North Face

Approach: From Lundy Lake Dam (Trailhead #5), cross the outlet of Lundy Lake and head west along the south shore for a short distance until you are below your line of choice. From here, skin as high as you can up the slope, then boot your way to the summit.

Gilcrest Exits: Follow your up-track back to the car.

↘ EAST COULOIR
Gilcrest Peak

Aspect	Consequence/Exposure	Slope
	3	38°

Summit Elevation	11,000'
Descent Vertical	2,000'
Total Vertical	3,100'
Hiking Distance	2 ½ miles
Terrain	Chute
Trailhead	5. Lundy Lake Dam
USGS Quad Maps	Lundy
GPS	38.014 / -119.227

The East Couloir of Gilcrest Peak is not visible from the trailhead, as it is hidden from view by the large buttress of rock on the looker's left side of the Northeast Face. As you climb up Deer Creek beneath Gilcrest's East Face and toward Mt. Warren, this striking line dominates the view to the west.

Approach: From Lundy Lake Dam (Trailhead #5), cross the outlet of Lundy Lake and continue due south up Deer Creek for approximate 1½ miles. The terrain is not as straightforward as it appears, as the middle portion of Deer Creek is comprised of a series of small benches, each of which is guarded by northeast or northwest faces covered with small brush. Travel can be challenging, but the best approach is to take high lines across these slopes and stay out of the creek bed.

Once beneath the East Face of Gilcrest, the couloir will be directly above you. Wander through the pine forest and up to the base of the couloir. Skin and boot up the chute, eventually choosing either the right or left hand branch of the Y at the top.

△ MT. WARREN *12,327'*

Sitting at the head of the Deer Creek Canyon, and forming the divide between Lee Vining and Lundy, is the broad and striking Mt. Warren. Though not fully visible from the trailhead, this peak offers a wide variety of easily accessed terrain choices.

↘ NORTH FACE
Mt. Warren

Aspect	Consequence/Exposure	Slope
	2	30°

Summit Elevation	11,700'
Descent Vertical	1,250'
Total Vertical	3,800'
Hiking Distance	2 ¾ miles
Terrain	Face, chute, ramps
Trailhead	5. Lundy Lake Dam
USGS Quad Maps	Lundy, Mt. Dana
GPS	37.996 / -119.225

Looking south at the Deer Creek Shoulder from Lundy Canyon Road

The North Face of Mt. Warren actually consists of several different terrain features. The main North Face, dropping from the true summit, is actually more like the Northeast Face. This line drops into the headwaters of Dechambeau Creek, which is just south of the Lundy Drainage. At the end of Mt. Warren's North Ridge is more terrain consisting of chutes and ramps that descend a shorter distance back into the headwaters of Deer Creek.

Approach: From Lundy Lake Dam (Trailhead #5), cross the outlet of Lundy Lake and continue due south up Deer Creek for approximately 2¾ miles. Though seemingly straightforward, the terrain in the middle portion of Deer Creek is comprised of a series of small benches, each of which is guarded by northeast or northwest faces covered with small brush. Travel can be challenging, but the best approach is to take high lines across these slopes and stay out of the creekbed.

Pass beneath the east face of Gilcrest Peak and continue up the drainage until you reach the base of Mt. Warren. From here a few different options exist, depending on your desired line.

It is possible to stay in the bottom of the creek and continue into the head of the drainage providing access to a bowl just west of the prominent rocky north ridgeline of Mt. Warren. This route offers a lower-angle route to the summit, but it is slightly less direct. If shooting for the chutes and ramps that cut through the North Face Ridge, it is easiest to just skin and boot directly up them. And if heading toward the Northeast Face, it is possible to gain a small saddle to the east of the ridge then skin/boot directly up the face.

Exit: Generally follow your up track back to the car. However, if skiing the Northeast Face, before dropping too low into Dechambeau Creek, work a series of benches down and left, trending northwest back toward the mouth of Lundy Canyon. After some significant traversing, you will eventually end up on the Roadside Attraction slopes directly above the Lundy Canyon Road and Lundy Dam Trailhead.

△ DEER CREEK SHOULDER 8,275'

As you reach the point of winter closure and the eastern end of Lundy Lake, a small east–west-running ridgeline appears on the south side of the canyon. The northern terminus of this ridge forms the southern edge of Deer Creek, which leads to the North Face of Mt. Warren.

↘ ROADSIDE ATTRACTION

Deer Creek Shoulder

Aspect	Consequence/Exposure	Slope
	1	30°

Summit Elevation	8,275'
Descent Vertical	500'
Total Vertical	500'
Hiking Distance	1 ¾ miles
Terrain	Trees
Trailhead	5. Lundy Lake Dam
USGS Quad Maps	Lundy
GPS	38.029 / -119.203

There are a number of glades, small gullies, and open faces that can be skied from the top of the ridgeline back to the road and your car. These are short-and-quick shots that can be banged out when time is limited or you're looking for a mellow day.

Approach: From Lundy Lake Dam (Trailhead #5), head south and into the mouth of Deer Creek. As you climb the lower portions, begin to veer east and eventually gain the ridgeline and bench. Once on top, head east until you find your desired drop-in point.

4 Lee Vining

Buffy Lloyd atop the Dana Plateau.

4. Lee Vining

LEE VINING REGION:

- Saddlebag Lake Area:
  - △ NORTH PEAK
  - △ MT. CONNESS
  - △ GREENSTONE RIDGE
  - △ WHITE MOUNTAIN
  - △ FALSE WHITE MOUNTAIN
- Tioga Pass Area:
  - △ GAYLOR PEAK
  - △ ELLERY BOWL
  - △ MT. DANA
  - △ DANA PLATEAU
  - △ LOWER PLATEAU BENCH
  - △ MT. GIBBS

Region Trailheads

7. Tioga Pass Lower Gate
8. Lee Vining Creek Bridge
9. Ellery Lake
10. Saddlebag Lake Road
11. Tioga Lake

Wedged between the Mono Basin and Yosemite National Park, the Lee Vining Region has some of the finest views (and skiing) of all the regions in this book. This area is characterized by rolling alpine meadows, High Sierra granite, and some incredibly diverse ski terrain.

During the winter months, Highway 120 (Tioga Pass Road) is closed three miles west of Lee Vining. While this makes for longer approaches to the descents in the Saddlebag Lake Area, the Tioga Pass Area descents are still within reach. In the spring when the road opens, the area comes alive with backcountry enthusiasts from all over the world. For a blissful few weeks, the Lee Vining Region becomes one of the heaviest used zones on the Eastside.

In years past, Tioga Pass Resort (located just a short distance up Highway 120 from its junction with Saddlebag Lake Road) ran a year-round operation, offering some of the finest ski-in-ski-out accommodations and terrain in the state. Unfortunately, the resort has been closed during the winter for several years and consequently the road is no longer groomed or otherwise maintained.

Getting There & Getting Going

Highway 120 west (Tioga Pass Road) leaves Highway 395 just south of the small community of Lee Vining, which is 25 miles north of Mammoth Lakes, and the same distance south of Bridgeport.

All of the descents in this region have different approaches for winter and spring access, so be sure to read each section carefully. We call out five separate trailheads, two of which (7 & 8) are used all winter, while the other three (9–11) are only available once CalTrans opens the lower gate on Tioga Pass Road, which typically happens right around the time of fishing opener in late April. Snowmobiles are allowed along the Tioga Pass Road to the boundary of Yosemite National Park. Be aware that the road does not always have enough snow at the bottom to allow this, and can be impassable higher up due to avalanche paths that cross it.

Though Tioga Pass Road is closed to vehicle traffic all winter long, Poole Power Plant Road in Lee Vining Canyon is plowed throughout the winter, except during periods of heavy snowfall. This road turns off of Tioga Pass Road just a few hundred feet before the winter-closure gate, and is frequented by ice climbers heading into Lee Vining Canyon.

7. Tioga Pass Lower Gate (Year-Round) *7,500'*

From its junction at Highway 395, head west on Tioga Pass Road approximately three miles to the winter-closure gate at the bottom of the pass. Parking is available on either side of the road just before the gate, or on Poole Power Plant Road at its intersection with Tioga Pass Road. Please do not block the gate!

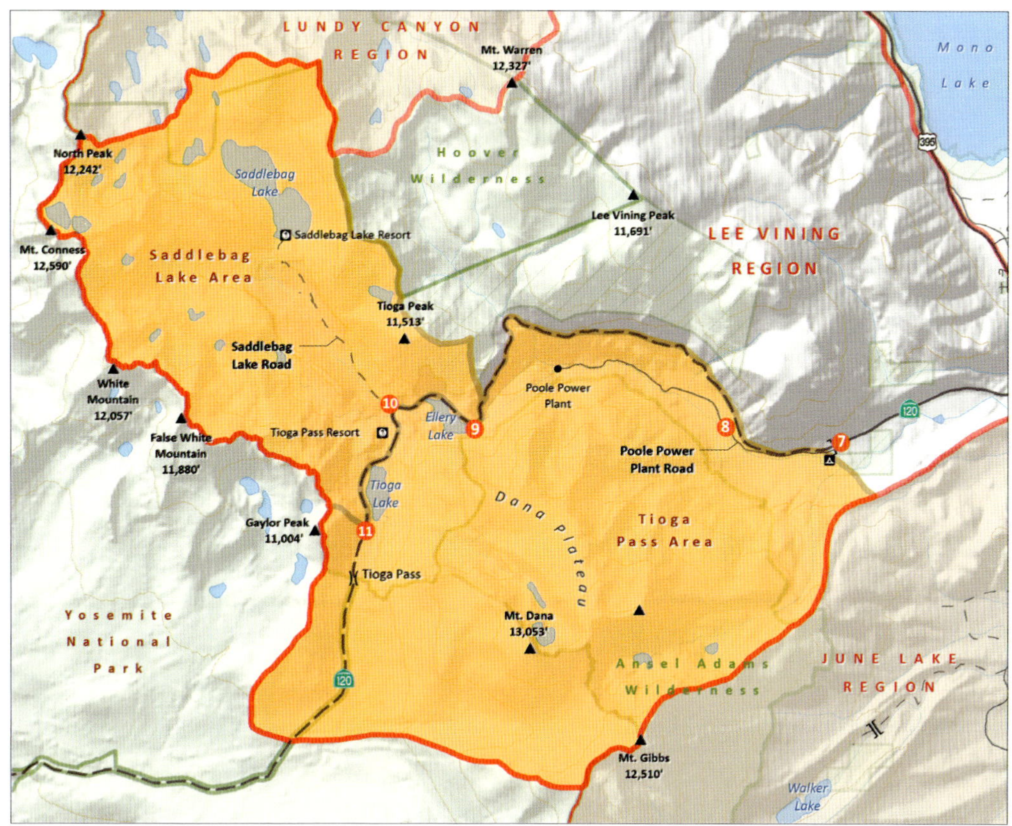

8. Lee Vining Creek Bridge (Year-Round) *7,800'*

Just before the lower gate (point of winter closure) on Tioga Pass Road, Poole Power Plant Road originates on the south side of the highway and parallels it as it winds into Lee Vining Canyon. This is a partially paved road that is used by Southern California Edison power company to access Poole Power Plant. Consequently it is plowed during the winter, though usually not during storms. The power plant at the end of the road is the preferred parking area for ice climbers accessing the frozen cliffs up-canyon, while several other parking areas along the way provide skiers with great access to the Dana Plateau and the Lower Plateau Bench year-round.

Depending on the amount of snow and how the road has been plowed, there are typically a number of small parking areas along the road between Tioga Pass Road and the power plant. The most popular of these is a larger parking area on the south side of Poole Power Plant Road, approximately ¾ miles west of its intersection with Tioga Pass Road. As you come out of the trees and curve to the right, keep an eye out for the plowed parking area to your left. There is a gate at the south side of the lot and a bridge that crosses Lee Vining Creek.

9. Ellery Lake (Spring Only) *9,500'*

Once the lower gate opens, access to the upper parking areas on Tioga Pass Road becomes available. The first popular trailhead is Ellery Lake, which is located 5½ miles west of the lower gate on Tioga Pass Road. As you approach the lake, the road curves sharply to the north and there is a large parking area on the south side of the road at the dam.

10. Saddlebag Lake Road (Spring Only) *9,540'*

The road to Saddlebag Lake is just one mile (6½ miles from the lower gate on Tioga Pass Road) west of the Ellery Lake parking area. This is a dirt road and is not plowed, so the timing of its opening depends entirely on temperatures and snowpack. In the early spring you will likely be able to skin most of the road, though it is generally on a southwest aspect—as the sun gets higher, the snow melts out.

11. Tioga Lake (Spring Only) *9,800'*

The uppermost trailhead on Tioga Pass Road frequented by backcountry skiers is at Tioga Lake, located eight miles from the lower gate. At the upper (western) end of Tioga Lake is a large pullout with a bathroom on

the south side of Tioga Pass Road. There is also typically a springtime closure on the pass road at this point and a lot of people staging out from the area.

Eats, Digs, Services, & Supplies

The small community of Lee Vining lies at the base of Tioga Pass and provides essentials such as gas, food, and lodging. As far as tourism goes, winter is typically the slow season for Lee Vining; the majority of its guests are summer visitors to Yosemite National Park. The Mobil Mart (located on Tioga Pass Road just up from its junction with Highway 395) and Mono Cone (in Lee Vining proper) are the hot spots for an *après* ski meal. Mono Market is the best spot for groceries.

If you are new to the area or looking for information, stop in to the Mono Lake Committee's bookstore, located in downtown Lee Vining on the west side of Highway 395. In the springtime, the Mono Basin Visitor Center opens up and offers great cultural exhibits and visitor information. It is located on the east side of Highway 395 as you leave Lee Vining going north.

▣ Saddlebag Lake Area

△ NORTH PEAK *12,242'*

Characterized by its formidable granite face, North Peak guards the eastern boundary of Yosemite National Park. From Saddlebag Lake, its southeast face is clearly visible, but doesn't look like much. Hidden from view, however, is its large north face, which is split by three large clefts. The right-hand of these is the popular North Couloir. All of these lines are heavily sought after by ice climbers and skiers alike, though in very different conditions.

North Peak Approaches: From the Saddlebag Lake Road trailhead (#10) continue along Saddlebag Lake Road for 2½ miles until you reach the dam at Saddlebag Lake. Cross the lake or ski around on the west shore if it isn't frozen.

North Peak Exits: Reverse the approach.

↘ SOUTHEAST FACE

North Peak

Aspect | Consequence/Exposure 2 | Slope 30°

Summit Elevation	12,242'
Descent Vertical	1,750'
Total Vertical	2,700'
Approach Distance	5 ½ miles
Terrain	Face
Trailhead	10. Saddlebag Lake Road
USGS Quad Maps	Tioga Pass
GPS	37.98 / -119.314

The Southeast Face of North Peak offers a moderate descent compared to the steep chutes on the other side. Though the upper portion of the peak tends to get scoured by the wind, it is possible to ski from fairly close to the summit.

Approach: After navigating around Saddlebag Lake, head west into a small basin and climb the Southeast Face.

↘ NORTH COULOIR

North Peak

Aspect | Consequence/Exposure 4 | Slope 45°

Summit Elevation	11,500'
Descent Vertical	1,200'
Total Vertical	2,000'
Approach Distance	5 ½ miles
Terrain	Chute
Trailhead	10. Saddlebag Lake Road
USGS Quad Maps	Tioga Pass
GPS	37.982 / -119.308

This is the right-hand of the three prominent couloirs that split the massive north face of North Peak. Though this doesn't drop right from the summit, it is one of the more classic lines in the region

Approach: After navigating around Saddlebag Lake, contour around to the west, climb a small bench to Greenstone Lake, and continue to the northwest toward the north face of the peak. From here, climb the couloir of choice.

It is also possible to get to the top of the couloirs via the Southeast Face approach.

Brian Robinette, Ken Coleman, and Brian Outhwaite walk along the Dana Plateau.

△ MT. CONNESS *12,590'*

Known equally for its rock climbing and skiing, the many sides of Mt. Conness hold a multitude of options for outdoor activities. Its sheer south face is visible from nearly any point in Tuolumne Meadows, while its hidden north face has a number of fine ski lines. These chutes drop down to the Conness Glacier, and in many years it's possible to ski them in the summer months.

Most of the skiing on Mt. Conness is found on its north face, which is comprised of a number of chutes and open faces that all end up on the Conness Glacier.

↘ SUMMIT COULOIRS — Mt. Conness

Aspect	Consequence/Exposure	Slope
N	3	40°

Summit Elevation	12,300'
Descent Vertical	2,000'
Total Vertical	3,000'
Approach Distance	5 miles
Terrain	Chute
Trailhead	10. Saddlebag Lake Road
USGS Quad Maps	Tioga Pass
GPS	37.967 / -119.319

Approach: From the Saddlebag Lake Road trailhead (#10), continue along Saddlebag Lake Road for 2½ miles until you reach the dam at the lake. Cross the lake or ski around on the west shore if it isn't frozen. At the far end of Saddlebag Lake, contour around to the west and climb a small bench to Greenstone Lake. From Greenstone Lake, continue west through a glacial valley to the Conness Lakes at the base of the Conness Glacier. From here, the north-facing chutes will be in view. To reach the summit plateau, either climb your intended descent or climb a short chute on the east ridge and continue up the moderate slope above.

The true summit of Mt. Conness is a short distance to the west of these chutes. The last little bit is exposed Class 3 and can potentially hold snow/ice into the summer months. Bear in mind that the Conness Glacier is quite large (by California standards, at least). As the season progresses, the bergschrunds at the base of each chute grow larger and larger. The cracks are much bigger than they look from afar and can pose a very serious threat. If you can see a crack forming on your desired descent, it is best to climb that chute first to inspect the danger.

It is also possible to summit Mt. Conness via the East Ridge. For this approach, follow Saddlebag Lake Road for 1½ miles from Trailhead #10 to Sawmill Campground. Go through the campground and across the

Jason Templeton riding the Coke Chute.

river, then continue heading west through the meadows of the Hall Natural Area. Approximately 1½ miles past the Sawmill Campground begin climbing the hillside on your right (north), aiming to the right of the large cliff face in the distance. Follow this to a small bench above Alpine Lake and then continue up the broad snowy slope of the east ridge. The top is the summit plateau, and the Conness Glacier is below you.

If doing this approach in the spring, remember that the bergschrunds may not be completely visible from the top of the chutes. Climbing the East Ridge does not give you the chance to inspect any of these dangers beforehand. If you see cracks forming below you, skiing down to them is not recommended.

Exit: Reverse the approach.

△ GREENSTONE RIDGE *10,750'*

Spanning the distance between Saddlebag Lake and Mt. Conness, this region has a wide variety of chutes and bowls.

Greenstone Ridge Approaches: From the Saddlebag Lake Road trailhead (#10) continue along Saddlebag Lake Road for 2½ miles until you reach the dam at Saddlebag Lake. Cross the lake or ski around on the west shore if it isn't frozen, then head west to the north side of the Greenstone Ridge.

Greenstone Ridge Exits: Reverse the approach.

↘ S CHUTE

Greenstone Ridge

Aspect	Consequence/Exposure	Slope
	3	35°

Summit Elevation	11,750'
Descent Vertical	500'
Total Vertical	1,200'
Approach Distance	2 ½ miles
Terrain	Chute
Trailhead	10. Saddlebag Lake Road
USGS Quad Maps	Tioga Pass
GPS	37.98 / -119.3

S Chute is the short, narrow cleft through a cliff band above the lakes. Its unmistakable "S" shape can be intimidating from below.

↘ GPS BOWL

Greenstone Ridge

Aspect	Consequence/Exposure	Slope
	3	38°

Summit Elevation	11,000'
Descent Vertical	900'
Total Vertical	1,500'
Approach Distance	2 ½ miles
Terrain	Bowl
Trailhead	10. Saddlebag Lake Road
USGS Quad Maps	Tioga Pass
GPS	37.98 / -119.3

Jon Crowley enjoys an early October dusting on the Conness Glacier.

GPS Bowl is the large bowl located on the eastern edge of the face, just a short distance below the S Chute.

↘ GREENSTONE RIDGE — Greenstone Ridge

Aspect	Consequence/Exposure	Slope
	2	30°

Summit Elevation	10,750'
Descent Vertical	750'
Total Vertical	1,200'
Approach Distance	2 ½ miles
Terrain	Mixed
Trailhead	10. Saddlebag Lake Road
USGS Quad Maps	Tioga Pass
GPS	37.982 / -119.301

The Greenstone Ridge comprises the terrain just east of GPS Bowl and offers a variety of open terrain. This terrain lies directly above Greenstone Lake.

△ WHITE MOUNTAIN *12,057'*

White Mountain is a classic example of "out of sight, out of mind." While people flock to the slopes of False White Mountain, White Mountain itself is often overlooked due to the fact that it isn't visible from the road.

↘ NORTH SLOPE — White Mountain

Aspect	Consequence/Exposure	Slope
	3	35°

Summit Elevation	11,700'
Descent Vertical	1,000'
Total Vertical	2,100'
Approach Distance	4 ¼ miles
Terrain	Chute
Trailhead	10. Saddlebag Lake Road
USGS Quad Maps	Tioga Pass
GPS	37.949 / -119.307

The North Slope descends from White Mountain's true summit. The long East Ridge that extends beyond the North Slope also holds a number of steep chutes.

Approach: Follow the Saddlebag Lake Road for 1½ miles to the Sawmill Campground. Go through the campground and across the river, then continue heading west through the meadows of the Hall Natural Area. Continue up this drainage to the base of the chutes. A short distance past these chutes is the broad North Slope of White Mountain. The North Slope is the easiest way to the summit, requiring just a short scramble on rock to reach the top.

↘ EAST FACE

White Mountain

Aspect	Consequence/Exposure	Slope
E	2	35°

Summit Elevation	12,057'
Descent Vertical	1,300'
Total Vertical	2,500'
Approach Distance	4 miles
Terrain	Face
Trailhead	10. Saddlebag Lake Road
USGS Quad Maps	Tioga Pass
GPS	37.946 / -119.309

The East Face of White Mountain offers a short rocky chute followed by a long open face.

Approach: From the Saddlebag Lake Road trailhead (#10), follow Saddlebag Lake Road for 1½ miles to the Sawmill Campground. Go through the campground and across the river, then continue heading west through the meadows of the Hall Natural Area. Approximately 1½ miles past the Sawmill Campground, head southwest to Green Treble Lake. Climb the short, steep hillside above Green Treble Lake to the bench below White Mountain's east face and Big Horn Lake. The gentle climb gradually steepens when you enter a chute that climbs to the summit.

White Mountain Exits: Reverse the approach.

△ FALSE WHITE MOUNTAIN *11,880'*

Highly visible from the parking lot at Saddlebag Lake, the moderate slope of False White attracts crowds like none other because it affords a range of skiing opportunities relatively close to the trailhead. False White holds snow well into the beginning of summer.

False White Approaches: From the Saddlebag Lake Road trailhead (#10), follow Saddlebag Lake Road a few hundred feet to a bridge on your left. Cross the river and begin a gentle climb to the northeast, past the meadow at Shell and Fantail lakes. From Fantail Lake, contour around to the southwest and climb the steep drainage to the base of False White.

↘ NORTH CHUTE

False White Mountain

Aspect | Consequence/Exposure: 3 | Slope: 35°

Summit Elevation	11,880'
Descent Vertical	1,500'
Total Vertical	2,300'
Approach Distance	3 miles
Terrain	Chute
Trailhead	10. Saddlebag Lake Road
USGS Quad Maps	Tioga Pass
GPS	37.936 / -119.294

This is a less commonly skied narrow chute that drops north from near the summit into the Skeleton Lakes basin. Getting into the chute may require a small amount of down climbing.

Exit: From the bottom of the chute, continue down the drainage, which will ultimately bring you to the exit for White Mountain.

↘ EAST FACE

False White Mountain

Aspect | Consequence/Exposure: 2 | Slope: 30°

Summit Elevation	11,880'
Descent Vertical	1,200'
Total Vertical	2,300'
Approach Distance	3 miles
Terrain	Face
Trailhead	10. Saddlebag Lake Road
USGS Quad Maps	Tioga Pass
GPS	37.939 / -119.293

This is the large, open face that is visible from the parking lot and is a very popular moderate descent. It is also the most common approach to the summit.

Exit: The bench below False White offers a number of bowls and chutes that will take you back toward the parking lot. Traversing to the skier's right after finishing the East Face will bring you to a moderate slope above the road, while continuing on the fall line will bring you to a handful of steeper chutes.

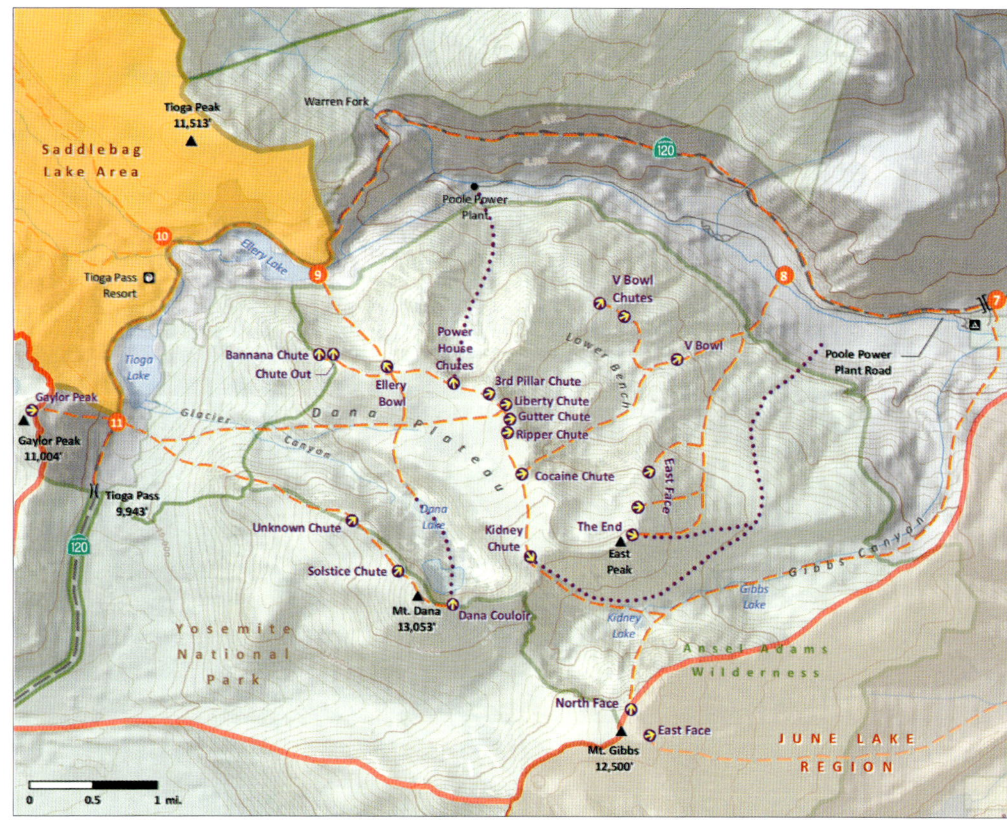

Tioga Pass Area

△ GAYLOR PEAK *11,004'*

Guarding Tioga Pass, Gaylor Peak is the major peak directly along the north side of Tioga Pass Road. It has a tremendous amount of terrain and is skied heavily during the spring when the road opens.

GAYLOR PEAK DESCENTS — Gaylor Peak

Aspect | Consequence/Exposure: 2 | Slope: 35°

Summit Elevation	11,004'
Descent Vertical	900'
Total Vertical	1,200'
Approach Distance	½ mile
Terrain	Mixed
Trailhead	11. Tioga Lake
USGS Quad Maps	Tioga Pass
GPS	37.92 / -119.265

A number of descent options exist off Gaylor's true summit and broad east ridge. As you approach the peak, you will be looking directly at the east face, which has a number of treed glades and shallow gullies. As you climb the peak, you will have full view of all the terrain off the northeast side, which generally includes lower-angle and shorter terrain. The east ridge yields a south-facing slope with lots of terrain features.

Approach: From Tioga Lake Trailhead (#11), travel a short distance up Tioga Pass Road to a prominent east–west-running ridge, which creates a number of south-facing descents before winding its way back to the south and main part of Gaylor Peak. Skin into the cleft that is formed between the actual summit and the east-west ridge and work generally south and west through gullies before gaining a low-angle ramp that leads south to the summit.

Exit: All descents off Gaylor Peak drop you onto Tioga Pass Road.

Kevin Smith drops into the Ripper Chute.

△ ELLERY BOWL *11,300'*

When Tioga Pass Road opens in the spring, the Ellery Bowl zone becomes one of the most popular destinations for roadside skiing. You can sleep until noon and still get a lap or two in the bowl. It is also quite popular to link one of these descents with something off Mt. Dana.

Ellery Bowl Approach: From Ellery Lake Trailhead (#9), skin and boot directly up Ellery Bowl. Beware of other skiers, wet slides, and cornices that loom above you.

It is also possible to reach the top of this area from the Dana Creek drainage after skiing Dana Couloir or the descents off Mt. Dana's north ridge. To reach Ellery, simply head northeast and climb a gradual slope that has large boulders scattered about it near the top.

↘ ELLERY BOWL DESCENT — Ellery Bowl

Aspect | Consequence/Exposure: 3 | Slope: 40°

Summit Elevation	11,300'
Descent Vertical	1,800'
Total Vertical	1,800'
Approach Distance	1 mile
Terrain	Bowl
Trailhead	9. Ellery Lake
USGS Quad Maps	Mt. Dana
GPS	37.925 / -119.2255

Ellery Bowl is the most popular descent in this area, and is the obvious large bowl above the dam. The top of the bowl is actually somewhat steep, is prone to wet slides in the spring, and often has large cornices that have been known to break off while people are standing on them, so beware.

↘ CHUTE OUT — Ellery Bowl

Aspect | Consequence/Exposure: 4 | Slope: 48°

Summit Elevation	11,300'
Descent Vertical	1,800'
Total Vertical	1,800'
Approach Distance	1 mile
Terrain	Chute
Trailhead	9. Ellery Lake
USGS Quad Maps	Mt. Dana
GPS	37.926 / -119.231

On the west flank of Ellery Bowl are a series of four chutes threading through the large rock buttress at the top. Depending on the year and conditions, all of these chutes may be skiable, though the skier's rightmost chute, Chute Out, fills in with the greatest consistency.

Approach: Once on top of Ellery Bowl, head west along the rim of the bowl, past the first gully (which cliffs out). Continue along the rim past a small rock buttress, beyond which another chute appears. Known as Chute Out, this is a great descent with nearly vertical rock walls on either side through the gut. The next logical entrance to the west is Banana Chute, so named because of a small dogleg that exists partway down

↘ BANANA CHUTE — Ellery Bowl

Aspect | Consequence/Exposure: 4 | Slope: 45°

Summit Elevation	11,300'
Descent Vertical	1,800'
Total Vertical	1,800'
Approach Distance	1 mile
Terrain	Chute
Trailhead	9. Ellery Lake
USGS Quad Maps	Mt. Dana
GPS	37.926 / -119.232

On the west flank of Ellery Bowl are a series of four chutes threading through the large rock buttress at the top. The skier's leftmost of these chutes is known as Banana Chute.

Approach: Follow the description provided for Chute Out from Ellery Lake Trailhead (#9). Continue west along the rim beyond Chute Out to the next logical entrance through the cliffs. This line is Banana Chute, named after the small dogleg halfway down the chute.

△ MT. DANA *13,053'*

The massive, rocky north face of Mt. Dana is split by two prominent couloirs, the Dana Couloir and Solstice Couloir. This popular peak holds some of the most classic lines on the Eastside.

While it is possible to access this terrain year-round, it is certainly more popular and civilized in the springtime. During the winter months, access to Mt. Dana is typically achieved by climbing Coke Chute then descending off the west side of the plateau into Glacier Canyon. From here, you can climb the line of choice from below. It is also possible to get to the top of Dana Couloir via Kidney Chute.

In the spring, most people choose to access the terrain from above via the Northwest Ridge, though it is also possible to access the terrain from below via Glacier Canyon.

↘ UNKNOWN CHUTE — Mt. Dana

Aspect	Consequence/Exposure	Slope
	4	45°

Summit Elevation	12,050'
Descent Vertical	1,000'
Total Vertical	2,250'
Approach Distance	1 ½ miles
Terrain	Chute
Trailhead	11. Tioga Lake
USGS Quad Maps	Mt. Dana
GPS	37.908 /-119.229

This narrow chute lies on Mt. Dana's shoulder a short distance below and to the northwest of Solstice Couloir. The fairly steep entrance is typically blocked by a large cornice, which can usually be passed on either side.

Looking west at Unknown Chute on Mt. Dana.

Dan Mingori drops into Solstice Couloir. *Photo: Brian Outhwaite.*

Approach: From the Tioga Lake Trailhead (#11), descend the short hill next to the bathroom, then head south through the meadow, skirting the west shore of Tioga Lake. The large, rotten rock buttress above marks the beginning of Mt. Dana's long Northwest Ridge. You can either go to the left or right of this buttress. The right is much easier, and climbs gently up the west side of the mountain. The left is a bit steeper at first, but will put you on the ridge very quickly.

As you top out on the ridge, the first prominent entry point you will reach is the one for Unknown Chute. Beyond this, the ridge climbs again slightly before reaching Solstice Couloir.

Exit: After skiing the line, hang a left and descend Glacier Canyon back to Tioga Lake. It is also possible to climb back up to the top of Ellery Bowl and ski one of the lines off the Dana Plateau with relative ease.

↘ SOLSTICE COULOIR

Mt. Dana

Aspect	Consequence/Exposure	Slope
	4	45°

Summit Elevation	12,500'
Descent Vertical	1,500'
Total Vertical	2,750'
Approach Distance	2 miles
Terrain	Chute
Trailhead	11. Tioga Lake
USGS Quad Maps	Mt. Dana
GPS	37.902 / -119.224

A large, overhanging cornice usually creates an intimidating entrance to the Solstice Couloir. While the skier's-left side can allow for an easier passage, it often demands some sort of air into the couloir. Just trying to inspect the entrance can mean walking out along this overhanging cornice. Stay very far away from the edge, especially in the middle sections: What appears to be solid ground can potentially be an overhang just waiting to let go. To safely inspect the entrance, either walk a few hundred feet above the couloir, or walk out on the ridge just below the couloir.

Skiing onto and below large cornices is generally not a very good idea. This is an exceptionally dangerous practice and should only be attempted during periods when you are certain of the snow stability. We are not

Chris Gallardo dropping into Solstice Couloir.

recommending or condoning this activity, though it is often a requirement if you want to ski this line. If conditions are less than appealing, continue on to the summit of Mt. Dana and ski the mellower Dana Couloir.

Approach: Beginning at the Tioga Lake Trailhead (#11), follow the approach to the Unknown Chute, then continue along the ridge to the top of the couloir.

Exit: After skiing the line, hang a left and descend Glacier Canyon back to Tioga Lake. It is also possible to climb back up to the top of Ellery Bowl and ski one of the lines off the Dana Plateau with relative ease.

↘ DANA COULOIR

Mt. Dana

Aspect	Consequence/Exposure	Slope
	3	40°

Summit Elevation	13,057'
Descent Vertical	2,000'
Total Vertical	3,250'
Approach Distance	2 ¼ miles
Terrain	Chute
Trailhead	11. Tioga Lake
USGS Quad Maps	Mt. Dana
GPS	37.899 / -119.217

Dana Couloir is the most popular descent off Mt. Dana and one of the more classic lines in the area. Though conditions vary, it is typically possible to ski directly off the summit and into this couloir.

The Dana Couloir has a large rock wall that shades it from the early morning sun. In the spring, the east face can be perfectly soft corn, while the Dana Couloir can hold bulletproof ice well past noon.

Approach: From the Tioga Lake Trailhead (#11), descend the short hill next to the bathroom, then head south through the meadow, skirting the west shore of Tioga Lake. The large, rotten rock buttress above marks the beginning of Mt. Dana's long Northwest Ridge. You can either go to the left or right of this buttress. The right is much easier, and climbs gently up the west side of the mountain. The left is a bit steeper at first, but will put you on the ridge very quickly.

Continue up the ridge beyond Unknown Chute and Solstice Chute to Mt. Dana's summit. From here, descend the east slope to the top of the Dana Couloir, located a few hundred feet below the summit in a small cleft.

Exit: After skiing the line, continue past Dana Lake and through Glacier Canyon back to Tioga Lake. It is also possible to climb back up to the top of Ellery Bowl and ski one of the lines off the Dana Plateau with relative ease.

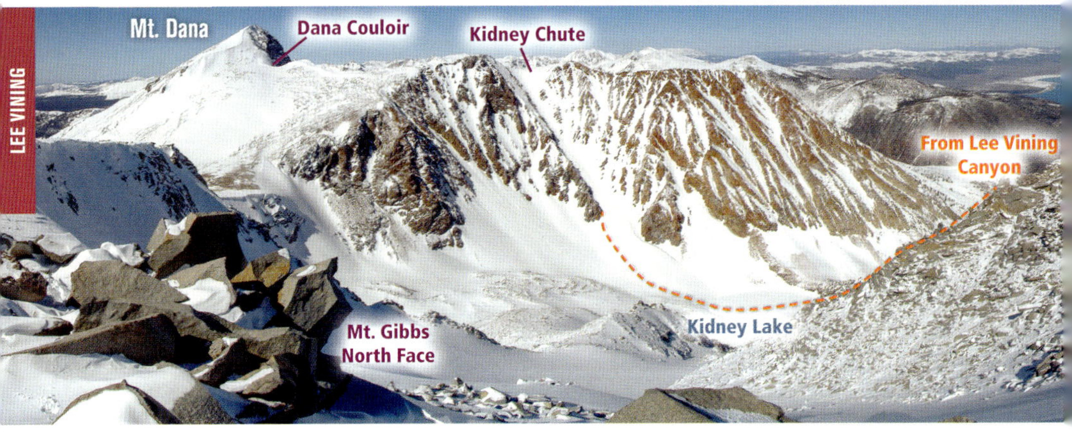

↘ KIDNEY CHUTE

Mt. Dana

Aspect	Consequence/Exposure	Slope
	3	40°

Summit Elevation	12,250'
Descent Vertical	2,000'
Total Vertical	4,750'
Approach Distance	3 miles
Terrain	Chute
Trailhead	7. Tioga Pass Lower Gate
USGS Quad Maps	Mt. Dana
GPS	37.904 / -119.209

Tucked away in the canyon between Mt. Gibbs and Mt. Dana, only a portion of the Kidney Chute is visible from Highway 395. The chute faces predominantly southeast and receives sunlight first thing in the morning. The Kidney Chute is the easiest way down from the Dana Plateau, and is a great linkup with Dana Couloir or the North Face of Mt. Gibbs.

Approach: There are many ways to get to the top of Kidney Chute, and the best choice is really dependent on the time of year and desired length of your day. During the winter months, it is arguable as to whether it is better to access from below or above. In the spring, most people choose to access from above.

Access from below is typically achieved from the lower gate on Tioga Pass (Trailhead #7). From here, skin through the campground to the south and find a suitable place to cross the river. There are a number of fallen trees to choose from, some of which have been turned into makeshift bridges by the people staying at the campground in the summer.

Once across the river, head south through the forest and begin climbing the treed gullies below the East Peak of the Dana Plateau. Contour around to the west, into the drainage from Gibbs Lake. From Gibbs Lake, a short climb will bring you to Kidney Lake at the base of the Kidney Chute.

To access from above in the winter months, utilize Cocaine Chute (page 98). From the Lee Vining Creek Bridge (Trailhead #8), skin up V Bowl and onto the Lower Bench. Continue southwest, staying left of the large, rocky ridge to the base of Coke Chute. Climb Coke Chute then head south along the plateau to the south end. As you get close to the narrow ridge that goes to the Dana Couloir, you will see a small, dark tower of rock at the end of the plateau. The Kidney Chute lies just to the left of that tower

In the spring, it is also possible to reach this point via Tioga Lake Trailhead (#11), following the approach up Glacier Canyon to the top of the Dana Plateau and Coke Chute. From here, follow the description above to Kidney Chute.

Exit: After skiing the line, keep a high line and contour to the east and eventually wrap back around to the north. A short skin or sidestep will provide you access back onto the lower bench below The End, from which it is possible to access the glades below the East Face of East Peak, or V Bowl proper.

△ DANA PLATEAU *11,500'*

The Dana Plateau is home to the highest concentration of steep terrain in the Sierra. Perched high above Mono Lake, this zone is characterized by narrow chutes cut through towering granite walls in an exposed environment—all of which makes for a surreal setting and some stellar skiing.

As raging Sierra storms come in from the west, the wind scours the giant plateau and drops all of that snow into the north- and east-facing chutes that line the

plateau. While this often fills the chutes rather nicely, it also creates incredibly large cornices and the potential for very serious consequences. As the season progresses, the sun weakens the cornices, and it is common for large blocks of snow and ice to come crashing down during the day. If climbing these chutes from the bottom, be aware of the terrain above you. Be sure to travel outside of the direct fall line and move quickly when it is warm or take an alternate approach.

Dana Plateau Access: During the winter months, access to the Dana Plateau is typically achieved via Poole Power Plant Road in Lee Vining Canyon. While many people choose to climb Coke Chute and then skin to the top of their descent, just as many prefer to climb via their descent of choice.

In the spring, it is not uncommon for there to be a few weeks when the lower gate on Tioga Pass Road is open and there is also snow all the way to Poole Power Plant Road. During these times, it is possible (if not preferable) to shuttle cars from Poole Power Plant Road to Ellery Bowl or the Tioga Lake staging area.

↘ POWERHOUSE CHUTES

Dana Plateau

Aspect	Consequence/Exposure	Slope
	3	45°

Summit Elevation	11,400'
Descent Vertical	3,500'
Total Vertical	3,600'
Approach Distance	2 ½ miles
Terrain	Chute
Trailhead	8. Lee Vining Creek Bridge
USGS Quad Maps	Mt. Dana
GPS	37.923 / -119.217

The Powerhouse Chutes lie at the head of a canyon directly above the Poole Power Plant. This mini drainage is squeezed between the Ellery Bowl zone and Dana Plateau.

There are a number of chutes that drop down into the Powerhouse Drainage, with the one in the center being the easiest. But "easy" is a relative term: This chute can form a cornice and be incredibly steep at the top. All of the chutes converge at the bottom, roughly 1,000' below the top of the plateau. Below this, a rolling valley brings you down to the power plant.

Approach: It is most popular to access Powerhouse from Ellery Lake (Trailhead #9), via Ellery Bowl, though also common to end up here after skiing something off Mt. Dana. From the top of Ellery, head slightly east,

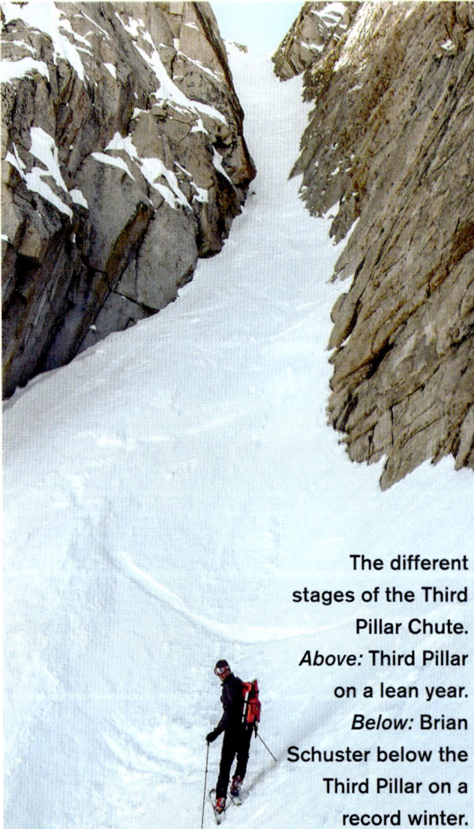

The different stages of the Third Pillar Chute. *Above:* Third Pillar on a lean year. *Below:* Brian Schuster below the Third Pillar on a record winter.

past the ridgeline that forms the skier's right-hand side of Ellery Bowl, and you will see the top of Powerhouse.

If accessing from Glacier Canyon, simply head northeast and climb a gradual slope that has large boulders scattered about it near the top to the top of Ellery Bowl, then follow the description above.

Exit: The Powerhouse Chutes are most commonly 'exited' by leaving a car at Poole Power Plant, then shuttling back to Ellery Lake. However, it is also possible to skin to Ellery Lake via Lee Vining Canyon. To do this, head around the north side of the power plant, then continue west up Lee Vining Canyon. Beware of avalanches in the upper reaches of the canyon.

↘ THIRD PILLAR CHUTE

Dana Plateau

Aspect	Consequence/Exposure	Slope
	5	55°

Summit Elevation	11,500'
Descent Vertical	2,000'
Total Vertical	4,000
Approach Distance	2 ½ miles
Terrain	Chute
Trailhead	8. Lee Vining Creek Bridge or 9. Ellery Lake
USGS Quad Maps	Mt. Dana
GPS	37.922 / -119.213

This steep, narrow chute lies just to the north of the Third Pillar of Mt Dana. A gentle, convex rollover provides a deceptively easy entrance into one of the steepest chutes listed in this book.

With a sustained angle of about 55° and ever-narrowing rock walls, just looking down the chute can be quite intimidating. And rightly so! The crux lies at the narrowest part, where a chockstone blocks the exit to the wide-open slope below. During big winters, this chockstone can become completely buried in snow, which significantly decreases the difficulty. But during most winters this crux section is fairly serious. It involves tight turns and possibly mandatory air on a steep slope. Though short and sweet, this descent is not to be taken lightly.

Approach: Third Pillar Chute is located on the immediate north side of Third Pillar of Mt. Dana, which is the large granite fin that extends out the east side of the Dana Plateau. (This holds some stellar climbing, by the way.)

In the spring, utilize the Ellery Lake Trailhead (#9) to access via Ellery Bowl. From the top of Ellery, head slightly southeast beyond the top of Powerhouse Chute, then continue slightly south. As you approach the rim of the plateau, you will notice several protrusions, the largest of which is Third Pillar— just north of it is the couloir.

During the winter, many people choose to access Third Pillar via the Coke Chute approach to the plateau, or by directly booting the line from below.

➘ LIBERTY CHUTE

Dana Plateau

Aspect	Consequence/Exposure	Slope
	4	45°

Summit Elevation	11,500'
Descent Vertical	2,000'
Total Vertical	4,000'
Approach Distance	2 ½ miles
Terrain	Chute
Trailhead	8. Lee Vining Creek Bridge or 9. Ellery Lake
USGS Quad Maps	Mt. Dana
GPS	37.921 / -119.212

The Liberty Chute gets its name from the resemblance it bears to the Statue of Liberty when seen from Highway 395. The "arm" of the statue is the crux of the chute, with the "torch" being a large, overhanging cornice.

The Liberty Chute doesn't get any direct sunlight during winter. In the spring, it begins to see a little bit of sun, but only in the very early morning. It's not until late spring that it receives enough light to soften the snow. However, skiing it this late in the season increases the risk of the cornice breaking. As the cornice slowly breaks down, it can create a large trough in the middle of this narrow chute and leave you with very unpleasant skiing conditions. This cornice also creates an incredible hazard if you are underneath it, as it has the potential to release huge chunks of ice.

Approach: Access to the Liberty Chute from above requires a rappel of 75–100 feet to reach the skiable terrain in the chute.

In the spring, utilize the Ellery Lake Trailhead (#9) to access via Ellery Bowl. From the top of Ellery, head slightly southeast. As you approach the rim of the plateau, you will notice several protrusions, the largest of which is Third Pillar. From here, walk a short distance east, passing by a wider chute that ends in a cliff. Liberty Chute is the narrow slot blocked by a cornice. A walk out on the north wall will give you a view of the descent.

Brett Lotz rapelling into Liberty Chute. *Photo: Nate Greenberg.*

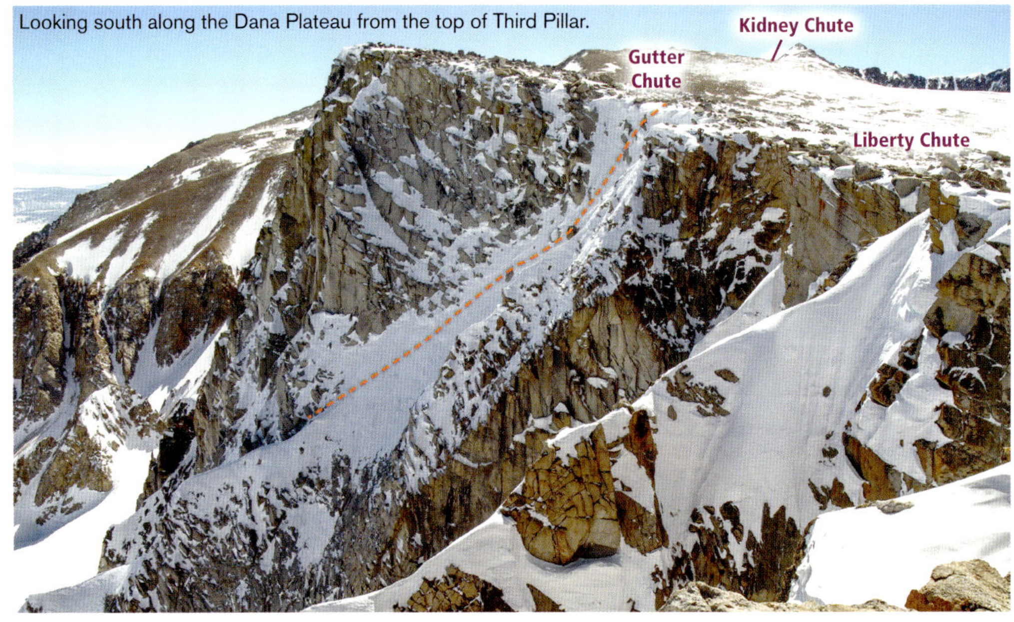

Looking south along the Dana Plateau from the top of Third Pillar.

On the north side of the chute are a number of large, solid blocks that make for good rappel anchors. This rappel isn't done very often, so any webbing up there has probably been cooking in the sun for quite some time and shouldn't be trusted.

Be sure to move quickly through the upper section, as there is nowhere to hide if the cornice breaks. Below the "arm" of the statue, the chute widens quite a bit and offers some protection, but there is still the risk of cornices from other locations.

During the winter, many people choose to access via the Coke Chute approach to the plateau. Booting the chute is not recommended due to hangfire from the cornices above.

↘ GUTTER CHUTE

Dana Plateau

Aspect	Consequence/Exposure	Slope
	5	45°

Summit Elevation	11,500'
Descent Vertical	2,000'
Total Vertical	4,000'
Approach Distance	2 ½ miles
Terrain	Chute
Trailhead	8. Lee Vining Creek Bridge
USGS Quad Maps	Mt. Dana
GPS	37.919 / -119.2115

Starting on an off-camber hanging snowfield, this line should only be attempted during periods of very stable snow. This slope is quite steep, and a lost edge here would most likely be fatal.

As you drop into the line, stay high along the top of the face, then descend to a spine of rock below you. An exit to skier's right gives access to the relative safety of the chute below.

During low snowfall, this spine of rock may not be covered in snow and could involve a bit of negotiating. Don't fall!

Approach: This line is located a short distance south of Liberty Chute.

In the spring, utilize the Ellery Lake Trailhead (#9) to access via Ellery Bowl. From the top of Ellery, head slightly southeast. As you approach the rim of the plateau, you will notice several protrusions, the largest of which is Third Pillar. From here, continue south along the rim for a few hundred more feet over to the top of the large, hanging slope that appears to end in a cliff.

During the winter, many people choose to access via the Coke Chute approach to the plateau. Booting the chute is not recommended.

Exits: After skiing Third Pillar, Liberty, or Gutter you have the option of skiing V Bowl, or one of the V Bowl Chutes down to Poole Power Plant Road.

Brett Lotz skiing the upper arm of Liberty Chute. *Photo: Nate Greenberg.*

Looking west at the Dana Plateau from the lower gate on Tioga Pass Road.

RIPPER CHUTE

Dana Plateau

Aspect | Consequence/Exposure: 4 | Slope: 45°

Summit Elevation	11,500'
Descent Vertical	2,000'
Total Vertical	4,000'
Approach Distance	2 ½ miles
Terrain	Chute
Trailhead	8. Lee Vining Creek Bridge or 9. Ellery Lake
USGS Quad Maps	Mt. Dana
GPS	37.918 / -119.211

Tucked deep in between granite walls, the Ripper Chute can be a little tricky to find from the top. It begins in the large cleft that is set back from the edge of the Dana Plateau, approximately ¼ mile north of Cocaine Chute.

The entrance is the steepest part, as it has the tendency to drift in and create a short but steep drop off the plateau. Below that, the wide chute goes around a corner, through a narrow choke, and out onto the apron below. Due to its rock walls, shape, and aspect, the whole of the chute is rarely in direct sunlight. If skiing it in spring corn, the best time to find soft conditions would be on a warm day, and before it has a chance to refreeze.

Approach: In the spring, utilize the Ellery Lake Trailhead (#9) to access via Ellery Bowl. From the top of Ellery, head slightly southeast. As you approach the rim of the plateau, you will notice several protrusions, the largest of which is Third Pillar. From here, continue south along the rim for a ¼ mile to a large cleft that is set back from the Dana Plateau. This feeds into a beautiful rock-lined chute that turns the corner out of sight.

During winter, many choose to access via the Cocaine Chute approach to the plateau. From the top of Cocaine Chute, head north about ¼ mile to the entrance.

COCAINE CHUTE

Dana Plateau

Aspect | Consequence/Exposure: 3 | Slope: 40°

Summit Elevation	11,500'
Descent Vertical	2,000'
Total Vertical	4,000'
Approach Distance	2 ½ miles
Terrain	Chute
Trailhead	8. Lee Vining Creek Bridge or 9. Ellery Lake
USGS Quad Maps	Mt. Dana
GPS	37.913 / -119.21

Slightly less steep than its neighbors, Cocaine (Coke) Chute is probably the easiest and safest way to reach the top of the plateau if climbing from Lee Vining Canyon. It is also the mellowest of the true plateau descents.

John Carleton climbing the Powerhouse Chutes.

Mike McHargue skiing off the East Face of East Peak. *Photo: Nate Greenberg.*

Coke Chute is the largest and looker's leftmost chute off the top of the Dana Plateau. There is an adjacent northeast face that eventually forms the skier's-right wall of Coke Chute and offers a different, slightly higher point of entry.

Approach: Coke Chute is very accessible during the entire year, but requires different approaches. During the winter months, access from the Lee Vining Creek Bridge (Trailhead #8). Skin up V Bowl and onto the Lower Bench, then continue southwest, staying left of the large, rocky ridge to the base of the chute. Skin and boot to the top, which is the steepest part.

In spring, it is nice to shuttle a car to Trailhead #8, then drive a second to the Ellery Lake Trailhead (#9). From here, climb Ellery Bowl to the plateau and head south along the ridgeline to the southern end and obvious entrance to Coke Chute.

Exits: After skiing Ripper or Cocaine Chute, you have the option of skiing V Bowl, or one of the V Bowl Chutes down to Poole Power Plant Road.

△ LOWER PLATEAU BENCH

The Lower Plateau Bench lies just below the prominent and dominant descents of the Dana Plateau, and offers some incredible skiing that is easily linked up with a plateau line, or done by itself. The bench is large—larger than most people realize. This area offers some incredible storm-skiing opportunities, with a variety of terrain, aspects, and exposures, and is some of our favorite easily accessible terrain.

↘ V BOWL — Lower Plateau Bench

Aspect | **Consequence/Exposure** 2 | **Slope** 30°

Summit Elevation	9,500'
Descent Vertical	2,000'
Total Vertical	2,000'
Approach Distance	1 mile
Terrain	Trees
Trailhead	8. Lee Vining Creek Bridge
USGS Quad Maps	Mt. Dana
GPS	37.926 / -119.196

The V Bowl zone offers great mid-elevation, easy access skiing with a variety of terrain and aspects to choose from. Its relatively low angle, low elevation, and tree cover make for great storm-day skiing when the descents higher up on the pass are getting hammered by snow or wind.

Approach: From Trailhead #8 at the Lee Vining Creek Bridge, cross the bridge, then head south and slightly west. There is a faint weakness that leads through the lower grove of trees and then eventually opens up to the south as you approach the lower flank of V Bowl. From here, most people choose to skin the lower flank, eventually heading to the south side of the bowl and back into the trees for some protection, and weaving their way to the top.

Exit: Ski right back to the car!

↘ V BOWL CHUTES — Lower Plateau Bench

Aspect | **Consequence/Exposure** 3 | **Slope** 35° 45°

Summit Elevation	10,050'
Descent Vertical	2,500'
Total Vertical	2,300'
Approach Distance	1 ¾ miles+
Terrain	Chute
Trailhead	8. Lee Vining Creek Bridge
USGS Quad Maps	Mt. Dana
GPS	37.926 / -119.196

As Poole Power Plant Road winds its way west away from the junction of Tioga Pass Road, it eventually gets closer to Lee Vining Creek and the base of the north face of the Lower Plateau Bench. As the north face of the bench comes into view, a series of chutes begin to become apparent, and span the entire distance between V Bowl and the power plant. All of these lines offer at least 2,000' of north-facing terrain that varies from steep rock-lined chutes, to exposed faces and complex terrain, to treed faces and gullies.

Though these lines offer stellar midwinter and midstorm skiing, they are not be underestimated or taken lightly. There is some serious terrain with serious consequences, and based on the location and aspect, it can harbor stability issues that require skilled assessment.

Looking south at the V Bowl chutes from the Tioga Pass Road.

Approach: The first chute to the looker's right of the ridge that separates V Bowl from the rest of the north face is a treed gully that is often referred to as Banana Chute (not to be confused with the chute of the same name in Ellery Bowl). To the right of that are two slightly more steep and exposed rock-lined chutes, the first of which is quite a good ski.

All of these lines are most easily accessed by parking at Lee Vining Creek Bridge (Trailhead #8).. Skin to the top of V Bowl, then gain a series of small benches and ridges as you head north. The first prominent point you reach in the trees directly above V Bowl is the start of Banana Chute, and the next couple benches above it provide entry into the following couple chutes.

Beyond these chutes, the bench curves a bit before the next series of lines appears. These lines are much more obscure, and are even somewhat challenging to pick out from the road. While it is possible to access these lines from the top of the bench (via the approach mentioned above), it is a bit of a trek to get back to your car, so climbing them from below may be a better bet.

Exit: Kick or skin back to your starting point. Be aware that you may have to trek a bit of a distance on flat terrain, and be sure to look out for the birdhouses.

△ EAST PEAK *13,053'*

As you turn onto Tioga Pass Road, the east-facing chutes and gullies off Mt. Dana's East Peak are some of the first things that come into view. When viewed from Highway 395, this area appears to be a separate peak from the Dana Plateau, but it is actually just an extension of the plateau.

On stormy days the treed gullies below the East Peak offer excellent sheltered skiing. There are also a few chutes tucked away on the north side, facing Cocaine Chute.

↘ EAST FACE

East Peak

Aspect	Consequence/Exposure	Slope
	3	35°

Summit Elevation	11,500'
Descent Vertical	1,500'
Total Vertical	4,000'
Approach Distance	1 mile
Terrain	Face
Trailhead	8. Lee Vining Creek Bridge
USGS Quad Maps	Mt. Dana
GPS	37.89965 / -119.22126

From the winter closure, the East Face lines loom overhead, offering a number of interesting terrain choices in deceptively long descents. There are true east-facing chutes and bowls, and some more northeast-facing lines that are a little steeper.

Approach: From Lee Vining Creek Bridge (Trailhead #8), cross the bridge then head south and slightly west. There is a faint weakness that leads through the lower grove of trees and then eventually opens up to the south as you approach the lower flank of V Bowl. As you climb the lower aspect of V Bowl and into the trees on the south flank, look for a logical path to the south over the ridgeline about a third of the way up.

First light on the Dana Plateau.

Continue south beyond the ridge into a small hanging valley that leads you to the base of the northeast chutes. If continuing on to the true East Face, climb the low-angle north-facing slope onto the bench beneath those lines, then boot the one of interest.

Exit: Reverse your steps and ski right back to the car!

↘ THE END — East Peak

Aspect	Consequence/Exposure	Slope
	3	35°

Summit Elevation	12,000'
Descent Vertical	2,000'
Total Vertical	4,500'
Approach Distance	2 ½ miles
Terrain	Chute
Trailhead	8. Lee Vining Creek Bridge
USGS Quad Maps	Mt. Dana
GPS	37.905 / -119.207

Approach: From Lee Vining Creek Bridge (Trailhead #8), cross the bridge then head south and slightly west. There is a faint weakness that leads through the lower grove of trees and then eventually opens up to the south as you approach the lower flank of V Bowl. As you climb the lower aspect of V Bowl and into the trees on the south flank, look for a logical path to the south over the ridgeline about a third of the way up.

Continue south beyond the ridge into a small hanging valley that leads you to the base of the northeast chutes, then up a low-angle north-facing slope onto the bench. Contour along the base of the East Face to the bottom of the chute located at the south end of the bench, just before Gibbs Canyon.

Exit: Reverse your steps and ski right back to the car!

△ MT. GIBBS *12,500'*

Mt. Gibbs is really part of the June Lake region, but its North Face is typically accessed from Lee Vining. Gibbs is the northernmost of the the three big peaks that flank the west side of Highway 395 between June Lake and Lee Vining (Mt. Wood, Mt. Lewis, and Mt. Gibbs). In addition to some amazing steep skiing off the East Face (covered in the June Lake chapter), the North Face offers big lines in a secluded setting with a stellar view of Kidney Chute.

Looking southwest at East Peak and Mt. Gibbs from Lee Vining Canyon.

↘ NORTH FACE

Mt. Gibbs

Aspect | **Consequence/Exposure** 4 | **Slope** 40°

Summit Elevation	12,500'
Descent Vertical	2,000'
Total Vertical	5,000'
Approach Distance	4 ¼ miles
Terrain	Chute
Trailhead	7. Tioga Pass Lower Gate
USGS Quad Maps	Mt. Dana
GPS	37.887 / -119.197

Mt. Gibbs' North Face holds amazing big-mountain lines. This face is really only visible from the north, with the best views from the Kidney Couloir or East Peak area. Though any of the lines on Gibbs' North Face are solid days themselves, they are also great linkups with Kidney Chute for the motivated adventurer.

Though there are a number of different ski options in the area, there are two main lines that are worthy objectives. The North Face is probably the most common of the descents. This is the large, open face that sits just west of the summit and that ultimately feeds into a chute at the bottom. The other line of note is the North Couloir, which drops in off the true summit via a steep chute onto an exposed face above some cliffs.

Approach: The most common approach for the North Face begins from the Lower Gate on Tioga Pass Road (Trailhead #7). From here, travel a short distance through the campground to the south, and find a suitable place to cross the creek. There are a number of fallen trees to choose from, some of which have been turned into makeshift bridges by the people staying at the campground in the summer.

Once across the river, head south through the forest and begin climbing the treed mouth of Gibbs Canyon. Continue up canyon past Gibbs Lake, where a short climb will bring you to Kidney Lake, which sits at the base of the north chutes. Either climb your chosen descent, or climb the large bowl at the head of the canyon and walk the rocky ridge to the top.

In the late spring it is also possible to have a slightly shorter approach via the Horse Meadows Road, which is accessed via the north end of the June Lake Region.

Exit: From Gibbs Lake it is most common to ski back down Gibbs Canyon to Trailhead #7. However, it is also possible to climb/traverse a short distance onto the bench beneath East Peak to access Lee Vining Creek Bridge (Trailhead #8).

5 June Lake

Carson Peak reflected in Silver Lake.

5. June Lake

JUNE LAKE REGION:

- ▣ Northern End:
  - △ MT. GIBBS
  - △ MT. LEWIS
  - △ KOIP PEAK
  - △ MT. WOOD
  - △ REVERSED PEAK
- ▣ Southern End:
  - △ CARSON PEAK
  - △ DREAM PEAK
  - △ SAN JOAQUIN MTN.
  - △ WHITE WING

Region Trailheads

12. Bohler Canyon
13. North June Loop Winter Closure
14. Silver Lake Winter Closure
15. Fern/Yost Trailhead
16. Four Seasons
17. Obsidian Dome

Home to June Mountain Ski Area, the small community of June Lake is only 20 minutes north of Mammoth Lakes but feels like a world away. Often referred to as the 'Switzerland of the Sierra', this region is characterized by dramatic craggy peaks that provide a beautiful backdrop to a quaint little town.

Getting There & Getting Going

From Mammoth Lakes, travel north on Highway 395 for roughly 15 miles. After descending off Deadman Summit, you will reach the south junction of Highway 158 (the June Lake Loop). There is a gas station and convenience store on the west side of the highway at this junction, and during the winter months this is the only access to June Lake, as the north end of the loop is closed between Silver Lake and Highway 395.

If you are heading toward destinations in the Southern End Area, turn west onto Highway 158 and follow it through the quaint downtown of June Lake to the trailhead associated with your destination. Roughly two miles past the ski area the highway is closed during winter months by a gate at Silver Lake, beneath the southern flanks of Mt. Wood.

For destinations in the Northern End Area, you will need to continue on 395 for a short distance. Since the Loop Road is closed during the winter months, these peaks are best accessed from the south side of the June Lake Loop. To reach this point, continue along 395 for another six miles. Just past a blinking light and just beyond the intersection with Highway 120 East, turn left onto Highway 158 and follow it a short distance to the gate. Please note that as spring hits, the June Lake Loop will open all the way through, which affords shorter approaches for peaks such as Mt. Wood, Koip Peak, and Mt. Lewis.

12. Bohler Canyon (Spring Only) *8,100'*

Continue north on Highway 395 past the northern turnoff for Highway 158 for 1¾ miles. Turn left onto Oil Plant Road. During the winter months, this road isn't plowed very far and you will have to park shortly after leaving Highway 395. As the snow begins to melt, you will be able to drive a bit closer to the base.

If the road is clear, follow Oil Plant Road for 1¼ miles, then turn right onto Forest Service Road 01N106. Follow this road 0.9 miles to a left-hand turn onto a secondary dirt road (01N16). This road is quite rough in sections and high clearance vehicles are recommended. You will most likely run into snowdrifts and probably won't be able to drive it to the end. Continue as far as possible into Bohler Canyon toward the base of the east face.

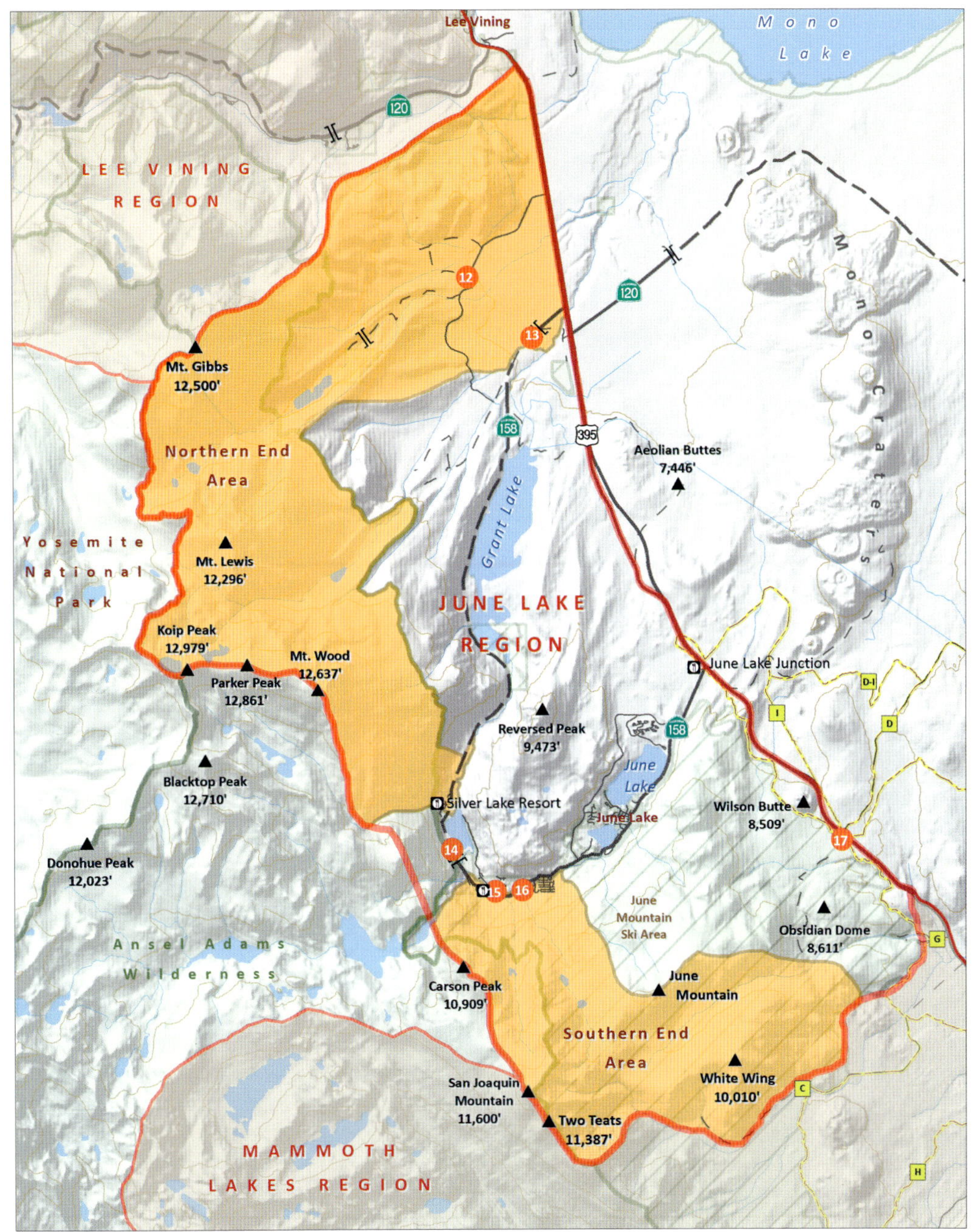

13. North June Loop Winter Closure (Year-Round)

7,050'

Continue north on Highway 395 past the southern junction for the June Lake Loop for six miles. Just past a blinking light and beyond the intersection with Highway 120 East, turn left onto Highway 158 and follow it a short distance to the gate. Please note that as spring hits, the June Lake Loop will open all the way through, which allows you to drive farther along this road and onto other Forest Service roads that afford shorter approaches.

Mt. Wood

Mt. Lewis

Parker Bench

Looking west from Highway 395 in the heart of the Mono Basin.

14. Silver Lake Winter Closure (Year-Round) *8,800'*

From Highway 395, turn onto Highway 158 (June Lake Loop) at the southern entrance and follow it through downtown June Lake. Continue past the ski area, and follow the road until it ends at the winter-closure gate at Silver Lake (approximately six miles).

In the spring, the June Lake Loop Road opens up completely and it is possible to drive all the way around the loop and onto other Forest Service roads that afford shorter approaches.

15. Fern/Yost Trailhead (Year-Round) *7,275'*

From Highway 395, turn west onto Highway 158 (June Lake Loop) at the southern entrance and follow it through downtown June Lake. Continue past the ski area and through a steep downhill S-curve. After a short distance, you will pass Venice Street (on your left) then Iowa Street (on your right). Shortly after Iowa Street, keep your eyes peeled for a small parking area on the south side of Highway 158. This is a summertime hiking trailhead, and is approximately six miles from the intersection of Highway 158 at Highway 395.

16. Four Seasons (Year-Round) *7,500'*

This trailhead is located just before Trailhead #15, and just beyond the bottom of the S-curve.

From Highway 395, turn west onto Highway 158 (June Lake Loop) at the southern entrance and follow it through downtown June Lake. Continue past the ski area and through a steep downhill S-curve. After a very short distance, Four Seasons Resort will appear on your left. While it is not legal to park at the resort itself, there is often street parking in the vicinity on the north side of June Lake Loop Road.

17. Obsidian Dome (Year-Round) *8,000'*

The Obsidian Dome trailhead is a popular winter staging area and is used by snowmachiners and Nordic skiers alike. The area to the west of the parking area offers several miles of free groomed Nordic ski trails, while the areas north, south, and east (across Highway 395) offer groomed snowmachine trails.

The Obsidian Dome trailhead is located 3½ miles south at the junction of Highway 395 and Highway 158, and 11 miles north of the junction of Highway 203 leading into Mammoth Lakes. Park on the west side of Highway 395 in the large plowed area. There is an information kiosk here with a winter-recreation map posted.

Eats, Digs, Services, & Supplies

Though June Lake is pretty sleepy during the winter months, there are a few local favorites that are definitely worth hitting up.

Trout Town Joe, located on the north side of Highway 158 toward the west end of June Lake village, has great coffee, muffins, and scones for starting your day off. And no June Lake tour is complete without beers, good storytelling, and tasty bar food at the local favorite Tiger Bar located in downtown June Lake.

If you are looking to spend the night in the June Lake Loop and are willing to spend a little more money, we definitely recommend checking out the Double Eagle Resort for incredible lodging, food, and a full-service spa.

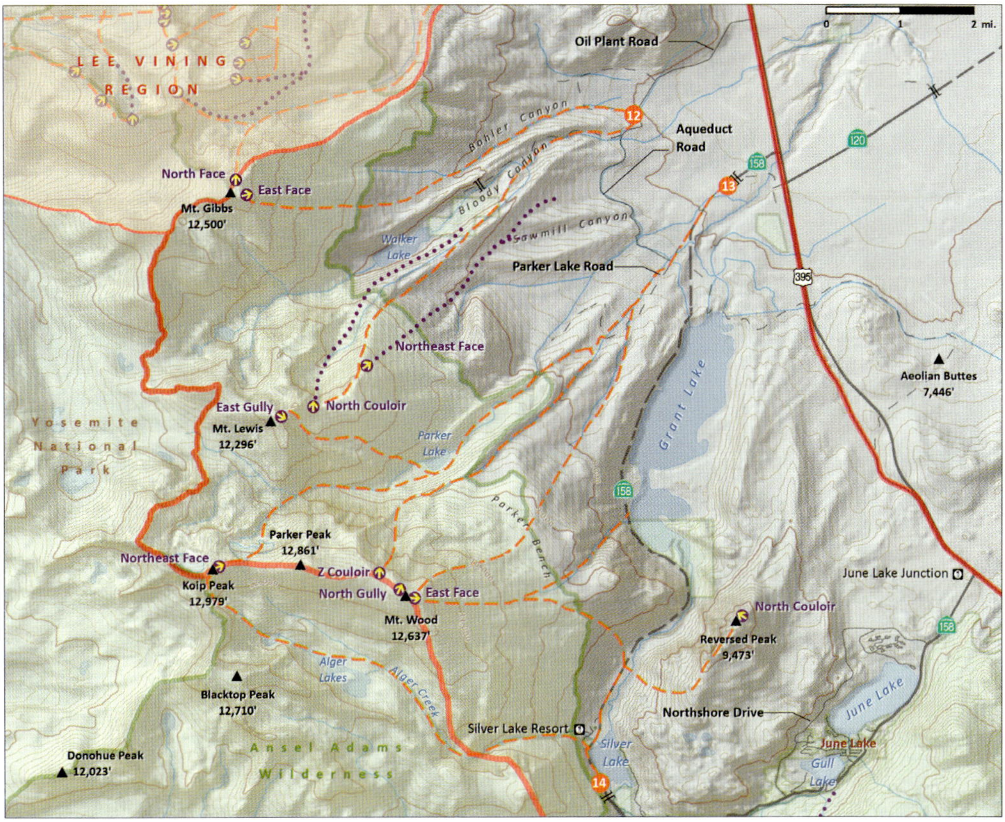

▣ Northern End

△ MT. GIBBS *12,500'*

Mt. Gibbs is the northernmost of the three peaks that span the distance of Highway 395 between Lee Vining and June Lake. The other two are Mt. Lewis and Mt. Wood, and are covered later in this chapter. Like its neighbors, Gibbs offers some stellar big-line skiing—most of which is visible from the highway and is reasonably accessible.

All of the ski descents that are referred to here actually sit on a sub-peak of Mt. Gibbs. The true summit lies another ¾ miles to the southwest and rarely holds enough snow to be skiable. Because of this, the sub-peak (call it Gibbs North) becomes the backcountry skier's high point.

See the Lee Vining Region chapter, page 103, for information on the North Face of Mt. Gibbs. Though accessible from the June Lake Region, this line is more frequently reached from Lee Vining Canyon.

Looking west at Mt. Gibbs from Highway 395.

Juan Gelpi skiing Mt Gibbs.

↘ EAST FACE CHUTES

Mt. Gibbs

Aspect	Consequence/Exposure	Slope
	3	40°

Summit Elevation	12,500'
Descent Vertical	2,400'
Total Vertical	4,400'
Hiking Distance	4 ½ miles
Terrain	Chute
Trailhead	12. Bohler Canyon
USGS Quad Maps	Mt. Dana, Lee Vining
GPS	37.884 / -119.195

The skiing on Mt. Gibbs' East Face is truly iconic, and the views of Mono Lake, Mt. Dana, and the surrounding area seen from the summit are some of the best you will find anywhere. The East Face is lined with more than a dozen chutes that beckon skiers who drive Highway 395 during the snowy months.

Approach: From Bohler Canyon Trailhead (#12), hike west through a lovely grove of aspen trees and eventually through a large meadow below the East Face. As you leave the west end of the meadow you will need to make a decision as to which chute (or general area) you want to ski, as you can choose the left or right branch of gullies, and then climb whichever chute looks best. At the top of the chutes, the angle kicks back quite a bit and a long, moderate slope brings you to the summit ridge.

Be aware that the top of this mountain is prime avalanche terrain. A large snowfield sits atop a convex rollover, with steep chutes below that. Extreme caution should be taken at the transition from the snowfield into the chutes.

△ MT. LEWIS *12,296'*

Sandwiched between Gibbs and Wood is Mt. Lewis, which at first glance is unimpressive since the obvious face is a broad tree-covered slope. However, the actual summit of Mt. Lewis is just beyond this slope, and in reality, all of the descents off Mt. Lewis are of high quality—and each offers a vastly different skiing experience.

↘ NORTH COULOIR

Mt. Lewis

Aspect	Consequence/Exposure	Slope
	3	35°

Summit Elevation	11,500'
Descent Vertical	3,000'
Total Vertical	4,400'
Hiking Distance	7 miles
Terrain	Chute
Trailhead	12. Bohler Canyon
USGS Quad Maps	Lee Vining, June Lake, Koip Peak
GPS	37.844 / -119.182

Tucked away behind the treed gullies of the Northeast Face, the North Couloir of Mt. Lewis offers a long, moderate, and protected run down toward Walker Lake, and is a really enjoyable ski.

Approach: From Bohler Canyon Trailhead (#12), continue south a short distance along Aqueduct Road to Walker Lake Road, which heads west into Bloody Canyon and the Walker Lake trailhead. This road is generally plowed during the winter, but parking can be difficult. Note that Walker Lake is private, and there is a gate blocking the road about one mile from the turnoff—please don't block the gate.

From the Walker Lake trailhead, skin west up the valley to its head, then weave uphill toward the south onto a morainal ridge. At the crest of the ridgeline, continue west through the Northeast Face to the summit ridge. Follow this ridge west to the top of the couloir beneath the impressive East Face of Mt. Lewis.

Exit: After reaching Walker Lake, continue east, down-canyon, until it becomes possible to roughly contour along the south wall of the canyon (on your right) and reach the ridgeline near the mouth. From here, head south and find your way back to your car (wherever you parked it).

↘ NORTHEAST FACE

Mt. Lewis

Aspect	Consequence/Exposure	Slope
	2	30°

Summit Elevation	10,800'
Descent Vertical	2,500'
Total Vertical	3,500'
Hiking Distance	5 ¼ miles
Terrain	Trees
Trailhead	13. N. June Loop Winter Closure
USGS Quad Maps	Lee Vining, June Lake, Koip Peak
GPS	37.861 / -119.171

Looking west at Mt. Lewis from Highway 395.

The treed slopes that cover the Northeast Face of Mt. Lewis are an excellent place to find protected powder skiing, though getting to the summit from here involves a long traverse and an exposed steep section at the top. Because of this, many people choose to just go to the top of the plateau above the trees and make the most of the snow quality and fun glade skiing.

Approach: From the Bohler Canyon Trailhead (#12), continue south a short distance along Aqueduct Road to Walker Lake Road, which heads west into Bloody Canyon and the Walker Lake trailhead. This road is generally plowed during the winter, but parking can be difficult. Note that Walker Lake is private, and there is a gate blocking the road about one mile from the turn-off—please don't block the gate.

From the Walker Lake trailhead, skin west up the valley to its head, then weave uphill toward the south onto a morainal ridge. At the crest of the ridgeline, continue west to the base of the Northeast Face, and weave your way through the trees to its top.

Exit: After skiing the upper portions of the Northeast Face, it is possible to contour left (north) into Sawmill Canyon, which will put you closer to your car.

↘ EAST GULLY

Mt. Lewis

Aspect | **Consequence/Exposure** 2 4 | **Slope** 30° 40°

Summit Elevation	12,296'
Descent Vertical	4,000'
Total Vertical	5,300'
Hiking Distance	7 miles
Terrain	Chute
Trailhead	13. N. June Loop Winter Closure
USGS Quad Maps	Lee Vining, June Lake, Koip Peak
GPS	37.842 / -119.189

The East Gully of Mt. Lewis offers some excellent moderate ski terrain in an alpine environment with incredible views of Mt. Wood and the Mono Basin. The main line is comprised of a large bowl on the eastern summit ridge of Mt. Lewis that feeds into a low-angle gully snaking its way all the way down to Parker Lake. There is also a more committing line that goes from the true summit of Mt. Lewis and feeds into the lower portions of the gully.

Approach: From the North June Loop Winter Closure (Trailhead #13), continue west along the highway for approximately 1¼ miles to the junction with Parker Lake Road, which is a large dirt road that may not be clearly visible with a thick snowpack.

As the snowline recedes in the spring, it is possible to drive a portion of Parker Lake Road, which will take you closer to your destination. If this is your course of action, follow the main dirt road (i.e., don't turn onto any side roads) until the road ends.

From here, follow the general path of the summer trail, which heads west along the north/east side of the stream until you reach a meadow near the outlet of the lake, then cross over to the south/west side. The stream that flows out of Parker Lake rarely forms a snow bridge at the lower elevations, so be sure to stay far away from its banks.

At Parker Lake, the East Gully will be above you to the north. Continue up the East Gully, climbing past a number of benches en route to the summit.

It is also possible to reach the upper bowl of the East Gully via the North Couloir approach.

Exit: Ski back down to Parker Lake then follow your tracks back to your car.

△ KOIP PEAK *12,979'*

Koip Peak sits at the head of the canyon between Mt. Wood and Mt. Lewis and offers excellent views of Mt. Ritter and Banner Peak, as well as Mt. Lyell and everything in between. It's a beautiful destination, and a nice long day tour.

Tracks below the summit of Mt Lewis.

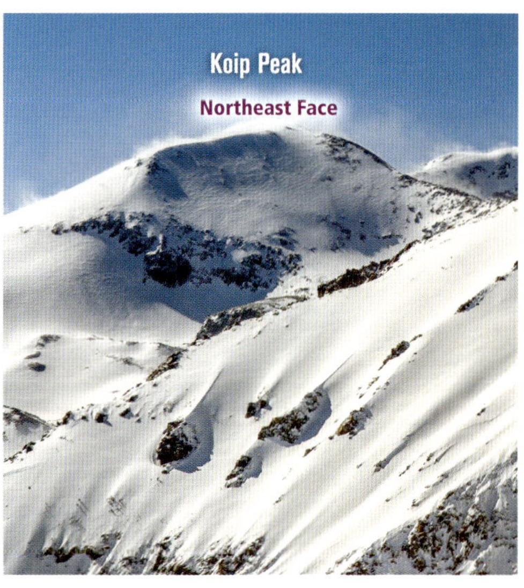

↘ NORTHEAST FACE

Koip Peak

Aspect	Consequence/Exposure	Slope
	2	30°

Summit Elevation	12,979'
Descent Vertical	4,500'
Total Vertical	4,700'
Hiking Distance	8 ½ miles
Terrain	Bowl
Trailhead	13. N. June Loop Winter Closure
USGS Quad Maps	Lee Vining, June Lake, Koip Peak
GPS	37.814 / -119.201

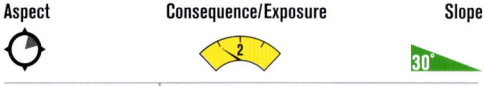

The most common descent off Koip Peak is the east face. On big snow years the steep North Face will also fill in and become skiable.

Approach: From the North June Loop Winter Closure (Trailhead #13), continue west along the highway for approximately 1¼ miles to the junction with Parker Lake Road, which is a large dirt road that may not be clearly visible with a thick snowpack.

As the snowline recedes in the spring, it is possible to drive a portion of Parker Lake Road, which will take you closer to your destination. If this is your course of action, follow the main dirt road (i.e., don't turn onto any side roads) until the road ends.

From here, follow the general path of the summer trail, which heads west along the north/east side of the stream until you reach a meadow near the outlet of the lake, then cross over to the south/west side. The stream that flows out of Parker Lake rarely forms a snow bridge at the lower elevations, so be sure to stay far away from its banks.

Continue past Parker Lake, beneath the north face of Mt. Wood, then begin climbing toward the head of the canyon. This canyon is notorious for forming small ice flows, and though it greatly depends on the season, be prepared to make some short detours to avoid the icy blue cliffs. Climb up the canyon, bearing to the southwest, which eventually brings you to a bench below the North Face of Koip Peak. The easiest way to the summit is via the East Ridge. Climb the bowl to the saddle between Parker Peak and Koip Peak and then continue up the ridge.

It is also possible to approach Koip Peak via Alger Creek from the Silver Lake Winter Closure (Trailhead #14).

Exit: Follow your tracks back to your car.

Δ MT. WOOD *12,637'*

Sitting directly across from the June Mountain Ski Area, the giant East Face of Mt. Wood beckons to skiers driving along Highway 395. With approximately 5,000' of vertical, Mt. Wood is one of the more coveted descents along the Highway 395 corridor, and offers a little bit of something for everyone.

During the peak of winter, the East Face gets the early morning sun and then goes into the shade in the afternoon. During the springtime, however, it holds sunlight almost all day. This also means that later in the season, lower sections of this face start melting out. Meanwhile, Mt. Wood's north face offers two impressive and high consequence lines.

↘ Z COULOIR

Mt. Wood

Aspect	Consequence/Exposure	Slope
	4	45°

Summit Elevation	12,500'
Descent Vertical	3,500'
Total Vertical	5,000'
Hiking Distance	7 miles
Terrain	Chute
Trailhead	13. N. June Loop Winter Closure
USGS Quad Maps	Lee Vining, June Lake, Koip Peak
GPS	37.813 / -119.170

The Z Couloir weaves its way improbably through the massive rock feature that comprises the North Face.

Approach: From the Northern June Loop Winter Closure (Trailhead #13) head west along Highway for approximately 1¼ miles to the junction of Parker Lake Road, which is a narrow dirt road that may not be clearly visible with a thick snowpack.

As the snowline recedes in the spring, it is possible to drive a portion of Parker Lake Road, which will take you closer to your destination. If this is your course of action, follow the main dirt road (i.e., don't turn onto any side roads) until its junction with 1S25A, approximately 1¾ miles from the Parker Lake Road/Highway 158 junction. Make a left onto this road, and follow it approximately ¾ miles to its end in a small canyon.

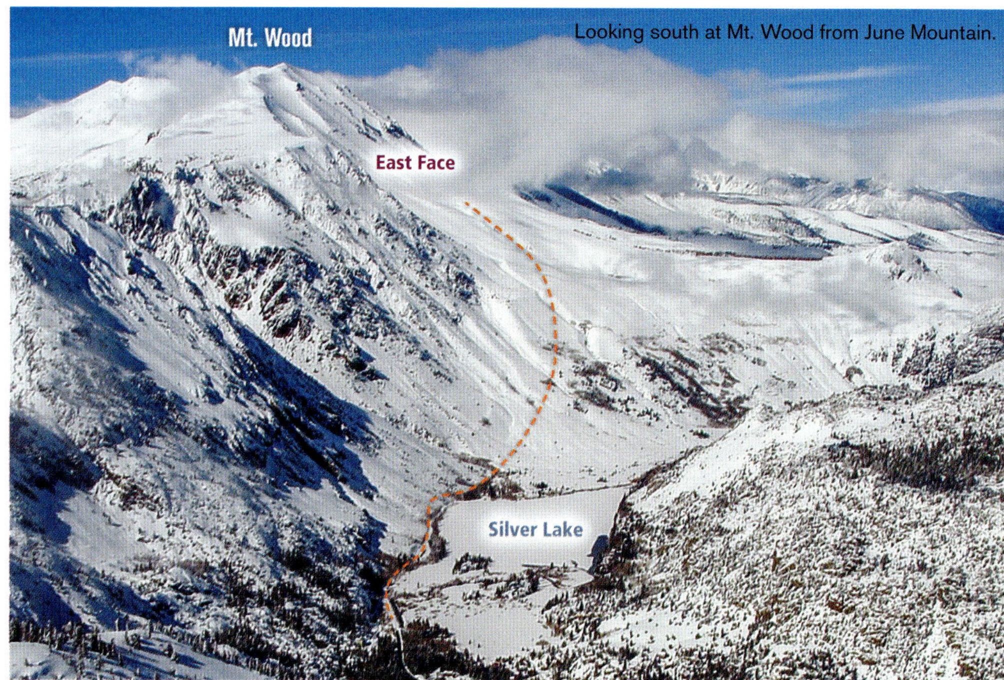

Looking south at Mt. Wood from June Mountain.

From here, continue up the canyon, negotiating your way around the stream (north side is better low down, south side is better higher up), until you reach a small bench above Parker Lake, and before a large ridge. Depending on the snowpack, either descend slightly or climb the right side a little ways until you find the best way around it. Once in the gully below the Z, start your boot-pack and rock-climbing journey up to the summit.

It is also possible to approach the lower gully via Parker Lake, or from the top via the East Face ascent.

Exit: Follow your tracks back to your car. It is also possible to ski to Parker Lake and then traverse out, though it requires a bit of climbing to get back to the end of 1S25A if you are parked there.

↘ NORTH GULLY

Mt. Wood

Aspect	Consequence/Exposure	Slope
N	4	40°

Summit Elevation	12,500'
Descent Vertical	3,500'
Total Vertical	5,000'
Hiking Distance	4 ½ miles
Terrain	Bowl
Trailhead	13. N June Loop Winter Closure
USGS Quad Maps	Lee Vining, June Lake, Koip Peak
GPS	37.810 / -119.166

The North Gully of Mt. Wood is one of those Eastside lines that gets looked at by everyone, but is rarely done by anyone. Though relatively innocuous in terms of steepness or technical difficulty, the exposure and consequences on this line are huge if you blow it. In moderate to high snow years, the gully fills in quite well, as does the skier's left-hand wall, which provides the only logical exit around the 100'+ cliff at the bottom.

Approach: There are a few ways to get to the summit of the North Gully, but the biggest issue becomes how you will get back to your car, depending on your starting point.

It is more direct to reach the top of the North Gully by following one of the East Face approaches, or by climbing the Z Couloir and walking a short distance to the southeast to the top of this line. The most logical for a car-to-car is from the Northern June Loop Winter Closure (Trailhead #13) via the Z Couloir. The simpler is via the East Face. Please refer to either of those descents for their specific approach information.

Once on the summit ridge, the North Gully lies at the northeast apex of Mt. Wood, just west of a large rock massif. The upper bowl of the North Gully is clearly evident from above

Exit: Depending on your starting point, this will vary. If starting from Trailhead #13, after skiing the line, stay left until it is possible to cross over the ridge to gain access back toward the Parker Lake Drainage. If

Brian Outhwaite climbing the Z Couloir.

Nate Greenberg pondering the next move in the Z Couloir. *Photo: Brett Lotz.*

approaching from the East Face, there are a variety of ways to ski the lower flank back to your car.

↘ EAST FACE

Mt. Wood

Aspect	Consequence/Exposure	Slope
	2	35°

Summit Elevation	12,637 '
Descent Vertical	5,300'
Total Vertical	5,300'
Hiking Distance	4 ½ miles
Terrain	Chute
Trailhead	14. Silver Lake Winter Closure
USGS Quad Maps	Lee Vining, June Lake, Koip Peak
GPS	37.808 / -119.163

The East Face of Mt. Wood is one of the more iconic faces on the Eastside, simply because of its exposure to Highway 395, and the amazing opportunities it provides skiers all season long. This face has a number of small chutes and large gullies that leave the summit ridge and end up down on the Parker Bench. All of these are of relatively the same aspect and angle.

Approach: There is no shortage of ways to reach the summit of Mt. Wood and the East Face, and your choice will likely depend on the time of year and how far you can drive. In the spring, or when it is possible to drive in beyond the north gate on Highway 158, most people choose to approach from the vicinity of the Northern June Loop Winter Closure (Trailhead #13), which is closer to Grant Lake Marina. In the winter months, many people choose to approach from Silver Lake Winter Closure (Trailhead #14).

If approaching from Grant Lake Marina, locate a moderately sized gully on the southwest side of the highway that climbs to the Parker Bench. From here, continue west up the bench below the East Face, and up one of its broad gullies to the summit ridge.

From Trailhead #14 at Silver Lake, skin north along the highway past Silver Lake until you are beneath the north face of Reversed Peak. In this vicinity, the slope to your north will begin to become more gentle, and it is possible to find your way up toward the ridgeline via a series of small gullies and canyons.

Once on top of the ridge, begin to head west and slightly north, until you find a gully that looks good to climb—all of them will take you to the ridgeline, from which you can access all the other east-facing lines.

Kevin Royal and Brian Schuster atop The Negatives.

△ REVERSED PEAK *9,473'*

The rather unimpressive Reversed Peak divides the northern and southern portions of the June Lake Loop from one another. From the south, the peak doesn't really look like much, though there is some fun glade skiing to be had off the summit back down toward Northshore Drive. From the north, however, Reversed Peak has a different quality, and as it drops down to the Aerie Crag Day Use Area, it forms a series of chutes, exposed faces, and other extreme terrain.

↘ NORTH COULOIR

Reversed Peak

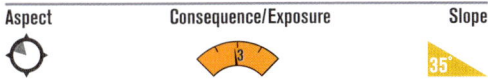

Aspect	Consequence/Exposure	Slope
	3	35°

Summit Elevation	9,473'
Descent Vertical	2,200'
Total Vertical	2,200'
Hiking Distance	3 ½ miles
Terrain	Chute
Trailhead	14. Silver Lake Winter Closure
USGS Quad Maps	June Lake
GPS	37.805 / -119.099

Cutting its way through the complex North Face of Reversed Peak, the North Couloir affords a relatively moderate ski through some interesting terrain with amazing scenery. A variety of other lines and options exist in this area as well, if you are interested in a bit of adventure.

Approach: From Silver Lake Winter Closure (Trailhead #14), continue north along Highway 158 past Silver Lake to the Aerie Crag Day Use Area. Above you at this point will be the north face and North Couloir of Reversed Peak. Boot the line from here.

It is also possible to gain the summit of Reversed Peak via the south ridge from Silver Lake, or the east face from Northshore Drive via the power-line road. While either of these approaches gets you to the summit, getting from there to the entry of the couloir can be a bit of an adventure, and requires a bit of work to get back to your starting point after skiing the line.

Exit: If you start at Silver Lake, simply follow your tracks back to the trailhead. If coming from Northshore Drive, it is best to head northeast around Reversed Peak, then climb the east ridge and ski down the east face to your car.

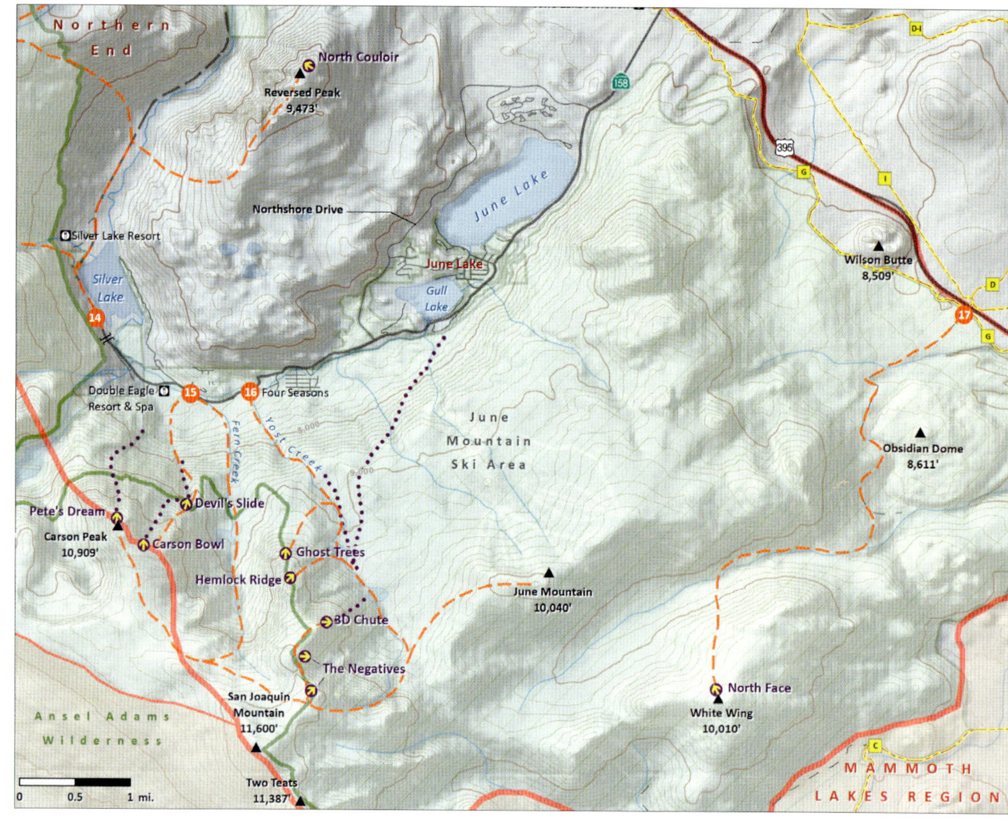

▣ Southern End

△ CARSON PEAK *10,909'*

Carson Peak is the iconic mountain that looms above Double Eagle Resort. It is an impressive, European-looking peak that hosts a variety of lines, ranging from moderate to extreme, all of which offer stellar skiing in an unsurpassed setting.

↘ PETE'S DREAM — Carson Peak

Aspect	Consequence/Exposure	Slope
	4	40°

Summit Elevation	10,909'
Descent Vertical	3,200'
Total Vertical	3,600'
Hiking Distance	5 ¾ miles
Terrain	Face
Trailhead	16. Four Seasons
USGS Quad Maps	June Lake, Mammoth Mountain
GPS	37.748 / -119.124

This line descends Carson Peak's true north face and requires a lot of snow in order to be skiable. Short, steep sections mix with easier chutes that cut through cliff bands and complex terrain features. Good route-finding skills are essential, especially if you decide not to climb the descent first.

Approach: There are two ways of reaching the top of Carson Peak. The shorter of the two is from Highway 158, but requires climbing approximately 3,500' to reach the summit. The longer is from the summit of June Mountain and involves more of a tour with considerably less elevation gain.

To access Carson Peak from June Mountain (which requires a lift ticket), ride J7 to the summit, then head southwest out along a prominent ridge. A short southwesterly traverse will bring you to the base of the Hourglass, which is the obvious gully at the southern end of the Negatives cirque. Climb through the Hourglass to the gentle slope above (please be aware of avalanche conditions while in this area, as the Hourglass is a major terrain trap and you are exposed to several avalanche-prone slopes here). From here, continue west, where a short descent takes you to a small saddle from which you can climb back northwest to the summit of Carson Peak.

To approach Carson from the highway, begin from Fern/Yost Trailhead (#15). Skin a short distance through the trees to the west until you reach the base of Devil's Slide, which is the obvious slide path to the south of the highway. Climb the face to the looker's left of the actual chute and work the ridgeline to the shoulder of Carson Peak. From here, some route-finding challenges exist, but eventually lead you to the summit.

Exit: If you start from Trailhead #15, you can ski right back to your car. If you accessed Carson Peak from June Mountain, it is generally possible to hitch a ride back to the base area of the resort with one of the friendly locals, or do a mega traverse back to the base area.

↘ NORTH BOWL

Carson Peak

Aspect	Consequence/Exposure	Slope
	3	35°

Summit Elevation	10,909'
Descent Vertical	1,800'
Total Vertical	3,600'
Hiking Distance	5 ¾ miles or 1 ¾ miles
Terrain	Bowl
Trailhead	15. Fern/Yost
USGS Quad Maps	June Lake, Mammoth Mountain
GPS	37.744 / -119.12

The North Bowl is the wide bowl on the eastern portion of Carson Peak, just down the ridge from the summit. While it's not incredibly steep or technical, it is possible to get into serious trouble in the middle section where a series of small cliffs exist. As you finish the main part of the descent, head east and wrap around the corner to access Devil's Slide. Be particularly cautious in the area of the cliff bands.

Approach: Follow the approach to Pete's Dream (page 120), but instead of continuing all the way to the true summit, contour over to the top of the obvious bowl.

Exit: If you start from the Fern/Yost Trailhead (#15), you can ski right back to your car. If you accessed Carson Peak from June Mountain, it is generally possible to hitch a ride back to the base area of the resort with one of the friendly locals.

↘ DEVIL'S SLIDE

Carson Peak

Aspect	Consequence/Exposure	Slope
	3	35°

Summit Elevation	9,100'
Descent Vertical	1,800'
Total Vertical	1,800'
Hiking Distance	1 ¼ miles
Terrain	Chute
Trailhead	15. Fern/Yost Trailhead
USGS Quad Maps	June Lake, Mammoth Mountain
GPS	37.749 / -119.115

Devil's Slide is obscured from view unless you are directly beneath it, in the vicinity of the Double Eagle Resort along Highway 158. There is a variety of terrain in this immediate area, in addition to the obvious gully of the slide itself. It is also the most common way to reach your car after skiing the North Bowl.

Approach: The most common way of accessing Devil's Slide is from the Fern/Yost Trailhead (#15). From here, skin a short distance through the trees to the west until you reach the base of Devil's Slide, which is the obvious slide path to the south of the highway. Climb the face to the looker's left of the actual chute until you reach the top of it.

It is also quite common to link Devil's Slide with the North Bowl of Carson Peak.

△ DREAM PEAK *10,000'*

Dream Peak is the often-overlooked northernmost peak of the San Joaquin/Negatives ridgeline. It sits just north of the end of the Negatives cirque, just beyond 3D Chute and a broad gully. It offers some excellent storm-skiing opportunities in its treed terrain.

Dream Peak Approach: It is possible to reach the top of Dream Peak from either Highway 158 via the Four Seasons Trailhead (#16) or June Mountain Ski Area. If you are accessing the area from June Mountain, most people choose to ski the Negatives first, though it is possible to ski into the Yost Creek Drainage directly from the top of the mountain.

If you are coming from the Negatives or the ski area, you will generally arrive at Yost Lake, which is located at the base of the Negatives. From here, continue downhill a short distance before heading west and climbing into a broad gully that eventually leads to the notch on the south side of Dream Peak. From here, traverse north and pick your line.

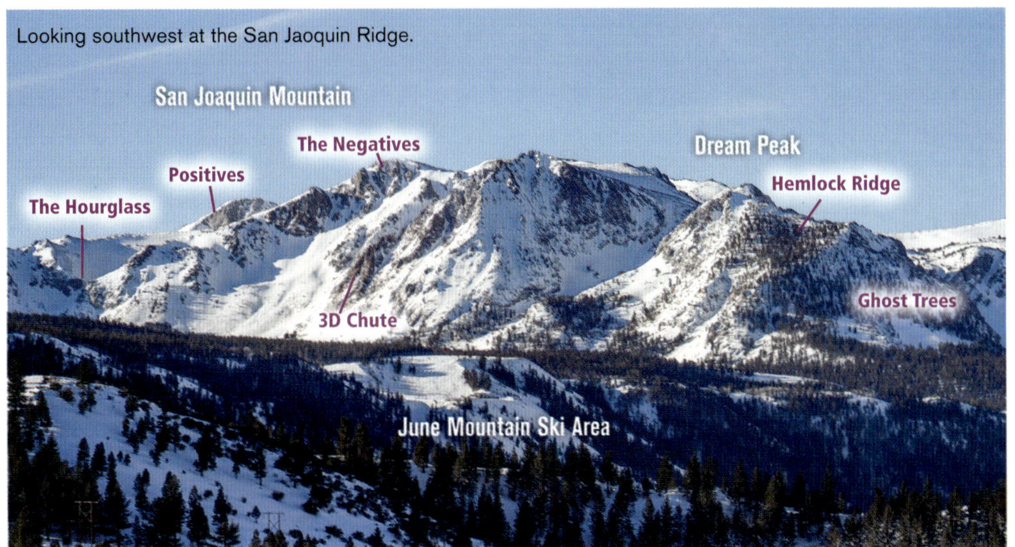

To approach Carson from the highway, begin from the Four Seasons Trailhead (#16). Skin up Yost Creek, generally following the creek drainage; find your way through the trees on either side of the canyon until you reach the open part of the canyon near the east flank of Dream Peak. As you reach the broad gully at the south end of Hemlock Ridge, begin your climb to the west until you have reached your high point. From here, traverse north and pick your line.

Dream Peak Exits: If you start from Trailhead #16, you can ski right back to your car. If you accessed Carson Peak from June Mountain, it is generally possible to hitch a ride back to the base area of the resort with one of the friendly locals.

➘ GHOST TREES

Dream Peak

Aspect	Consequence/Exposure	Slope
	3	30°

Summit Elevation	10,000'
Descent Vertical	1,000'
Total Vertical	2,500'
Hiking Distance	1 ½ miles
Terrain	Trees
Trailhead	16. Four Seasons
USGS Quad Maps	June Lake, Mammoth Mountain
GPS	37.743 / -119.102

The Ghost Trees provide tree skiing at the northern end of San Joaquin Mountain. This area is most frequently skied by folks coming off the Negatives, as one last short climb offers an additional thousand feet of fall-line skiing before working your way out via the Yost Creek Drainage.

➘ HEMLOCK RIDGE

Dream Peak

Aspect	Consequence/Exposure	Slope
	2	30°

Summit Elevation	10,500'
Descent Vertical	1,500'
Total Vertical	3,000'
Hiking Distance	1 ½ miles
Terrain	Trees
Trailhead	16. Four Seasons
USGS Quad Maps	June Lake, Mammoth Mountain
GPS	37.74 / -119.101

Hemlock Ridge affords some fantastic tree skiing in moderately spaced old growth on the northern flank of San Joaquin Mountain. This area is most frequently skied on the way out of the Negatives, as the skin-up to the ridge is relatively short but offers you considerable vertical descent in quality terrain.

Approach: Follow the approach provided for Dream Peak (see previous page) up canyon beyond the Ghost Trees. Once beneath the East Face of Dream Mountain, skin your way to the ridgeline.

△ SAN JOAQUIN MOUNTAIN *11,600'*

Lying just west of the June Mountain Ski Area, this is the most prominent lift-accessed backcountry spot in the Eastern Sierra. The slopes of San Joaquin Mountain afford a collection of opportunities regardless of conditions.

↘ THE NEGATIVES

San Joaquin Mountain

Aspect	Consequence/Exposure	Slope
	4	42°

Summit Elevation	11,150'
Descent Vertical	1,800'
Total Vertical	3,650'
Hiking Distance	3 ½ miles
Terrain	Mixed
Trailhead	16. Four Seasons
USGS Quad Maps	June Lake, Mammoth Mountain
GPS	37.726 / -119.099

The Negatives offers some of the best lift-served backcountry terrain in the Sierra. The Negatives are an 1,800' cirque riddled with chutes, faces, and other terrain choices that range from north to south aspects, with everything between moderate and extreme terrain.

Approach: It is possible to reach the top of San Joaquin Mountain (the Negatives) from either the Four Seasons Trailhead (#16) or June Mountain Ski Area. While the June Mountain approach is by far the preferred method, it does require a lift ticket—and the mountain being open. The approach from the highway, however, is considerably longer with substantially more elevation gain.

If you are approaching via the ski area, ride J7 to the top of June Mountain, and then head southwest out along a prominent ridge. A short southwesterly traverse will bring you to the base of the Hourglass, which is the obvious gully at the southern end of the Negatives cirque. Climb through the Hourglass to the gentle slope above and continue on to the top of your chosen descent. Please be aware of avalanche conditions while in this area, as the Hourglass is a major terrain trap and you are exposed to several avalanche-prone slopes here.

If you choose to approach the Negatives from the Four Seasons Trailhead (#16), cross the highway and skin up through small aspen trees and into the Yost Creek Drainage until you arrive at the base of the Negatives cirque. From here, climb southwest slightly up onto a bench and rejoin the standard approach route up through the Hourglass.

Once atop the Negatives, pick your poison and drop in. Some of the most popular lines are on the south end of the cirque, though the north end offers some incredible terrain options as well.

Exit: If you start from the Four Seasons Trailhead (#16), you can ski right back to your car. If you accessed Carson Peak from June Mountain, it is possible to traverse your way back to the east and end up at the base of June Mountain.

↘ 3D CHUTE

San Joaquin Mountain

Aspect	Consequence/Exposure	Slope
	4	55°

Summit Elevation	10,750'
Descent Vertical	1,500'
Total Vertical	3,250'
Hiking Distance	4 miles
Terrain	Chute
Trailhead	16. Four Seasons
USGS Quad Maps	June Lake, Mammoth Mountain
GPS	37.735 / -119.097

Lisa Mather climbing Hemlock Ridge during a storm.

The East Face of Carson Peak, as seen from atop The Negatives.

3D Chute is a narrow and steep chute that breaks the buttress that forms the northern end of the Negatives cirque. It is best viewed from the bottom, on the way out of the Yost Creek Drainage. It is usually necessary to rappel or lower yourself into the chute. A fixed rope is sometimes present at the top, although one should not assume it will be there, or necessarily trust it.

Approach: Follow the approach to the Negatives (previous entry). Once atop the Negatives, curve your way around to the northern end of the cirque (the Hourglass approach leaves you on the southern end of the cirque). As you reach the north end, continue east out to the end of the cirque to a rocky outcrop. From here, down-climb slightly and look for the entrance to 3D Chute, which often has a fixed rope atop it.

Exit: If you start from the Four Seasons Trailhead (#16), you can ski right back to your car. If you accessed San Joaquin Mountain from June Mountain, it is possible to traverse your way back to the east and end up at the base of June Mountain.

△ WHITE WING *10,010'*

White Wing is the clearly visible peak that sits above Obsidian Dome as you are driving Highway 395, and is also prominently visible from the summit of June Mountain (to the southeast). While there isn't a ton of terrain to be sought after on the peak, it does offer some great opportunity for lower-angle, lower-commitment backcountry skiing in the Owens River Headwaters.

↘ NORTH FACE

White Wing

Aspect	Consequence/Exposure	Slope
	1	30°

Summit Elevation	10,010'
Descent Vertical	1,200'
Total Vertical	2,000'
Hiking Distance	4 ¾ miles
Terrain	Face
Trailhead	17. Obsidian Dome
USGS Quad Maps	June Lake, Mammoth Mountain
GPS	37.726 / -119.047

The North Face of White Wing is probably the most heavily sought-after of all the terrain on the peak, though there is also some good skiing off the east face of the peak. In general, all of the skiing off White Wing is moderate in steepness, and open in terms of terrain.

Approach: Most people choose to ski White Wing via Trailhead #17, though it is also possible to ski off the back of June Mountain and climb the west ridge or North Face of White Wing.

From Trailhead #17, follow the Nordic trails around the back (west) side of Obsidian Dome, then continue west, weaving your way up the canyon. As you enter the canyon proper, cross the creek and begin your climb up the North Face of White Wing.

Exit: If you start from the Obsidian Dome Trailhead (#17), you can retrace your steps back to your car. If you came from June Mountain, most people choose to boot directly back up to the ski-area boundary, or skin toward the western boundary and reenter the ski area from that side.

6 Mammoth Lakes

Crystal Crag.

6. Mammoth Lakes

MAMMOTH REGION:

- ▣ Minaret Vista Area:
  - △ MT. RITTER
  - △ SAN JOAQUIN RIDGE
- ▣ The Sherwins Area:
  - △ SHERWIN RIDGE
- ▣ Mammoth Crest:
  - △ RED CONE ZONE
  - △ TJ BOWL ZONE
  - △ HAMMIL BOWL ZONE
  - △ BLUE CRAG ZONE
- ▣ Duck Pass Area:
  - △ DUCK PASS
  - △ PIKA PEAK
- ▣ Sherwin Creek Area:
  - △ PUNTA BARDINI
  - ◎ SOLITUDE CANYON
    - △ SOLITUDE PEAK
    - △ PYRAMID PEAK
  - ◎ VALENTINE CANYON
    - △ PYRAMID PEAK
    - △ VALENTINE PEAK
    - △ NO NAME PEAK
- ▣ Laurel Canyon Area:
  - △ NO NAME PEAK
  - △ BLOODY MOUNTAIN
  - △ LAUREL MOUNTAIN

Though Mammoth Lakes is probably best known for Mammoth Mountain Ski Area, it is also arguably the premiere backcountry skiing destination in the West. Situated in a small valley at 8,000', the Town of Mammoth Lakes is surrounded on all sides by prominent peaks and significant ridgelines. At the western end of the valley is Mammoth Mountain, which straddles the crest of the Sierra Nevada and sits proudly at the head of the San Joaquin River Drainage. As a result of this geography, there is a tremendous amount of skiing located within a 10-minute drive of downtown coffee shops. While abundant weather patterns from the Pacific Ocean funnel right into Mammoth, burying the region in snow.

There are several different trailheads that service the terrain in this region, some of which are plowed to 9,000' and others that give access to smaller and more protected areas. All in all, Mammoth is an excellent spot for half days, morning laps, or easy access to deep powder. There are, of course, plenty of longer tours spread throughout this region as well.

With the exception of the Mammoth Crest and some of the higher peaks surrounding town, the majority of the terrain in this chapter tends to melt out relatively early in the spring. So when Bloody Mountain and The Sherwins begin to look ugly, it's time to move on to higher ground.

Amenities are abundant, including lodging, dining, full-service ski-shops, camping, and entertainment (see Eats, Digs, Services, & Supplies, next page). Check with the Mammoth Lakes Welcome Center located on Highway 203 on your way into town for information, or stop by Mammoth Mountaineering Supply on Main Street for complete details about what's going on.

Getting There & Getting Going

The Town of Mammoth Lakes sits three miles west of scenic Highway 395, and is accessed via Highway 203. Mammoth is roughly five hours north of the Los Angeles area, one hour north of Bishop, and three hours south of Reno, NV, all along Highway 395. The Bay Area is roughly a six-hour drive (the best access in the winter from the Bay Area is via Highway 50 and 88 through South Lake Tahoe).

18. Main Lodge – Mammoth Mountain Ski Area (Year-Round) *8,600'*

The Main Lodge of Mammoth Mountain Ski Area is the primary starting point for most resort skiers, making this area rather crowded. Luckily, with the crowds come ample parking, public transit, and amenities, should you need them.

To reach the Main Lodge from the Welcome Center, continue west on Main Street through Mammoth until you reach the second stoplight at the intersection of Minaret Road. Take a right here and follow Minaret Road for approximately four miles until you reach the roadside parking near Main Lodge. There is a parking shuttle that will take you (for free) from your car to the actual Main Lodge area, if you are parked a little ways away.

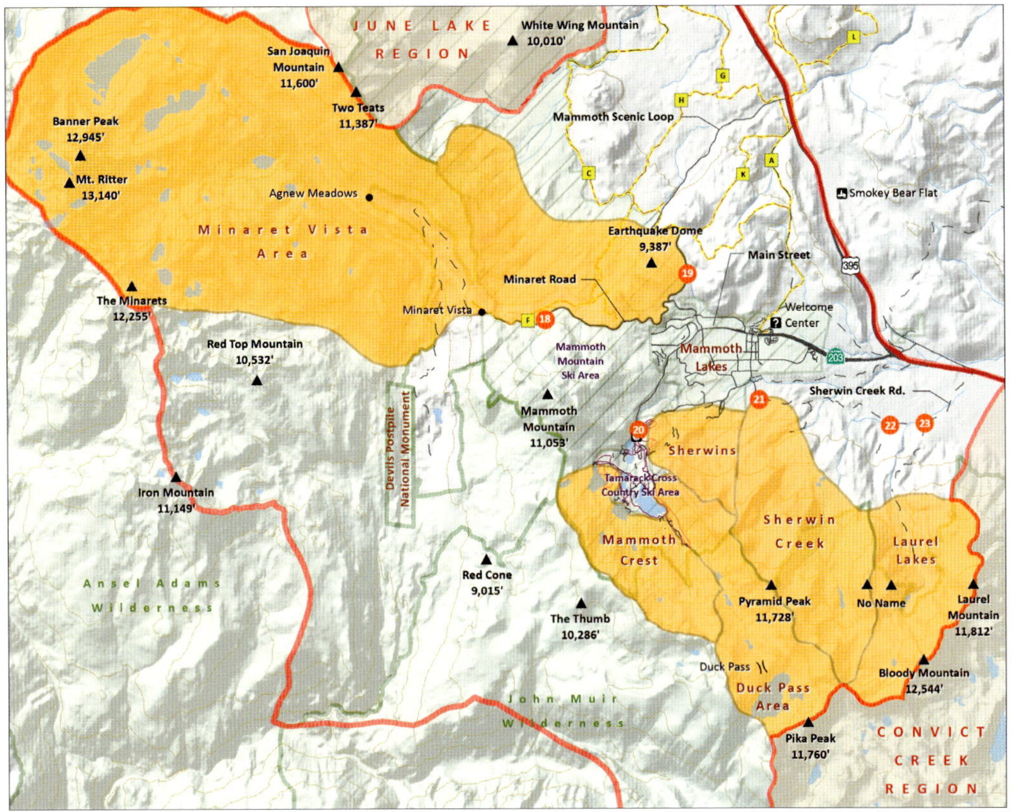

19. Mammoth Scenic Loop (Year-Round) *8,200'*

The Mammoth Scenic Loop is a secondary access road that connects Minaret Road (between The Village and Main Lodge) to Highway 395 a few miles north of Highway 203. It was built as a secondary exit from town, in the event that a volcanic event actually took place in town (Mammoth is an active volcano).

From the Welcome Center, follow Main Street west to the second stoplight at the Minaret Road intersection. Turn right here and follow Minaret Road for approximately one mile. Pass The Village and Mammoth Knolls Drive, then keep your eyes peeled for the right-hand turn onto Mammoth Scenic Loop. Follow this road for ¾ mile or so, up a small hill and around a sweeping left-hand corner, then look for a long, plowed parking lane located along the east side of the road. The parking area is located almost due east of a prominent hill (Earthquake Dome), and before you begin curving your way around and down its north face.

20. Tamarack XC Ski Area (Year-Round) *8,600'*

Tamarack XC Ski Area offers groomed Nordic trails in the serene setting of the Mammoth Lakes Basin on the back side of Mammoth Mountain.

From the Welcome Center, follow Main Street west uphill through both stoplights. At the second light (Minaret Road intersection), Main Street turns into Lake Mary Road. Continue on Lake Mary Road about three more miles. After crossing the bridge at the outlet for Twin Lakes, the road forks. The right fork (Twin Lakes Loop Road) takes you to Tamarack Lodge proper, while the left dead-ends after a short distance at a gate and serves as the preferred winter staging area.

Region Trailheads

18. Main Lodge – MMSA
19. Mammoth Scenic Loop
20. Tamarack XC Ski Area
21. Sherwin Creek Staging Area
22. Valentine Canyon Trailhead
23. Laurel Canyon Trailhead

21. Sherwin Creek Staging Area (Year-Round) 7,900'

Sherwin Creek Road stretches along the southeast side of town, ultimately connecting Old Mammoth Road with Highway 395. In the winter, the road is closed a short distance in from either end and is used for winter-staging areas. This trailhead is located at the top end of Sherwin Creek Road (closer to Old Mammoth Road).

From the Welcome Center, continue west on Main Street to the first stoplight at the intersection of Old Mammoth Road. Turn left here and head south on Old Mammoth Road through the next stoplight at the intersection at Meridian Blvd. Continue along Old Mammoth Road past Vons and a series of shopping centers. As Old Mammoth heads out the south end of town, you will pass Mammoth Creek Park (on the west side) and the road will start to curve. The second intersection in the curve to the east is Sherwin Creek Road. A sign for Sierra Meadows Ranch is located at the intersection of Sherwin Creek and Old Mammoth Roads.

Continue along Sherwin Creek Road past the Sierra Meadows Ranch (on your left) and down a small hill. As you descend you will notice a plowed parking area to the south of the road at the base of The Sherwins. Park here, out of the middle of the road. Please do not park in front of the pack station or in the propane depot.

22. Valentine Canyon Trailhead (Spring Only) 7,400'

Along the lower reaches of Sherwin Creek Road, closer to Highway 395, are a handful of smaller Forest Service roads that provide access into the mountains—specifically Valentine and Laurel canyons.

From the Welcome Center, head east out of town on Highway 203, then south on Highway 395. After 1½ miles is an exit on the west side of the highway for Sherwin Creek Road. In the peak of winter, you may not be able to drive much farther than this intersection, and it is common to see people stage snowmobiles from this location (you can snowmobile to this trailhead, and #23).

To reach the Valentine Canyon trailhead in the springtime (or with your skis or sled), travel west along Sherwin Creek Road for 2¼ miles total, passing the Laurel Lakes Road after 1½ miles. After you pass the Laurel Lakes Road (a steep uphill road heading south across a cattle guard), the road to Valentine Canyon trailhead will be the next left you can make. It is Forest Service Road 04S08G, and should be marked with a small post. Turn left onto this road and follow it to the end.

23. Laurel Canyon Trailhead (Spring Only) 7,300'

Along the lower reaches of Sherwin Creek Road, closer to Highway 395, are a handful of smaller Forest Service roads that provide access into the mountains—specifically Laurel and Valentine canyons.

From the Welcome Center, head east out of town on Highway 203, then south on Highway 395. After 1½ miles is an exit on the west side of the highway for Sherwin Creek Road. In the peak of winter, you may not be able to drive much farther than this intersection, and it is common to see people stage snowmobiles from this location (you can snowmobile to this trailhead, and #23).

To reach the Laurel Lakes trailhead in the springtime (or with your skis or sled), travel west along Sherwin Creek Road for 1½ miles where the steep Laurel Lakes Road heads uphill to the south across a cattle guard. If you have a high-clearance vehicle and the road is clear (read: fall or spring months), it is possible to drive a long way up this road (3½–4miles) to the summertime trailhead for Laurel Lakes. If there is snow anywhere on the road, or you are not interested in 4x4ing your rig, park where you can, closer to the intersection with Sherwin Creek Road.

Eats, Digs, Services, & Supplies

Mammoth Lakes offers an assortment of options for eating, drinking, sleeping, and getting what you need for your tour. Check with the Mammoth Lakes Welcome Center on the way into town for more complete information about lodging and camping. There are also a variety of camping options out of town in the Owens Valley.

We are particularly fond of the baked goods and coffee at Stellar Brew, sushi at Shogun, crepes, paninis, and wine at the Side Door Café, gourmet dining at Restaurant Skadi, and and quick, cheap, and tasty Mexican food at Salsa's.

Be sure to stop by Mammoth Mountaineering Supply on Main Street for the most complete selection of gear on the Eastside and information about conditions from their friendly staff.

If you have time, or are looking for something to do on a rest day, go practice your beacon-search skills at one of the two Beacon Basins, located behind the Mammoth Lakes Welcome Center and at the Main Lodge of Mammoth Mountain Ski Area.

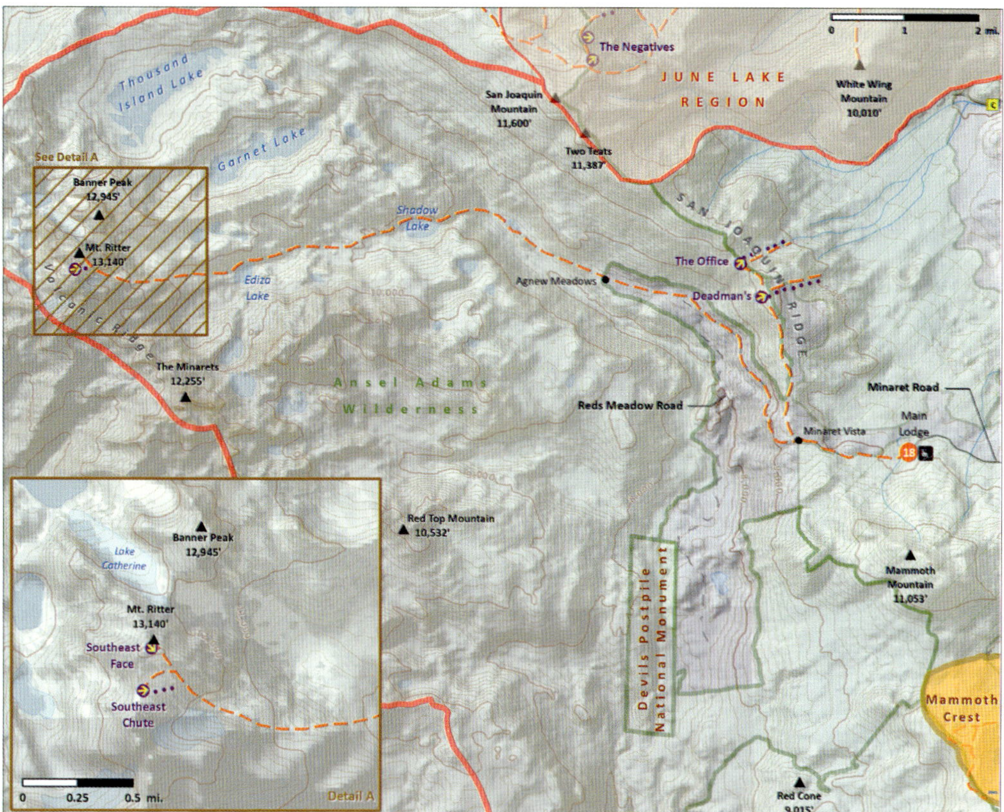

▣ Minaret Vista Area

This is a large area that stretches from the iconic Mammoth skyline (The Minarets) to the Minaret Vista, located at the top of Minaret Road, approximately one mile west from the Main Lodge at Mammoth Mountain Ski Area.

△ MT. RITTER *13,140'*

Forming the backdrop for the Town of Mammoth Lakes, Mt. Ritter, Banner Peak, and The Minarets are some of the most recognizable peaks in the Sierra. Highly visible from the ski area, Mt. Ritter's Southeast Face is also highly sought-after among backcountry skiers.

Though it appears to be close to town, the Ritter Range is fairly remote, particularly during the winter, when the road to Red's Meadow is closed. A trip to Mt. Ritter typically involves at least two days, but with all of the skiable terrain out there, you'll probably want to take even more time than that.

The Southeast Face of Mt. Ritter is the obvious, large face that leaves the summit of the peak to the south and eventually funnels down to a small chute onto the lower slopes. This is a prized line by many, as it stares you in the face around town and in the region as a whole. Located just to the south of the Southeast Face at the south end of the upper bowl is the entrance to the Southeast Chute, which drops plumb through the craggy north face of Mt. Ritter.

↘ SOUTHEAST FACE — Mt. Ritter

Aspect	Consequence/Exposure	Slope
	3	40°

Summit Elevation	13,140'
Descent Vertical	3,000'
Total Vertical	7,000'
Hiking Distance	11 ¼ miles
Terrain	Face
Trailhead	18. Main Lodge
USGS Quad Maps	Mammoth Mountain, Mt. Ritter
GPS	37.689 / -119.199

Though not very technically difficult, these are committing lines with relative steepness, where consequences could be bad and a rescue could take a long time.

↘ SOUTHEAST CHUTE

Mt. Ritter

Aspect	Consequence/Exposure	Slope
	3	40°

Summit Elevation	13,000'
Descent Vertical	2,800'
Total Vertical	7,000'
Hiking Distance	11 ¼ miles
Terrain	Chute
Trailhead	18. Main Lodge
USGS Quad Maps	Mammoth Mountain, Mt. Ritter
GPS	37.689 / -119.197

Approach: The most common approach begins at Main Lodge (Trailhead #18). Currently, the Mammoth Mountain Inn offers backcountry parking for those headed out overnight.

From Main Lodge, skin along what would be the summer alignment of Minaret Road, which is typically groomed all the way to Minaret Summit. Pass the small entrance station to Red's Meadow, where you will begin descending into the valley. Follow the road as it traverses the steep hillside and then flattens out near Agnew Meadow. At Agnew Meadow, the main road will make a nearly 180-degree turn. At this point you will leave it and head across the meadow. Continue west through the campground at Agnew Meadow. After approximately one mile, descend a short distance into the drainage from Olaine Lake, roughly following the location of the summer trail. Continue up this drainage and across Olaine Lake. A short distance past Olaine Lake, begin looking for the bridge across the San Joaquin River. Once across, climb the steep drainage to the south up to Shadow Lake. The final stretch of this traverses a steep hillside at a point where the river is typically not frozen over. The exposed slope above rushing water can be quite intimidating, and extra caution should be taken to safely make it through this passage. Just past the waterfall, a snow bridge typically forms, which while convenient, can be very hazardous as well.

Cross Shadow Lake and continue another 2½ miles up the canyon to Lake Ediza. From Lake Ediza, begin climbing toward the saddle between Mt. Ritter and Banner Peak. A short, steep slope on the left will give access to the moderate slope of the southeast glacier. Ascend the glacier and climb the chute to the giant Southeast Face. A moderate skin will bring you to the summit.

It is also possible to access the south side of Mt. Ritter from the June Lake Loop. While this distance is shorter, it involves gaining and losing more elevation.

It is also sometimes possible to snowmobile to Agnew Meadow, which will save a bit of time going in and a ton of time coming out. Snowmobile staging is available via the CalTrans facility located on the north side of Minaret Road near the Chair 4 parking lot, and a network of trails

Brian Schuster, Bill Ossofsky, and Zach Schneider climbing the Southeast Face of Mt Ritter.

will lead you back to Minaret Vista. If you are unfamiliar with this area, check with the Forest Service Visitor's Center in Mammoth for a snowmobile map.

Snowmobiling the road to Red's Meadow is no easy task. Side hilling on steep slopes combined with numerous wind drifts make for very challenging driving. Snowmobiles are allowed to travel over the summer roads only. Driving off the roadway is prohibited in this area.

Exit: Follow the approach in reverse.

△ SAN JOAQUIN RIDGE *10,000'*

The San Joaquin Ridge is the massive ridgeline that stretches between Minaret Summit north to June Lake and divides the west and east side of the range in the Mammoth Region. Along with having some stellar touring (skiing from Mammoth to June is a popular outing for many looking to put a little distance under their skis), the ridge boasts some deserving and often-overlooked ski terrain.

↘ THE OFFICE

San Joaquin Ridge

Aspect	Consequence/Exposure	Slope
	3	35°

Summit Elevation	10,000'
Descent Vertical	1,000'
Total Vertical	1,000'
Hiking Distance	2 ½ miles
Terrain	Mixed
Trailhead	18. Main Lodge
USGS Quad Maps	Mammoth Mountain
GPS	37.687 / -119.07

The Office is located at the far north end of the lower portion of San Joaquin Ridge, just before the ridge begins its climb toward San Joaquin Mountain. This is a relatively small northeast-facing cirque that drops from the ridgeline down to the upper portion of Glass Creek and offers a variety of terrain choices in chutes and gullies. It is a popular short day destination, especially with snowmobilers, as you can ride directly to the top of the cirque.

Approach: From Main Lodge (Trailhead #18), skin along what would be the summer alignment of Minaret Road, which is typically groomed all the way to Minaret

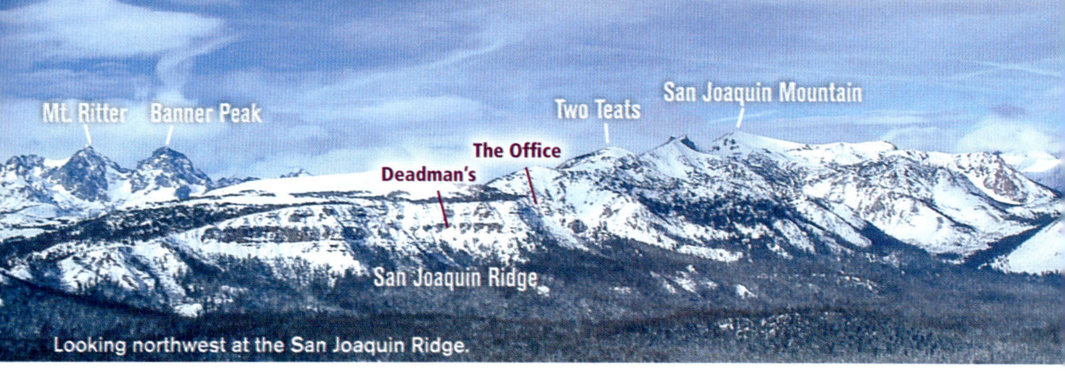

Looking northwest at the San Joaquin Ridge.

Vista. At the small entrance station to Red's Meadow, turn north and begin climbing the ridgeline past the Minaret Vista summer picnic area, and up the ridge. This skin is rather nondescript and generally stays along the ridgeline itself up a series of small benches until you reach a rather prominent headwall at the northern end of the lower portion of the San Joaquin Ridge.

If you are taking a snowmobile, stage from the Caltrans sand shed, which is located just downhill from the Chair 4 parking lot, on the north side of Minaret Road. Follow the C Trail north then west to the junction with the F Trail, which you can follow past Main Lodge and to the groomed road that leads to Minaret Vista. Please note that while the top of the San Joaquin Ridge is open to snowmobiles, there is a boundary line located down the east face of the ridge at approximately 9,800', beyond which is wilderness. It is also illegal to take your sled north beyond The Office.

Exit: After skiing The Office, skin and boot your way back to the ridge, then follow your route back to Main Lodge.

↘ DEADMAN'S
San Joaquin Ridge

Aspect	Consequence/Exposure	Slope
	4	35°

Summit Elevation	10,000'
Descent Vertical	1,500'
Total Vertical	1,500'
Hiking Distance	2 miles
Terrain	Face
Trailhead	18. Main Lodge
USGS Quad Maps	Mammoth Mountain
GPS	37.681 / -119.065

Just before The Office cirque lies the summit of Deadman's, the east face of which hosts some high-risk bigline skiing that is riddled with complex terrain features, including a series of large cliff faces. There are a handful of lines that weave their way through this terrain feature, with some of the more obvious lying on the immediate northern and southern ends of the formation itself.

Approach: From Main Lodge (Trailhead #18), skin along what would be the summer alignment of Minaret Road, which is typically groomed all the way to Minaret Vista. At the small entrance station to Red's Meadow, turn north and begin climbing the ridgeline past the Minaret Vista summer picnic area, and up the ridge. This skin is rather non-descript and generally stays along the ridgeline itself. Follow this up a series of small benches to the first real prominent open peak you come to on the ridge. Directly to your east will be the Deadman's Cliffs.

Due to the complexity of this terrain, it may be wiser to approach the area from the bottom, via the Inyo Craters staging area off Mammoth Scenic Loop, then boot the line of choice.

If you are taking a snowmobile, stage from the Caltrans sand shed, which is located just downhill from the Chair 4 parking lot, on the north side of Minaret Road. Follow the C Trail north then west to the junction with the F Trail, which you can follow past Main Lodge and to the groomed road that leads to Minaret Vista. Please beware that while the top of the San Joaquin Ridge is open to snowmobiles, there is a boundary line located down the east face of the ridge at approximately 9,800', beyond which is wilderness.

Exit: After skiing Deadman's, skin and boot your way back to the ridge, then follow your route back to Main Lodge.

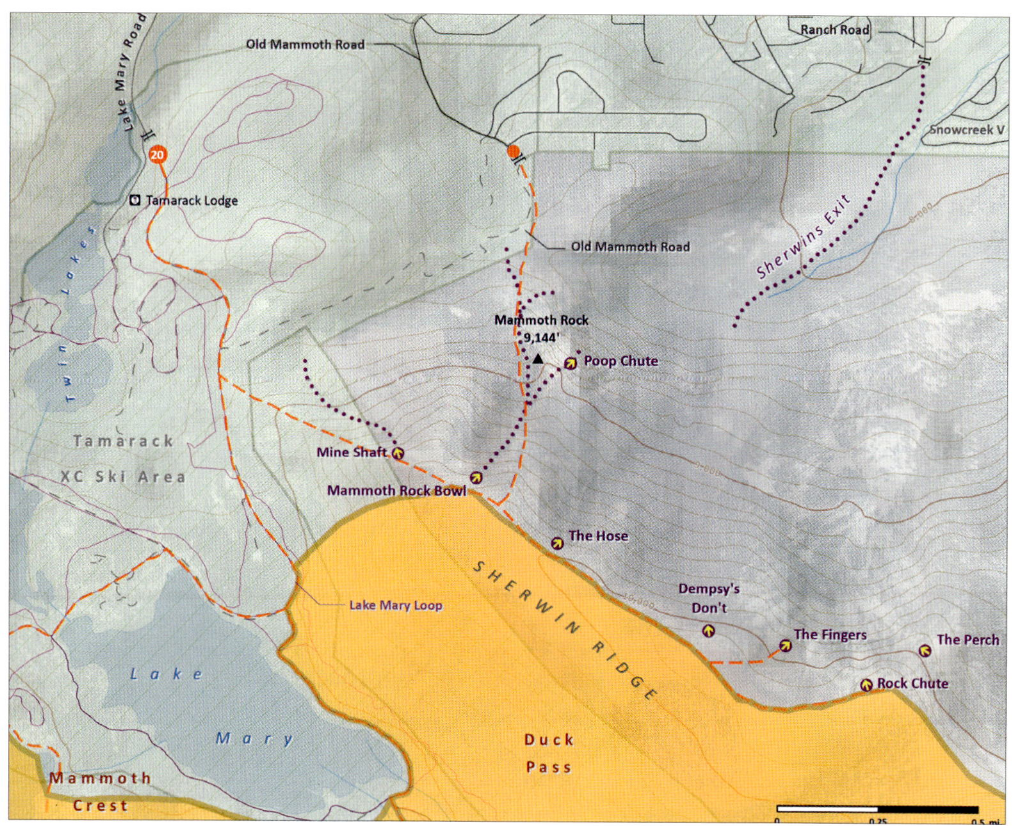

▣ The Sherwins Area

Though it is considered by many to be more of a "front-country" destination, The Sherwins offer easy access to excellent powder skiing on treed north-facing slopes. With the option of either a car shuttle or public transit from the end point to the trailhead, The Sherwins see a lot of action, especially after storm cycles. Due to its proximity to town and ease of access, many Sherwins users view this area as being almost an extension of the ski area. Because of this, it is not uncommon to come across users who are unfamiliar with backcountry protocols, including those without beacons, shovels, or probes. If you are seeking the complete backcountry wilderness experience, The Sherwins are probably not for you. That being said, with some effort it is not too difficult to find your own peace and solitude along this ridge.

∆ SHERWIN RIDGE *10,000'*

One of the most appealing aspects of The Sherwins is that a car shuttle or public transit can be used to eliminate roughly half of the elevation on the approach. Access issues have popped up in the past couple of years in this area, but Ranch Road is still the most popular ending location for The Sherwins. There are a few places to park cars near Snowcreek Athletic Club, but please be mindful of property rights. If you have any question about the legitimacy of your parking, or are conscientious of your carbon footprint, opt to take the Red Line bus, which picks up in the parking lot of the athletic club every 20 minutes and can be taken all the way to The Village. The Orange Line then departs The Village roughly every hour and takes riders to and from Tamarack Cross Country Ski Center, the trailhead for The Sherwins.

Sherwins Approach: Tamarack Lodge grooms and maintains the roads around the Lakes Basin for cross-country skiing during the winter months. While open to the non-paying public for access, please be mindful of the rules—the well-groomed right-hand track is for cross-country and skate skiing; traveling in this lane requires a pass from Tamarack. The left-hand lane is for hikers, snowshoers, and backcountry skiers. All dogs must be on a leash.

From Tamarack XC Ski Resort (Trailhead #20), hike approximately ½ mile, just past the snowed-over upper terminus of Old Mammoth Road, to where a prominent rocky ridge appears on your left. Leave the groomed path and head left (east) up the rocky, wind-scoured ridge. The first short section is usually the only part to drift in with snow. There is typically a boot pack put in already and sometimes a skin track. If you are booting, please respect the skin track and stay out of it. A few hundred feet up you will be hiking along rocks, following the discontinuous trails above the site of the old mine. Traverse right below the large cliff band and follow a short, loose chute to the summit plateau.

Sherwins Exit: After skiing the lower flanks of The Sherwins, you will find yourself on the south side of the Snowcreek Golf Course. Please note that this is private land—respecting proper egress is imperative to protect future access.

The best exit is via Ranch Road, which can be reached by skinning east over to the corner of the Snowcreek V subdivision (the large cluster of townhomes on the east end of the meadow). From this point, head due north to the bend in Ranch Road, then follow the road north to its intersection with Old Mammoth Road. There are generally signs on the golf course that indicate the approved exit route.

Note for Snowboarders: The Sherwins are one of the few spots that typically do not require a splitboard or snowshoes to climb. The rocky, windswept ridge makes for an easy ascent, and the short snowy sections get a solid bootpack very quickly. The bottom of the run can be a different story. Crossing this meadow with fresh, untracked snow can be a chore. While your skier friends are poling across the flats, you'll be wallowing up to your armpits. If you are riding The Sherwins shortly after a storm, it is recommended that you bring a pair of snowshoes or at least some poles, just in case. Within a few days there will be plenty of tracks, both from skiers and snowmobilers, to allow for an easy ride out

MINE SHAFT

Sherwin Ridge

Aspect	Consequence/Exposure	Slope
	3	35°

Summit Elevation	9,600'
Descent Vertical	1,000'
Total Vertical	1,000'
Hiking Distance	2 miles
Terrain	Chute
Trailhead	20. Tamarack
USGS Quad Maps	Bloody Mountain
GPS	37.613 / -118.9995

Though often overlooked, Mine Shaft is a nice, aesthetic line that can be accessed quickly and even done as a first lap before doing something farther out along the ridge. The line is most obvious from the junction of Old Mammoth Road and Lake Mary Road before you reach the actual western end of the ridge—it is a small, rocky chute descending the northwest shoulder.

Approach: Access Mine Shaft via skier's left of Mammoth Rock Bowl and ski or hike down and left to its entrance. The chute is relatively short, but finishes almost right back at the boot pack, making it a great option for a quick first lap.

Exit: Mine Shaft drops you directly below the north end of The Sherwins on Old Mammoth Road. From this point, you can easily skin up Old Mammoth Road to its junction at Lake Mary Road, then follow Lake Mary back to the trailhead.

MAMMOTH ROCK BOWL

Sherwin Ridge

Aspect	Consequence/Exposure	Slope
	2	30°

Summit Elevation	9,700'
Descent Vertical	1,500'
Total Vertical	1,500'
Hiking Distance	2 miles
Terrain	Bowl
Trailhead	20. Tamarack
USGS Quad Maps	Bloody Mountain
GPS	37.612 / -118.997

Mammoth Rock Bowl is the prominent bowl that lies just west of Mammoth Rock. There are a number of options in the upper bowl, with the left side affording less committing entrances and mixed tree and glade skiing. The center and right sides see a considerable amount of wind-loading and should be treated with care depending on conditions. The upper bowl collects onto a small bench just above and west of Mammoth Rock, which ultimately becomes the Bluffs subdivision. From here, there are a number of options, with easier exits trending toward Mammoth Rock and more complex terrain forming in the cliff band to skier's left.

Approach: As you crest out on the ridge, you will see a moderately sized bowl above Mammoth Rock—this is the aptly named Mammoth Rock Bowl.

Melissa Buehler climbing the Sherwins with Mammoth Crest in the background.

The Sherwin Ridge as seen from Old Mammoth Road.

Many people also choose to park at the top of Old Mammoth Road at the point of winter closure, and skin directly up Mammoth Rock Bowl.

Exit: The exit from the Mammoth Rock area is dependent on the location of your car. If you parked at the end of Old Mammoth Road, the best option is to skin the short slope to the west which gains a bench just above the end of the road. From here, continue north, downhill, until you reach your car. If you parked at Trailhead #20, you can continue west from this same point along Old Mammoth Road to the intersection with Lake Mary Road, then glide back to the trailhead.

↘ POOP CHUTE

Sherwin Ridge

Aspect	Consequence/Exposure	Slope
	3	40°

Summit Elevation	9,700'
Descent Vertical	1,500'
Total Vertical	1,500'
Hiking Distance	2 miles
Terrain	Chute
Trailhead	20. Tamarack
USGS Quad Maps	Bloody Mountain
GPS	37.611 / -118.994

Poop Chute is an obscure, short, and relatively steep chute located on the east (skier's right) side of Mammoth Rock. Access Poop Chute by dropping into the upper Mammoth Rock Bowl via the center or skier's-right side, and continue working right, staying directly above Mammoth Rock. As the terrain steepens, it somewhat naturally funnels into a couple of logical slots, one of which is the Poop Chute. Be aware that straying too far to skier's right will put you on top of a large cliff band.

↘ THE HOSE/THE PROW

Sherwin Ridge

Aspect	Consequence/Exposure	Slope
	2	30°

Summit Elevation	9,900'
Descent Vertical	1,800'
Total Vertical	1,800'
Hiking Distance	2 ¼ miles
Terrain	Trees
Trailhead	20. Tamarack
USGS Quad Maps	Bloody Mountain
GPS	37.608 / -118.991

From town, The Hose almost looks like a cut ski run or an old lift line. While it is neither of these, it is a well-protected, very enjoyable descent. The area immediately surrounding The Hose is notorious for large cornices and severe wind-loading. Be extremely cautious when dropping in here—the safer approaches are those that stay in the trees and enter in from the sides so as to avoid the cornice.

The prominent point that lies just beyond the hose yet west of Dempsy's Don't is referred to as The Prow. There are several lines on the ridgeline that descends from this point, as well as back toward The Hose or toward Dempsy's.

All of these lines generally converge on an open slope below, beyond which you will find a steep, convex, rocky rollover that avalanches frequently. Extreme care should be taken here. The safest exit is to the right and into the toe of The Prow or farther toward Dempsy's. The lowest portions of these descents end in a fairly dense section of aspen trees. While this forest typically gets covered in snow later in the season, it can be quite a nuisance in the early season.

Approach: Once atop the Sherwin Ridge, continue for another ¼ mile or so to the top of a small, rocky knoll. Near the far (east) side of this knoll is The Hose.

DEMPSY'S DON'T (AKA MAIN AVY PATH) — Sherwin Ridge

Aspect | Consequence/Exposure: 1 | Slope: 30°

Summit Elevation	9,800'
Descent Vertical	1,800'
Total Vertical	1,800'
Hiking Distance	2 ¼ miles
Terrain	Bowl
Trailhead	20. Tamarack
USGS Quad Maps	Bloody Mountain
GPS	37.607 / -118.988

The most prominent line on The Sherwins is the Main Avy Path or Dempsy's Don't, which is the large open bowl/face that was formed by a climax natural slide that occured during the 1986 season. The skier's-left side of the path is the easiest way down The Sherwins. It goes through a forest of new growth, which gets completely covered during big winters. The skier's-right side of the Avy Path is similar to the left, except for a steeper entrance that is more prone to wind-loading.

In the early season, the lower section of this area is a maze of old trees and stumps that were swept down the mountain in the slide, so use caution. After big storms, large avalanches are still quite common here, occasionally running the entire length of the mountain down to the meadow below.

Approach: Once atop the Sherwin Ridge, continue another ½ mile until you reach the edge of the Main Avy Path.

Located just east of the Main Avy Path is the beginning of the rocky outcrop that forms Rock Chute. Just before this obvious outcrop are three small chutes known as The Fingers. Each of the three chutes is similar in terms of steepness and length, but due to slightly different aspects and positions, they capture snow differently. It is not uncommon for the ridge leading down to the top of the chutes to be stripped of snow. Most of this snow is deposited immediately below, and caution should be exercised when skiing in this area following a storm or large wind event. In 2004, a local snowboarder triggered a small slide in The Fingers that swept him into trees below, breaking both of his femurs.

THE FINGERS — Sherwin Ridge

Aspect | Consequence/Exposure: 3 | Slope: 35°

Summit Elevation	9,700'
Descent Vertical	1,500'
Total Vertical	1,500'
Hiking Distance	2 ½ miles
Terrain	Chute
Trailhead	20. Tamarack
USGS Quad Maps	Bloody Mountain
GPS	37.605 / -118.983

The Fingers end up in the toe of Rock Chute, which affords several more turns in the nicely gladed trees below. As you ski this terrain, continue working left and over a series of benches to eventually meet up with the bottom of the Main Avy Path.

Approach: Once atop the Sherwin ridge, continue for another ¾ mile, and past the far side of the Main Avy Path. The first chute of The Fingers begins just beyond the eastern end of the Main Avy Path. All of the lines start several hundred feet below the actual ridgeline.

ROCK CHUTE — Sherwin Ridge

Aspect | Consequence/Exposure: 3 | Slope: 45°

Summit Elevation	9,700'
Descent Vertical	1,500'
Total Vertical	1,500'
Hiking Distance	2 ½ miles
Terrain	Chute
Trailhead	20. Tamarack
USGS Quad Maps	Bloody Mountain
GPS	37.604 / -118.98

Rock Chute is probably the most striking ski descent visible from town. It splits the major rock buttress at

Forest Cross atop the Mammoth Crest.

the looker's left end of the Sherwin Ridge. Though it is not quite as steep as it looks from afar, the entrance can be challenging enough for the most talented skiers and riders. Rock Chute is a prime candidate for windloading, with the long flat fetch of the Sherwin Ridge leading right to the buttress. A number of sizeable skier-triggered slides have occurred here over the past several years, so be aware of conditions.

Take pleasure in the steep granite walls on either side of you as you ski the chute and end in the protected treed bowl at the bottom. Once in the bowl, continue working left and over a series of benches and eventually meet up with bottom of the Main Avy Path.

Approach: Once atop the Sherwin Ridge, continue for another mile or so, passing the bowl that forms The Fingers to the large rock outcrop that marks the top of Rock Chute.

↘ THE PERCH

Sherwin Ridge

Aspect	Consequence/Exposure	Slope
	2	35°

Summit Elevation	9,700'
Descent Vertical	1,500'
Total Vertical	1,500'
Hiking Distance	2 ½ miles
Terrain	Trees
Trailhead	20. Tamarack
USGS Quad Maps	Bloody Mountain
GPS	37.604 / -118.979

The small hanging bowl and terrain just east of Rock Chute is referred to as The Perch. This portion of the Sherwin Ridge is rarely skied, but offers some fine turns in moderately spaced trees. Many people ski The Perch and connect it with a run on Punta Bardini (page 154) due to its proximity.

Though the Sherwin Ridge continues to the east beyond this point, what is commonly referred to as "The Sherwins" ends at The Perch. The descents beyond The Perch are referred to as "Punta Bardini."

Approach: Continue along the ridge past the bowl that forms The Fingers to the large rock outcrop that marks the top of Rock Chute. Just beyond this, to the east, are the upper ridges that form The Perch.

▣ Mammoth Crest

The Mammoth Crest (or The Crest, as it is often referred to) is quintessentially Mammoth, and is heavily visited by locals and travelers looking for a quick half-day fix. Flanking the southwestern edge of the Mammoth Lakes Basin, The Crest forms the backdrop for the area between Mammoth Mountain and The Sherwins. Through the steep granite walls cut dozens of lines and variations of lines along generally north-facing aspects, offering some superb and varied skiing options.

While the distance from the trailhead might seem a little far, the approach to The Crest is mostly on the groomed Nordic trails of Tamarack XC Ski Area, which allow for a relatively quick approach and exit. In fact, for many of the exits, it is possible to glide most of the way back to the car at the end of the day. The top of The Crest is fairly flat and is generally easily navigable, so if you arrive on top of a chute or line that doesn't look good, it is easy enough to just continue on to the next one.

Because of the wind, the chutes along the Mammoth Crest typically have firm, frozen, or wind-packed snow in the upper sections of the descents. While the snow quality will often improve as soon as you get below the leeward deposition area, you should be prepared for hard pack on your drop in.

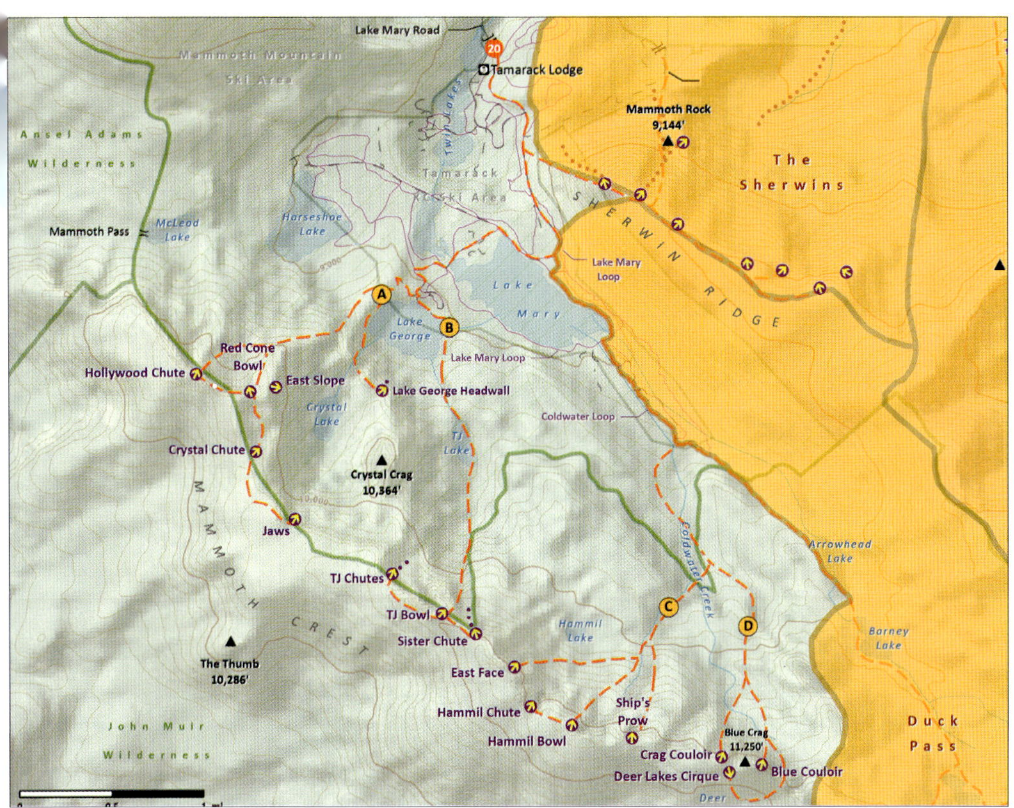

△ RED CONE ZONE *10,200'*

Defining the northern end of the Mammoth Crest is Red Cone, a small and relatively unassuming peak that is aptly named due to its dark-red coloration, which is clearly visible in the summertime on its north face. Red Cone is also one of the more prominent (and hence popular) areas of The Crest, as it is clearly visible from the top of Mammoth Mountain, and its north flank offers some great moderate skiing terrain.

Red Cone Access (Approach A on map): From Tamarack XC Ski Resort (Trailhead #20), skin along the groomed Lake Mary trail, staying to the left along the way and off the paid side of the trail system. Follow this main trail past the pack station and Lake Mary, then turn left at Pokonobe Lodge and head southwest on the Lake Mary Loop trail. At the back side of the lake, take a right at the T intersection onto the Lake George Loop trail and climb uphill to Lake George. As you enter the Lake George basin, stay to the right (northwest) and climb through the cluster of cabins that belong to Woods Lodge. Eventually this will lead you to a broad ridge that separates the north and east faces of Red Cone. Continue up this ridge until it leads you to Red Cone Bowl.

Red Cone Exits: After skiing the main line off The Crest, the terrain that lies below offers some great tree-skiing opportunities with fun gullies and rollers. Keep your *eyes open* as you weave through this benchy maze. There are a number of very large cliffs tucked away in these gullies.

The standard exit from the Red Cone area is via the eastern shore of Horsehoe Lake where you can reconnect with the groomed trail system of Tamarack. A short skate or skin up gradual terrain leads you back to Lake Mary, where you can glide back to the trailhead.

↘ HOLLYWOOD CHUTE — Red Cone Zone

Aspect	Consequence/Exposure	Slope
	3	40°

Summit Elevation	10,200'
Descent Vertical	1,000'
Total Vertical	1,700'
Hiking Distance	3 ½ miles
Terrain	Chute
Trailhead	20. Tamarack
USGS Quad Maps	Crystal Crag
GPS	37.597 / -119.029

Jon Crowley dropping into Red Cone.

Looking south at the Red Cone zone of the Mammoth Crest.

Hollywood Chute is the prominent diagonal cleft that cuts through the portion of The Crest above Horseshoe Lake. While the chute itself is relatively short, the treed, rocky gullies that lie below it and Red Cone Bowl offer fun and varied terrain down to Horseshoe Lake. In this area, rolling hills lead to short, steep drops and small gullies that can sneak up on you if you are not paying attention.

Approach: Most people choose to access Hollywood Chute by cutting northwest across Red Cone Bowl into Hollywood Bowl, then booting the chute directly. It is also possible to climb Red Cone Bowl, then skin along the ridge top over to the entrance for Hollywood Chute.

↘ RED CONE BOWL

Red Cone Zone

Aspect	Consequence/Exposure	Slope
	1	30°

Summit Elevation	10,200'
Descent Vertical	800'
Total Vertical	1,700'
Hiking Distance	3 miles
Terrain	Bowl
Trailhead	20. Tamarack
USGS Quad Maps	Crystal Crag
GPS	37.596 /-119.025

Highly visible from the top of Mammoth Ski Area, and with fairly easy access, Red Cone Bowl is the most popular spot along the Mammoth Crest. It offers a great moderate pitch that is often the first terrain in the region to have enough snow in it to actually ski.

Approach: The best access to the top of Red Cone Bowl is found by skinning the skier's-right wall (east side) along the small, rocky ridge. Unfortunately, you are somewhat exposed in this area. The other side of the ridge, in the vicinity of the East Slope, can also be used to get to the top, though depending on coverage, navigating the trees in this area may be a bit challenging.

↘ EAST SLOPE

Red Cone Zone

Aspect	Consequence/Exposure	Slope
	2	30°

Summit Elevation	10,000'
Descent Vertical	750'
Total Vertical	1,500'
Hiking Distance	3 miles
Terrain	Trees
Trailhead	20. Tamarack
USGS Quad Maps	Crystal Crag
GPS	37.596 / -119.022

The East Slope of Red Cone is the small east-facing treed face that drops down into Crystal Lake Basin from the summit of Red Cone. It is often overlooked, but offers some nice sheltered and moderately pitched tree skiing.

Approach: From the top of Red Cone Bowl, traverse east, toward Crystal Lake below you. A series of treed gullies will come into view.

Exit: From Crystal Lake, either follow the drainage out, or a short climb/traverse will bring you back to your skintrack.

Looking south at Crystal Crag and surrounding terrain.

↘ CRYSTAL CHUTE

Red Cone Zone

Aspect	Consequence/Exposure	Slope
	3	40°

Summit Elevation	10,300'
Descent Vertical	800'
Total Vertical	1,800'
Hiking Distance	3 miles
Terrain	Chute
Trailhead	20. Tamarack
USGS Quad Maps	Crystal Crag
GPS	37.591 / -119.024

Crystal Crag is the prominent granite thumb that divides the eastern and western portions of The Crest. There are a handful of terrain choices in the Crystal Lake basin to the west of the crag, as well as on the slopes below it. This is the short, narrow chute that breaks the headwall directly above Crystal Lake.

Approach: Just past the rocky section above Crystal Lake, you will find the entrance to Crystal Chute.

Exit: After skiing the chute, continue through the Crystal Lake Basin to the north. At the outlet of Crystal Lake is another short chute that descends to Lake George. It is not uncommon for this chute to be filled with roller balls or other debris—navigating it can sometimes be challenging.

Continue around the western edge of Lake George, being mindful of thin ice that often abuts the lake in this area. Once around the lake, reconnect with the groomed trail system and follow the Lake George Loop downhill to the western edge of Lake Mary. At the intersection, turn left and head north on the Lake Mary Loop trail until it reaches the T intersection with Lake Mary trail. Turn right and follow this back to your car.

↘ JAWS

Red Cone Zone

Aspect	Consequence/Exposure	Slope
	2	40°

Summit Elevation	10,200'
Descent Vertical	600'
Total Vertical	1,700'
Hiking Distance	4 miles
Terrain	Bowl
Trailhead	20. Tamarack
USGS Quad Maps	Crystal Crag
GPS	37.586 / -119.0216

Jaws is the locals' name for the large bowl behind Crystal Lake. Sitting at a low point on The Crest, Jaws is notorious for forming an extremely large cornice. At times it may be possible to pass the cornice on either side, but use extreme caution when skiing this bowl, regardless.

Approach: Once atop the ridge, continue south and east, past Crystal Chute to the back of the basin/bowl. Pay attention to the cornice that often forms here, giving it a wide berth.

Lake George Headwall as seen from Lake George.

↘ LAKE GEORGE HEADWALL

Red Cone Zone

Aspect | Consequence/Exposure: 3 | Slope: 40°

Summit Elevation	9,500'
Descent Vertical	500'
Total Vertical	1,000'
Hiking Distance	2 ½ miles
Terrain	Face
Trailhead	20. Tamarack
USGS Quad Maps	Crystal Crag
GPS	37.596 / -119.014

The terrain that immediately surrounds Lake George's south and western sides is known as the Lake George Headwall. In the southern portion of this area is the summertime climbing area known as the Dike Wall. This should be a clue that this area has lots of steep terrain and granite cliffs. Take extreme caution. That being said, there is some great free-skiing terrain in this zone, especially for those looking for technical lines or big air.

Approach: If you are headed to the terrain below Crystal Crag, you can either climb through the small chute/cleft that is the outlet of Crystal Lake (to the west of Crystal Crag), or follow the East Slope approach for Red Cone, then continue east to the top of the headwall terrain.

△ TJ BOWL ZONE *11,000'*

TJ Bowl Access (Approach B on map): Follow the groomed trails to Lake George. As you enter the Lake George Basin, head east through the campground.

At Lake George's south end is the inlet from TJ Lake. Continue heading south, up the gully to reach TJ Lake.

Be aware that the section between Lake George and TJ Lake can remain unfrozen well into the winter due to running water. Typically, the open water will be a small section and can be avoided, but keep your distance!

↘ TJ BOWL

TJ Bowl Zone

Aspect | Consequence/Exposure: 2 | Slope: 35°

Summit Elevation	11,000'
Descent Vertical	1,500'
Total Vertical	2,500'
Hiking Distance	3 ¾ miles
Terrain	Bowl
Trailhead	20. Tamarack
USGS Quad Maps	Crystal Crag
GPS	37.582 / -119.009

TJ Bowl is the western of the two prominent bowls that sit between Crystal Crag and Duck Pass. The bowl itself offers some great moderately pitched skiing on north and northeastern aspects.

Approach: From TJ Lake, either climb the bowl or the slopes to the left of the bowl.

Kevin Smith riding the Mammoth Crest.

Looking south at TJ Bowl from Lake Mary.

TJ Bowl Exits: Follow your tracks back to Lake George, then reverse your approach back to the trailhead.

↘ TJ CHUTE

TJ Bowl Zone

Aspect	Consequence/Exposure	Slope
	3	40°

Summit Elevation	10,700'
Descent Vertical	1,200'
Total Vertical	2,300'
Hiking Distance	4 miles
Terrain	Chute
Trailhead	20. Tamarack
USGS Quad Maps	Crystal Crag
GPS	37.582 / -119.013

TJ Chute is the small yet relatively steep chute at the back-center of TJ Bowl proper. Located just west of the Sister Chutes, this provides one of the more direct entrances into TJ Bowl.

↘ SISTER CHUTES

TJ Bowl Zone

Aspect	Consequence/Exposure	Slope
	3	35°

Summit Elevation	11,000'
Descent Vertical	1,500'
Total Vertical	2,500'
Hiking Distance	4 miles
Terrain	Chute
Trailhead	20. Tamarack
USGS Quad Maps	Crystal Crag
GPS	37.577 / -119.007

Sister Chutes are the pair of northwest-facing chutes that descend from the point at the eastern end of TJ Bowl, just east of TJ Chute.

Approach: At the south end of Lake George is the inlet from TJ Lake. Continue heading south, up the gully. Once at TJ Lake, skin into TJ Bowl and climb as though you were going to TJ Chute. As you approach the base of the cliff, you can choose to either boot TJ Chute or climb one of the Sisters directly.

∆ HAMMIL BOWL ZONE *11,300'*

Steep, rock-lined chutes are the name of the game in this portion of The Crest. Some are wider than others, and some are steeper than others, so you shouldn't have a problem finding one to suit your tastes. All of the lines flow into the large Hammil Bowl, which sits just east of TJ Bowl.

In this area, Hammil Bowl provides the easiest route to the top of The Crest. However, be aware that the last 100' or so have a tendency to drift in and become quite steep.

Hammil Bowl Access (Approach C on map): From Tamarack XC Ski Resort (Trailhead #20), skin along the groomed Lake Mary trail, staying to the left along the way and off the paid side of the trail system. Follow this main trail past the pack station and take the first left turn onto the Lake Mary Loop trail just before Lake Mary. Ski around the lake to its far end and turn left onto the Coldwater Loop trail. This groomed trail goes through the Coldwater Campground and ends at the summer trailhead.

From the summer trailhead at Coldwater, head south, up a gentle treed slope. Continue south and cross the creek. There is a footbridge, but in the winter it can be

Looking south at the Hammil Bowl zone of the Mammoth Crest.

difficult to locate if you are unfamiliar with the area. As the season goes on, a number of snowbridges will form, so finding a safe way across the creek shouldn't be too much of a task. Ski across a small meadow and begin climbing the trees and gullies to the west, heading toward the base of the Mammoth Crest.

As you enter the Hammil Lake Basin, Ship's Prow will be directly above you, and Hammil Bowl slightly to the west. Continue up into Hammil Bowl, and find the cleanest line to the top, which in the case of the East Face may mean booting your line directly.

Hammil Bowl Exits: Follow your tracks back the way you came, being sure to keep your eyes peeled for some great tree skiing along the way.

EAST FACE OF HAMMIL BOWL

Hammil Bowl Zone

Aspect	Consequence/Exposure	Slope
	3	40°

Summit Elevation	11,300'
Descent Vertical	1,400'
Total Vertical	2,800'
Hiking Distance	5 miles
Terrain	Face
Trailhead	20. Tamarack
USGS Quad Maps	Bloody Mountain
GPS	37.575/ -119.004

This is one of the sunnier spots on The Crest, which means that conditions on this face can be a little variable. There are a number of different lines on this generally open face.

HAMMIL BOWL

Hammil Bowl Zone

Aspect	Consequence/Exposure	Slope
	2	35°

Summit Elevation	11,300'
Descent Vertical	1,400'
Total Vertical	2,500'
Hiking Distance	4 miles
Terrain	Bowl
Trailhead	20. Tamarack
USGS Quad Maps	Bloody Mountain
GPS	37.570 / -118.999

Surrounded by large rock walls, Hammil Bowl barely sees any direct sunlight until late in the season. It is one of the few spots along The Crest that can hold snow or ice year-round. When conditions are good, it is a great ski descent.

↘ HAMMIL CHUTE

Hammil Bowl Zone

Aspect | Consequence/Exposure: 3 | Slope: 40°

Summit Elevation	11,100'
Descent Vertical	1,200'
Total Vertical	2,600'
Hiking Distance	4 ½ miles
Terrain	Chute
Trailhead	20. Tamarack
USGS Quad Maps	Bloody Mountain
GPS	37.572 / -119.002

This is the short, narrow chute that drains directly into Hammil Bowl. Depending on the wind, there are two other chutes in this vicinity that can potentially fill in and become skiable.

↘ SHIP'S PROW

Hammil Bowl Zone

Aspect | Consequence/Exposure: 3 | Slope: 40°

Summit Elevation	11,200'
Descent Vertical	1,200'
Total Vertical	2,700'
Hiking Distance	5 miles
Terrain	Chute
Trailhead	20. Tamarack
USGS Quad Maps	Bloody Mountain
GPS	37.569 / -118.994

Ship's Prow is one of the longest continuous runs on The Crest, and one of the most obvious rock outcrops visible from the Lakes Basin. There are stellar skiing options on either side of Ship's Prow, though most choose the chute that is skier's left (west side) of the main prow.

△ BLUE CRAG ZONE *11,250'*

The prominent rock buttress that defines the eastern end of the Mammoth Crest is referred to as Blue Crag. Located on either side of the crag are two chutes that offer some great, albeit short, descents from the top of The Crest.

Blue Crag Access (Approach D on map): Follow the directions in the previous section to Hammil Bowl (page 147). As you climb out of Coldwater Creek, Ship's Prow will be directly above you. From this point, begin to head slightly east toward Sky Meadow, and ultimately the benches beneath Blue Crag. Once at the base of the crag, boot your line directly.

Exit: Follow your tracks back the way you came, being sure to keep your eyes peeled for some great tree skiing along the way.

CRAG COULOIR

Blue Crag Zone

Aspect | Consequence/Exposure 3 | Slope 40°

Summit Elevation	11,200'
Descent Vertical	1,000'
Total Vertical	2,700'
Hiking Distance	5 miles
Terrain	Chute
Trailhead	20. Tamarack
USGS Quad Maps	Bloody Mountain
GPS	37.568 / -118.988

This is the steep and narrow chute located on the west side of Blue Crag. This chute has a tendency to get scoured by the wind in its midsection. Because of this, we highly recommend that you climb the chute prior to skiing it, so you are aware of conditions and coverage.

BLUE COULOIR

Blue Crag Zone

Aspect | Consequence/Exposure 2 | Slope 35°

Summit Elevation	11,400'
Descent Vertical	1,000'
Total Vertical	2,900'
Hiking Distance	5 miles
Terrain	Chute
Trailhead	20. Tamarack
USGS Quad Maps	Bloody Mountain
GPS	37.567 / -118.984

This is the larger and less intimidating of Blue Crag's two chutes, located on the east side of the buttress.

DEER LAKES CIRQUE

Blue Crag Zone

Aspect | Consequence/Exposure 3 | Slope 40°

Summit Elevation	11,200'
Descent Vertical	1,000'
Total Vertical	2,700'
Hiking Distance	5 miles
Terrain	Mixed
Trailhead	20. Tamarack
USGS Quad Maps	Bloody Mountain
GPS	37.568 / -118.988

The Deer Lakes Cirque is a small hidden cirque that sits directly behind Blue Crag and feeds into the Deer Lakes. This cirque has a variety of terrain—though it's mostly open, and much being somewhat steep and technical—that faces mostly east and south.

Approach: Climb Blue Couloir (above) and continue southwest toward the Deer Lakes Cirque.

It is also possible to access Deer Lakes via Duck Pass or the Barney Lake area, then continue back west once around the south side of the ridge. The benefit of this approach is you get a better view of the lines in the cirque before skiing them.

Exit: The best way out of the Deer Lakes basin is via the terrain above Barney Lake, or Duck Pass. From here, continue down the Coldwater Creek drainage until you reach the Duck Pass trailhead and the groomed trails of Tamarack.

Mike Wright, Jewls Wright, and Jason Templeton on their way to TJ Bowl.

Joe Stewart, Toby Schwindt, and Buddy drop into Hammil Chute.

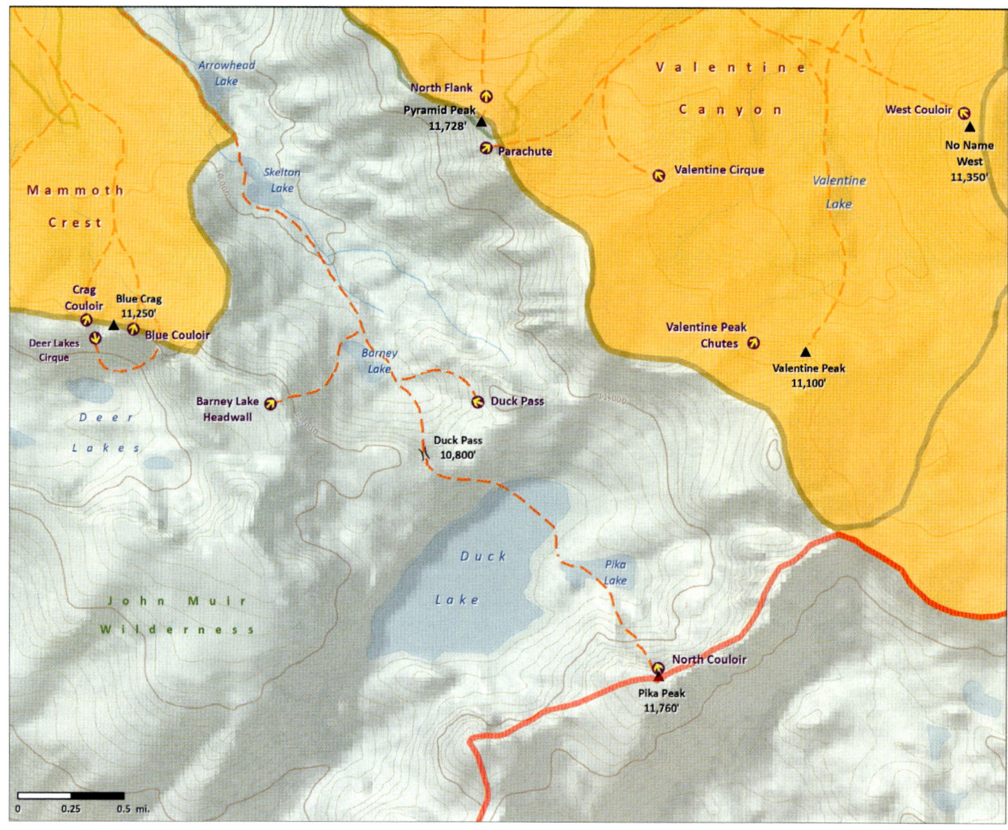

▣ Duck Pass Area

This is the most remote section of the Mammoth Crest and Lakes Basin. While it is not incredibly far, the crowds have a tendency to stick to the closer and more prominent portions of The Crest, leaving the terrain in this area generally untracked.

Approach: From Tamarack XC Ski Resort (Trailhead #20), skin along the groomed Lake Mary trail, staying to the left along the way and off the paid side of the trail system. Follow this main trail past the pack station and take the first left turn onto the Lake Mary Loop trail just before Lake Mary. Ski around the lake to its far end and turn left onto the Coldwater Loop trail. This groomed trail goes through the Coldwater Campground and ultimately ends at the summer trailhead for Duck Pass.

Roughly following the summer trail, continue southeast from the trailhead into the drainage, keeping to the east of the ridge that separates Mammoth Creek from Coldwater Creek. Eventually cross Arrowhead Lake and continue on past Skelton Lakes, until you eventually reach Barney Lake and the basin below Duck Pass.

From this point, the Barney Lake Headwall lies just above you, and you can choose to either pick a line and boot it directly, or climb Duck Pass then continue on to your line of choice.

Δ DUCK PASS *10,800'*

The runs in this small zone are generally more wide-open as opposed to the narrow chutes that are typical of the rest of The Crest. That being said, there is a variety of terrain and different aspects to choose from.

↘ BARNEY LAKE HEADWALL — Duck Pass

Aspect | Consequence/Exposure: 3 | Slope: 40°

Summit Elevation	11,300'
Descent Vertical	1,000'
Total Vertical	2,800'
Hiking Distance	4 ½ miles
Terrain	Mixed
Trailhead	20. Tamarack
USGS Quad Maps	Bloody Mountain
GPS	37.562 / -118.961

This terrain is comprised of a series of chutes and technical faces that lie directly above Barney Lake to the south and west.

↘ DUCK PASS

Duck Pass

Aspect	Consequence/Exposure	Slope
	2	35°

Summit Elevation	11,000'
Descent Vertical	1,000'
Total Vertical	2,500'
Hiking Distance	4 ½ miles
Terrain	Mixed
Trailhead	20. Tamarack
USGS Quad Maps	Bloody Mountain
GPS	37.562 / -118.961

The terrain around Duck Pass is rolling and gentle in nature, with a series of small, broad ridges and shallow gullies. Combined with multiple different aspects to choose from, this terrain offers great options for a novice backcountry skier looking to get out and explore a bit.

△ PIKA PEAK *11,760'*

Situated on just the other side of Duck Pass, Pika Peak offers a remote experience in a relatively close location. Its north face has two chutes that converge into a large bowl above Pika Lake, both of which are clearly visible from the top of Mammoth Mountain—making them highly desired by many local skiers.

Nate Greenberg below Pika Peak.

Looking south at Pika Peak.

NORTH COULOIRS

Pika Peak

Aspect | Consequence/Exposure: 3 | Slope: 40°

Summit Elevation	11,760'
Descent Vertical	1,500'
Total Vertical	3,500'
Hiking Distance	6 miles
Terrain	Chute
Trailhead	20. Tamarack
USGS Quad Maps	Bloody Mountain
GPS	37.545 / -118.949

Two prominent couloirs surround the large rock buttress on the north face of Pika Peak. The couloirs are similar in nature to each other, both with steep headwall entrances that lead to long, blissful, perfect steep skiing all the way down to Pika Lake.

Approach: From Tamarack XC Ski Area (Trailhead #20), follow the approach for Duck Pass (previous page). Descend a short distance off the back of the pass down to Duck Lake. Depending on coverage, either skin across or skirt around the eastern edge of the lake, then climb a small bench up to Pika Lake.

From here you can choose to boot directly up your chute of choice, or skin around the west shoulder of Pika Peak and gain its summit that way.

Exit: Follow your tracks back to your car.

Sherwin Creek Area

This area spans the distance between the eastern end of The Sherwins and Laurel Canyon, and is comprised of three zones: Punta Bardini, Solitude Canyon, and Valentine Canyon. Some of this terrain feels very much in the front-country, and some feels quite remote, despite being relatively close to town.

△ PUNTA BARDINI *9,400'*

Punta Bardini is the ridgeline to the north of Solitude Canyon and is one of the more popular quick hits in this region. Due to its proximity to town, the Punta Bardini area is a very popular destination, especially during storms. The prominent chutes and gullies on its north face are the main attraction, though some of the finest old-growth tree skiing in the area can be found here as well. North facing and protected from the wind, the trees and gullies are a great place to ski in inclement weather and a terrific place to find powder long after a storm.

BARDINI CHUTES

Punta Bardini

Aspect | Consequence/Exposure: 3 | Slope: 40°

Summit Elevation	9,400'
Descent Vertical	1,500'
Total Vertical	2,000'
Hiking Distance	1 ¾ miles
Terrain	Chute
Trailhead	21. Sherwin Creek Staging Area
USGS Quad Maps	Bloody Mountain
GPS	37.608 / -118.963

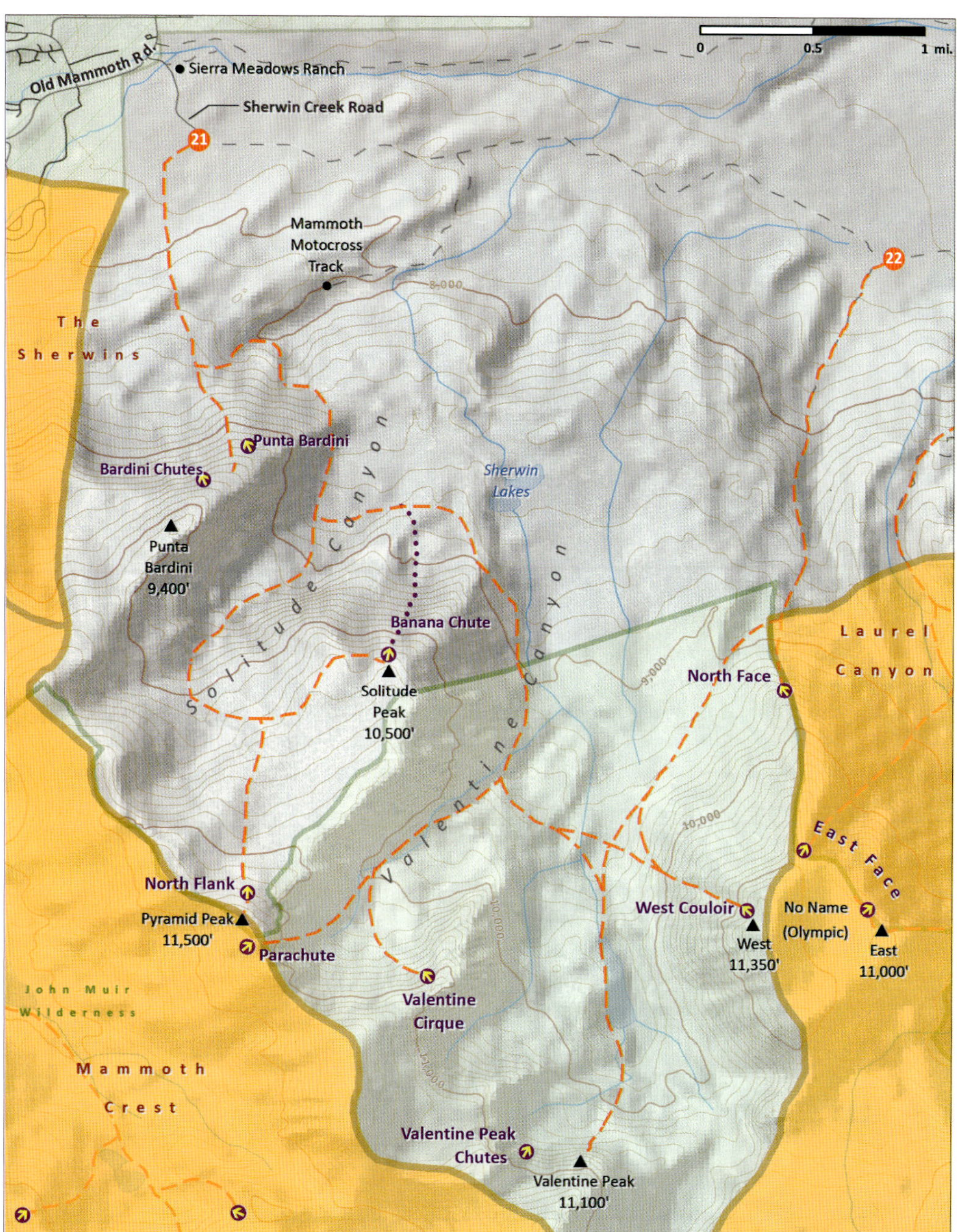

Two main chutes descend the north face of Punta Bardini, beginning about 300' below the summit. They are similar in length, terrain, and difficulty. In addition to the two main chutes, there are a number of smaller chutes on either side that feed into them. The entrances to all of the chutes are steep, convex rollovers with rocky cliffs above them. These avalanche regularly, and extreme care should be taken when entering any of them.

Approach: From the Sherwin Creek Staging Area (Trailhead #21), head to the south across the flat terrain, then climb to the top of a small, rolling hill. Once atop, veer right through a small drainage, over another small ridgeline, then descend into an open meadow near the base of Bardini's north ridgeline. At the south end of the meadow are some old cross-country-ski-trail signs; the standard approach follows these, then goes up through the trees to climber's right of the Tele Bowls

and continues roughly along the ridgeline until it becomes impassable. From here, head slightly east and into the trees, finding the best route to the ridge.

Once on the ridge, continue climbing up and heading slightly west. As the ridge starts to peter out and turn into more of the north face, you will find the entry to the first of the Bardini Chutes. The second is a short distance west of this point.

Exit: From the chutes' base, head slightly east and over a small ridgeline until you reconnect with your skin track.

↘ OLD GROWTH & TELE BOWLS — Punta Bardini

Aspect	Consequence/Exposure	Slope
	2	30°

Summit Elevation	9,200'
Descent Vertical	1,200'
Total Vertical	1,400'
Hiking Distance	1 ¾ miles
Terrain	Trees
Trailhead	21. Sherwin Creek Staging Area
USGS Quad Maps	Bloody Mountain
GPS	37.610 / -118.961

The old-growth tree skiing that comprises Bardini's north face is some of the finest on the Eastside, and offers a wonderful protected alternative to the chutes on a nasty-weather day. This treed slope naturally trends down and reaches two obvious bowls below, known as the Tele Bowls.

Approach: Follow the directions for the Bardini Chutes (previous page). The Old Growth will be found alongside the skintrack, and will ultimately end up in the Tele Bowls as you descend.

Exit: Most people choose to ski the Tele Bowls after the Old Growth, which puts you at the Mammoth Motocross Track. From this small valley, climb up the hill on the north side, trending into a small gully at its western end, which will put you back on your skin track. You can also choose to pull out of the Tele Bowls a bit early (if skiing the skier's-left bowl), and maintain a high traverse to this same point.

◎ SOLITUDE CANYON

Solitude Canyon itself is typically just as the name suggests—a quiet canyon that not many people venture into. The area lies outside the wilderness, however, and is popular among snowmobilers. While they may detract from the solace, their tracks provide easy access to this area and the surrounding peaks without having to break any trail.

Solitude Canyon provides access to Solitude and Pyramid peaks, both of which have moderate descents off their north faces. Outside of these two destinations, the canyon offers a wide variety of aspects and terrain choices and makes for a terrific half-day tour.

△ SOLITUDE PEAK *10,500'*

Solitude Peak sits at the end of a small ridgeline on the south side of Solitude Canyon and has several lines cut through its treed northern slope. There are a number of descent options off Solitude Peak, but most skiers and riders are attracted to the slopes around Banana Chute, which is the most prominent treed chute on the north face.

↘ BANANA CHUTE — Solitude Peak

Aspect	Consequence/Exposure	Slope
N	2	40°

Summit Elevation	10,500'
Descent Vertical	1,600'
Total Vertical	2,800'
Hiking Distance	4 ½ miles
Terrain	Chute
Trailhead	21. Sherwin Creek Staging Area
USGS Quad Maps	Bloody Mountain
GPS	37.599 / -118.951

This chute is clearly visible on your way into town, as it cleanly cuts through the trees directly from the summit of Solitude Peak, stretching all the way into the canyon below. This line and the area immediately surrounding it are very similar to the terrain on Punta Bardini, but the slightly longer approach means significantly less traffic.

Approach: From the Sherwin Creek Staging Area (Trailhead #21), head south across flat terrain, then climb to the top of a small rolling hill. Once atop, veer right through a small drainage, over another small ridgeline, then descend into an open meadow near the base of Bardini's north ridgeline. At the south end of the meadow are some old cross-country-ski-trail signs leading into an opening in the trees. Skin into this opening, then descend the back side of this ridge to the Motocross Track located in the valley beyond this ridge and at the base of the Tele Bowls. It is also possible to reach this point on a snowmobile by following Sherwin Creek Road to the Mammoth Motocross Track Road.

From here, head south across the track where you will find a small road with a gate. Follow this road uphill and along the east flank of the Tele Bowls , then around the shoulder of Punta Bardini and into the mouth of Solitude Canyon.

Once in the canyon, continue south a short distance until you are at the base of Solitude Peak. From here, you can climb the chute directly, though most people choose to continue up the canyon to the west ridge of Solitude Peak, which provides much easier access to the summit.

Exit: From the base of the chute, follow your tracks back to the car.

△ PYRAMID PEAK *11,500'*

This mountain gets its name from its pyramidal shape as viewed from town. Lying along the Sherwin Range, Pyramid seems to be just a short distance past Rock Chute, though in actuality it creates the divide between Solitude and Valentine canyons. The most popular descent off the peak is Parachute, which is covered in the Valentine Canyon Zone, though the North Face of Pyramid also provides a nice moderate ski.

↘ NORTH FACE

Pyramid Peak

Aspect	Consequence/Exposure	Slope
N	2	30°

Summit Elevation	11,500'
Descent Vertical	1,200'
Total Vertical	3,900'
Hiking Distance	5 ¼ miles
Terrain	Face
Trailhead	21. Sherwin Creek Staging Area
USGS Quad Maps	Bloody Mountain
GPS	37.583 / -118.961

The North Face of Pyramid Peak offers picturesque and relatively easy skiing opportunities back into Solitude Canyon. While most people do not ski this line, it can afford some nice turns on a great tour. If the conditions in Parachute are grim and you approached via Solitude Canyon, this is your way out.

Approach: Pyramid Peak sits behind and above Solitude Peak. Follow the directions to Solitude (previous page). As you get closer to Solitude Peak, begin to climb the canyon on your right, beneath the back side of Punta Bardini. Follow this to the summit.

◎ VALENTINE CANYON

Valentine Canyon in the winter is an amazing place. Despite its proximity to town, it feels remote. The approach into Valentine Canyon is slightly longer than surrounding areas. This distance thins out the traffic, but a tour into this area can still be easily completed in a day.

As one of the few north–south-trending canyons in the Mammoth Lakes Area, Valentine offers a variety of aspects, elevations, and terrain for virtually all abilities of skiers.

△ PYRAMID PEAK *11,500'*

Though the North Face has the namesake pyramidal shape, the east side of Pyramid Peak holds its signature descent: Parachute.

↘ PARACHUTE

Pyramid Peak

Aspect	Consequence/Exposure	Slope
E	4	50°

Summit Elevation	11,500'
Descent Vertical	1,500'
Total Vertical	4,000'
Hiking Distance	5 ½ miles
Terrain	Chute
Trailhead	21. Sherwin Creek Staging Area
USGS Quad Maps	Bloody Mountain
GPS	37.579 / -118.961

Steep and narrow, Parachute is one of the more challenging and proud runs in the Mammoth Lakes Region. This rocky chute requires quite a bit of snow in order to be completely skiable. There is a major chockstone lodged in the middle of the chute, and a few other crux sections that must be negotiated as well. It's a good idea to bring a short section of rope along, just in case, as there are a handful of rap stations along the walls of the chute created by people who have arrived to find the chute in a less-than-ideal condition.

Looking west at Parachute from Valentine Canyon.

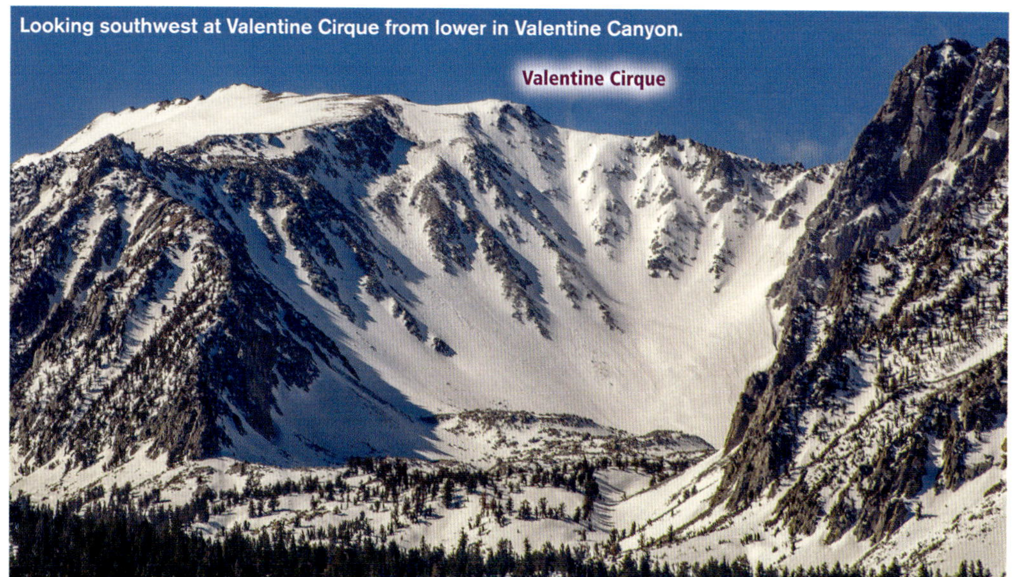

Looking southwest at Valentine Cirque from lower in Valentine Canyon.

Approach: Though it is possible to reach Parachute from the summit of Pyramid Peak via Solitude Canyon and the North Face approach, most people choose to boot the line from below so they know the conditions. If you are approaching from above, refer to the North Flank of Pyramid Peak for the approach description. From the summit of Pyramid, descend the narrow and exposed 3rd Class ledges on the west face until you reach a gunsight-like notch below you. This notch is the start of the chute. It is also highly recommended that you take a rope and small selection of rock protection if using this approach.

Access to Parachute from below is via Valentine Canyon, which can be entered from either Trailhead #21 or #22. From Trailhead #21, proceed into the mouth of Solitude Canyon (see description for Solitude Peak provided earlier). Once at the base of the north face of Solitude Peak, head east onto a bench at the base of the Banana Chute, then drop off the east side of this and into Valentine Canyon.

You can reach this same location via Trailhead #22 (typically done in the springtime). To do so, continue south from the trailhead around the west flank of No Name Peak until you are in the bottom of Valentine Canyon.

From this point, continue south, staying generally on the west side of the drainage. Eventually Valentine Cirque and the notch of Pyramid Peak will come into view to the west. Parachute is the prominent cleft that drops from the notch. Simply boot the couloir from this point, then carve out a spot to put your skis on up top.

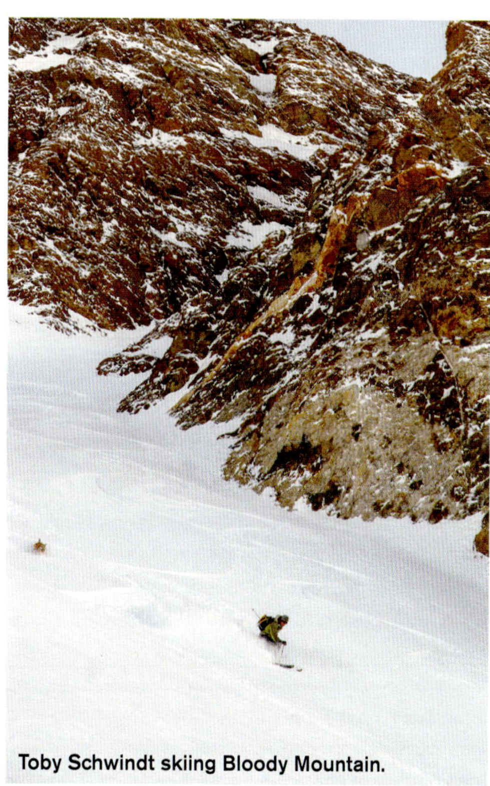
Toby Schwindt skiing Bloody Mountain.

△ VALENTINE PEAK *11,100'*

Valentine Peak sits directly above Valentine Lake, situated roughly three-quarters of the way up the drainage. It is a remote peak that is rarely skied, but has a few great lines.

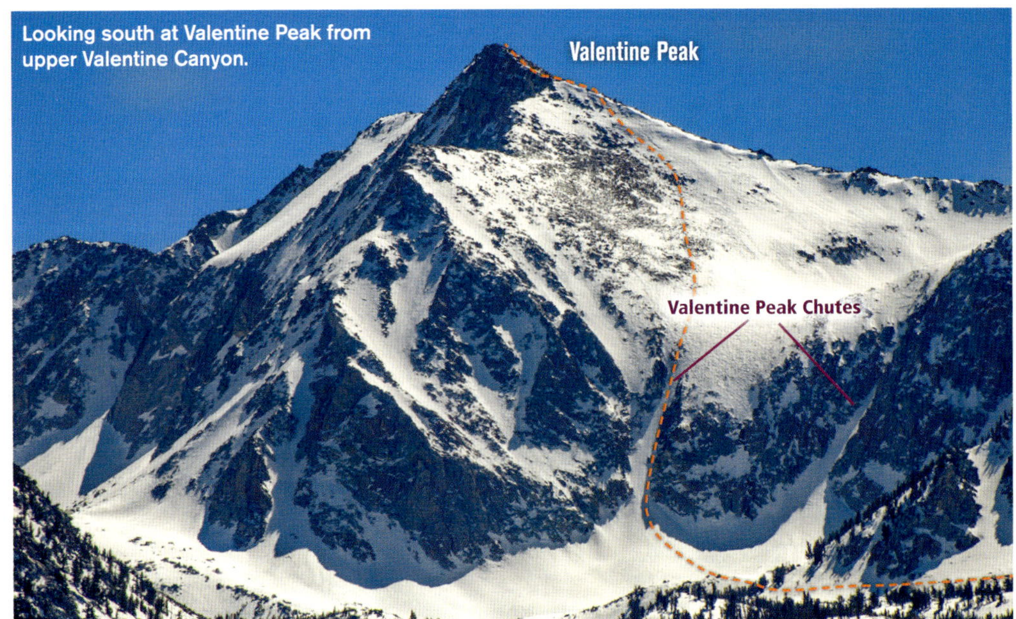

Looking south at Valentine Peak from upper Valentine Canyon.

↘ VALENTINE CIRQUE

Valentine Peak

Aspect	Consequence/Exposure	Slope
N	3	35°

Summit Elevation	10,950'
Descent Vertical	1,000'
Total Vertical	1,200'
Hiking Distance	5 ½ miles
Terrain	Face
Trailhead	21. Sherwin Creek Staging Area
USGS Quad Maps	Bloody Mountain
GPS	37.579 / -118.949

Disconnected from Valentine Peak itself, Valentine Cirque is a backcountry skier's paradise—laden with multiple high-quality north-facing lines. The cirque actually is situated in the small canyon above Lost Lake that leads to the base of Parachute.

Approach: Valentine Cirque can be accessed from either Trailhead #21 or #22. From Trailhead #21, proceed into the mouth of Solitude Canyon (see description for Solitude Peak provided earlier). Once at the base of the north face of Solitude Peak, head east onto a bench at the base of the Banana Chute, then drop off the east side of this and into Valentine Canyon.

You can reach this same location via Trailhead #22 (typically done in the spring ime). To do so, continue south from the trailhead around the west flank of No Name Peak until you are in the bottom of Valentine Canyon.

From this point, continue south, staying generally on the west side of the drainage. Eventually Valentine Cirque and the notch of Pyramid Peak will come into view to the west. From the basin at the bottom of Valentine Cirque, there are a dozen or more different lines to choose from. Pick your poison and start booting. If you are looking to spend a day in the cirque, think about punching one boot pack in that you can reuse to access neighboring chutes

Exit: Follow your tracks back to the car.

↘ VALENTINE PEAK CHUTES

Valentine Peak

Aspect	Consequence/Exposure	Slope
N	3	40°

Summit Elevation	11,100'
Descent Vertical	1,300'
Total Vertical	3,600'
Hiking Distance	6 ½ miles
Terrain	Mixed
Trailhead	21. Sherwin Creek Staging Area
USGS Quad Maps	Bloody Mountain
GPS	37.566 / -118.943

Looking south at the North Face of No Name Peak.

Dropping from the true summit of Valentine Peak are two prominent chutes. Located on the north face, these lines are visible from town, and are the most frequently skied descents in this immediate vicinity. There are also a number of other options on the east face, farther up the canyon.

Approach: Follow the directions to Valentine Cirque (previous page) and continue up the drainage to the base of your chosen descent.

Exit: Follow your tracks back to the car.

ΔNO NAME PEAK (WEST SUMMIT) *11,350'*

This is the relatively unassuming peak (which we have been unable to find an official name for) that separates Valentine Canyon from Laurel Canyon, and is ever present in the views to the east from town and other locations in the Mammoth Lakes Region. There are actually two summits to this peak: The west of the two is better accessed from Valentine Canyon, while the east is typically accessed from Laurel Canyon.

This first descent is an often-overlooked north-facing line that is comprised of open faces and gladed trees. It is relatively short, with multiple stopping points along the way, and also fairly easy to access from the car (in the spring), so makes for a great quick ski.

↘ NORTH FACE — No Name Peak

Aspect	Consequence/Exposure	Slope
	2	30°

Summit Elevation	9,700'
Descent Vertical	1,000'
Total Vertical	2,000'
Hiking Distance	2 miles
Terrain	Trees
Trailhead	22. Valentine Canyon Trailhead
USGS Quad Maps	Bloody Mountain
GPS	37.579 / -118.9496

Approach: From Trailhead #22 head south up the canyon through the trees to the base of the North Face. Weave your way through the trees and up the open faces to your desired stopping point along the ridge.

Exit: Follow your tracks back to the car.

Looking west at No Name Peak from Laurel Canyon.

↘ WEST COULOIR

No Name Peak

Aspect	Consequence/Exposure	Slope
	2	35°

Summit Elevation	11,350'
Descent Vertical	2,000'
Total Vertical	3,800'
Hiking Distance	3 ¼ miles
Terrain	Chute
Trailhead	22. Valentine Canyon Trailhead
USGS Quad Maps	Bloody Mountain
GPS	37.579 / -118.949

This line is clearly visible from town, though is generally overlooked and unrecognized by most backcountry skiers. The reality is that it is one of the few west-facing couloirs in the area, and offers a great, remote-feeling 2,000' descent back to the canyon bottom.

Approach: Though possible to access the couloir from Trailhead #21 by following the Valentine Canyon approach, it is typically accessed from Trailhead #22. To do so, head south from the trailhead up the north flank of No Name Peak, then wrap around its west side until you are at the base of the couloir. From this point, boot the line to its summit.

■ Laurel Canyon Area

The Laurel Lakes Drainage is home to one of the most recognizable peaks in the Mammoth Region (if not the Eastside), Bloody Mountain. It is an extremely beautiful canyon with some amazing terrain on the major and minor peaks that comprise it. The canyon is relatively easy to access during all times of the year, and is a popular destination for snowmobilers. The meadows area in the upper portion of the canyon also offers some superb camping spots in the springtime.

∆NO NAME PEAK (EAST SUMMIT) 11,100'

From town, lines on its west face are clearly visible and prominent, though the real gems of this peak are on the east face and drop into the bottom of the Laurel Lakes.

↘ EAST FACE CHUTES

No Name Peak

Aspect	Consequence/Exposure	Slope
	3	40°

Summit Elevation	11,050'
Descent Vertical	1,800'
Total Vertical	3,700'
Hiking Distance	3 ¾ miles
Terrain	Bowl
Trailhead	23. Laurel Canyon
USGS Quad Maps	Bloody Mountain
GPS	37.579 / -118.949

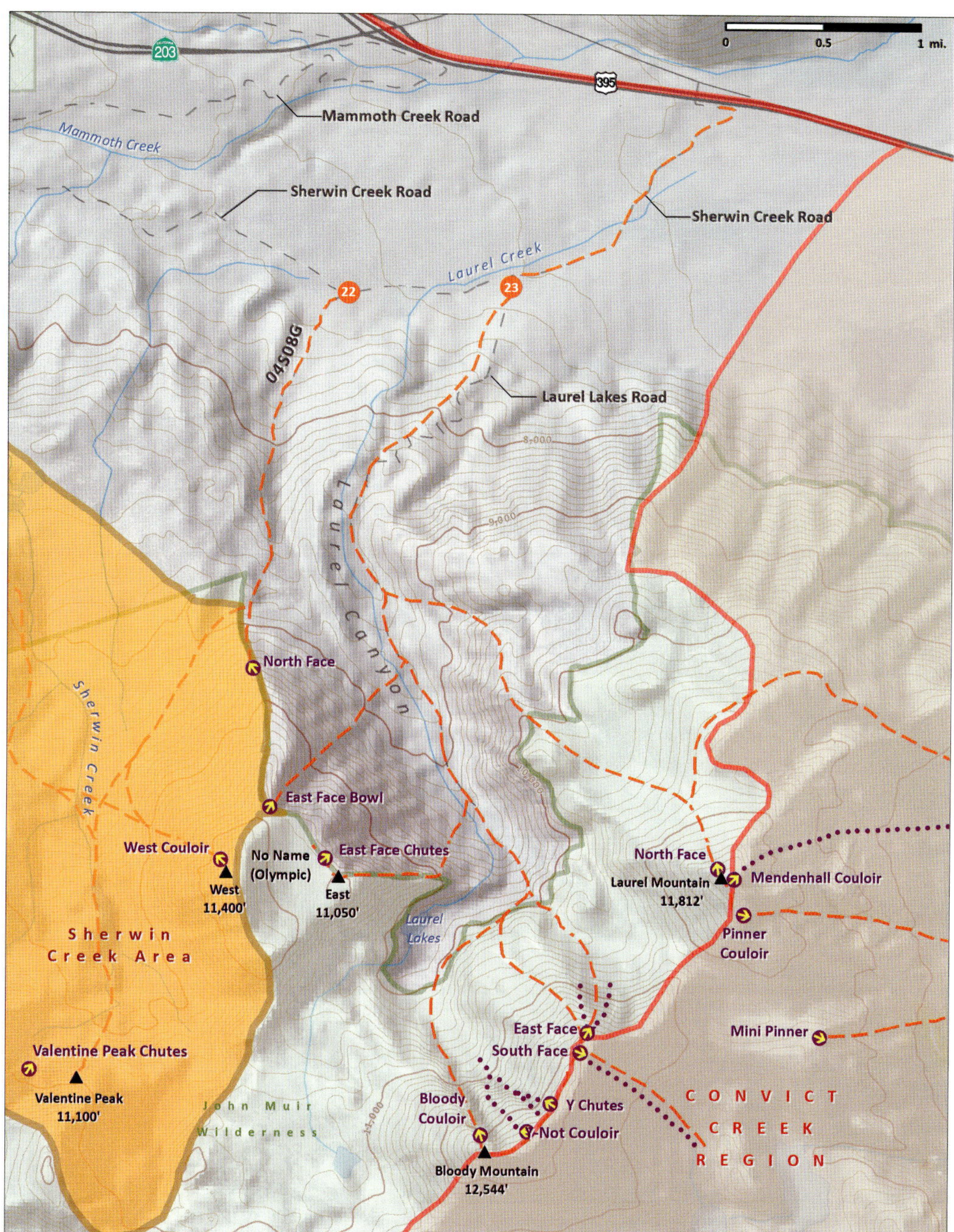

Deeper in Laurel Canyon, and near the southern end of No Name Peak, lie a series of steep east-facing chutes that descend directly from the summit of the peak to the canyon floor. This is big-mountain terrain, and some of finest and most easily accessed chute skiing in the region.

Approach: From the Laurel Canyon Trailhead (#23), follow the general alignment of the summer road up the north face of the moraine at the mouth of the Laurel Lakes Drainage. Climb to the top of this feature and into the mouth of the canyon. Continue up the canyon toward the southeastern ridge of No Name Peak, from where the chutes are clearly visible above.

From here it is possible to boot the lines directly, or climb around the south face and access them from the top. To do this, climb onto a small bench at the toe of the southeast ridge of No Name, then continue west onto its south face. Traverse the south face for a short

Looking south at Bloody Mountain from Sherwin Creek.

distance, then begin booting up and left. The first chute in the series is accessible through a small notch low on the ridgeline above you, while the rest are accessed by climbing to the summit via a small gully farther up the ridgeline.

Exit: Follow your tracks back to the car.

↘ EAST FACE BOWL
No Name Peak

Aspect	Consequence/Exposure	Slope
	3	35°

Summit Elevation	11,000'
Descent Vertical	1,800'
Total Vertical	3,700'
Hiking Distance	3 miles
Terrain	Bowl
Trailhead	23. Laurel Canyon
USGS Quad Maps	Bloody Mountain
GPS	37.585 / -118.925

At the northern end of No Name Peak's eastern summit is a moderately sized bowl with a chute-lined cirque above it. This terrain typically provides great skiing conditions on some reasonably steep east-facing terrain.

Approach: From Trailhead #23, follow the general alignment of the summer road up the north face of the moraine at the mouth of the Laurel Lakes drainage. Climb to the top of this feature and into the mouth of the canyon. As you enter the canyon itself, the lines off the eastern face of No Name Peak become clearly visible, the first of which is the East Face Bowl. Cross the creek and skin/boot the line of choice to the top.

Exit: Follow your tracks back to the car.

△ BLOODY MOUNTAIN *12,544'*

Bloody Mountain is one of the icons of the Eastside. Clearly visible from many points in the region, the lines on Bloody Mountain are coveted by locals and visitors alike.

Approach: From Trailhead #23, follow the general alignment of the summer road up the north face of the moraine at the mouth of the Laurel Lakes Drainage. Climb to the top of this feature and into the the canyon, staying to the east of the creek. As you get toward the head of the canyon, climb the eastern slopes that eventually lead to the Laurel/Bloody Col, then begin trending west.

Brett Lotz climbing the West Couoir of No Name Peak. *Photo: Nate Greenberg.*

Looking south at Bloody Mountain from Sherwin Creek Road.

↘ BLOODY COULOIR

Bloody Mountain

Aspect	Consequence/Exposure	Slope
	3	45°

Summit Elevation	12,522'
Descent Vertical	2,500'
Total Vertical	5,200'
Hiking Distance	5 miles (w) | 6 ½ miles (s)
Terrain	Chute
Trailhead	23. Laurel Canyon
USGS Quad Maps	Bloody Mountain
GPS	37.562 / -118.909

Without a doubt, the most prominent line on Bloody Mountain is the Bloody Couloir. Named as one of the *Fifty Classic Ski Descents of North America* by Chris Davenport (www.wolverinepublishing.com) and also in Paul Richins' *50 Classic Descents of California* book, this is a line to put on your tick list.

Depending on the amount of snow and time of year, the couloir ranges in steepness from 40° to 45° at the top, before funneling into a seemingly endless lower section lined by beautiful rock walls.

Approach: If you are interested in booting the couloir, continue traversing west along the summer-road alignment past Laurel Lake, and eventually into the basin below the couloir. It is also possible to reach the couloir from the top by climbing the snowfield on Bloody's north face, just east of the Y Chutes, then walking along the ridgeline.

Bloody Exits: Follow your tracks back to the car.

↘ Y-NOT COULOIR

Bloody Mountain

Aspect	Consequence/Exposure	Slope
	5	45°

Summit Elevation	12,522'
Descent Vertical	2,500'
Total Vertical	5,200'
Hiking Distance	5 miles (w) | 6 ½ miles (s)
Terrain	Chute
Trailhead	23. Laurel Canyon
USGS Quad Maps	Bloody Mountain
GPS	37.562 / -118.907

The Y-Not Couloir descends a large hanging snowfield that ends in a 200' cliff, where you enter the chute. From afar, it seems improbable, and while it is clearly a ski line, it should only be attempted during times of good snow stability.

As you ski down this snowfield, finding your way into the chute can be a little tricky. Skiing too far down will

Ali Feinberg skiing Bloody Couloir. *Photo: Nate Greenberg.*

bring you to the top of the cliff, so it is recommended that you climb this chute before skiing it, or have a keen sense of where the chute starts.

Approach: As you enter this basin, climb toward the left of the large rocky buttress above you. Beneath the chutes, the Y-Not will appear on your right.

Y CHUTES

Bloody Mountain

Aspect	Consequence/Exposure	Slope
	3	40°

Summit Elevation	12,000'
Descent Vertical	2,000'
Total Vertical	4,700'
Hiking Distance	5 miles (w) | 6 ½ miles (s)
Terrain	Chute
Trailhead	23. Laurel Canyon
USGS Quad Maps	Bloody Mountain
GPS	37.564 / -118.904

Dropping from the eastern end of Bloody's ridgeline are two chutes that form a Y. They are located just to the east of the hanging snowfield and the Y-Not Couloir, and offer a slightly less committing yet equally attractive alternative to the standard Bloody Couloir.

Approach: As you enter this basin, climb toward the left of the large, rocky buttress above you. Continue up this slope and into the chutes.

EAST FACE

Bloody Mountain

Aspect	Consequence/Exposure	Slope
	3	40°

Summit Elevation	11,900'
Descent Vertical	1,500'
Total Vertical	4,600'
Hiking Distance	5 miles (w) | 6 ½ miles (s)
Terrain	Chute
Trailhead	23. Laurel Canyon
USGS Quad Maps	Bloody Mountain
GPS	37.564 / -118.904

From the car and other distant points, the East Face of Bloody Mountain looks steep and formidable—almost Alaska-like. Though riddled with steep faces and fun technical chutes, the face is overall rather short, and not nearly as complex as it seems. In fact, there is some great moderate–advanced terrain in this area that can be accessed easily in three-quarters of a day.

Approach: To access the East face of Bloody, follow the Bloody Couloir approach up into the head of the Laurel Lakes Drainage. At the head of the drainage, continue south and slightly east from the trailhead, following the path of least resistance (generally the alignment of the summer trail) into the large basin below the East Face.

Once in the basin, locate your line of choice, then skin and boot to the top.

SOUTH FACE

Bloody Mountain

Aspect	Consequence/Exposure	Slope
	3	40°

Summit Elevation	12,000'
Descent Vertical	1,700'
Total Vertical	4,700'
Hiking Distance	5 miles (w) | 6 ½ miles (s)
Terrain	Chute
Trailhead	23. Laurel Canyon
USGS Quad Maps	Bloody Mountain
GPS	37.564 / -118.904

Often overlooked, the South Face of Bloody Mountain offers some great moderate terrain in a series of broad gullies and faces. There are several varied lines off the South Face, beginning at the eastern end of the Bloody Ridge and stretching west to the actual summit of the peak. All of these lines drop you onto the Lake Genevieve bench, from where you can either skin back up to the Bloody ridgeline or access terrain that drops into Convict Creek.

Approach: It is possible to access the South Face either via the standard Bloody Couloir/Y Couloir approach,or by following the East Face approach to gain the Bloody Mountain ridgeline. From here, continue along the ridge to the top of your line, and enjoy the ride down to the Genevieve Bench.

Exit: Once on the Lake Genevieve bench, it is possible to either re-skin back up the South Face or access one of the many lines that drop into Convict Creek.

Joe Stewart above the Y Chutes.

Kevin Smith dropping into Jaws.

△ LAUREL MOUNTAIN *11,812'*

Laurel Mountain is the easternmost peak in the Mammoth Lakes Region, and also has descents off its east face that are covered in the Convict Creek Region. Though less popular than the lines that drop into Convict Canyon, the North and West Faces of Laurel Mountain offer some classic descents, which stare at you as you are trolling around Mammoth.

↘ NORTH FACE

Laurel Mountain

Aspect	Consequence/Exposure	Slope
N	2	30°

Summit Elevation	11,812'
Descent Vertical	1,700'
Total Vertical	4,500'
Hiking Distance	4 miles
Terrain	Face
Trailhead	23. Laurel Canyon
USGS Quad Maps	Bloody Mountain, Convict Lake
GPS	37.581 / -118.892

The broad, low-angle North Face of Laurel Mountain drops nearly 2,500' feet down perfect wide-open terrain as it falls into the lower reaches of Laurel Canyon. This is an excellent ski descent for those looking for moderate terrain. Unfortunately, its openness and exposure also mean that it tends to get stripped or have challenging skiing conditions on it.

In addition to the North Face of Laurel Mountain, there are a couple of small chutes on the West Face, one of which offers a great quick second lap that can be easily accessed on your way out from Bloody or other terrain higher up the canyon.

Approach: The North Face can be approached from either Trailhead #26 in the Convict Creek drainage (with a skin or a car shuttle) or from Trailhead #23. For access from Convict Creek, see the descriptions for the Mendenhall Couloir or other Laurel Mountain descents.

From Trailhead #23, follow the general alignment of the summer road up the north face of the moraine at the mouth of the Laurel Lakes Drainage. Climb to the top of this feature and into the mouth of the canyon. As you head up the canyon, stay to the east of the creek and begin climbing onto the slope to your west (east). Eventually this leads to a bench below the North Face. From here, skin right to the top.

7 Convict Creek

Mt. Morrison looms over Mini Morrison after an early season snowfall.

7. Convict Creek

CONVICT REGION:

- ▣ Lower Convict Canyon:
  - △ BATCH PLANT BOWLS
  - △ LAUREL MOUNTAIN
  - △ MINI MORRISON
  - △ MT. MORRISON NORTH
  - △ MT. MORRISON SOUTH
  - △ WHITE FANG
  - △ MT. AGGIE
- ▣ Upper Convict Canyon:
  - △ MT. MORRISON NORTH
  - △ MT. BALDWIN
  - △ RED SLATE

Region Trailheads

24. Hot Creek Hatchery Road
25. Convict Creek Trailhead Parking
26. Convict Lake Marina

Named by *Powder* magazine as "California's Trophy Backcountry Area," the Convict Creek Region is a popular destination at any time of year—and upon your first visit, it's easy to understand why. Nestled in a deep valley between towering peaks, Convict Lake is one of the most stunning locations on the Eastside. The standard High Sierra granite is noticeably absent here, and is instead replaced by some of the most colorful rock in the range. The Sevehah Cliff on Laurel Mountain and the walls of Convict Canyon are adorned with layers of red, orange, and brown igneous and metamorphic rock.

With Convict Lake Road being plowed and open year-round, and situated just a few short miles south of the town of Mammoth Lakes, it is a popular region for backcountry skiers. There are a number of "classic" and demanding descents packed into this small area, many of which are fairly close to the trailhead.

The terrain immediately surrounding the lake is covered in the Lower Convict Canyon section. This terrain has a tendency to melt out relatively early in the spring, so these descents are best explored during midwinter and early spring. The lines deeper in the canyon, including Red Slate, are higher in elevation and can hold snow well into the spring or summer. This area is covered in the Upper Convict Canyon section.

The lake itself can remain unfrozen well into the winter, and some years may not freeze at all. Because of this, we recommend following the summer trail on the north shore of the lake to get to Laurel Mountain and everything back in Convict Canyon. Be very cautious if you choose to cross the lake, as it has claimed multiple lives over the years.

Getting There & Getting Going

Convict Creek is located 4½ miles south of Mammoth Lakes via Highway 395. Most of the skiing that is referenced in this chapter is accessed via trailheads in the canyon itself, though it is also possible to access the Batch Plant Bowls directly from Highway 395.

24. Hot Creek Hatchery Road (Year-Round) 7,100'

Though it's not frequently used, it is possible to stage from the intersection of Hot Creek Hatchery Road and Highway 395. To reach this point, head south on Highway 395 four miles from the town of Mammoth Lakes. Hot Creek Hatchery Road provides access to the Mammoth-Yosemite Airport, located on the north side of Highway 395. There is typically some parking plowed out near the junction that can be used for daytime parking.

25. Convict Creek Trailhead Parking (Year-Round) 7,500'

This trailhead is located at the summertime overnight parking area that is provided for folks heading deeper into Convict Canyon, and is located at the mouth of the canyon prior to reaching Convict Lake Resort.

From Mammoth Lakes, travel south on Highway 395 for 4½ miles, then turn right (south/west) onto Convict Lake Road. Follow the road for approximately 1¾ miles until it begins to flatten out in the upper reaches of the canyon. As this happens, keep your eyes peeled for a parking area on your right that is marked with a parking sign.

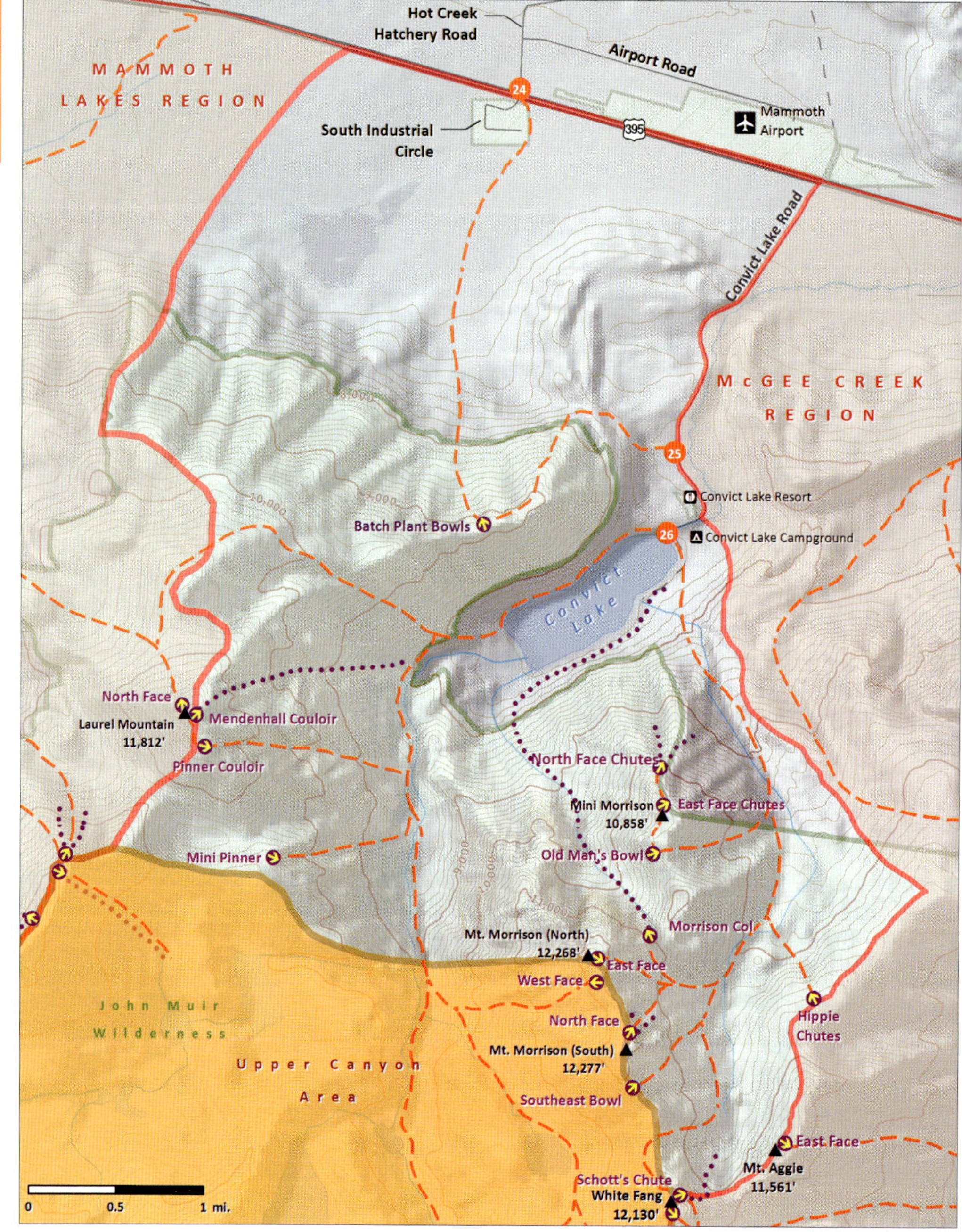

26. Convict Lake Marina (Year-Round) *7,600'*

The most popular staging area is at the Convict Lake Marina parking lot, which is located at the outlet of Convict Lake.

From Mammoth Lakes, travel south on Highway 395 for 4½ miles, then turn right (south/west) onto Convict Lake Road. Follow the road for approximately two miles. Pass the Convict Lake Resort and continue until the road ends at the lake. There is typically parking in either of the lots to the north or south.

Eats, Digs, Services, & Supplies

Though Convict Creek seems a bit off the beaten path, it is a very popular summertime destination for fishermen, campers, and hikers. Catering to these people is the Convict Lake Resort, which luckily for skiers is open year-round. The resort features a top-notch restaurant, small general store with basic provisions, and some rental cabins. It is a great place to post up for a couple days with friends or family and have some great skiing access right out your front door.

▣ Lower Convict Canyon

△ BATCH PLANT BOWLS *9,100'*

The Batch Plant Bowls consist of a half dozen or so open chutes and gullies that face Highway 395. The bowls are just north of the Convict Lake Road, directly across from the airport. They offer relatively easy access to fun terrain that can be a good morning or half-day affair.

↘ BATCH PLANT BOWLS

Aspect	Consequence/Exposure	Slope
	2	35°

Summit Elevation	9,100'
Descent Vertical	1,800'
Total Vertical	1,800'
Hiking Distance	2 ½ miles | 1 ¼ miles
Terrain	Bowl
Trailhead	24. Hot Creek Hatchery Rd or 25. Convict Creek
USGS Quad Maps	Convict Lake
GPS	37.595 / -118.867

Approach: You can reach the Batch Plant Bowls either directly from Highway 395 via Trailhead #24 at Hot Creek Hatchery Road, or by climbing onto the back side of the ridgeline from the Convict Lake Trailhead (#25).

From Trailhead #24, cross the highway and skirt the eastern edge of the industrial park. Skin to the base of the bowl and find the safest route to the ridge.

From Trailhead #25 in Convict Canyon, head slightly northwest and find the natural line that leads up the back side of the small peak that forms the Batch Plant Bowls until you gain the ridgeline. This is an ideal access point if you have two cars and can run a shuttle.

Exit: If coming from Trailhead #24, simply follow your skin-track back to the car. If you parked at Trailhead #25, head southeast, past the small ridgeline that forms the right flank of the bowl, then follow your track back to the car.

△ LAUREL MOUNTAIN *11,812'*

Unlike its north face, the portion of Laurel Mountain that drops into Convict Canyon is steep and rugged. Named the Sevehah Cliff, the east face is riddled with rocky spines that create complex, steep, and exposed gullies that descend thousands of feet to the drainage below. This face is clearly visible from Highway 395, and is what you are staring at as you drive into Convict Canyon.

This side of Laurel hosts some very popular and quite challenging descents that top the tick lists of many backcountry enthusiasts.

↘ MENDENHALL COULOIR

Laurel Mountain

Aspect	Consequence/Exposure	Slope
	4	50°

Summit Elevation	11,812'
Descent Vertical	3,750'
Total Vertical	3,750'
Hiking Distance	3 ½ miles
Terrain	Chute
Trailhead	26. Convict Lake Marina
USGS Quad Maps	Convict Lake, Bloody Mountain
GPS	37.580 / -118.890

Also referred to as the Northeast Gully, the Mendenhall Couloir is a landmark in Sierra climbing history, as its first ascent marked the first time a proper belay was used. First climbed by John Mendenhall and James Van Patten in 1930, the couloir provides modern climbers with a popular and moderate 5th Class rock climb during the summer months. During the winter months, the short vertical sections of rock fill in with snow, creating a skiable line that cuts steeply through the face. The difference between summer and winter is quite drastic: A rotten, 5th Class pile of choss becomes one of the most appealing ski descents in the Eastern Sierra.

This is a highly visible line and is relatively close to the road, but often remains untracked through the majority of the winter, as everyone waits for the rocks to get covered. In the early season or during a low snow year, these cliffs will not be covered with snow and a descent in these conditions will require mandatory air and/or rappels. The majority of the crux sections can be seen from the parking lot at Convict Lake, and it is highly recommended that you scope this line with a pair of binoculars before an attempt. If unsure of conditions or snow depth, it is best to climb the route before skiing it.

The main crux of the descent is negotiating a section that often forms an ice bulge about halfway down the couloir. From afar, this can appear as snow, so beware. Also bear in mind that Laurel Mountain is mostly comprised of loose rock. The solid granite that is typical of most of the Sierra is missing in this small region. As a result, setting up rappels over some of these crux sections could be dangerous or even impossible.

The descent begins directly from the summit of Laurel Mountain, off the northeast face. A steep, wide-open bowl gradually funnels down into the couloir itself, and the first crux. A handful of short narrow sections will keep you on your toes for the majority of this run as it winds and weaves steeply down the face.

Looking west into the Convict Lake drainage from Benton Crossing Road.

The exposure also adds a bit of excitement. In addition to the pitch of the couloir, the east-facing rocks/chutes above the line are a particular avalanche hazard to be aware of. The steep, rocky face catches the sun first thing in the morning, and has a tendency to heat up very quickly and release its snow. Because of this, the middle section of this route is an incredible terrain trap and extreme caution should be taken, particularly during the warm days of spring or immediately after a storm cycle. In addition, it may be filled with frozen avalanche debris, making some of the most technical and challenging portions of the descent that much more serious.

Approach: From the Convict Lake Marina (Trailhead #26), skin around the northwest side of the lake, following the general alignment of the summer trail. After passing the inlet to the lake near the head of the canyon, climb over a small outcrop/ridgeline, putting you at the base of the Mendenhall. If you are interested in booting the couloir, start hiking from here—but beware of the terrain that lurks above you, particularly the possibility of getting hit by a slide.

Most people choose to approach Mendenhall from above, via the northeast ridge of Laurel. To do so, climb the hillside on your right (north) just before reaching the base of the couloir, which eventually puts you on a bench on the upper ridge. From here, a small hanging gully/bowl stands in your way. Avoid this by skirting it to the north, gaining another small ridgeline, then travel back west across the top of the headwall and up the rocky face to the summit.

Mendenhall is the prominent east-facing line that drops directly from the summit of the peak.

Exit: Skin right back to your car.

↘ PINNER COULOIR

Laurel Mountain

Aspect	Consequence/Exposure	Slope
	3	40°

Summit Elevation	11,812'
Descent Vertical	3,500'
Total Vertical	3,500'
Hiking Distance	3 ½ miles
Terrain	Chute
Trailhead	26. Convict Lake Marina
USGS Quad Maps	Bloody Mountain, Convict Lake
GPS	37.578 / -118.89

Looking west at Laurel Mountain from Convict Lake.

The Pinner Couloir provides an unlikely natural passage through the colorful rock of Laurel Mountain's east face. This line is hidden from viewers looking at Laurel from the highway or Convict Lake, but is clearly visible from the peaks to the south. While not particularly steep, the Pinner rarely exceeds 100' in width as it twists and turns through a multi-colored canyon. Deep within the heart of Laurel Mountain, you will barely be able to see more than a few turns ahead at any given time.

A wide-open bowl sits atop the main portion of the couloir and is prime avalanche terrain. A slide here would be catastrophic, as you would likely be swept all the way down the line and deposited several thousand feet below in the canyon bottom. Due to the rocky terrain and the aspect of Laurel, large slides are not uncommon in this area. Nor are roller balls formed by sun-warmed snow from the many gullies and fins that feed into the line.

Approach: From the Convict Lake Marina (Trailhead #26), skin around the north (west) side of the lake, following the general alignment of the summer trail. After passing the inlet to the lake near the head of the canyon, climb over a small outcrop/ridgeline, putting you at the base of the Mendenhall. From here, you have the choice to either continue to the base of the Pinner and boot it directly or climb the northeast ridge and access it from the top.

To reach the base of the couloir, continue along the west side of Convict Creek, hugging the eastern flank of Laurel Mountain. After rounding the corner, the canyon climbs slightly, and as it does, the Pinner comes into view. It is the first significant line on your right after the Sevahah Cliffs.

If accessing from above, follow the summit approach directions listed in the Mendenhall Couloir (previous page). From the summit, continue down the ridge, past the entire upper bowl of the Mendenhall. Just beyond this to the south you will find the large bowl that serves as the entrance for the Pinner.

Exit: Continue down Convict Canyon, staying west of Convict Creek, until you reach your approach track.

Looking north at Laurel Mountain from Mt. Morrison.

↘ MINI PINNER

Laurel Mountain

Aspect	Consequence/Exposure	Slope
	3	35°

Summit Elevation	10,800'
Descent Vertical	2,500'
Total Vertical	3,300'
Hiking Distance	3 ½ miles
Terrain	Chute
Trailhead	26. Convict Lake Marina
USGS Quad Maps	Bloody Mountain, Convict Lake
GPS	37.576 / -118.888

Tucked away in Convict Canyon, this line is like a miniature version of the Pinner Couloir. Similar in shape, size, and aspect, it tops out on the south shoulder of Laurel Mountain.

Finding the entrance to this chute could be tricky from the top, so it is highly recommended that you climb it first, from the bottom. While it does not quite reach the top of Laurel Mountain, when climbing the chute, it is possible to continue on and go to the summit via the south face. From this point, it is also possible to go up Bloody Mountain via its southeast face.

Approach: From the Convict Lake Marina (Trailhead #26), skin around the north (west) side of the lake, following the general alignment of the summer trail. Continue along the west side of Convict Creek, hugging the eastern flank of Laurel Mountain. After rounding the corner, the canyon climbs slightly, and as it does, the Pinner comes into view. Continue a short distance on the canyon floor to the entrance of the Mini Pinner.

Ali Feinberg dropping into the Pinner in some of the best conditions you could ask for. *Photo: Pete Clark.*

Exit: Continue down Convict Canyon, staying west of Convict Creek, until you reach your approach track.

△ MINI MORRISON *10,858'*

Located in the shadow of its bigger brother, Mini Morrison provides a worthy set of options for those interested in high-value quick hits in an alpine-like setting. A variety of terrain and aspect choices make this peak a popular destination for locals and travelers alike.

Though the peak is physically close to the trailhead at Convict Lake, accessing it can be somewhat of a challenge, at times. In the early season, the moraine section to the south of the lake can be a bit of a nightmare. Dense brush and a typically shallow snowpack will make navigation difficult, among the endless hollow spots in the snowpack.

The bench which this moraine provides access to, located on the east flank of Mini Morrison, is known as Tobacco Flat. It is also possible to approach this bench via the Tobacco Flat Road from Mt. Morrison Road, which is frequently used by snowmobiles heading on top of McGee Peak. The common trailhead for this approach is the small wellhouse located behind the cemetery on Mt. Morrison Road, just south of the Convict Lake Road.

↘ NORTH & EAST FACE CHUTES

Mini Morrison

Aspect | **Consequence/Exposure** 3 | **Slope** 38°

Summit Elevation	10,858'
Descent Vertical	2,500'-3,200'
Total Vertical	3,300'
Hiking Distance	2 ¼ miles
Terrain	Face
Trailhead	26. Convict Lake Marina
USGS Quad Maps	Convict Lake
GPS	37.573 / -118.852

The North & East Face Chutes are the collection of chutes that lie to the north of Old Man's Bowl, dropping from the ridgeline of Mini Morrison. While each of these lines offers slightly different terrain and aspect options, they are all generally similar in nature, and can all be clearly seen from Convict Lake or the approach.

The east-facing descents drop you back onto Tobacco Flat, while the north-facing descents drop more directly to Convict Lake.

Approach: While it is possible to boot your line of choice directly from below, most people choose to

Moonset over Laurel Mountain.

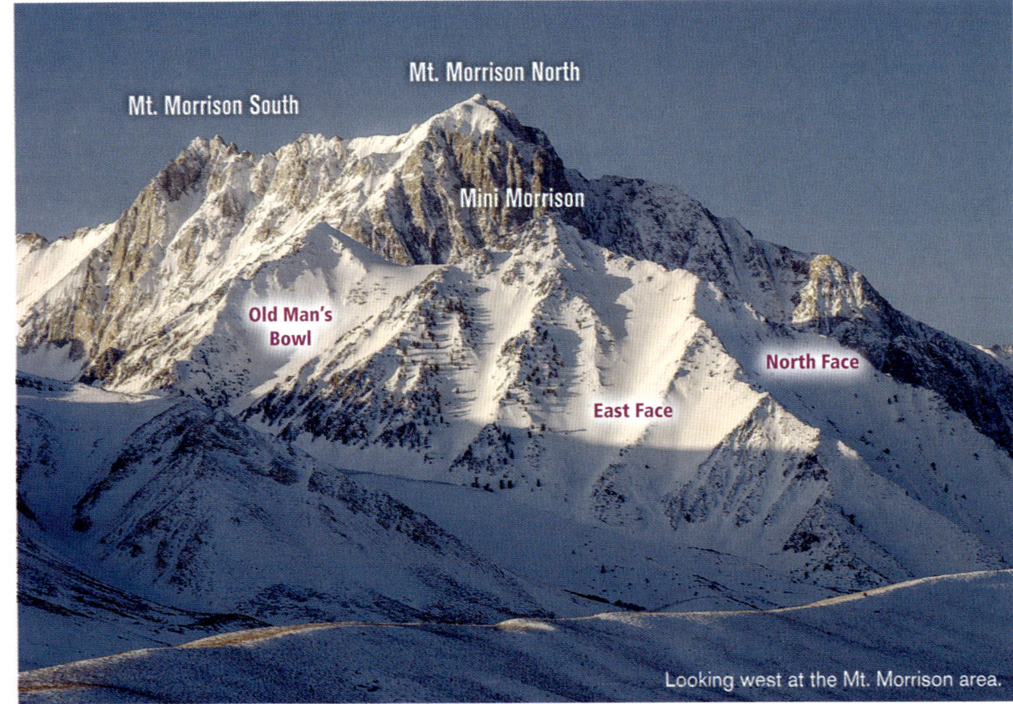

Looking west at the Mt. Morrison area.

approach from above. If you are heading toward some of the more north-facing lines, head around the south shore of Convict Lake and traverse the steep hillside until you reach the base of your line.

To approach the more east-facing lines, or the standard summit approach, from Trailhead #26 at Convict Lake Marina, head south along the east shore of Convict Lake. At the southeast corner of the lake climb a short pitch up the moraine that leads to Tobacco Flat. Continue south across the bench via a shallow gully, which climbs gently along the base of Mini Morrison's East Face. This gully is a huge terrain trap. One of the authors saw it get filled with avalanche debris literally in front of him while skinning up it. The best approach is to stay high on the left (east) wall, though the endless side-hill wears on you after a while.

About halfway up the gully, a large bowl (Old Man's Bowl) appears to your right, and affords relatively easy skinning to the summit of Mini Morrison. The best route up Old Man's is via the climber's right (north) side where there is a little more protection and anchoring.

Once atop the peak, it's relatively easy to walk the ridgeline to your chosen descent. To reach the north-facing descents, drop a short distance from the summit and traverse across the large east-facing bowl, staying as high as possible. Cross a small ridge to reach the north face.

Exit: Ski right back to the car.

↘ OLD MAN'S BOWL

Mini Morrison

Aspect	Consequence/Exposure	Slope
E	2	35°

Summit Elevation	10,700'
Descent Vertical	1,500'
Total Vertical	3,200'
Hiking Distance	2 miles
Terrain	Bowl
Trailhead	26. Convict Lake Marina
USGS Quad Maps	Convict Lake
GPS	37.569 / -118.853

Old Man's Bowl is one of the classic descents in this area, and rightly so. In addition to being the primary approach route for all descents on Little Morrison, the bowl offers a consistent yet moderate pitch for nearly its entire length. Though not a difficult or high-consequence descent, avalanche potential in this bowl should not be overlooked. Its due-east-facing aspect collects a lot of sun, as well as a considerable amount of snow during wind events.

Jim Wintermyre and Ray Ellis climbing Laurel Mountain.

Approach: Follow the directions for the North & East Face Chutes (previous section).

Exit: Ski right back to the car.

↘ MORRISON COL

Mini Morrison

Aspect	Consequence/Exposure	Slope
	3	35°

Summit Elevation	10,670'
Descent Vertical	2,800'
Total Vertical	3,100'
Hiking Distance	3 miles
Terrain	Bowl
Trailhead	26. Convict Lake Marina
USGS Quad Maps	Convict Lake
GPS	37.563 / -118.853

At the head of the large canyon that separates Mini Morrison and Mt. Morrison North is the Morrison Col. This striking canyon trends north-south, and the neighboring peaks provide protection from both the sun and wind. This is a great tour that circumambulates Mini Morrison, with a moderate amount of climbing and an enjoyable ski back to Convict Lake.

Approach: Follow the directions to the base of Old Man's Bowl (previous page) and continue up the gully until it ends on the south flank of Mini Morrison. From here, climb directly toward the notch that lies at the base of the northeast face of Mt. Morrison. The notch is the col, and your descent.

Exit: If the lake isn't frozen and the snowpack is shallow, reaching the bottom of this run can be a little tricky and may involve a short, steep traverse through a few rocky sections. Falling in these areas would be bad and likely drop you in the lake, though luckily they are short and put behind you quickly.

Looking northwest at Mt. Morrison from the Hippie Chutes.

△ MT. MORRISON NORTH *12,268'*

Mt. Morrison is probably the most recognizable peak in the area. Driving on Highway 395 from the north, it is the first thing you see as you near Mammoth Lakes.

Given its sheer north face, it's hard to imagine that anything off Mt. Morrison's North Summit would be skiable, and most of the mountain is indeed not. Cliff bands of loose rock abound, with only a handful of moderate passages in between. Hidden from view until you are practically just below it, the East Face holds one of these passages. While not incredibly steep or technical, this descent does require some route-finding.

↘ EAST FACE — Mt. Morrison

Aspect | Consequence/Exposure | Slope: 40°

Summit Elevation	12,268'
Descent Vertical	2,000'
Total Vertical	2,700'
Hiking Distance	3 miles
Terrain	Face
Trailhead	26. Convict Lake Marina
USGS Quad Maps	Convict Lake
GPS	37.561 / -118.858

The East Face descends directly from Mt. Morrison's North summit through moderate yet exposed terrain. Due to the complexity of this face, a fall would likely result in significant injury. This line generally follows the upper bowl, which eventually splits, with the skier's-left version being the typical approach route, and likely the way you came. The skier's-right side descends to a cliff band, which may or may not be filled in. During big snow years, many other lines on this face will fill in and become skiable. There is a great little diagonal chute near the bottom of the east face that provides a fun exit to the exposed terrain from above.

This face gets sunlight first thing in the morning, which makes it a great run to do in the early spring, or to try to catch some sunlight in the midwinter. But because of its aspect, it goes into the shade quite quickly in the midwinter and melts out very early in the spring.

In addition to this descent, the Death Couloir has been skied in the past, involving a rappel at the bottom. This is the steep, narrow chute that drains down into the Morrison Col (previous page).

Approach: From the Convict Lake Marina (Trailhead #26), head south along the east shore of Convict Lake and proceed up the Tobacco Flat Drainage as though you were heading to Morrison Col.

Once on the south of Mini Morrison, proceed directly west and uphill to the East Face. As you approach the

Looking south at Mt. Morrison from Morrison Col.

rocky ledges above, a southeast-facing chute will come into view, splitting the dark-red cliffs. Climb this chute, and follow the steep slopes to the summit. This mountain is unique in that the crux section lies at the bottom, and the upper section of the mountain gets less steep as you ascend.

△ MT. MORRISON SOUTH *12,277'*

Mt. Morrison's South Summit is taller, but often gets overlooked due to the impressive north face of its little brother. For those who are looking for committing and extreme big-mountain terrain, tthis area holds a handful of steep and technical lines.

This summit sits approximately ½ mile to the south of Mt. Morrison North, with a knife-edge ridge separating the two peaks.

↘ EAST FACE CHUTES — Mt. Morrison

Aspect	Consequence/Exposure	Slope
	5	55°

Summit Elevation	12,277'
Descent Vertical	2,500'
Total Vertical	2,700'
Hiking Distance	1 ¼ miles
Terrain	Face
Trailhead	26. Convict Lake Marina
USGS Quad Maps	Convict Lake
GPS	37.556 / -118.856

Jim Barnes booting the East Face Chutes.
Photo: Nate Greenberg.

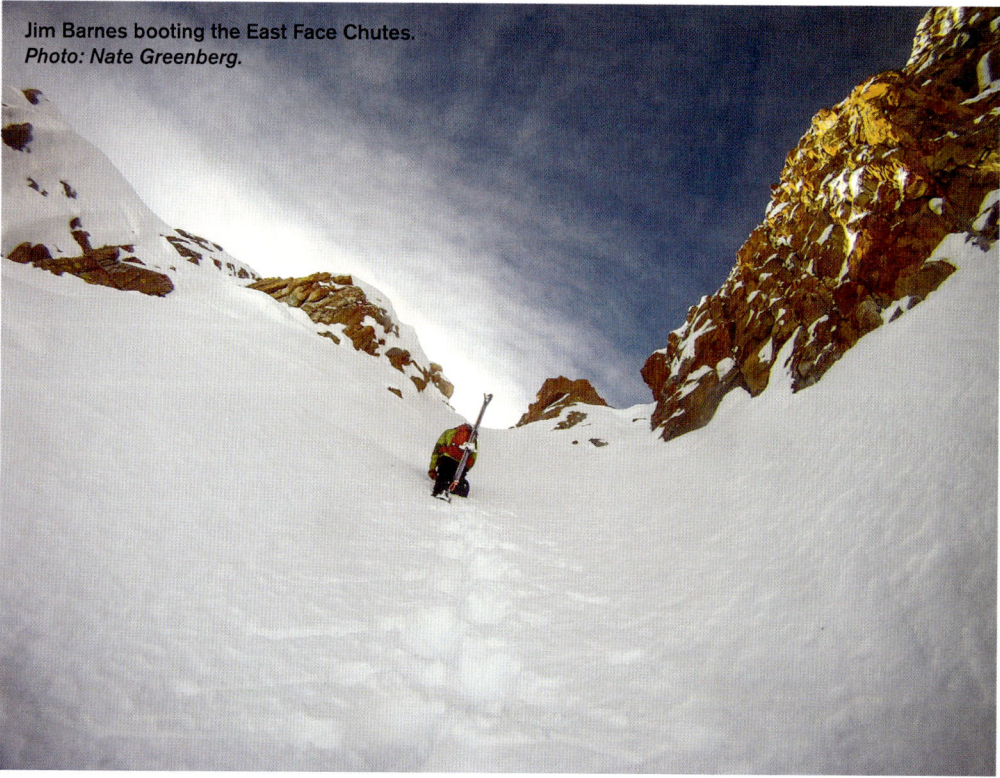

Nate Greenberg climbing into the East Face Chutes.
Photo: Jim Barnes.

Steep and exposed, the lines of the North Face should only be attempted when you are very confident in the stability of the snow and your abilities to ski technical terrain. The upper chute requires a deep snowpack before it becomes skiable, so this run may be best suited for later in the season.

This is serious terrain, in which a fall would likely be fatal. The complexity of the line begins with the entrance chutes, which are typically steep and rather narrow. After exiting the entrance chute(s), the terrain opens up considerably and you will find yourself on the giant North Face. Pick your way around the many rocks and cliffs, taking care not to descend too far. The face ultimately ends in a 200' cliff, and extreme care must be taken to safely traverse above the danger.

As you near the bottom of the face, stick to the skier's left and do a short but highly exposed traverse above the cliff band. While not incredibly steep at this point, a fall from here would not be good. For this reason, you may want to consider bringing a rope and a selection of rock pro for the final traverse. Past the cliff, you are in the relative safety of the lower flank and your up-track.

There are a handful of other entrances that fill in along the ridgeline between Morrison's two summits,

some of which are even more committing and exposed than the true North Face entrance.

Approach: From Convict Lake Marina (Trailhead #26) head south along the east shore of Convict Lake and proceed up the Tobacco Flat Drainage as though you were heading to Morrison Col.

Continue south beyond the approach for the Morrison Col and the East Face toward the large cliffs that skirt the bottom of the North Face. It is advised that you boot the line you intend to ski, so that you have a route to follow on the way down.

Exit: Follow your track back to the car.

SOUTHEAST BOWL

Mt. Morrison

Aspect	Consequence/Exposure	Slope
	2	35°

Summit Elevation	11,800'
Descent Vertical	1,300'
Total Vertical	4,500'
Hiking Distance	3 ¼ miles
Terrain	Bowl
Trailhead	26. Convict Lake Marina
USGS Quad Maps	Convict Lake
GPS	37.550 / -118.855

The Southeast Bowl is a broad, slightly convex face that spans the distance between Mt. Morrison South and White Fang. In some years this face may not fill in completely, and there may only be one passage through the middle. On big snow years, however, this terrain becomes a giant bowl.

Approach: From Convict Lake Marina (Trailhead #26) head south along the east shore of Convict Lake and proceed up the Tobacco Flat Drainage as though you were heading to Morrison Col.

Continue south beyond the approach for the Morrison Col, passing the East Face and the large cliffs that skirt the bottom of the North Face. Just south of this point, the Southeast Bowl will come into view. Skin and boot your way to the top.

△ WHITE FANG 12,130'

White Fang is the large, prominent peak that lies just to the south of Mt. Morrison. It is comprised of an impressive and steep tower on its northern end, with a broad and equally steep face to the south.

There are two prominent lines off White Fang: Schott's Chute, which descends off the northeast face of the peak and is described here; and the Z/Lightning Bolt Couloir, which drops into McGee Creek and is described in the next chapter on page 208.

This descent is named after longtime Mammoth local Matthew Schott, who scoped and likely nabbed the first descent of this line in 2003, along with local friends "Powder" Dan Molnar, Cedric Bernardini, and John Wentworth.

↘ SCHOTT'S CHUTE

White Fang

Aspect	Consequence/Exposure	Slope
	5	50°

Summit Elevation	12,000'
Descent Vertical	1,500'
Total Vertical	1,500'
Hiking Distance	4 miles
Terrain	Chute
Trailhead	26. Convict Lake Marina
USGS Quad Maps	Convict Lake
GPS	37.543 / -118.852

This is the steep, exposed, high-consequence, and extremely aesthetic line that graces White Fang's northeastern face and descends along the northern side of the prominent tower. The main chute ends in a large, impassible cliff band, which creates the high-consequence nature of the line. As a result, a traverse out through technical terrain is needed to complete the actual descent.

Due to the location, exposure, and consequence of this line, it should only be attempted during times of high snow stability when chances of a slide do not exist.

Approach: From Convict Lake Marina (Trailhead #26) begin the approach as though you are heading to the Southeast Bowl of Mt. Morrison. Head south along the east shore of Convict Lake and proceed up the Tobacco Flat Drainage as though you were heading to Morrison Col. Continue south beyond the approach for the Morrison Col, the East Face, and the large cliffs that skirt the bottom of the North Face. Just south of this point, the Southeast Bowl will come into view.

Continue past this point, just beyond the small ridge that makes up the skier's right-hand side of the Southeast Bowl into a small cleft that forms a small couloir from the Morrison/White Fang ridgeline. Climb this couloir, then proceed to the west side of the ridgeline and head south and up the north ridge of White Fang. As you near the summit, the entrance for the chute will become apparent.

Exit: After skiing the main upper "gut" of the couloir, look for a weakness in the skier's-left wall that provides exposed passage to the north via a high traverse above rocks. Continue north (left) across the face as it opens up beyond this to the next large, prominent ridgeline. From here, the best option is to sidestep or boot uphill a short distance until you can cross this ridge into another hanging pocket (which also ends in a cliff band). Ski a short distance down this pocket via a couple of different chute options, then find your first exit left through the final prominent ridgeline. Once through this ridge, you will find yourself back in the vicinity of your up-track and the relative safety of that couloir.

△ MT. AGGIE 11,561'

Most of the lines that are skied off Mt. Aggie descend off its southeast face into McGee Creek. The north face of Mt. Aggie is a rather unimpressive area, though it hosts a handful of chutes that are quick, short descents in moderately steep north-facing terrain.

Nate Wallace atop Schott's Chute. *Photo: Matt Schott.*

↘ HIPPIE CHUTES

Mt. Aggie

Aspect	Consequence/Exposure	Slope
	3	38°

Summit Elevation	10,700'
Descent Vertical	1,000'
Total Vertical	3,200'
Hiking Distance	2 ½ miles
Terrain	Chute
Trailhead	26. Convict Lake Marina
USGS Quad Maps	Convict Lake
GPS	37.559 / -118.841

These are the obvious set of north-facing chutes that you see as you skin past Old Man's Bowl beyond Tobacco Flat. They are also visible from various locations in the Mammoth Lakes Region, particularly in the Laurel Lakes drainage.

Approach: From Convict Lake Marina (Trailhead #26), head south along the east shore of Convict Lake and proceed up the Tobacco Flat Drainage as though you were heading to Morrison Col.

Continue south beyond the approach for the Morrison Col and other Mt. Morrison descents directly toward the chutes. You can choose to either skin to the base and boot up them directly, or approach from the top. To do this, head east and climb the shallow southwest–northeast-trending ridge that leads to their summit.

Exit: Follow your track back to the car.

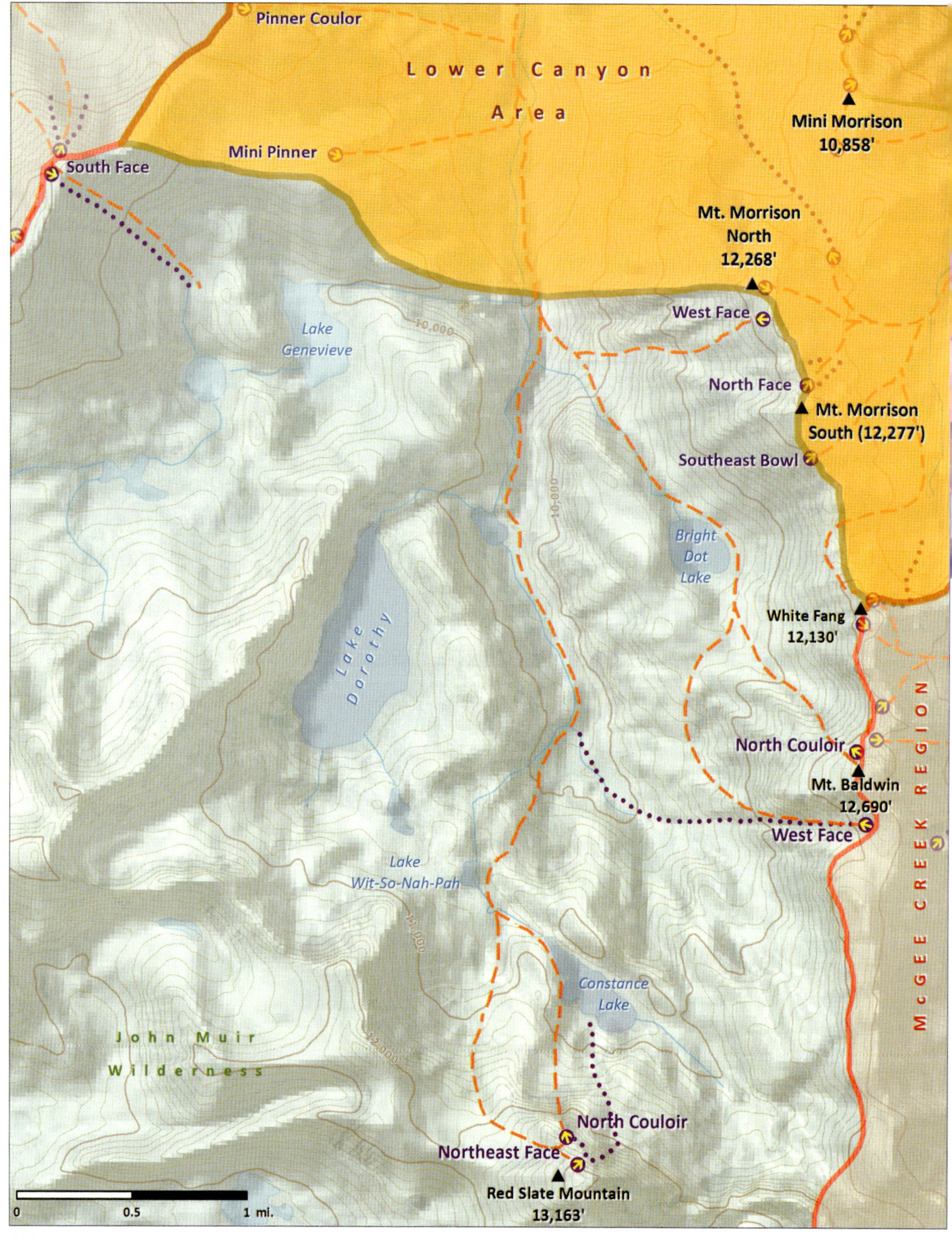

Upper Convict Canyon

△ MT. MORRISON NORTH *12,268'*

It is rather strange for snow to stick to the west face of a mountain in the Sierra, as this aspect typically gets hammered by the wind, and what little snow accumulates is almost always scoured by the following storm. Though seemingly exposed to that wind, the West Face of Mt. Morrison North has just enough protection to hold snow. Having a west aspect also means this slope receives sun fairly late, a bonus for those short days of December and January.

Since it is impossible to know the conditions of this descent until you are on it, we recommend climbing it from the bottom, which requires a different approach than the other descents on this peak.

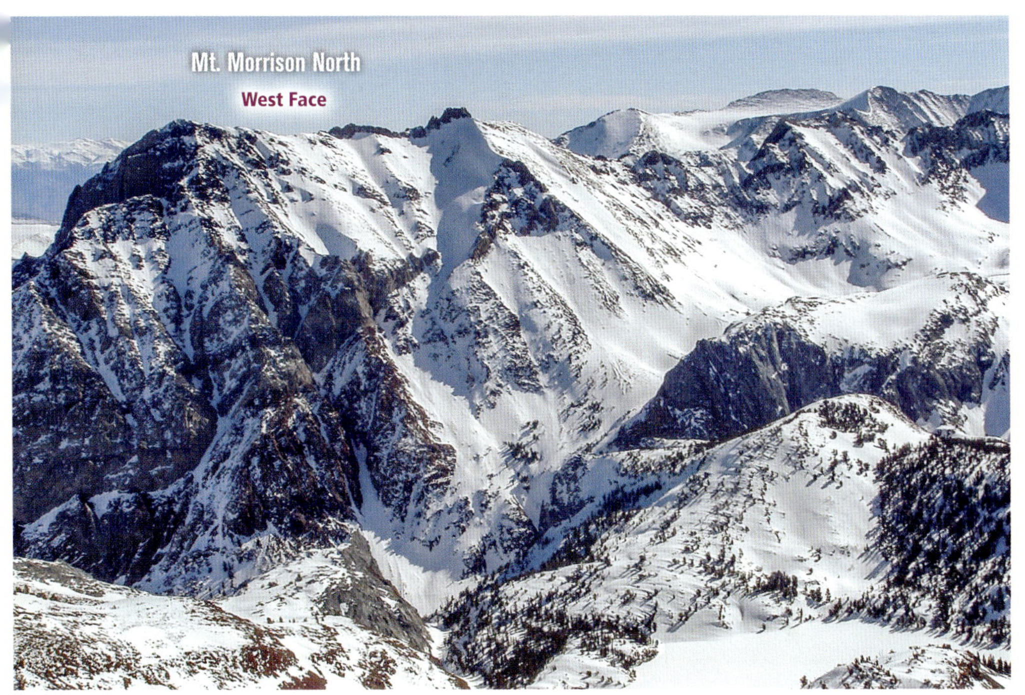

↘ WEST FACE

Mt. Morrison

Aspect	Consequence/Exposure	Slope
	3	35°

Summit Elevation	12,000'
Descent Vertical	2,500'
Total Vertical	4,500'
Hiking Distance	4 miles
Terrain	Face
Trailhead	26. Convict Lake Marina
USGS Quad Maps	Convict Lake
GPS	37.559 / -118.859

Approach: From Convict Lake Marina (Trailhead #26), skin around the north (west) side of the lake, following the general alignment of the summer trail and up into Convict Canyon.

Staying on the north side of the creek, you will eventually pass through a meadow with aspen trees. Past the meadow, the canyon begins to climb again, where you should begin looking for a safe place to cross the creek. During a typical winter, it is common for this section to have a snow bridge over the water. In periods of low snow, however, this could be the crux of your day.

Once across the river, begin climbing the southeast wall of the canyon. The most obvious and wide-open way will bring you to Bright Dot Lake, which is not where you want to go. Instead of continuing up the drainage to Bright Dot, begin heading east, below the colorful cliffs on the west side of Mt. Morrison. Follow the path of least resistance up the West Face to the summit ridge.

You can also reach this same point via the standard East Face approach, though you will not be able to see the coverage of the West Face until you have already committed to the descent.

Exit: Follow your track back to the car.

△ MT. BALDWIN *12,690'*

Sitting between the two classic peaks of Mt. Morrison and Red Slate, Mt. Baldwin is an often-overlooked gem. The seemingly narrow North Couloir is actually quite wide, followed by a long ride all the way down into Convict Canyon. A climb up the west ridge offers front-row seats for viewing Red Slate and the upper portions of Convict Canyon.

Looking south into the upper Convict Creek drainage from Laurel Mountain.

↘ NORTH COULOIR

Mt. Baldwin

Aspect	Consequence/Exposure	Slope
	3	35°

Summit Elevation	12,300'
Descent Vertical	1,800'
Total Vertical	4,800'
Hiking Distance	5 ½ miles
Terrain	Face
Trailhead	26. Convict Lake Marina
USGS Quad Maps	Convict Lake
GPS	37.533 / -118.853

Approach: From Convict Lake Marina (Trailhead #26), skin around the north (west) side of the lake, following the general alignment of the summer trail and up into Convict Canyon.

Staying on the north side of the creek as you climb, you will eventually pass through a meadow with aspen trees. Past the meadow, the canyon begins to climb again. At this point, you should begin looking for a safe place to cross the creek. During a typical winter, it is common for this section to have a snow bridge over the water. In periods of low snow, however, this could be the crux of your day.

Once across the river, begin climbing the southeast wall of the canyon, following the drainage to Bright Dot Lake. At Bright Dot, Mt. Baldwin will be directly in front of you. Either climb the couloir directly, or ascend the west ridge. Due to its exposure to the wind, the west ridge rarely holds snow, and can involve a short scramble on steep, icy rock. Past that short scramble, the remainder of the slope is quite moderate all the way to the summit. From the ridge at the top of the couloir, the summit is just a short distance above you.

Exit: Follow your track back to the car.

↘ WEST FACE

Mt. Baldwin

Aspect	Consequence/Exposure	Slope
	3	35°

Summit Elevation	12,300'
Descent Vertical	2,300'
Total Vertical	4,800'
Hiking Distance	5 ½ miles
Terrain	Face
Trailhead	26. Convict Lake Marina
USGS Quad Maps	Convict Lake
GPS	37.533 / -118.853

Just south of the North Couloir and west ridge of Mt. Baldwin is the broad, open slope that comprises the West Face. The position of this peak provides for excellent views as you drop a couple thousand feet into the bottom of the drainage.

Approach: Follow the approach for the North Couloir of Baldwin, continuing south past the west ridge to the base of the West Face. Climb this face/gully to the summit.

Exit: Follow your track back to the car.

Mt. Baldwin, as seen from the shoulder of Mt. Morrison South.

△ RED SLATE *13,163'*

Red Slate dominates the skyline from just about any point in the region. The peak towers above its neighbors, and its giant North Couloir stands out from afar. Red Slate's popularity and classic status come mainly from the sheer aesthetics of the peak and the notorious exposure associated with the entrance to the North Couloir. This peak is a destination on many people's tick lists.

Red Slate lies deep in Convict Canyon. While it is possible (and certainly not uncommon) to ski the lines on Red Slate in a day from car-to-car, most people choose to spend the night in the basin in order to give them more time on the peak.

↘ NORTH COULOIR — Red Slate

Aspect	Consequence/Exposure	Slope
	5	50°

Summit Elevation	13,163'
Descent Vertical	2,100'
Total Vertical	5,600'
Hiking Distance	7 ½ miles
Terrain	Chute
Trailhead	26. Convict Lake Marina
USGS Quad Maps	Convict Lake
GPS	37.510 / -118.870

While the North Couloir on Red Slate is one of the more popular and sought after descents in the region, its distance and danger tend to keep traffic in check.

Many who gaze upon this line make the mistake of assuming it is thin and narrow, but this is a classic example of "bigger than it looks." The North Couloir is a consistent 100' (or wider) as it drops for nearly 2,000' to Constance Lake below.

Jesse Horn traversing across the North Face gullies on way to the summit of Red Slate. *Photo: Josh Feinberg.*

The crux of the descent (and all of the exposure) lies in the drop-in from the summit. This involves descending the obvious chute on the northeast side of the peak, then traversing to the skier's left as soon as possible. While not incredibly technical or difficult, this section is not to be taken lightly. Hold as high a line as possible, and continue traversing to the left across three chutes. Each of these chutes ends in a large cliff about 100' below you, and a fall from here would most likely be fatal.

The traverse eventually ends in (relative) safety at the top of the couloir. A small staging area allows you to collect your wits and begin the fun—2000' of the most classic, sustained 50-degree couloir that awaits you below.

Note that on good snow years, it is also possible to access the top of the couloir via a steep (50°) 200' long chute that drops from the north ridge of Red Slate directly to the top of the chute. While this is less exposed, falling in this terrain would also have serious consequences.

Approach: From the Convict Lake Marina (Trailhead #26), skin around the north (west) side of the lake, following the general alignment of the summer trail and up into Convict Canyon.

Staying on the north side of the creek as you climb, you will eventually pass through a meadow with aspen trees. Past the meadow, the canyon begins to climb again, where you should begin looking for a safe place to cross the creek. During a typical winter, it is common for this section to have a snow bridge over the water. In periods of low snow, however, this could be the crux of your day.

From here, continue to follow the canyon to Mildred Lake, cross the lake, and begin climbing the treed hillside below the north face of Red Slate. This will bring you to a bench at Lake Wit-So-Nah-Pah, where you can either head toward the North Couloir directly (and boot it to the summit) or climb the large bowl on the northwest flank of the peak. If this is your choice, the top of the bowl rarely holds snow, and it is likely that you will have a rocky walk to summit

There is also a sneak entrance into the top of the North Couloir (below the technical summit entrance) along the north ridge, though it may not fill in with snow on some years. From the summit, walk along the ridge a few hundred feet until you are directly above the start of the couloir. The entrance will be below you. This shot is steep and narrow, but offers a much safer entrance to the main couloir than dropping in the Northeast Face.

Exit: Follow your track back to the car.

Looking south up Convict Creek from Laurel Mountain.

Red Slate
Baldwin and West Face
of Morrison Approach
Red Slate Approach
Laurel Mountain

Looking west across Convict Lake at Mt. Morrison (left) and Laurel Mountain (right).

↘ NORTHEAST FACE

Red Slate

Aspect	Consequence/Exposure	Slope
	5	55°

Summit Elevation	13,163'
Descent Vertical	2,400'
Total Vertical	5,600'
Hiking Distance	7 ½ miles
Terrain	Face
Trailhead	26. Convict Lake Marina
USGS Quad Maps	Convict Lake
GPS	37.508 / -118.869

Steep and exposed, this line is a much more challenging alternative to the popular North Couloir. Bear in mind that this face requires a deep snowpack in order to be skiable, and is quite exposed to the wind, so even after a heavy snowfall it may not be filled in. Patience and timing are very important for this one. It is absolutely necessary to get a look at the line before attempting it, and highly recommended that you bring a rope and a selection of rock pro. The upper section has a handful of technical cruxes, and a fall at any point would almost certainly be fatal.

From the summit, ski a short distance down the large chute on the northeast side of the peak. This is also the start for the North Couloir, and there may be tracks on it that will most likely traverse to the left. A few hundred feet below the summit, you will encounter one of the first crux sections. At this point, it is still possible to escape over to the North Couloir by traversing left. If this section isn't filled in, chances are the other sections are not filled in below, and it would be best to retreat.

From here, continue a short distance straight down the fall line. A brief, narrow section will bring you to a pillar of rock, where you will begin working your way to the skier's right, aiming for the large crescent-moon-shaped chute below you. An exposed traverse over a cliff will bring you to this chute, and relative safety. Follow this through a rocky section onto the lower apron, and down into Convict Canyon.

Approach: Follow the directions to the North Couloir (previous section). Once below the peak, you will have the option to climb the line directly or climb the ridge.

8 McGee Creek

Kevin Smith below Esha Peak.

8. McGee Creek

MCGEE CREEK REGION:

- Lower Canyon Area:
  - △ MCGEE MOUNTAIN
  - △ MCGEE CREEK PEAK
  - △ MT. AGGIE
- Upper Canyon Area:
  - △ WHITE FANG
  - △ MT. BALDWIN
  - △ RED & WHITE MOUNTAIN
  - △ ESHA PEAK
- Mt. Morgan Area:
  - △ NEVAHBE RIDGE
  - △ MT. MORGAN
  - △ RED MOUNTAIN

Region Trailheads

27. Mt. Morrison Cemetery
28. McGee Mountain Rope Tow
29. McGee Creek Road
30. Crowley Lake Campground
31. Aspen Springs

McGee Creek is one of the quieter regions described in this book. Though a road provides access to a summertime trailhead in the heart of the canyon, winter access begins at Highway 395, 3½ miles away. The distance is just far enough to keep the crowds away. It is not uncommon for people to access the canyon with snowmachines, which does make the ski travel a bit easier for those without.

Though relatively small in size, the McGee Creek Drainage has plenty of worthy lines to explore, and will likely be the site of much future exploration. If you are looking for some interesting, aesthetic, and even challenging lines that are off the beaten path, you will not be disappointed by a trip up this canyon.

This chapter is broken into three areas: the Lower Canyon Area, the Upper Canyon Area, and the Mt. Morgan Area, which are all distinctly different from one another and offer varied terrain choices. Some of the descents featured in the Lower Canyon and Mt. Morgan areas are adjacent to the road, while others in all three areas lie deep in the canyons and require a more significant time investment to explore.

Getting There & Getting Going

Five separate trailheads are used to access the terrain described in this region. In general, all of these trailheads are located roughly nine miles south of Mammoth Lakes on Highway 395 just beyond the Green Church and at the northern end of Long Valley. McGee Creek itself is accessed via McGee Creek Road, which heads west from Highway 395 a short distance south of the CalTrans maintenance station located on Highway 395. Specific directions to the trailheads in this region are covered below.

27. Mt. Morrison Cemetery (Year-Round) *7,000'*

This is a popular staging area for snowmachines, and for those looking to access McGee Mountain's North Face or reach the summit of the peak via Tobacco Flat.

From the junction of Highway 203 (Mammoth Lakes), travel south on Highway 395 for approximately six miles. Just beyond the Green Church and Benton Crossing Road, take a right turn (south/west) onto Mt. Morrison Road. Follow this road a short distance past a small cemetery. On the far (north) side of the cemetery is a small road that provides access to a well-shed building. Park in the plowed area near the building without blocking access to it for service workers.

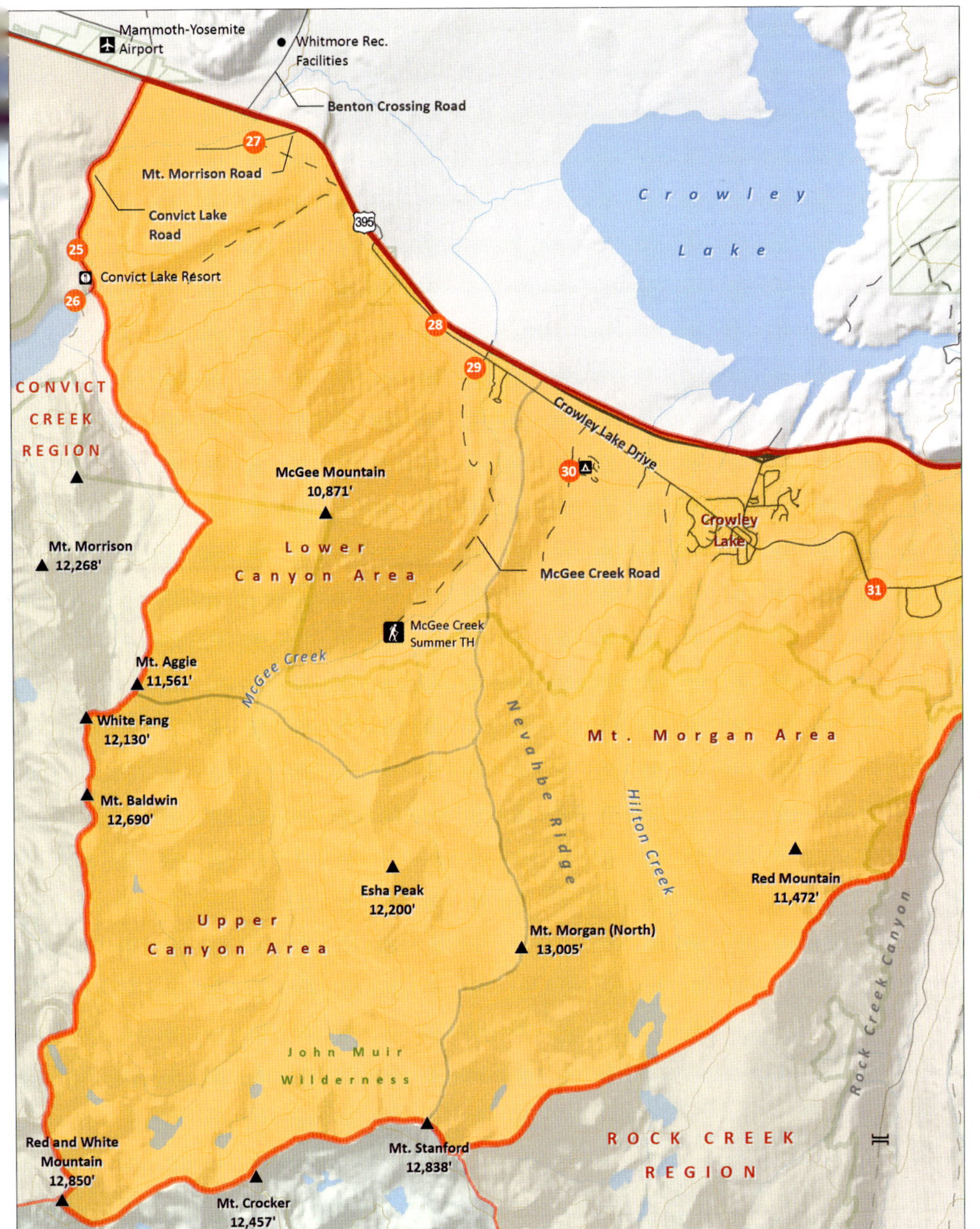

28. McGee Mountain Rope Tow (Year-Round) 6,900'

This trailhead is located along Crowley Lake Drive, which parallels the west/southern side of Highway 395 through Long Valley. The rope-tow site is a small plowed parking area on the south/west side of Crowley Lake Drive with a monument in it that marks the location of the original site of "Mammoth Mountain Ski Area" and the legacy that Dave McCoy established on the Eastside.

From the junction of Highway 203 (Mammoth Lakes), travel south on Highway 395 for approximately 8½ miles. Pass the Green Church at Benton Crossing Road and descend into Long Valley. Take the second right for McGee Creek Road, then turn right onto Crowley Lake Drive. Continue a short distance (approximately ½ mile) to a small plowed turnout on the west side of the road.

Looking southwest across the valley at McGee Creek.

29. McGee Creek Road (Year-Round) *6,900'*

This trailhead is located at the point of winter closure of McGee Creek Road, just west/south of Highway 395, adjacent to a small trailer park. In the spring, this road will be plowed to a summertime trailhead located approximately 3½ miles up-canyon. This is also a popular staging area for snowmachines.

From the junction of Highway 203 (Mammoth Lakes), travel south on Highway 395 for approximately 8½ miles. Pass the Green Church at Benton Crossing Road and descend into Long Valley. Take the exit for McGee Creek Road. Continue through the stop sign at Crowley Lake Drive to the end of the road just beyond and adjacent to some trailers. Please park to one side of the road to provide access for other users.

30. Crowley Lake Campground (Year-Round) *7,000'*

This trailhead is located at the point of winter closure of the road which provides summertime access to the Crowley Lake Campground. The campground is located on the south/west side of Crowley Lake Drive, roughly equidistant between McGee Creek and the community of Crowley Lake.

From the junction of Highway 203 (for Mammoth Lakes), travel south on Highway 395 approximately 8½ miles. Pass the Green Church at Benton Crossing Road and descend into Long Valley. Take the exit for McGee Creek Road. At the stop sign, turn left onto Crowley Lake Drive, then head south/east along this road for approx. one mile. On your right will be a sign for the Crowley Lake Campground and a small road that provides summertime access. Turn onto this road and find parking off the road.

31. Aspen Springs (Year-Round) *7,000'*

This trailhead is between the communities of Crowley Lake (to the north) and Aspen Springs (to the south). Though it may not be plowed out immediately after a storm, there is typically a reasonably sized parking area on the south side of Crowley Lake Drive at the bottom of the small hill that separates Crowley Lake from

Aspen Springs. Please do not park along Crowley Lake Drive if this parking area is not plowed.

From the junction of Highway 203 (Mammoth Lakes), travel south on Highway 395 for approximately 8½ miles. Pass the Green Church at Benton Crossing Road and descend into Long Valley. Take the second right-hand exit from the highway onto McGee Creek Road. At the stop sign, turn left onto Crowley Lake Drive, then head south/east along this road for approximately 4½ miles. Continue through the community of Crowley Lake (including the fire station and sheriff substation—*please observe the speed limit)* and through the stop sign at South Landing Road. Climb over a small hill, at the bottom of which on the right-hand (south) side is a plowed parking area.

It is also possible to reach the South Landing Road/ Crowley Lake Drive via the main Crowley Lake community exit off Highway 395. And if coming from the south, you can exit 395 at Tom's Place, and then continue north on Crowley Lake Drive.

Eats, Digs, Services, & Supplies

If you are in the area between Thursday and Monday, be sure to stop at the Eastside Bake Shop located in the historic McGee Creek Lodge at the corner of Crowley Lake Drive and McGee Creek Road for some fresh coffee and some of the best baked goods on the Eastside. The community of Crowley Lake also has a small gas station and general store that has basic items. The store is located on South Landing Road, which connects Highway 395 to Crowley Lake Drive a few miles south of the McGee Creek Road.

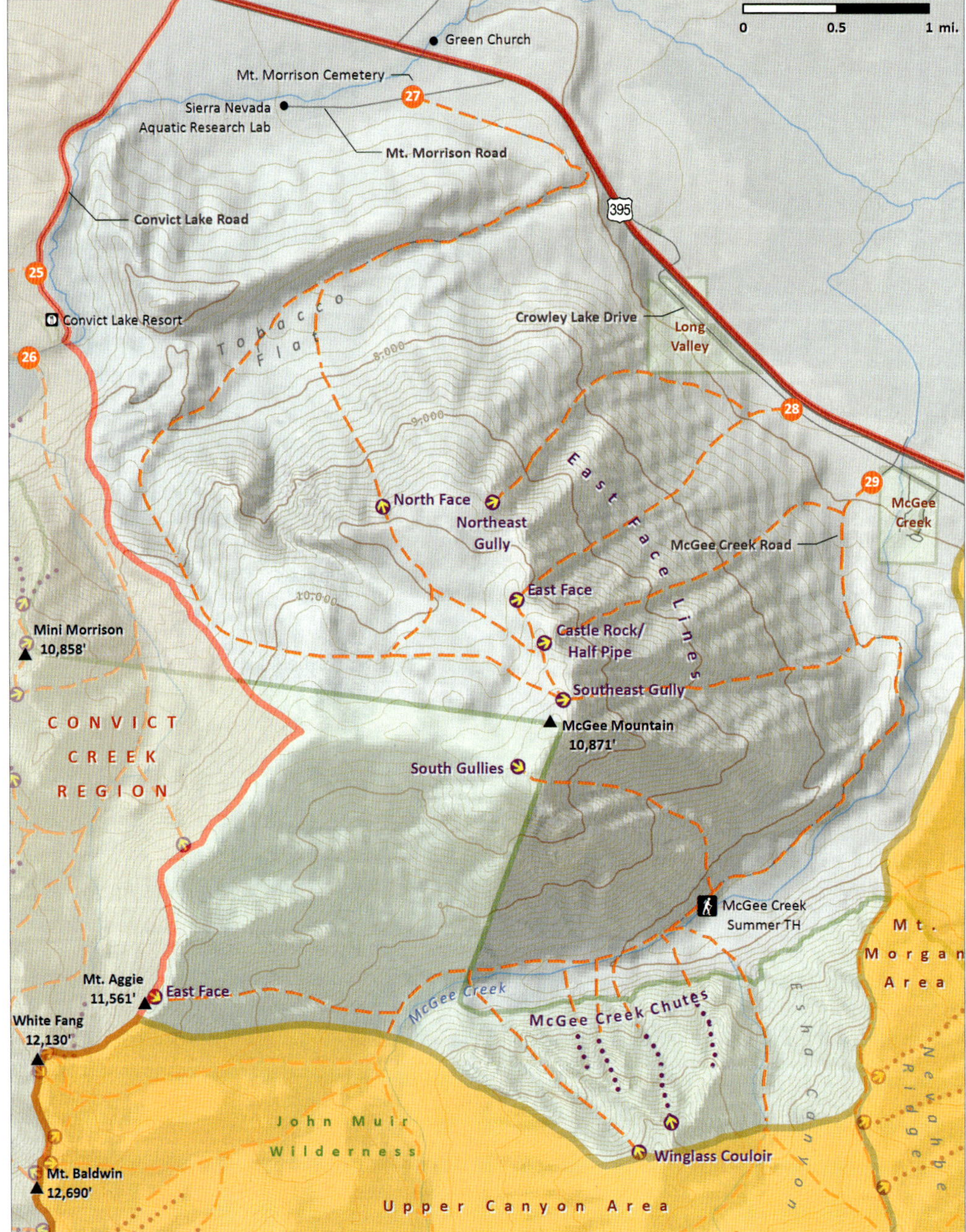

▣ Lower Canyon Area

The Lower Canyon Area comprises the terrain immediately surrounding McGee Mountain, as well as the lines in the lower mouth of the McGee Creek Drainage. For the most part, these lines can be easily accessed from the roads/trailheads that service them.

△ MCGEE MOUNTAIN *10,871'*

The first rope tow in the Eastern Sierra was on the lower east slopes of McGee Mountain. The only thing that remains today is a disheveled building, and a small monument on the south side of Crowley Lake Drive at the winter trailhead.

Though paid skiing is no longer an option on McGee, backcountry skiing, riding, and snowmobiling are still alive and well here. With its relatively large size, variety

Looking southwest across the valley at McGee Mountain.

of aspects and terrain, ease of access, and high visibility from Highway 395, McGee remains one of the favorites for many locals.

McGee Mountain is also one of the few mountains on the Eastside where snowmobiles are allowed, so be aware if you are looking for solitude, as you may not be alone.

↘ NORTH FACE

McGee Mountain

Aspect	Consequence/Exposure	Slope
	3	35°

Summit Elevation	10,000'
Descent Vertical	2,000'
Total Vertical	3,000'
Hiking Distance	3 ½ miles
Terrain	Chute
Trailhead	27. Mt. Morrison Cemetery
USGS Quad Maps	Convict Lake
GPS	38.064 / 37.583

The North Face of McGee Mountain is characterized by a series of small yet relatively steep and aesthetic chutes, a large sweeping gully, and a broad, open face with an old mining road carved through it. Its terrain is popular for snowmobile skiers or those coming from Tobacco Flat looking to turn a quick lap.

Approach: The most popular approach for the North Face is via Mt. Morrison Cemetery (Trailhead #27), though it is also possible to climb the East Face and descend the north.

From Trailhead #27, head south along the base of a moraine along the power-line road. Before the road drops downhill, climb up and over the moraine toward Mt. Morrison onto Tobacco Flat, which puts you in a small canyon below the North Face of McGee Mountain. Continue up this canyon, and choose from one of the following two options:

One option is to climb the line of your choice directly: the broad, open face at the eastern end of the North Face or the low-angle gully that splits this open face from the steeper chutes on the western edge of the North Face.

The other option is to follow a slightly longer but lower-angle approach around the northwest shoulder of McGee. For this approach, continue up the Tobacco Flat Drainage toward the East Face of Little Morrison. As you reach the western end of McGee's North Face, turn south, then continue up a broad gully/face back toward the east that eventually leads to the summit. At the top of this slope is a large plateau. Head north across this plateau to the top of the line of your choice.

Exit: After skiing the North Face, continue back to your car at Trailhead #27. Based on the snow coverage on the south side of the bench that separates Tobacco Flat from the trailhead, it may be possible to shortcut the long trek around its east end by going up and over, though this slope is covered with sagebrush and it can be a wallowing nightmare.

EAST FACE LINES

McGee Mountain

Aspect	Consequence/Exposure	Slope
	3	35°

Summit Elevation	10,500'
Descent Vertical	3,200'
Total Vertical	3,700'
Hiking Distance	2 miles
Terrain	Mixed
Trailhead	28. McGee Mountain Rope Tow
USGS Quad Maps	Convict Lake
GPS	37.569 / -118.81

There are myriad lines that drop several thousand feet from the summit of McGee Mountain all the way down to Crowley Lake Drive. These are the prominent gullies and faces that are clearly visible as you travel along Highway 395 and are very popular among local skiers because of the variety of terrain and aspect options that they offer.

Approach: The most popular approach for the East Face is via the McGee Mountain Rope Tow (Trailhead #28), though it is also possible to reach the top of McGee from Trailhead #27 via the approach described for the North Face.

The standard approach heads west from Trailhead #28 across the flats to the toe of McGee's East Face. From here, choose one of the gullies and climb it up to the summit ridge.

Beware that McGee sees quite a bit of wind and frequent large avalanches, so in days immediately following a storm, be cautious of avalanche hazard in this area. Slides are known to reach the flats and even the road itself.

Exit: Ski the line right back to your car.

SOUTH GULLIES

McGee Mountain

Aspect	Consequence/Exposure	Slope
	2	35°

Summit Elevation	10,800'
Descent Vertical	3,000'
Total Vertical	3,900'
Hiking Distance	4 miles
Terrain	Chute
Trailhead	29. McGee Creek Road
USGS Quad Maps	Convict Lake
GPS	37.564 / -118.814

The south gullies on McGee Mountain are rarely skied, partially due to their aspect and exposure, and partially due to obscurity. Regardless, some great terrain exists in the two major gullies that descend from the true summit of McGee Mountain down the south face into McGee Creek.

Approach: From the winter closure on McGee Creek Road (Trailhead #29), continue around the southeast shoulder of McGee Mountain. Just after entering the mouth of McGee Creek, the first of the South Gullies will appear on your right. The second gully lies up-canyon beyond the pack station and summertime trailhead. Choose your line and climb to the summit.

It is also possible to reach these lines from the summit of McGee Mountain via the approaches described for the North or East Face earlier in this section.

Exit: Ski the line right back to your car.

△ MCGEE CREEK PEAK *11,000'*

Flanking the southern side of the McGee Creek canyon is a rather innocuous peak that is riddled with north-facing chutes and technical, steep terrain. Though many people ski directly below this terrain while heading toward objectives deeper in McGee Creek and never even notice it, these lines are worthy missions in and of themselves. It is also possible and relatively common to link one of these lines with a tour up Esha Canyon/Peak for a little extra vertical or a nice alternative to skiing the lower mellow portions of Esha Canyon at the end of your day.

General Approach: The most common approach to the McGee Creek Peak is via the winter closure on McGee Creek Road (Trailhead #29). From here, continue up

Looking south at McGee Creek Peak.

into the McGee Creek Drainage. After you pass the mouth of the Esha Canyon Drainage, a series of chutes will appear on your left.

↘ MCGEE CREEK CHUTES

McGee Creek Peak

Aspect	Consequence/Exposure	Slope
	3	40°

Summit Elevation	11,000'
Descent Vertical	3,000'
Total Vertical	4,000'
Hiking Distance	4 miles
Terrain	Chute
Trailhead	29. McGee Creek Road
USGS Quad Maps	Convict Lake
GPS	37.539 / -118.801

Along the unassuming peak flanking the south wall of McGee Canyon are a series of chutes and complex terrain features comprised of open faces filled with rocks, ramps, and small trees that drop up to 2,000' down to the canyon bottom. There are a couple of aesthetic lines along this face, the most obvious of which is the first one you come to, just beyond the mouth of Esha Canyon.

Approach: Follow the general approach referenced at left for the McGee Creek Chutes. Near the mouth of Esha Canyon find a suitable location to cross to the south side of the creek and begin climbing the chute of your choice. It is also possible to reach the top of most of this terrain from the back side via Esha Canyon. This approach is most commonly used by people who ski one of Esha Peak's North Face Chutes.

Exit: After skiing your line, continue down canyon and back to your car.

↘ WINEGLASS COULOIR

McGee Creek Peak

Aspect	Consequence/Exposure	Slope
	3	32°

Summit Elevation	11,300'
Descent Vertical	3,000'
Total Vertical	4,300'
Hiking Distance	5 miles
Terrain	Chute
Trailhead	29. McGee Creek Road
USGS Quad Maps	Convict Lake
GPS	37.534 / -118.804

Looking east at the Wineglass Couloir from across McGee Creek canyon.

Brian Robinette skiing the Wineglass.

The Wineglass Couloir is one of the more popular and aesthetic lines along the northern face hosting the McGee Creek Chutes. Though not as steep as it looks from afar, it also doesn't offer many escape options should you trigger a slide, so extra care should be taken when attempting this route. Due to its westerly aspect, conditions can vary greatly from storm to storm, and at the different elevations of the line. Throughout the winter, the Wineglass doesn't receive any sunlight. In the spring, it is shaded in the morning and gets sunlight late in the day.

Approach: The most common approach to the Wineglass is via the McGee Creek Road trailhead (#29). From the point of winter closure, follow the McGee Creek Road to the summer trailhead. Continue west up toward the crook of McGee Creek Canyon, following the river approximately a mile to the site of an old campground.

Cross to the south side of the creek as carefully as you can and begin climbing the southeast side of the canyon. Above you will be a narrow spine of rock, which forms the north wall of the Wineglass Couloir. The start of the chute isn't visible until you are just below it, but as you round its corner the narrow confines will come into sight. Climb the "stem" of the Wineglass to a bench and the large bowl above. Because of its aspect, the upper bowl doesn't hold snow all of the time. The west side is the best bet for coverage.

It is also possible to reach the top of the Wineglass Couloir from the back side via Esha Canyon. This approach is most commonly used by people who ski one of Esha Peak's North Face Chutes.

Exit: After skiing the line, continue down-canyon and back to your car.

△ MT. AGGIE *11,561'*

An often overlooked gem, Mt. Aggie sits on the ridge between McGee Mountain and White Fang. This peak divides the Convict Creek Region from the McGee Creek Region. Several east-facing gullies offer fun terrain and are deceptively long, dropping over 3,000' into McGee Creek Canyon. The views from the summit of Mt. Aggie are stellar, offering a perspective into the Mt. Morrison Area, Upper McGee Canyon, and across the Owens Valley.

↘ EAST FACE

Mt. Aggie

Aspect	Consequence/Exposure	Slope
	2	35°

Summit Elevation	11,561'
Descent Vertical	3,000'
Total Vertical	4,500'
Hiking Distance	5.25 miles
Terrain	Gullies
Trailhead	29. McGee Creek Road
USGS Quad Maps	Convict Lake
GPS	37.546 / -118.842

Mt. Aggie's East Face is characterized by a series of shallow gullies and broad ridges that descend from its summit into the heart of the McGee Creek Drainage. These offer some great options for those looking for moderate terrain.

Approach: From the winter closure on McGee Creek Road (Trailhead #29), head into the canyon to where it turns south, following the rough alignment of the summer trail over several small benches on the north side of the canyon. As the canyon turns south, begin to head west, ultimately climbing the west wall of the canyon, which forms the East Face of Mt. Aggie. A relatively wide chute/bowl leads to the summit and can typically be skinned up directly.

Kevin Smith skins along the Esha Peak ridgeline with the Lower McGee Canyon area in the background.

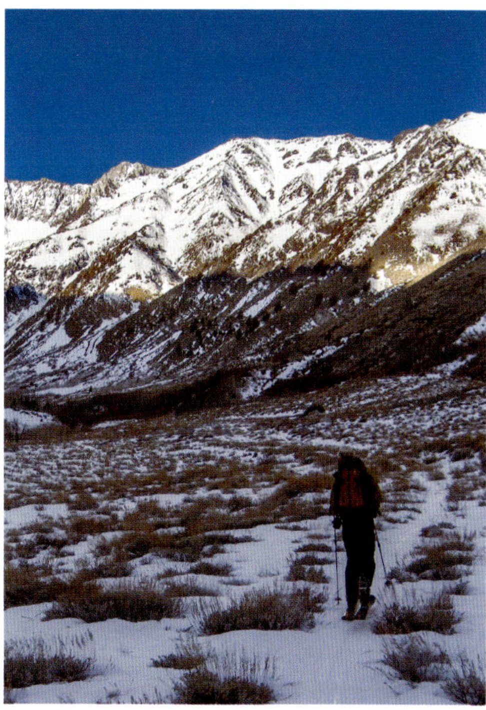

Ali Feinberg skins into McGee Creek with Mt. Baldwin and Mt. Aggie in the background.

Exit: Follow your tracks back to your car.

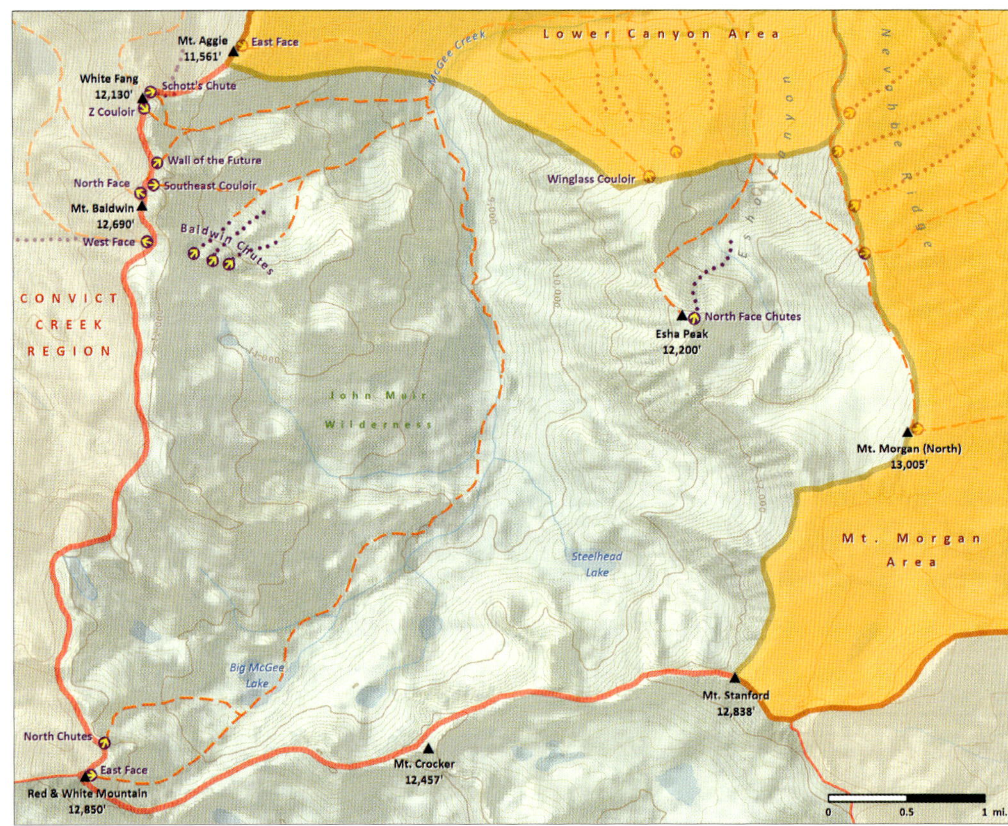

Upper Canyon Area

The Upper Canyon Area of McGee Creek comprises the terrain that lies beyond the crook of the drainage, where the canyon changes direction and heads south.

General Approach: The next several lines are all accessed from the wintertime closure on McGee Creek Road (Trailhead #29) (or the summertime trailhead in the spring). From here, continue west up to the crook of McGee Creek Canyon, following the rough alignment of the summer trail. Along the way you will travel over several small benches on the north side of the canyon. As you reach the point where the canyon turns south, the approaches break off, and each is described more specifically in its individual section below.

△ WHITE FANG *12,130'*

White Fang is the large, prominent peak that lies just to the south of Mt. Morrison. It is comprised of an impressive, steep tower on its northern end, with a broad and equally steep face to the south. In summer, or without snow, the peak is predominantly white in color (a result of a combination of a unique, rare mixture of limestone and marble, which is notoriously loose), hence its name.

In the winter, two exciting and demanding lines grace the northern and southern sides of White Fang's formidable east face: Schott's Chute and Z Couloir (also referred to as Lightning Bolt or Sneaker Line). Schott's Chute is covered in the Convict Creek chapter, page 188.

↘ Z/LIGHTING BOLT COULOIR — White Fang

Aspect	Consequence/Exposure	Slope
	4	50°

Summit Elevation	12,000'
Descent Vertical	2,000'
Total Vertical	5,000'
Hiking Distance	6 miles
Terrain	Chute
Trailhead	29. McGee Creek Road
USGS Quad Maps	Convict Lake
GPS	37.542 / -118.851

Dropping off the southern summit of White Fang is a prominent Z-shaped couloir that precariously cuts through steep terrain as it dodges large cliff bands on either side. Though exceptionally aesthetic, this line is

Sean Haverstock topping out on the ridge of White Fang after booting the Z Couloir. *Photo: Nate Greenberg.*

not skied very frequently, as it is not easily viewed from many locations and is rather serious in nature.

Approach: Follow the general approach mentioned above to where the canyon turns south, then continue west, ultimately climbing the west wall of the canyon, just to the south of the Mt. Aggie ridge.

Continue up this drainage into an impressive cirque at the base of the Lightning Bolt & Wall of the Future. At the back (west end) of this cirque is a small couloir that leads to the summit ridge just south of the Z/Lightning Bolt. Climb this couloir, then proceed north a short distance along the ridge to the entrance of the couloir.

Exit: Follow your tracks back to the car.

Looking northwest at White Fang from Esha Peak.

△ MT. BALDWIN *12,690'*

Mt. Baldwin is the striking and highly visible peak that looms over the lower reaches of McGee Creek Canyon as seen from Highway 395. There are lines on the northwest side of Mt. Baldwin that are covered in the Convict Creek Region, but Baldwin's east face is home to some high-quality couloirs, and some of the steepest and most committing terrain featured in this book.

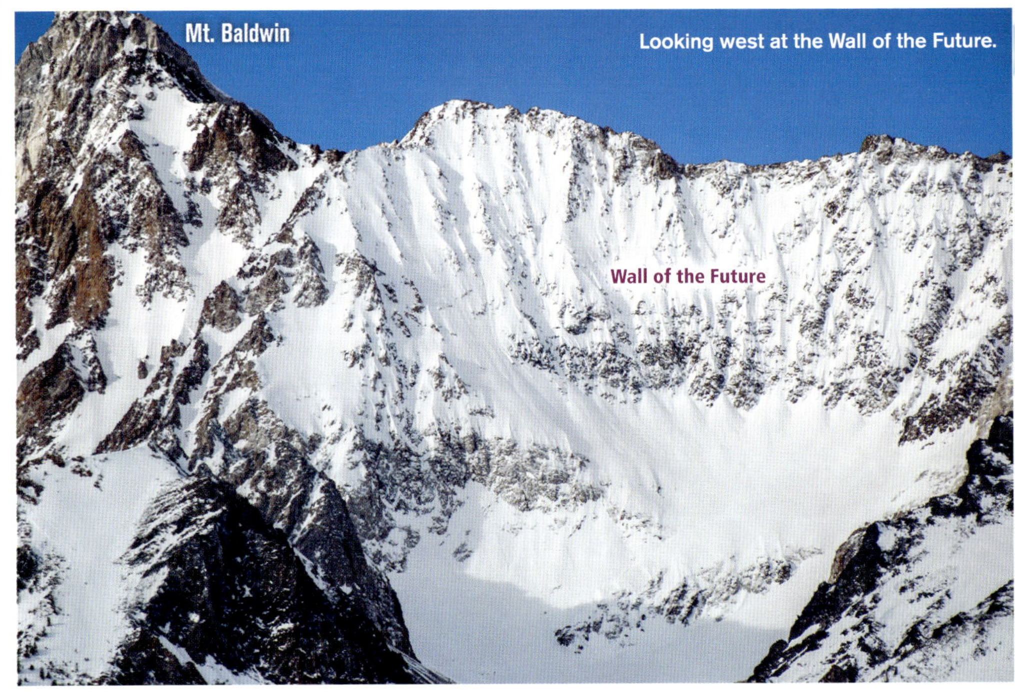

↘ WALL OF THE FUTURE

Mt. Baldwin

Aspect | Consequence/Exposure 5 | Slope 55°

Summit Elevation	12,000'
Descent Vertical	2,000'
Total Vertical	5,000'
Hiking Distance	6 miles
Terrain	Face
Trailhead	29. McGee Creek Road
USGS Quad Maps	Convict Lake
GPS	37.536 / -118.85

This was named by Mammoth local Matthew Schott, who along with "Powder Dan" Molnar pioneered a couple of visionary lines down its face in 2003. The face itself hosts a series of line options, all of which are exceptionally steep, exposed, and very committing, as the wall ends in a huge cliff band that you would be swept over if you were to fall.

Though technically part of Mt. Baldwin, the Wall of the Future is positioned in the cirque to the north of the other Baldwin lines mentioned, just south of the Z/ Lighting Bolt Couloir on White Fang.

Approach: It is possible to reach the Wall of the Future from the top of the Southeast Couloir of Mt. Baldwin (which is the safer approach), or by booting directly up it. To approach from the top, follow the general approach mentioned above to where the canyon turns south. From here, continue a short distance beyond Mt. Aggie and the approach for the Z/Lightning Bolt Couloir.

As you pass the drainage from Horsetail Falls, begin climbing the west side of McGee Canyon. The lower part of Horsetail Canyon has a section of very dense aspen trees that should be avoided. The best way to avoid this is to continue hiking a short distance past the creek and then climb through the forest just to its south. Continue up through the trees, then traverse back into the canyon to a bench just above an aspen grove. From here, continue climbing to the south and west, up a steep slope to the next bench, which is the entrance to the Baldwin Cirque.

Once in the cirque, the Southeast Couloir of Mt. Baldwin will be clearly in front of you on the cirque's northern side. This couloir provides direct and easy access to the summit ridge that divides Mt. Baldwin from White Fang, and ultimately the top of the Wall of the Future.

It is also possible to approach the Wall of the Future from below. To do so, follow the description provided for the Z/Lightning Bolt Couloir on White Fang.

Exit: Descend into the cirque that is formed by the Wall and White Fang, then travel down this canyon back into McGee Creek where you will pick up your skin track.

Brett Lotz skiing the upper portion of the Z Couloir. *Photo: Sean Haverstock.*

Jason Templeton and Ryan Copenhagen beneath the Baldwin Cirque.

SOUTHEAST COULOIR

Mt. Baldwin

Aspect | Consequence/Exposure: 3 | Slope: 38°

Summit Elevation	12,100'
Descent Vertical	2,000'
Total Vertical	5,000'
Hiking Distance	6 ¼ miles
Terrain	Chute
Trailhead	29. McGee Creek Road
USGS Quad Maps	Convict Lake
GPS	37.534 / -118.851

The Southeast Couloir of Mt. Baldwin is frequently overlooked, despite being clearly visible from afar. This aesthetic line drops from the summit of Mt. Baldwin 2,000' down a continuously pitched chute and is a gem of a line.

Approach: Refer to the approach for the Wall of the Future on previous pages to gain access to the Baldwin Cirque. Once in the cirque, the Southeast Couloir is the obvious line on the northern side which climbs to the ridgeline looker's right of the summit of Mt. Baldwin.

Exit: Retrace your steps back to the car.

BALDWIN CIRQUE

Mt. Baldwin

Aspect | Consequence/Exposure: 3 | Slope: 40°

Summit Elevation	11,600'
Descent Vertical	1,500'
Total Vertical	4,400'
Hiking Distance	6 ¼ miles
Terrain	Chutes and bowls
Trailhead	29. McGee Creek Road
USGS Quad Maps	Convict Lake
GPS	37.530 / -118.851

The Baldwin Cirque offers a series of north- and east -facing chutes, which are relatively protected from the wind due to the surrounding peaks and the rocky walls of each chute. While the lines in the center of the cirque hold the best snow, the southern ones (on the looker's left) fill in occasionally, depending on which way the wind has been blowing. The chutes below Mt. Baldwin's actual summit are also excellent options, though none of them go all the way to the top.

Approach: Follow the approach referenced previously for the Wall of the Future or the Southeast Couloir, which leads you into the Baldwin Cirque. Once in the cirque choose the line you are interested in and climb it to the top.

Jon Crowley skiing beneath Mt Baldwin.

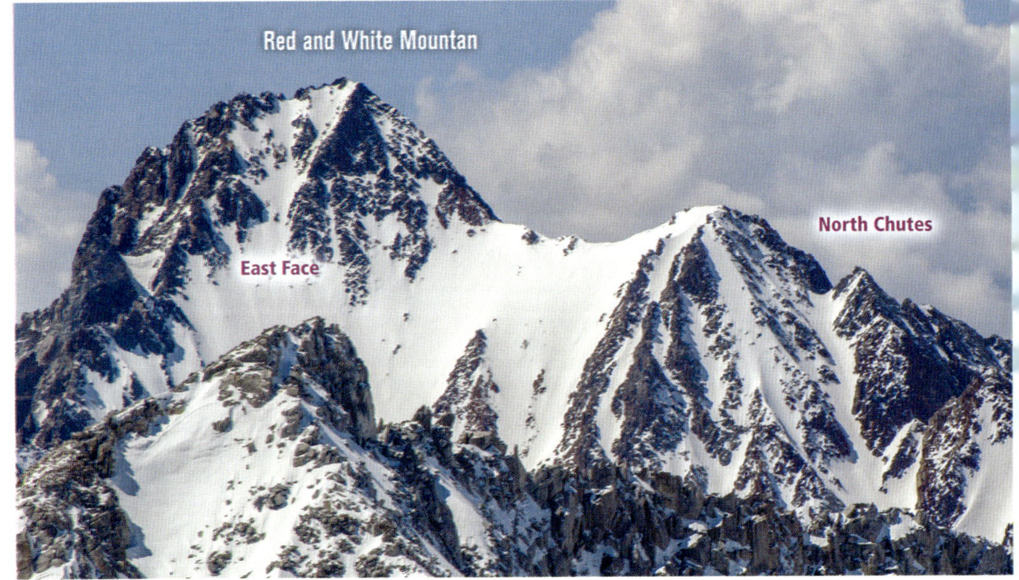

△ RED AND WHITE MOUNTAIN *12,850'*

Red and White Mountain lies deep within McGee Canyon and is guarded from view from Highway 395 by Mt. Morgan (North) and the Nevahbe Ridge. It is far from any roads, particularly during midwinter, and as a result doesn't see much traffic.

↘ NORTH CHUTES — *Red & White Mountain*

Aspect | Consequence/Exposure: 3 | Slope: 40°

Summit Elevation	12,300'
Descent Vertical	1,800'
Total Vertical	5,200'
Hiking Distance	8 ½ miles
Terrain	Chute
Trailhead	29. McGee Creek Road
USGS Quad Maps	Convict Lake, Mt. Abbot
GPS	37.483 / -118.855

These are the series of chutes that cut through the small northern sub-peak of Red and White Mountain. They offer several attractive options.

Approach: Follow the general approach mentioned above to where the canyon turns south, continuing past Mt. Aggie and Mt. Baldwin deeper into the canyon. At the head of the canyon lies Big McGee Lake, and as you arrive, the dark red sub-peak of Red and White will be in front of you, with the true summit just behind that.

From Big McGee Lake, continue to climb toward the peak, heading slightly north and to the right of the dark-red buttress in front of you. A short distance up this slope the North Chutes will come into view and you will have the opportunity to see which one looks best. Climb a chute to the top of the sub-peak.

If you are interested in gaining the actual summit, traverse the large northwest-facing bowl and then climb a short distance until the snow runs out. From here, an exposed 3rd Class scramble brings you to the summit of Red and White Mountain. To get back to the chutes, return to your skis and traverse all the way to top of the sub-peak, where a short walk along the ridge will bring you to your chosen descent.

Exit: Follow the approach back to the car.

↘ EAST FACE — *Red & White Mountain*

Aspect | Consequence/Exposure: 3 | Slope: 40°

Summit Elevation	12,850'
Descent Vertical	2,500'
Total Vertical	6,000'
Hiking Distance	9 ½ miles
Terrain	Face
Trailhead	29. McGee Creek Road
USGS Quad Maps	Convict Lake, Mt. Abbot
GPS	37.480 / -118.856

Looking southwest at Red and White Mountain.

The rocky and exposed East Face rises out of the small drainage to the south of the prominent dark-red subpeak of Red and White Mountain.

Approach: Follow the approach described above for the North Chutes to Big McGee Lake. From Big McGee Lake, continue southwest up the small drainage to the base of the large East Face. Follow this to the top. The last little bit to the summit is very exposed to the wind and may not be filled in with snow.

Exit: Follow the approach back to the car.

Δ ESHA PEAK *12,200'*

Esha Peak is recognizable by its large North Face, which looms above McGee Creek, and is clearly visible while traveling south on Highway 395 through the Crowley Lake Area. From a distance, the chutes that cut through this face resemble the Wahoo Gullies (in the Bishop Creek Region)—five distinct chutes that drop roughly 2,000' continuously into the canyon below. Though it's seemingly close to the road, accessing Esha can be a bit of a trek. It is nestled deep in the hanging valley behind the Nevahbe Ridge, and the approach climbs past a series of benches before ultimately reaching the base.

Chris Gallardo on Esha Peak.

Looking south up Esha Canyon.

Esha Peak

North Face Chutes

↘ NORTH FACE CHUTES

Esha Peak

Aspect	Consequence/Exposure	Slope
	3	40°

Summit Elevation	12,200'
Descent Vertical	1,700'
Total Vertical	5,200'
Hiking Distance	2 ½ miles
Terrain	Chute
Trailhead	29. McGee Creek Road
USGS Quad Maps	Convict Lake
GPS	37.515 / -118.801

Approach: From the wintertime closure on McGee Creek Road (Trailhead #29), follow the road into the canyon until you reach the summer trailhead. The entrance to Esha Canyon is directly south of this point, across the creek. There is no ideal way to cross the river, but there are a handful of narrow sections and a few fallen trees that should allow safe passage. The best way will depend on the creek level and depth of snow.

Once across the river, climb the gentle slope into the mouth of Esha Canyon. As you enter the canyon, a short, narrow section gives passage to the wider slopes above. Follow the canyon past a number of benches to the base of the North Face.

At the base of the North Face, choose your line and climb it directly, or gain the ridge to the west of the true summit of Esha by skinning up an open face then booting the ridge.

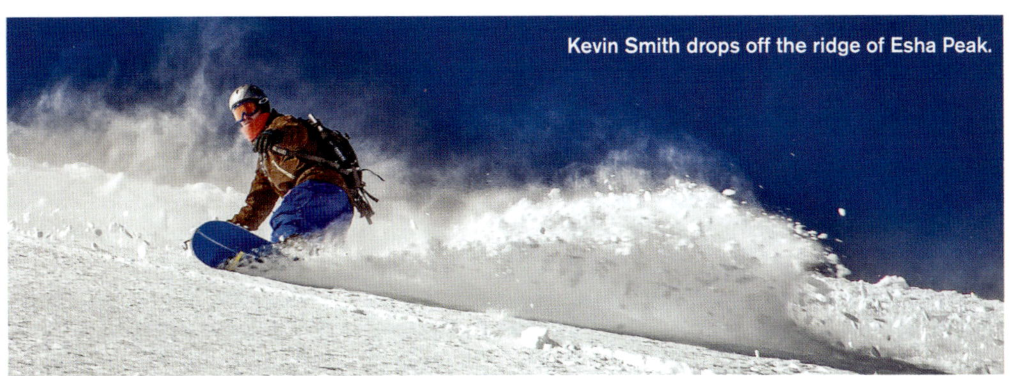

Kevin Smith drops off the ridge of Esha Peak.

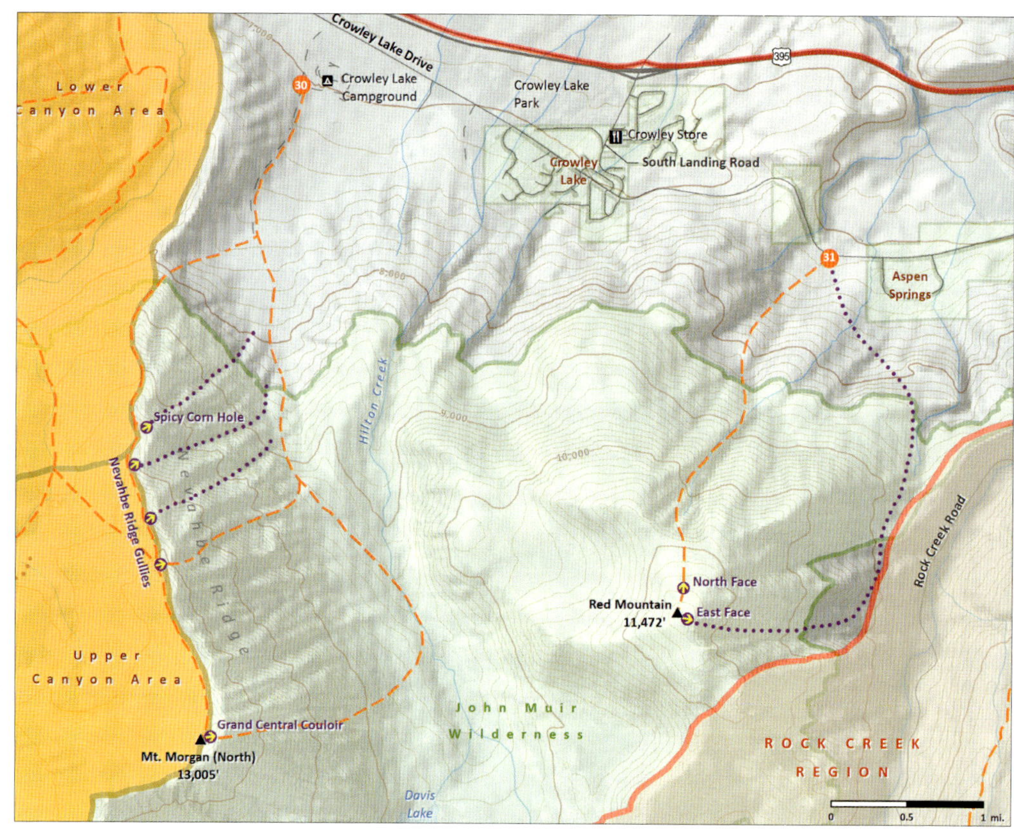

Mt. Morgan Area

The Mt. Morgan Area lies just outside and slightly to the south of McGee Creek itself and borders the northeastern edge of the Rock Creek Region. This is an often-overlooked wrinkle of an area, but hosts a good amount of terrain to choose from.

△ NEVAHBE RIDGE *12,000'*

Towering above the community of Crowley Lake, the massive Nevahbe Ridge dominates the skyline as it spans the distance between McGee Creek and the summit of Mt. Morgan (North) nearly four miles away. Along this ridge are countless chutes and bowls, with a variety of terrain and aspect options.

Spicy Corn Hole is a more obscure line that was likely first skied by Mammoth locals Martin Kuhn, Frank Fazzino, and Brett Lotz in the early 2000s. The line roughly descends the rocky ridge that separates the first and second northernmost prominent gullies on Nevahbe.

↘ SPICY CORN HOLE — Nevahbe Ridge

Aspect | Consequence/Exposure: 3 | Slope: 40°

Summit Elevation	10,500'
Descent Vertical	2,500'
Total Vertical	3,500'
Hiking Distance	2 ½ miles
Terrain	Chute
Trailhead	30. Crowley Lake Campground
USGS Quad Maps	Convict Lake
GPS	37.54 / -118.786

Approach: The line is best accessed from the ridgeline of Nevahbe, though it is also possible to boot it directly from below. The most common approach leaves from the Crowley Lake Campground (Trailhead #30) and travels southwest up a gentle slope toward the northern toe of the ridge. As you approach the toe, begin climbing toward the west, up a slope that leads into a northeast-facing chute that provides access to the ridgeline above. Once atop the ridgeline, continue south past the top of the first prominent gully at the north end of Nevahbe.

Looking northwest at the Nevahbe Ridge from Red Mountain

After crossing over the peaklet that forms the top of the ridge that separates the first and second gullies, find a drop-in point on the skier's-left wall. Drop into the gully as though you are going to ski its main gut, heading more south than straight down. After passing the first island of rock, trend back toward the skier's left toward the left-hand ridgeline of the main gully.

From here, a series of entry points exist that drop into a prominent chute that cuts through the rock band dividing the first and second gullies and drops into the valley below.

It is also possible to reach the top of the Nevahbe Ridge and the drop-in point mentioned via Esha Canyon.

Exit: Travel down-valley back to the car.

↘ NEVAHBE RIDGE GULLIES

Nevahbe Ridge

Aspect	Consequence/Exposure	Slope
	3	35°

Summit Elevation	12,000'
Descent Vertical	3,500'
Total Vertical	5,000'
Hiking Distance	3 ½ miles
Terrain	Chute
Trailhead	30. Crowley Lake Campground
USGS Quad Maps	Convict Lake
GPS	37.527 / -118.784

Aside from the Spicy Corn Hole line mentioned above, there are countless other northeast-facing gullies and chutes that slice through the Nevahbe Ridge as they drop several thousand feet to the valley below. Choose your own adventure.

Approach: The Nevahbe Ridge is most commonly approached from the Crowley Lake Campground (Trailhead #30). From here, travel southwest up a gentle slope that leads into the Hilton Creek Drainage that flanks the eastern toe of the Nevahbe Ridge. As you travel up this drainage, find your line of choice, then skin and boot to the top.

It is also possible to reach the top of the Nevahbe Ridge and the drop-in point mentioned via Esha Canyon.

Exit: Travel down-valley back to the car.

△ MT. MORGAN (NORTH) *13,005'*

At the southern end of the massive Nevahbe Ridge is the rather unassuming Mt. Morgan (North). With a summit over 13,000 feet, this peak offers views into Rock Creek, as well as a giant skiable line on its east face.

Brain Outhwaite above the clouds on Red Mountain.

Amber Fazzino drops into the 3,500' Grand Central Couloir. *Photo: Nate Greenberg.*

↘ GRAND CENTRAL COULOIR

Mt. Morgan North

Aspect	Consequence/Exposure	Slope
	3	35°

Summit Elevation	13,005'
Descent Vertical	3,500'
Total Vertical	6,000'
Hiking Distance	5 ½ miles
Terrain	Chute
Trailhead	30. Crowley Lake Campground
USGS Quad Maps	Convict Lake
GPS	37.512 / -118.779

This is an often-overlooked though exceptional classic descent on the Eastside. As it drops 3,500' from the true summit to Davis Lake below, it offers a consistent moderate pitch. Due to its aspect and elevation, this is a classic spring ski that can hold some spectacular corn snow.

Approach: From the Crowley Lake Campground (Trailhead #30), travel southwest up a gentle slope that leads into the Hilton Creek Drainage. Continue south beneath the massive east face of Nevahbe Ridge toward the head of the canyon at Davis Lake. Before reaching the lake, begin to head west, climbing atop a small bench. From this point, the couloir should be clearly visible and you can head straight up it to the summit.

It is also possible to reach the summit of Mt. Morgan (North) from other gullies on the Nevahbe or via Esha Canyon. Beware, however, that Morgan North is notorious for having a deceptively long ridgeline with many false summits. Depending on where you arrive along the ridge, be prepared for a long and potentially frustrating walk to the summit. The ridge is mostly 2nd and 3rd Class talus, and it is best to stay just below the ridge on its west side. Be aware that if you top out on the ridge farther to the north, you may encounter some 4th Class climbing. The 4th Class is short, and centered on the false summit that is visible from Highway 395—it can generally be avoided by dropping down the west side and climbing along the talus.

Exit: Travel down-valley back to the car.

Δ RED MOUNTAIN *11,472'*

Perched above the small community of Aspen Springs, Red Mountain has a large variety of terrain that is fairly easy to access and is a popular local attraction for those in this portion of the county. Flanking the west mouth of Rock Creek Canyon and sitting just off Highway 395, this peak has excellent views of Mt. Morgan (North), the Nevahbe Ridge, and the Hilton Creek Drainage. Red Mountain has a tendency to melt out fairly early in the season and is therefore more of a midwinter or early spring destination.

Looking south at the North Face of Red Mountain from Aspen Springs.

↘ NORTH FACE

Red Mountain

Aspect | Consequence/Exposure: 2 | Slope: 35°

Summit Elevation	11,472'
Descent Vertical	4,000'
Total Vertical	4,400'
Hiking Distance	2 ½ miles
Terrain	Trees
Trailhead	31. Aspen Springs
USGS Quad Maps	Tom's Place
GPS	37.532 / -118.736

The North Face of Red Mountain hosts a handful of small gullies and moderately pitched treed slopes that are all clearly visible from Highway 395 and Crowley Lake Drive.

Approach: From the Aspen Springs staging area (Trailhead #31), head southwest up the obvious gully to its top. It is common to ski from this point, or you can continue a short distance to the summit and ski from there.

Exit: Ski right back to your car.

↘ EAST FACE

Red Mountain

Aspect | Consequence/Exposure: 2 | Slope: 35°

Summit Elevation	11,472'
Descent Vertical	2,000'
Total Vertical	4,400'
Hiking Distance	2 ½ miles
Terrain	Trees
Trailhead	31. Aspen Springs
USGS Quad Maps	Tom's Place
GPS	37.528 / -118.73

The East Face of Red Mountain drops into the lower reaches of Rock Creek Canyon proper and offers skiing in treed bowls. It is a less frequently skied line, as it is not as clearly visible and far less obvious than the North Face.

Approach: From the Aspen Springs staging area (Trailhead #31), head southwest up the obvious gully to the summit of Red Mountain. Once on top of the peak, contour to the east and gain a small bench that leads you to the true summit of Red Mountain.

Exit: Drop off the east side of Red Mountain into Rock Creek Canyon, though be sure not to go too far. Instead, when you reach a small bench near the toe of the East Face, begin to head left and contour back north/east. The bench ultimately leads you back to the lower reaches of the North Face, which you can follow back to your car.

9 Rock Creek

Springtime in Rock Creek Canyon.

9. Rock Creek

ROCK CREEK REGION:

- Outer Canyon Area:
  - △ MT. HUNTINGTON
  - △ POINTLESS PEAK
  - △ WHEELER CREST
- Inner Canyon Area:
  - △ MT. STARR
  - △ MT. ABBOT
  - △ TREASURE PEAK
  - △ MT. DADE
  - △ PIPSQUEAK SPIRE
  - △ MT. GABB
  - △ MT. MORGAN

Region Trailheads

32. Rock Creek Sno-Park
33. Hilton Lakes Trailhead
34. Sky Meadows Road
35. Ainslee Spring

Rock Creek Canyon is one of the most spectacular regions in this book. From Highway 395, Rock Creek Road rises over 3,000' to the summer trailhead at Mosquito Flat. Along the way the canyon is lined with jagged ridges and filled with dozens of alpine lakes and streams. During the summer months, this area is heavily visited by hikers, campers, fishermen, and climbers. But winter in the canyon is comparatively quiet, offering some incredible solace for intrepid backcountry enthusiasts looking for winter adventure.

Much of the skiing here is characterized by classic Sierra Nevada alpine terrain, consisting of a mix of endless open bowls interspersed with steep, rock-lined chutes. Because of the rugged nature of the terrain, many of the peaks in Rock Creek are not skiable from their actual summit, and in some cases just climbing to the summit may require a rope.

During the winter months, Rock Creek Road is only plowed to the Sno-Park located at East Fork Campground. Though this trailhead is six miles up the canyon from Highway 395, it is still roughly five miles shy of the summertime trailhead at Mosquito Flat. Rock Creek Lodge grooms the road from the Sno-Park to Mosquito Flat as part of their winter operation, making the long approach more manageable.

As spring hits and the snow turns to corn, approaches become easier and the backcountry traffic increases a bit. In the late spring, the plow crews begin removing the snow from the road, and ultimately allow you to drive an additional three miles to the Hilton Creek trailhead. While the timing of this varies from year to year (and depends greatly on the snowpack), you can generally expect it to be plowed for the fishing opener at the end of April.

Beyond the summer trailhead at Mosquito Flat the canyon levels out dramatically until you reach the base of the peaks at the head of the canyon. This area, known as Little Lakes Valley, is comprised of dozens of lakes and an intricate network of streams. These pose a serious threat in both the early and late season, as there is often not much snow and the ice on the lakes may not support your weight. When the lakes are melted out, it can become a bit more difficult to get into and out of the upper reaches of the canyon, and by late spring, be prepared for a number of detours that can add time to your trip. Often it is easier to follow the summer trail alignment and simply carry your skis for the first mile or two, rather than deal with the countless stops and dangers.

A note about water hazards: It is best to give lake shores a wide berth and move quickly and carefully through the inlets and outlets of these water bodies. In the springtime, you may be able to comfortably ski across the ice in the early morning, and find yourself breaking through on your way out hours later. If any blue ice is showing on lakes or other water features, it is best to avoid crossing at that location. When in doubt—avoid the area and go around.

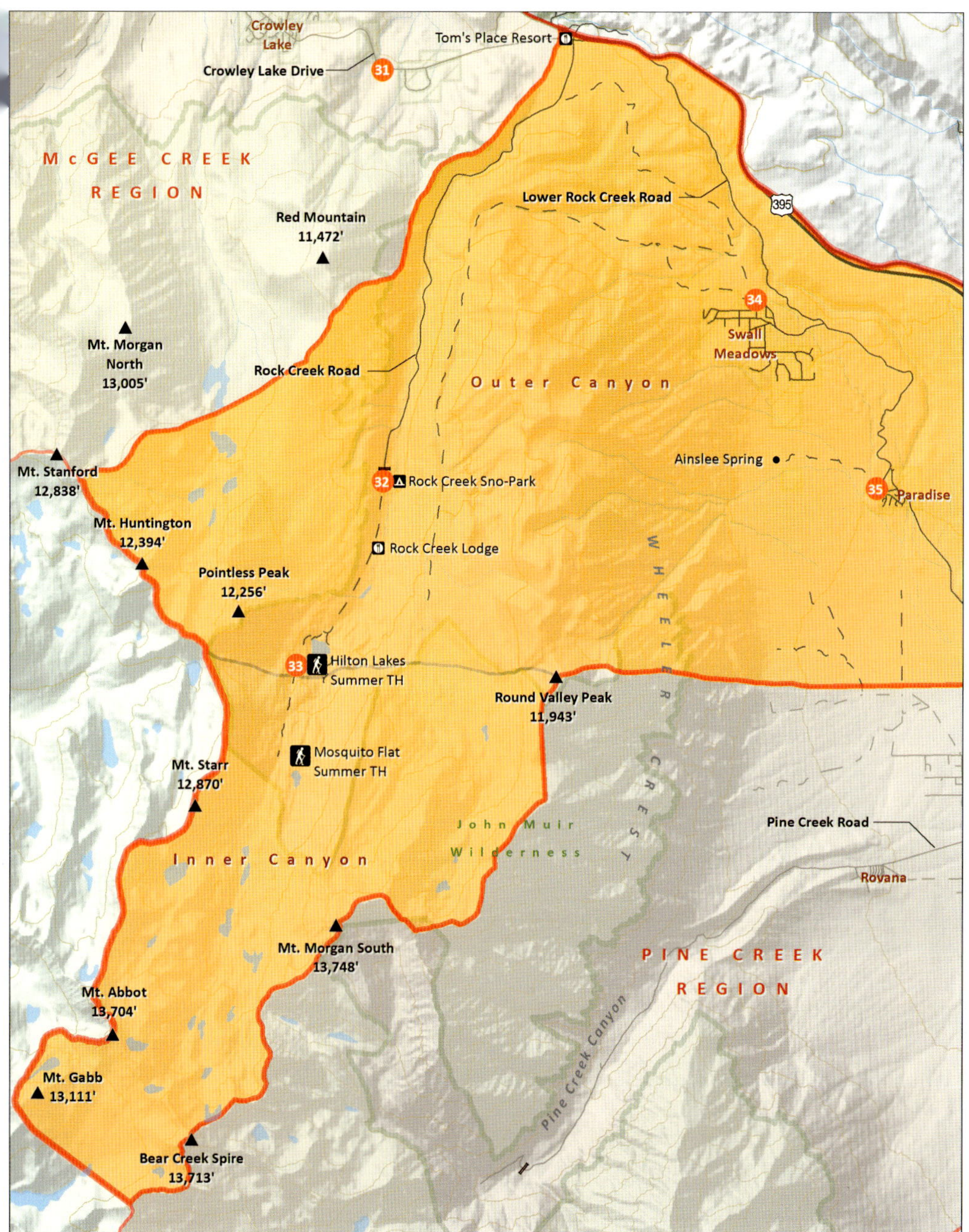

Getting There & Getting Going

The terrain covered in this chapter is concentrated in and around Rock Creek Canyon, which is located about 20 minutes south of Mammoth along Highway 395. There is also some terrain referenced in this chapter on the northern end of the Wheeler Crest, which forms the eastern wall of Rock Creek Canyon and is the massive, rocky ridge that looms over the Sherwin Grade.

32. Rock Creek Sno-Park (Year-Round) 9,300′

From the Town of Mammoth Lakes, head south on Highway 395 for 15 miles to Tom's Place. Turn right (south) onto Rock Creek Road and follow it for six miles to the point of winter closure. This is the sole California Sno-Park in the Eastern Sierra, and requires a fee of $5 per day, which is self-issued at the trailhead. Season permits can be also be purchased at Tom's Place Resort before coming up the hill.

From the trailhead at East Fork, the remaining five miles of the road are groomed for cross-country skiing by the Rock Creek Resort. Currently there is no fee for using the groomed trails. Rock Creek Resort holds a special-use permit to operate during the winter months and because of this, private snowmobiles are not allowed on the road.

Note that during periods of heavy snowfall, plowing the Rock Creek Road is not a priority and it can remain unplowed for quite some time. If you are planning a multi-day trip into the backcountry, pay close attention to the weather as your car may be inaccessible at the end of your journey.

33. Hilton Lakes Summer Trailhead (Spring) 9,900′

As spring hits the Sierra, Mono County begins to plow the mountain roads, providing access to the high country. This work typically begins in mid-April in order to meet the demands of the fishing opener. As this happens, it becomes possible to drive a short distance farther up Rock Creek Canyon to the vicinity of the summertime trailhead for Hilton Lakes and the Rock Creek Pack Station—roughly three miles farther up-canyon from Trailhead #32 at the Rock Creek Sno-Park.

34. Sky Meadows Road (Year-Round) 6,500′

This trailhead leaves Sky Meadows Road at the northern end of the community of Swall Meadows. Swall Meadows is located about 20 minutes south of Mammoth and 10 minutes south of Tom's Place off Lower Rock Creek Road.

From Tom's Place, continue south on Highway 395 for approximately 1 mile, then take the next right-hand (west) exit off the highway onto Lower Rock Creek Road. Follow the winding road down along the creek for 4¼ miles, then turn right onto Swall Meadows Road. Follow this for approximately ¾ mile westward. Just before you enter the community, veer right at the fork onto Sky Meadows Road. After about ½ mile Sky Meadows Road reaches an intersection with Valley View Drive, where you should be able to find some off-street parking on the north side of the road.

35. Ainslee Spring (Year-Round) 5,100′

Located at the base of the Wheeler Crest, just west of the community of Paradise, this trailhead is located at the point of winter closure along the summertime road to Ainslee Spring. Paradise is a small community located about 30 minutes south of Mammoth (and 30 minutes north of Bishop), along Lower Rock Creek Road.

From Tom's Place, continue south on Highway 395 for approximately 1 mile, then take the next right-hand (west) exit off the highway onto Lower Rock Creek Road. Follow Lower Rock Creek Road for approximately 7½ miles downhill. You will pass the turnoff for the community of Swall Meadows after about 4¼ miles, then begin a steep descent toward the community of Paradise. As you come into the upper end of the community, you will pass a fire station, and the upper end of Westridge Road. Continue along Lower Rock Creek Road for another ¼ mile or so, and look for a small right-hand turn (west) onto a dirt road with a large circular loop/parking area. If you reach the lower end of Westridge Road, you have gone too far.

It is also possible to reach the Ainslee Spring Road from the south. From downtown Bishop, follow Highway 395 north for approximately 12 miles. A short distance after the highway takes a rightward bend and begins heading up the Sherwin Grade, take a left turn onto Gorge Road. This is the first left-hand (west) turn you can make off Highway 395 after passing Pine Creek Road. Follow Gorge Road a short distance west to the T-intersection with Lower Rock Creek Road. Turn right and head north for approximately three miles. As you enter the small community of Paradise, the road will snake around a steep rock outcrop, then climb uphill. After passing the lower end of Westridge Road, keep your eyes peeled for a left-hand turn (west) onto a dirt road with a large circular loop/parking area. If you reach the upper end of Westridge Road, you have gone too far.

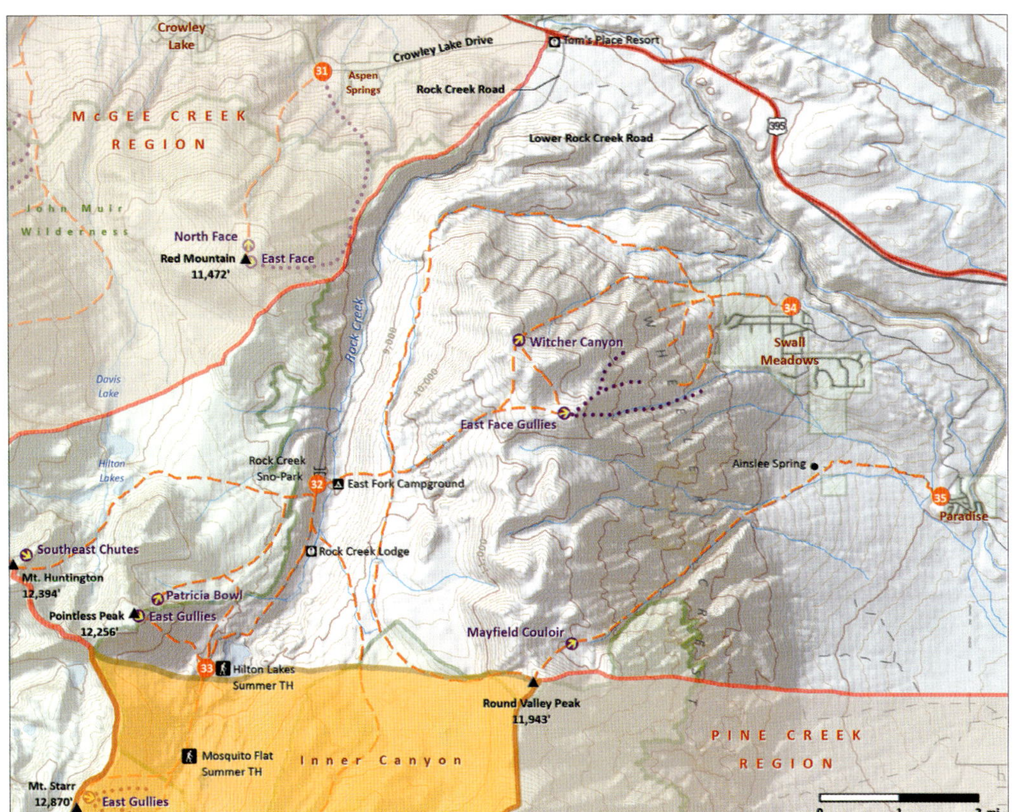

Eats, Digs, Services, & Supplies

At the intersection of Highway 395 and Rock Creek Road is Tom's Place Resort. Tom's Place offers a year-round store, restaurant, and lodging, and is a great place to stop after your tour for a burger and a beer.

Rock Creek Lodge (one mile up the road from the Rock Creek Sno-Park) is a full-service operation during both summer and winter, and grooms the entirety of Rock Creek Road from East Fork Campground all the way to Mosquito Flat trailhead. This makes travel along the road quite easy and popular among cross-country skiers. Winter accommodations at the lodge are comfortable and moderately priced. If you are looking for a weekend getaway, or just a night of dining after a full day of skiing, give them a call at (877) 935-4170 or visit www.rockcreeklodge.com.

▣ Outer Canyon Area

The Outer Canyon Area comprises the terrain that is more easily accessible from the Rock Creek Sno-Park, or the descents along the Wheeler Crest. These are all significantly easier to access compared to the peaks and terrain described in the Inner Canyon. Also, the character of this terrain is less alpine than that of the Inner Canyon, though it still offers some amazing views, opportunities for solitude, and of course, great skiing. Most of the descents listed in this section are best suited for midwinter, as they tend to melt out relatively early in the spring.

△ MT. HUNTINGTON *12,394'*

Tucked away in a seemingly obscure drainage, Mt. Huntington sees very little traffic compared to the more visible peaks in the area. Though a little farther off the beaten path, this peak offers some great skiing, with excellent views into the Third and Fourth Recesses and Pioneer Basin.

In addition to the terrain on Mt. Huntington itself, there are a number of chutes and bowls along the ridge to the north and south of the peak. These bowls continue on to neighboring Mt. Stanford and Mt. Morgan (North). While these chutes do not offer much vertical, they are plentiful, making this area an excellent spot for a weekend basecamp.

Jason Templeton beneath Mt Huntington.

SOUTHEAST CHUTES

Mt. Huntington

Aspect	Consequence/Exposure	Slope
	2	35°

Summit Elevation	12,394'
Descent Vertical	1,400'
Total Vertical	3,000'
Hiking Distance	3 ½ miles
Terrain	Chutes
Trailhead	32. Rock Creek Sno-Park
USGS Quad Maps	Mt. Morgan, Mt. Abbot
GPS	37.471 / -118.775

Along either side of Mt. Huntington's northeast-trending ridgeline are a series of chutes that drop either back into the upper Hilton Lakes Basin, or off the north side toward the Huntington/Stanford Basin.

Approach: From the Rock Creek Sno-Park (Trailhead #32), skin up the groomed Rock Creek Road for just a few hundred feet to where the road crosses to the west side of the creek. Just beyond this point, leave the road and head west, climbing a treed east-facing slope to a large bench above the road. The majority of this slope gets a lot of sun and has a tendency to melt out fairly early in the spring, but there are a number of sheltered gullies and riverbeds along this slope that are protected from the sun and wind.

Looking west across Rock Creek Canyon from the Wheeler Crest.

Once atop the bench, continue west for approximately 1½ miles toward the Hilton Lakes. As you near the lakes, the terrain will begin to drop down to the northeast to the lowest of the lakes. Instead of dropping down, traverse around the rocky slope in front of you, staying on the southeast side of the lakes and as high as possible, which will bring you to the upper lakes. Following the drainages of each lake, climb into the canyon that is just to the east of Mt. Huntington. Mt. Huntington's southeast face will be on your right, with numerous chutes and cliffs cut through it. Continue below this face to the head of the canyon, where you will find a handful of east- and northeast-facing chutes that lead to the summit.

Exit: Retrace your steps, making sure not to drop down into the lower portion of the Hilton Lakes basin.

△ POINTLESS PEAK *12,256'*

Pointless Peak flanks the northwestern side of the canyon directly above Rock Creek Lake. While the peak itself is not terribly impressive, there are a handful of descents down both its east face and in the Patricia Bowl vicinity that offer some great short-day ski-touring options.

Looking southwest across Rock Creek Canyon from the Wheeler Crest.

PATRICIA BOWL

Pointless Peak

Aspect	Consequence/Exposure	Slope
	2, 3	30°–40°

Summit Elevation	11,000'
Descent Vertical	800'
Total Vertical	1,100'
Hiking Distance	2 ¼ miles
Terrain	Chutes
Trailhead	33. Hilton Lakes Trailhead
USGS Quad Maps	Mt. Morgan, Mt. Abbot
GPS	37.463 / -118.751

Hidden from the canyon bottom, Patricia Bowl is a popular summertime climbing area that also offers some great wintertime skiing opportunities. The bowl itself is actually part of a reasonably sized cirque on the northeast side of Pointless Peak.

On the south side of the bowl are a handful of steep chutes that cut through the steep north-facing granite walls that are frequented by climbers in summer months. Most of these chutes do not go all the way to the summit ridge of Pointless, but the lower reaches offer some great steep skiing opportunities in a stellar setting.

Up higher in the canyon/cirque are a collection of east- and south-facing terrain options, comprised mostly of moderate-angled chutes that descend alongside beautiful rock spires and buttresses.

Approach: It is possible to access Patricia Bowl from either Trailhead #32 or #33, depending on the time of year. Though coming from Trailhead #33 does allow you to start a little higher up the canyon, the approach from either trailhead is quite similar in terms of travel time.

From Rock Creek Sno-Park (Trailhead #32), skin up the groomed Rock Creek Road for just a few hundred feet until the road crosses to the west side of the creek. Just beyond this point, leave the road and head west, climbing a treed east-facing slope to a large bench above the road. The majority of this slope gets a lot of sun and has a tendency to melt out fairly early in the spring, but there are a number of sheltered gullies and riverbeds along this slope that are protected from the sun and wind.

Once atop the bench, travel south (up-canyon) along its top through some broad treed slopes. After about ½ mile, the terrain to the south and east begins to gradually fall away back toward the canyon floor. At this point, head slightly west and into the small valley that is home to Patricia Lake and Patricia Bowl.

It is also possible to reach Patricia Bowl from the Hilton Lakes Trailhead (#33). From this point, head northwest, aiming for the end of the eastern ridgeline off Pointless Peak. Round the corner of this ridgeline,

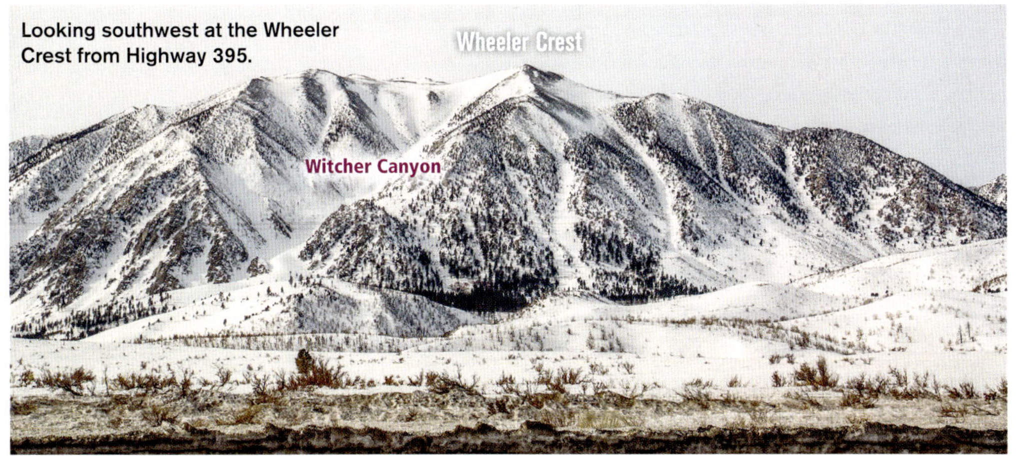
Looking southwest at the Wheeler Crest from Highway 395.
Wheeler Crest
Witcher Canyon

and head back west into Patricia Bowl. Once in the bowl, choose your line and climb it to the top.

Exit: Retrace your steps back to the car.

↘ EAST GULLIES

Pointless Peak

Aspect | Consequence/Exposure | Slope

2 | 35°

Summit Elevation	12,256'
Descent Vertical	2,300'
Total Vertical	2,300'
Hiking Distance	3 ½ miles
Terrain	Chutes
Trailhead	33. Hilton Lakes Trailhead
USGS Quad Maps	Mt. Morgan, Mt. Abbot
GPS	37.46 / -118.755

The East Gullies that drop off the summit ridge of Pointless Peak provide some great moderate ski terrain that is relatively quick-and-easy to access during the winter or spring. Though not terribly technical in nature, these gullies are prime avalanche terrain, so be aware of conditions before considering your line.

Approach: It is possible to access the East Gullies from either Trailhead #32 or #33, depending on the time of year. However, the best place to begin climbing the east face of Pointless is within the vicinity of the Hilton Creek Trailhead (#33).

From Trailhead #32, skin up Rock Creek Road for approximately three miles to the Rock Creek Pack Station. From Trailhead #33, continue down the road a short distance toward the pack station. From this point, head west, climbing onto the bench that guards the lower reaches of Pointless Peak's east face.

At this point you should be able to see all of the East Gullies. Choose your line and climb it to the summit ridge.

△ WHEELER CREST *11,675'*

The Wheeler Crest has a seemingly endless supply of chutes, gullies, and treed runs along its eastern face. Serving as the front of the range between Pine Creek and Rock Creek, the Wheeler Crest is stoutly perched above the Sherwin Grade along Highway 395. The summit ridge provides excellent views of the Owens Valley and across to the White Mountains, as well as front-row views of Rock Creek Canyon.

Because of its lower elevation and easterly aspect, the lower portions of the Wheeler Crest tend to melt out very early in the spring, making most of the descents along this ridge better suited for early to midseason.

↘ WITCHER CANYON

Wheeler Crest

Aspect | Consequence/Exposure | Slope

2 | 35°

Summit Elevation	11,400'
Descent Vertical	4,500'
Total Vertical	4,900'
Hiking Distance	3 miles
Terrain	Bowl
Trailhead	34. Sky Meadows Road
USGS Quad Maps	Tom's Place
GPS	37.509 / -118.686

Located at the northern end of the Wheeler Crest, Witcher Canyon is the prominent northeast-facing canyon that drops from the ridgeline down to Swall Meadows. There are actually a number of east-facing gullies that drop more directly into Swall, Witcher being the largest and most northern of all of them.

Approach: It is possible to access Witcher Canyon a variety of ways; these include starting in Swall Meadows (at Trailhead #34), or in Rock Creek Canyon (at Trailhead #32) and running a car shuttle.

The most direct and obvious approach begins at Sky Meadows Road (Trailhead #34) in Swall Meadows. From this point, head north slightly and follow the summer Sand Canyon Road across a small creekbed, then west toward the northeastern flank of the Wheeler Crest. As the road begins to head around the northern end of Wheeler Crest, Witcher Canyon will come into view to your left (west). Leave the road and continue directly up the canyon, skinning your way to the summit ridge.

It is also possible, and equally popular, to reach the Wheeler Crest ridge above Witcher Canyon from the Rock Creek Sno-Park (Trailhead #32). From this point head east, dropping down slightly to cross the creek, then climb the slopes above it onto the Sand Canyon bench (the large moraine located several hundred feet above the canyon bottom). Continue slightly northeast as you approach the summit ridgeline of the Wheeler Crest, aiming for the north side of a broad peak that divides Witcher Canyon from the remaining terrain of the Wheeler Crest to the south.

Incidentally, it is also possible to follow the Sand Canyon Road from Trailhead #34 around the back side of the Wheeler Crest and into Rock Creek Canyon, then follow the description provided that begins at Trailhead #32.

Exit: Retrace your steps back to the car, and reverse the car shuttle if you started in Rock Creek Canyon.

EAST FACE GULLIES

Wheeler Crest

Aspect	Consequence/Exposure	Slope
	2	35°

Summit Elevation	11,500'
Descent Vertical	4,500'
Total Vertical	5,000'
Hiking Distance	4 miles
Terrain	Gullies
Trailhead	34. Sky Meadows Road
USGS Quad Maps	Tom's Place, Mt. Morgan
GPS	37.496 / -118.678

Located just south of Witcher Canyon on the Wheeler Crest, the East Face Gullies are the series of lines that drop from the Wheeler ridgeline down into Swall Meadows and the valley below. There is a wide variety of options in this terrain, and it is BIG—you can make the line as challenging or interesting as you would like, or choose to stick to the more obvious and direct gullies themselves.

Approach: The approach for East Face Gullies really depends on which line you choose to ski. The Witcher Canyon approach provides the most moderate route to the summit ridge of Wheeler Crest from the east, though that may be a fair distance from the drop-in point for your line. It is also worth noting that the Wheeler Crest is big and filled with complex terrain features, meaning that the line that you think you want to ski from below may be challenging to locate from above. Clearly, the best bet is to climb your line of choice from below, though that may require 4500' of wallowing and a fair bit of energy.

To utilize the Witcher Canyon approach from Swall Meadows, follow the approach directions at left.

Exit: Ski right back down to the car in Swall Meadows.

MAYFIELD COULOIR/HELLCAT CANYON

Wheeler Crest

Aspect	Consequence/Exposure	Slope
	3	35°

Summit Elevation	11,943'
Descent Vertical	6,000'
Total Vertical	6,800'
Hiking Distance	5 ½ miles
Terrain	Chute
Trailhead	35. Ainslee Spring Road
USGS Quad Maps	Tom's Place, Mt. Morgan
GPS	37.455 / -118.677

Dropping off the Wheeler Crest from its southern end near Round Valley Peak, the Mayfield Couloir is undoubtedly the most prominent line on the east face of the Wheeler Crest. It sits in a deep canyon that runs from the top of the crest to the valley floor, and is clearly

Wheeler Crest, Mayfield Couloir.

visible as you travel up and down the Sherwin Grade on Highway 395.

Approach: Depending on the conditions and the snowline, people choose to approach Mayfield either from below, booting the couloir directly, or from the back via the Sand Canyon bench.

If you choose to approach from below, starting from Ainslee Spring Road (Trailhead #35). Depending on the snowline, it may be possible to travel on this road for a while, or even to its end at the actual spring. Regardless, find parking in this area and begin heading west toward the Wheeler Crest. By now, you should have the prominent Mayfield Couloir in sight. Skin to the base of the couloir and climb it to the summit.

If you choose to approach from Rock Creek Canyon, you can park at either Trailhead #34 and follow the Sand Canyon Road around the back side of the Wheeler Crest onto the moraine/bench in the canyon, or start at Trailhead #32 and gain the bench by skinning up the slopes above the creek.

Once on the bench, follow it south and up-canyon until it generally ends at the toe of a moderately treed slope that drops down to Rock Creek Lake. From this point, continue south a short distance, then climb east up the slope, ultimately aiming for a prominent gully that drops west from the summit of Round Valley Peak. Gain the ridgeline at the top of this gully, then proceed around the north side of Round Valley Peak. The couloir drops through a bowl directly below the northeast face of Round Valley Peak.

Exit: Ski right back down to the valley and Ainslee Spring.

▣ Inner Canyon Area

The terrain included in the Inner Canyon Area of Rock Creek is typically skied in the spring when Rock Creek Road opens to the Hilton Creek trailhead, or as part of a multiday tour deeper into the reaches of the canyon. The descents covered in this section lie in the "heart" of Rock Creek Canyon, where you will find a number of chutes, bowls, and peaks, all packed into this remote valley.

With the exception of Mt. Morgan (South), approaches for all of the descents covered here pass by the Mosquito Flat summer trailhead, which is at the end of Rock Creek Road. This point is roughly five miles from the winter road-end at the Rock Creek Sno-Park, and about

Brian Robinette skiing the Wheeler Crest.

two miles from the Hilton Lakes summer trailhead. We have chosen to begin the approaches for these lines at Hilton Lakes, as the road is not always plowed all the way to Mosquito Flat during prime spring ski season.

Δ MT. STARR *12,870'*

Mt. Starr offers terrain that is very similar to its down-canyon brother, Pointless Peak. The prominent East Gullies that drop from the summit ridge offer a consistent pitch with a variety of terrain options to choose from. Other, less popular descents exist off Mt. Starr's north and southeast faces, and can be accessed via the base of those descents.

Looking southwest up Rock Creek Canyon from Mt. Morgan South.

↘ EAST GULLIES

Mt. Starr

Aspect | Consequence/Exposure: 3 | Slope: 35°

Summit Elevation	12,870'
Descent Vertical	2,500'
Total Vertical	2,970'
Hiking Distance	1 mile
Terrain	Chutes
Trailhead	33. Hilton Lakes Trailhead
USGS Quad Maps	Mt. Morgan, Mt. Abbot
GPS	37.429 / -118.764

Mt. Starr's East Gullies drop down to the canyon bottom just above the Mosquito Flat summer trailhead.

Approach: From Hilton Lakes Trailhead (#33), continue up the Rock Creek Road to Mosquito Flat. As you arrive, the multiple gullies of Mt. Starr's east face will be in plain view. The best approach is to climb your intended descent. The base of the peak is most easily accessed through the Mosquito Flat Campground, just up the road from the trailhead.

Exit: Retrace your steps back to the car.

△ MT. ABBOT *13,704'*

Mt. Abbot and neighboring Mt. Mills dominate the skyline above Mills Lake and form the northern portion of the Treasure Peak backdrop. The two most common descents in this area are actually found along the ridgeline between the two peaks, rather than off either of their summits.

↘ PETIT GRIFFON

Mt. Abbot

Aspect | Consequence/Exposure: 3 | Slope: 40°

Summit Elevation	12,800'
Descent Vertical	1,000'
Total Vertical	2,900'
Hiking Distance	4 ¼ miles
Terrain	Chute
Trailhead	33. Hilton Lakes Trailhead
USGS Quad Maps	Mt. Abbot
GPS	37.39 / -118.788

In the small saddle between Mt. Mills and Mt. Abbot is a beautiful granite spire known as Le Petit Griffon. In the cleft beneath this spire is a nice, moderately sloped couloir that offers a 1,000' descent from its col down to Mills Lake.

Approach: From Hilton Lakes Trailhead (#33), continue up the Rock Creek Road to Mosquito Flat. From here, continue up canyon for roughly ½ mile, then begin climbing a drainage to the northwest toward Ruby Lake. Follow the south shore of the lake, cross a small ridge, and drop into the Mills Lake Drainage.

You will be directly below the couloir at this point—climb it to the summit ridge.

Exit: Retrace your steps back to the car.

↘ NORTHEAST COULOIR

Mt. Abbot

Aspect	Consequence/Exposure	Slope
	3	40°

Summit Elevation	13,400'
Descent Vertical	2,500'
Total Vertical	3,800'
Hiking Distance	4 ¼ miles
Terrain	Chute
Trailhead	33. Hilton Lakes Trailhead
USGS Quad Maps	Mt. Abbot
GPS	37.389 / -118.785

Juan Gelpi dropping into Mt Abbot.

Mt. Abbot is a vertical face of granite, split only by the Northeast Couloir on the ridge between the summit and Le Petit Griffon. Going to the summit of Mt. Abbot can be time-consuming, as the Northeast Couloir ends at a rock headwall and the standard route to the summit is mostly on rock, offering little skiing on the way down.

Approach: From the Hilton Lakes Trailhead (#33), continue up the Rock Creek Road to Mosquito Flat. From here, continue up-canyon for roughly ½ mile, then begin climbing a drainage to the northwest toward Ruby Lake. Follow the south shore of the lake, cross a small ridge, and drop into the Mills Lake Drainage.

From Mills Lake, gain a large bench at the base of Mt. Abbot. Climb up the apron and into the Northeast Couloir. As the slope steepens, you will have to decide if you are going up the couloir or up the ridge to the summit.

If you are going up the couloir, be aware that the top of it ends with a rock headwall. The point where the snow meets the rock is quite steep and you do not get the luxury of a "staging area." Putting your skis on will likely require digging out a small platform.

If you are going to the summit, climb up the couloir just a few hundred feet above the apron and then head out to the right toward the rocky ledges. You will want to access the rocks at the lowest ledge system possible. The upper ledge systems all lead to vertical rock faces, so don't climb too high up the couloir. Continue out the lowest ledge system and climb Class 3 rock and snow toward the summit.

On big snow years this face can fill in with enough snow to be skiable, but don't count on it. Under most conditions it is best to leave your skis and continue on foot to and from the summit. The climb can be tedious—the face rarely fills in very well, and the shallow snow can create endless hollow spots and glide cracks around the big rocky blocks. There is no exact way to go—your route will depend on the conditions of the day.

Toward the top of the face, where the angle kicks back, begin traversing to the south (left), which will bring you to a short, narrow section of ridge that is the most exposed and potentially complicated section. The west side of the ridge is slightly less exposed, and it is best to stay low through this section to avoid the steepest parts. Past that it is smooth sailing to the top.

Exit: Retrace your steps back to the car. An alternate way out is to continue to the south toward Mt. Dade and then ski one of the gullies down to Treasure Lakes.

△ TREASURE PEAK *12,837'*

Treasure Peak sits just in front of Rock Creek's Inner Canyon ridgeline. Its large, funnel-shaped East Face can be a little intimidating when viewed from the canyon below.

↘ EAST FACE

Treasure Peak

Aspect	Consequence/Exposure	Slope
	3	35°

Summit Elevation	12,837'
Descent Vertical	2,200'
Total Vertical	2,900'
Hiking Distance	3 ½ miles
Terrain	Face
Trailhead	33. Hilton Lakes Trailhead
USGS Quad Maps	Mt. Abbot
GPS	37.392 / -118.777

The bottom of the East Face doesn't always fill in with snow and has a tendency to melt out quickly, leaving an exposed section of near-vertical rock. Luckily, a narrow passage along a large ledge provides easy access to the slope above, with just a few feet of walking on rock.

Approach: From the Hilton Lakes Trailhead (#33), continue up the Rock Creek Road to Mosquito Flat. From the summertime trailhead, continue up the canyon to Long Lake. Shortly after the lake, begin climbing up to the right (north), aiming for the base of Treasure Peak. A gentle slope will change suddenly as you enter a steep, narrow chute. Follow this chute to a bench at the base of the East Face. If the lower section of the face is not filled in, climb the short, snow-filled gully on your right and walk a very short distance across a large, solid rock ledge to reach the snow again. Continue up the East Face to the summit ridge. The true summit of Treasure Peak lies far to the west and is quite difficult to reach from this point, so the ridge is the most logical stopping point.

Exit: Retrace your steps back to the car.

△ MT. DADE *13,400'*

Mt. Dade sits at the center of Rock Creek's ridgeline. It is probably best known for its Hourglass Couloir, which is the classically obvious descent just south of the actual summit. Mt. Dade's broad north face is characterized by many small chutes (including the Cat Ears Couloir), split by pillars of clean Sierra granite. On big snow years, some of the chutes in between the Hourglass and Cat Ears Couloir might fill in and become skiable. On lean years, they may not be skiable from the summit, but the lower sections of these can be fun on their own.

↘ CAT EARS COULOIR

Mt. Dade

Aspect	Consequence/Exposure	Slope
	3	40°

Summit Elevation	13,000'
Descent Vertical	1,000'
Total Vertical	3,100'
Hiking Distance	4 miles
Terrain	Chute
Trailhead	33. Hilton Lakes Trailhead
USGS Quad Maps	Mt. Abbot
GPS	37.382 / -118.779

The Cat Ears Couloir is the prominent line on Mt. Dade's North Face. The top of the couloir is situated between the two "ears" of rock.

With a sufficient snowpack, a small ribbon of snow forms just to the looker's right of the Cat Ears Couloir, known as the Cat Whisker Couloir. This run is steep and narrow and has two crux sections that require a lot of snow to fill in. As you approach the north face, it will be very apparent whether or not this line is skiable.

Approach: From the Hilton Lakes Trailhead (#33), continue up the Rock Creek Road to Mosquito Flat. Continue up the canyon past Long Lake and into the basin just south of Treasure Peak—the location of Treasure Lakes. From this point, the Hourglass and Mt.

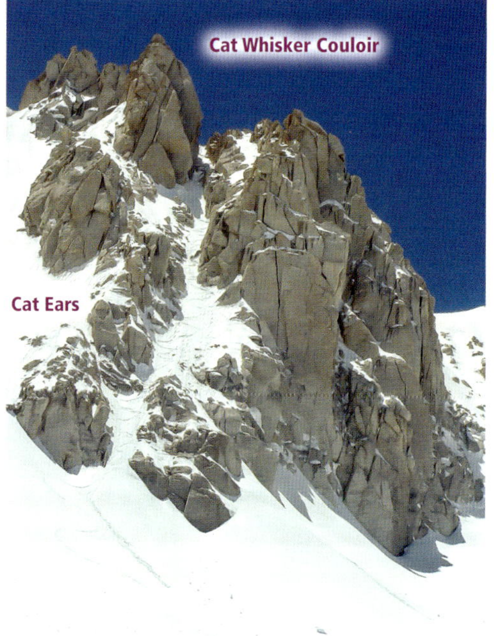

continue up the gradually steepening slope, then climb directly up the couloir to the notch. Going to the summit will most likely require a rope, as it is Class 4–5 along the ridge and is rarely done by people in ski boots.

Exit: Retrace your steps back to the car.

↘ HOURGLASS COULOIR

Mt. Dade

Aspect	Consequence/Exposure	Slope
	2	35°

Summit Elevation	12,325'
Descent Vertical	1,000'
Total Vertical	2,400'
Hiking Distance	4 miles
Terrain	Chute
Trailhead	33. Hilton Lakes Trailhead
USGS Quad Maps	Mt. Abbot
GPS	37.379 / -118.773

Dade sit directly above you.

From Treasure Lakes climb the steep hillside to the west and gain a small bench at the base of Mt. Dade's north face. It is also possible to reach this point via Ruby Lake and the approaches described for Mt. Mills/Mt. Abbot earlier in this section.

From the terminal moraine at the base of Mt. Dade,

The Hourglass Couloir is the prominent large chute that divides Mt. Dade from Pipsqueak Spire to the south, and is a classic Rock Creek Canyon spring-skiing line.

Approach: From the Hilton Lakes Trailhead (#33), continue up the Rock Creek Road to Mosquito Flat. Continue up the canyon past Long Lake and into the

basin just south of Treasure Peak—the location of Treasure Lakes. From this point, The Hourglass and Mt. Dade sit directly above you.

From Treasure Lakes, climb to the southwest directly up the aptly named Hourglass Couloir.

It is occasionally possible to ski directly from the summit of Mt. Dade down the south face to the top of the Hourglass, though this can be a little tricky and requires timing and luck. The standard route up the Hourglass holds snow to a certain elevation, but above that it has a tendency to get stripped by the wind.

If the summit is your objective, this is the easiest way to go, but be prepared for a bit of walking up and down on rocks. At the bench above the Hourglass, you can climb to the summit via Mt. Dade's large south-facing bowl.

Exit: Retrace your steps back to the car.

△ PIPSQUEAK SPIRE *12,607'*

Sitting between Bear Creek Spire and Mt. Dade, Pipsqueak Spire is seemingly just a bump on the ridge. But in the winter, when its slopes fill in with snow, this sub-peak takes on a life of its own. Pipsqueak Spire is visually known for the bands of multicolored rock that decorate its north face. Dikes of alternating black and gray granite distinguish this peak from its neighbors. Spanning the distance between Cox Col and the Hourglass on Mt. Dade, this peak holds a number of bowls on its northeastern flanks.

↘ NORTH FACE

Pipsqueak Spire

Aspect	Consequence/Exposure	Slope
	3	40°

Summit Elevation	12,607'
Descent Vertical	1,500'
Total Vertical	2,700'
Hiking Distance	4 miles
Terrain	Chutes/Face
Trailhead	33. Hilton Lakes Trailhead
USGS Quad Maps	Mt. Abbot
GPS	37.379 / -118.773

Approach: From the Hilton Lakes Trailhead (#33), continue up Rock Creek Road to Mosquito Flat. Ski into Rock Creek Canyon past Long Lake, where a short climb will bring you to Treasure Lakes. From here, the colorful cliffs of Pipsqueak Spire will be directly above.

For a slightly different approach (or exit), it is also possible to reach Dade Lake by following the Chickenfoot Lake drainage.

△ MT. GABB *13,741'*

Mt. Gabb lies over the crest, just outside of Rock Creek Canyon, and is one of the more remote peaks listed in this book. Simply reaching its base involves climbing over a 13,000' pass, from which the bottom of the North Couloir

Bear Creek Spire.

Joe Stewart skiing Mt Gabb.

is still one more pass away. The surrounding peaks of Mt. Julius Caesar and Mt. Hilgard have plenty of other skiable options, making this an excellent place to spend a few days.

NORTH COULOIR

Mt. Gabb

Aspect	Consequence/Exposure	Slope
N	4	45°

Summit Elevation	13,741'
Descent Vertical	1,500'
Total Vertical	3,800'
Hiking Distance	8 miles
Terrain	Chute
Trailhead	33. Hilton Lakes Trailhead
USGS Quad Maps	Mt. Abbot, Mt. Hilgard
GPS	37.378 / -118.803

The North Couloir of Mt. Gabb is arguably one of the most attractive lines in the Eastern Sierra, but due to its distance from the road, doesn't see very much traffic. It drops 1,500' from the summit of Mt. Gabb through the striking and steep north face into the remote Mills Creek Drainage.

Due to its aspect and rock walls, the north couloir sees very little direct sunlight, even in the spring. If you are concerned about snow conditions, you may want to choose to approach via Gabbot Pass. Gabbot Pass is quite moderate on both sides and doesn't require very much extra work—just a bit more distance.

Approach: From the Hilton Lakes Trailhead (#33), continue up the Rock Creek Road to Mosquito Flat. From the summertime trailhead, continue up Rock Creek Canyon past Long Lake, where a short climb will bring you to Treasure Lakes. Pass Treasure Lakes, then begin contouring left (east) and climb to Dade Lake. It is also possible to reach this point via the Chickenfoot Lake drainage.

From Dade Lake, climb the gentle slopes below Bear Creek Spire, then continue up the large bowl above you to reach Cox Col. Cox Col is the low point on the ridge to the north of Bear Creek Spire, and provides fairly easy access to the Lake Italy Drainage to the west. The east side of the col is a moderately steep slope at the top but gives way to a broad plateau on the west side. The west side tends to get scoured by the wind—there is typically enough snow to ski on, but be prepared to do a little route-finding through some of the snow patches.

From the top of Cox Col, follow the snow down and right to a short, steep rollover. Below this, be sure to keep

Looking north from Toe Lake.

to the skier's right-hand side. Follow the snow down to Toe Lake, and the base of Mt. Gabb's East Face.

From Toe Lake, the easiest way to the North Couloir is to climb the East Face to the summit of Mt. Gabb, where you will be able to see down into the couloir. From the summit of Mt. Gabb, walk a short distance along the ridge to the west, where a narrow slot in the rocks provides access to the upper snowfield and the start of the couloir.

Exit: From the base of the couloir above Upper Mills Creek Lake, it is necessary to climb back over Gabbot Pass to get back into the Italy Lake Drainage. This can be accomplished by heading slightly east, then climbing the north slope of Gabbot Pass.

From the Italy Lake Drainage, it is best to simply retrace your steps over Cox Col back to the trailhead.

↘ EAST FACE

Mt. Gabb

Aspect	Consequence/Exposure	Slope
E	3	35°

Summit Elevation	13,741'
Descent Vertical	2,500'
Total Vertical	3,800'
Hiking Distance	8 miles
Terrain	Face
Trailhead	33. Hilton Lakes Trailhead
USGS Quad Maps	Mt. Abbot, Mt. Hilgard
GPS	37.376 / -118.801

The East Face of Mt. Gabb has a number of steep gullies and chutes dropping from its rocky summit to Toe Lake. The blocks on the summit ridge rarely hold snow, so if you are interested in reaching the actual summit, you may have some talus to negotiate near the top.

Approach: Follow the directions to the North Couloir, on the previous page.

Exit: From the Italy Lake Drainage, it is best to simply retrace your steps over Cox Col back to the trailhead.

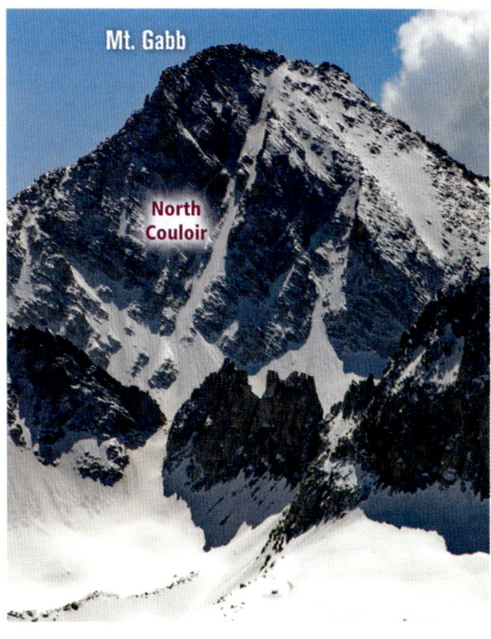

△ MT. MORGAN (SOUTH) *13,748'*

Mt. Morgan (South) appears as the dominant long ridgeline that forms the east wall of Rock Creek Canyon between Rock Creek Lake and Morgan Pass. The true summit of the peak lies at the southern end of this ridgeline. The north face of Mt. Morgan (South) offers moderate skiing in bowls, trees, and small chutes. Depending on snow coverage and conditions, it is also possible to ski a number of different lines off the west side of the peak.

↘ WEST FACE *Mt. Morgan*

Aspect | Consequence/Exposure: 2 | Slope: 35°

Summit Elevation	13,000'
Descent Vertical	2,500'
Total Vertical	31,00'
Hiking Distance	2 ½ miles
Terrain	Trees
Trailhead	33. Hilton Lakes Trailhead
USGS Quad Maps	Mt. Morgan, Mt. Abbot
GPS	37.408 / -118.736

The West Face of Mt. Morgan (South) offers a variety of tree skiing opportunities along the generally broad and open face.

Approach: From the Hilton Lakes Trailhead (#33), continue up the Rock Creek Road to Mosquito Flat. From the summertime trailhead, continue up Rock Creek Canyon toward Long Lake. After approximately ½ mile the West Face of Mt. Morgan (South) will be above you on the left. Find the best line to the top, and skin your way up it.

↘ FRANCIS GULLIES *Mt. Morgan*

Aspect | Consequence/Exposure: 2 | Slope: 35°

Summit Elevation	13,748'
Descent Vertical	2,000'
Total Vertical	4,400'
Hiking Distance	6 miles
Terrain	Bowls, Trees, Chutes
Trailhead	32. Rock Creek Sno-Park
USGS Quad Maps	Mt. Morgan, Mt. Abbot
GPS	37.407 / -118.733

The Francis Gullies are a series of moderate gullies that cut through the bench below the summit of Mt. Morgan (South)'s North Face. There is also a good bit of terrain in the basin below the north face that you can choose from.

Approach: From the Rock Creek Sno-Park (#32), continue up Rock Creek Road to Rock Creek Lodge. Skin through the lodge and find a place to cross the creek (there should be a number of snow bridges). Once on the other side, begin climbing the east side of Rock Creek Canyon. Continue southeast to a bench, ultimately heading south past Kenneth Lake and into the canyon below the north face.

From here, either stay in the bottom of the canyon and climb the gullies on the north face or head west to the ridge and follow it to the summit, which has a tendency to get wind scoured. It usually has a small ribbon of snow to ski.

10 Pine Creek

Dan Molnar, Denise Molnar, and Jim Zellers climbing into the Tungstar Bowls.

10. Pine Creek

PINE CREEK REGION:

- Lower Canyon Area:
  - △ BROKEN FINGER PEAK
  - △ MT. TOM
- Upper Canyon Area:
  - △ FOUR GABLES
  - △ FEATHER PEAK

Region Trailheads

36. Scheelite Canyon
37. Pine Creek Trailhead
38. Vanadium Ranch Road
39. Horton Creek Campground

Rising dramatically out of the lateral moraines that fan out into Round Valley, Pine Creek Canyon is nestled between the massive southern end of the Wheeler Crest and the North Face of Mt. Tom. The steep canyon walls guard impeccable alpine basins and thousands of feet of skiing opportunities. Pine Creek is truly one of the biggest untapped and overlooked skiing resources on the Eastside. While a few classic descents exist in and around this canyon, there are opportunities for dozens more everywhere you look.

This is one of the quieter regions of the range. Blame it on huge climbs, lack of well-known lines, or a greater distance from Mammoth Lakes, but Pine Creek doesn't see nearly the number of skiers as other regions in this book. Ironically, access into Pine Creek Canyon trumps almost every other area in the range, as the Pine Creek Road is maintained year-round.

The plowed road provides access to the Tungstar Mine, which sits just beyond the summer trailhead. Though now closed, Tungstar was once one of the largest tungsten-mining operations in the western U.S. As you climb out of the higher reaches of Pine Creek and look back into the canyon, it is impressive to see the amount of earth that has been extracted from deep within the heart of the Wheeler Crest.

Getting There & Getting Going

From Mammoth Lakes, travel south on Highway 395 for roughly 30 miles. As you reach the bottom of the Sherwin Grade (dropping from Rock Creek toward Bishop), keep an eye out for a right-hand (west) turn to Rovana. Exit the highway here and follow the directions to one of the trailheads referenced below.

36. Scheelite Canyon (Year-Round) 7,000'

From the intersection of Highway 395, continue southwest up Pine Creek Road for approximately seven miles. Along the way you will pass Round Valley School and the small community of Rovana before entering the canyon. As the road starts to level out in the canyon, look for a dirt road on the right-hand (north) side of the road that is just beyond the mouth of Scheelite Canyon. This is an obvious canyon filled with steep rock walls and Scheelite Chute towering high above. Turn right onto a small dirt road and follow it a short distance north to a parking area.

37. Pine Creek Trailhead (Year-Round) 7,500'

Follow Pine Creek Road to its end (roughly nine miles from the intersection with Highway 395). As you approach the end of the road at the head of the canyon, you will encounter a gate, beyond which is the mine. Just before the gate on the south side of the road is a large parking lot for the Pine Creek Pack Station and the trailhead.

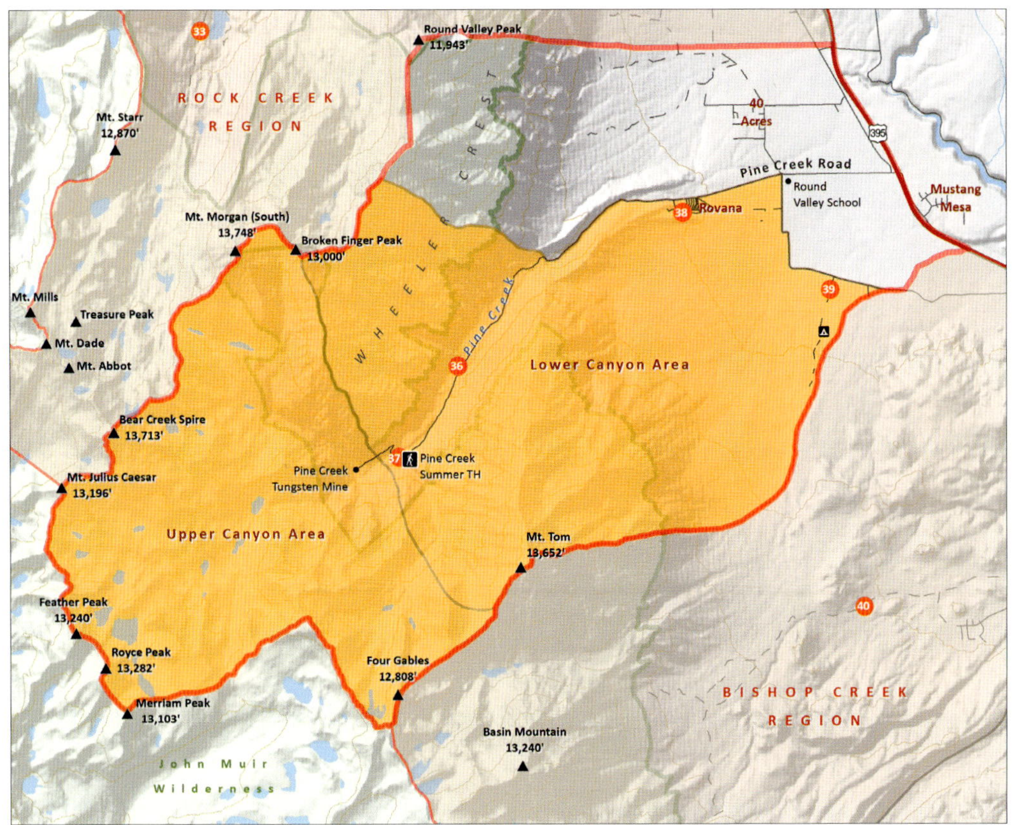

38. Vanadium Ranch Road (Year-Round) 5,200'

From the intersection at Highway 395, follow Pine Creek Road west for approximately three miles to the small community of Rovana. At the uphill end of this community is Vanadium Ranch Road, which serves as the jumping-off point for Elderberry Canyon.

Turn left onto Vanadium Ranch Road. Follow this road for ½ mile, then take your first right and continue along this road, bearing to the right toward the base of Elderberry Canyon. If the road is clear of snow, you will notice that it continues up the steep slope and eventually into the lower reaches of the canyon. Though you can drive a good ways up this road with a 4WD vehicle, driving the switchbacks is not recommended, as the road gets narrow and eventually runs into a dead end with limited places to turn around.

39. Horton Creek Campground (Year -Round) 4,700'

From Highway 395, follow Pine Creek Road west for 1¾ miles. When you reach Round Valley School, turn left onto North Round Valley Road. Follow this for two miles, then turn right onto Horton Creek Road. Follow Horton Creek Road through the campground and to the base of the canyon.

Eats, Digs, Services, & Supplies

There are no services in Pine Creek Canyon. The closest resource for fuel, food, and equipment is Bishop, another 15 miles south along Highway 395.

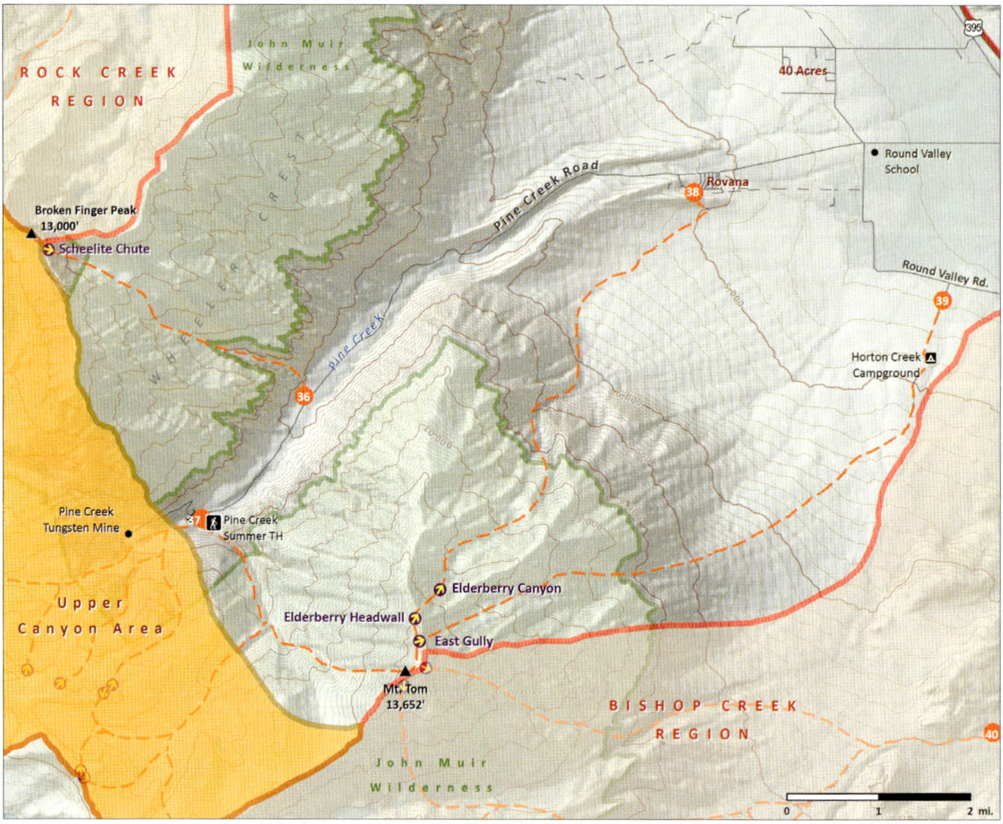

▣ Lower Canyon Area

This area comprises the lower reaches of Pine Creek Canyon—namely Mt. Tom and Scheelite Canyon. This is big terrain, with relief of 6,000'+ rising immediately off the canyon floor and filled with many more opportunities than are described here.

△ BROKEN FINGER PEAK 13,000'

The dramatic Wheeler Crest looms high above Round Valley, and marking its southern terminus is Broken Finger Peak. Because of the way the crest is positioned, the peak is often overlooked as it blends in with the surrounding terrain. As it spills into Pine Creek Canyon, it is broken into a series of steep and rugged ridges and canyons, one of which is Scheelite Canyon—home to Scheelite Chute.

The relief in Scheelite Canyon is significant, and with low elevations at the bottom of the slopes, it can be difficult to find decent skiing conditions top to bottom in this area. There is an endless supply of chutes, bowls, and ridges in this zone; the most well known is Scheelite Chute.

Looking north up Scheelite Canyon from the parking area.

↘ SCHEELITE CHUTE

Broken Finger Peak

Aspect	Consequence/Exposure	Slope
	4	40°

Summit Elevation	12,800'
Descent Vertical	6,000'
Total Vertical	5,800'
Hiking Distance	3 miles
Terrain	Chute
Trailhead	36. Scheelite Canyon
USGS Quad Maps	Mt. Morgan
GPS	37.403 / -118.714955

This chute starts from just below the summit of Broken Finger Peak and ends up at the Pratt's Crack climbing area at the bottom of Scheelite Canyon. A maze of minor chutes and gullies that are regular slide paths drain down into the Scheelite Chute. With its southeast aspect getting so much sun, the rocky chutes tend to shed on the first sunny day after a storm, filling the chute with roller balls, and quite frequently glazing it over altogether. Finding good conditions is almost as challenging as the skiing itself.

Approach: From the Scheelite Canyon Trailhead (#36), walk up an old dirt mining road into the mouth of the canyon. Depending on the snowline, it may be possible to follow a climber's trail well up into the depths of the canyon, putting you a short distance from the base of the chute. From here, skin and climb the chute to the summit.

Exit: Retrace your track back to the car.

△ MT. TOM *13,652'*

Sitting at the base of the Sherwin Grade and looming over Round Valley, Mt. Tom's impressive size and stature welcome those traveling south along Highway 395 between Mammoth and Bishop. It is one of the most prominent and pronounced peaks in the entire range, with a vertical relief of nearly 8000'. This Eastside giant is slightly separated from the main Sierra Crest, creating a peak that stands alone and towers above the valley. Because of this, the drop from summit to base is almost entirely fall line, with virtually no approach.

Mt. Tom is very popular among backcountry skiers and can be a thoroughly humbling first introduction to the deceptively large peaks of the Eastern Sierra. As many have learned, this is the quintessential *sandbag* of the range. It is bigger than it looks, and reaching the true summit, which many people do not achieve, typically involves a full day. Luckily, the terrain on Mt. Tom could easily keep a backcountry skier busy for an entire season, if not a lifetime—even without going to

Forest Cross climbing Mt Tom.

the summit. Tucked away in its two major canyons are 4,000–5,000' descents in a mixture of terrain and on a variety of aspects.

Timing can be a challenge for this mountain. Since the base and lower flanks are so low in elevation, they tend to melt out very early in the spring. Even in the midwinter, the snowline may not be low enough to enable you to ski all the way down into the desert. Luckily, there are several dirt roads that go to the base of the two major east-facing canyons, which can reduce the amount of bushwhacking that typically accompanies these low-elevation approaches.

In addition to the descents listed in this region are those on the south face of Mt. Tom, which are covered in the Bishop Creek chapter.

ELDERBERRY CANYON

Mt. Tom

Aspect	Consequence/Exposure	Slope
	2	30°

Summit Elevation	11,000'
Descent Vertical	7,500'
Total Vertical	5,800'
Hiking Distance	5 miles
Terrain	Gully
Trailhead	38. Vanadium Ranch Road
USGS Quad Maps	Mt. Tom, Mt. Hilgard, Rovana
GPS	37.351 / -118.653092

The most prominent (and popular) descent on Mt. Tom is the obvious northeast-trending Elderberry Canyon, which drops from the north summit ridge to the valley floor. The terrain in the canyon itself is relatively low angle, making it a great long, big mountain tour, without the typically associated consequences and exposure.

It is worth noting, however, that while the terrain in the gully isn't difficult, you are exposed to significant avalanche hazard from much of the surrounding terrain. Since the gully is essentially a huge terrain trap, this is probably not the best place to be immediately after a large storm. In fact, in 2005, two skiers (one local to the Bishop area) were caught and tragically killed in a major slide on the headwall of the canyon.

If you are interested in skiing steeper terrain, or summiting Mt. Tom, see the next descent listed for the Elderberry Headwall.

Approach: If you are interested in sticking to the gut of Elderberry Canyon and not summiting Mt. Tom, it is best to approach from Vanadium Ranch Road (Trailhead #38). Follow the road into the mouth of the canyon, then skin up into the depths of the canyon.

Exit: Retrace your track back to the car.

ELDERBERRY HEADWALL

Mt. Tom

Aspect	Consequence/Exposure	Slope
	3	40°

Summit Elevation	12,800'
Descent Vertical	1,800'
Total Vertical	7,600'
Hiking Distance	5 ½ miles
Terrain	Chutes, face
Trailhead	38. Vanadium Ranch Road
USGS Quad Maps	Mt. Tom, Mt. Hilgard, Rovana
GPS	37.347 / -118.657011

At the head of Elderberry Canyon lies an impressive and formidable east-facing headwall that is split by multiple chutes and open faces. This upper slope is considerably more severe than that of the actual canyon itself and should not be taken lightly. Due to its aspect and elevation, this headwall sees a considerable amount of wind-loading during storm cycles and is the site of frequent large avalanches during and immediately after such storms. As previously mentioned, in 2005 two skiers were killed in a major slide on the headwall on their way down from the summit ridge.

If you're interested in attaining the summit from Elderberry, this is also the most common route to the top. Once atop the ridge, many make the mistake of thinking they are close to the summit. While most of the elevation is gained once you reach the ridge, there is a considerable amount of distance to cover, which can take a couple hours.

Approach: Most people choose to approach the headwall from below, following the approach described for Elderberry Canyon, then booting the headwall directly.

It is also possible to reach the top of the headwall via the northwest face. This approach begins at the Pine Creek Trailhead (#37), and requires shuttling a car to Vanadium Ranch Road (Trailhead #38) for the end of the day. If you choose this route, beware that the upper half of the northwest face is very exposed to the wind and doesn't hold snow very well.

Looking west at Mt. Tom from Ed Powers Road.

From the Pine Creek Trailhead (#37), head south up the prominent drainage, as though you are approaching the Four Gables area. As the drainage splits, head left (east) and pick your way through the talus, passing by an old mine, and on to the summit. You may encounter some exposed Class 3 climbing if you stick too close to the West Ridge. From the summit, Elderberry Canyon is still far away, though it is all downhill.

Exit: Descend one of the many chutes into Elderberry Canyon, then enjoy the long ski down to your car.

↘ EAST GULLY

Mt. Tom

Aspect	Consequence/Exposure	Slope
	3	35°

Summit Elevation	13,000'
Descent Vertical	8,000'
Total Vertical	8,300'
Hiking Distance	6 ¼ miles
Terrain	Gully
Trailhead	39. Horton Creek Campground
USGS Quad Maps	Mt. Tom, Rovana, Tungsten Hills
GPS	37.343 / -118.656331

The canyon just to the south of Elderberry is quite similar in character, but a bit wider with an equally large amount of terrain. The East Gully has the advantage of

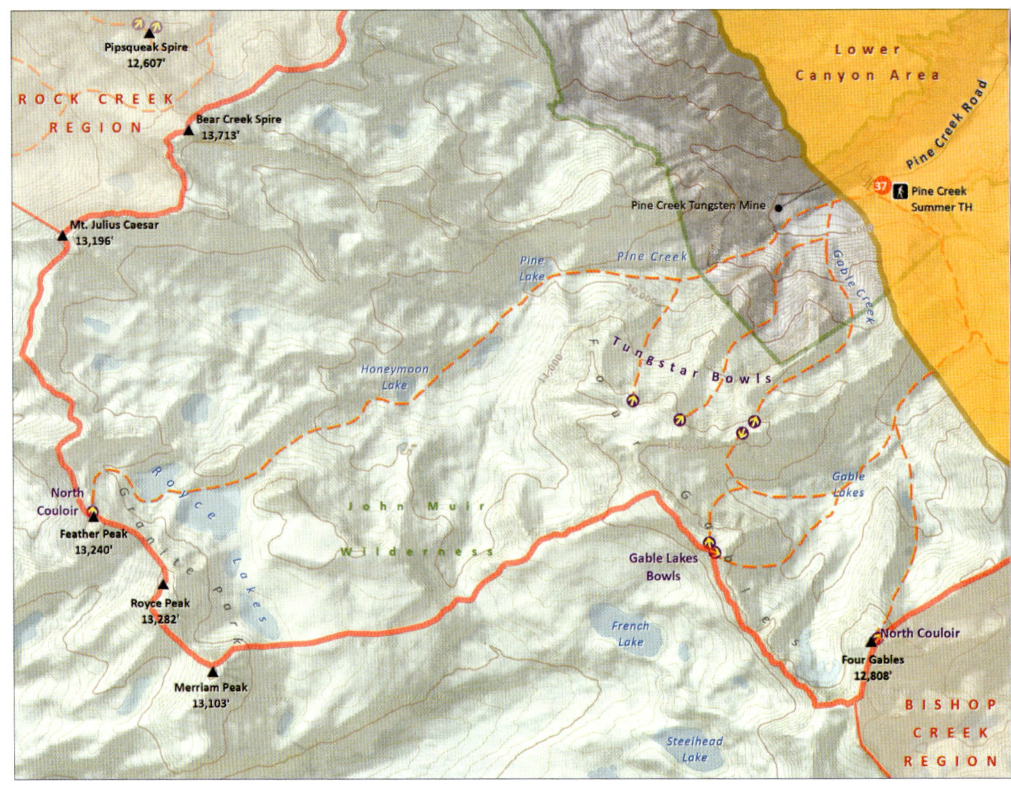

topping out much closer to the summit than Elderberry, though the lower stretches tend to melt out much earlier in the season.

Approach: Though it's possible to reach the East Gully from the north via Pine Creek Trailhead (#37), most choose to climb directly up it, starting at Horton Creek Campground (Trailhead #39). Follow Horton Creek Campground Road through the back of the campground and up onto the lower slopes of Mt. Tom leading to the East Gully. Skin up the gully to the ridgeline.

Exit: Retrace your track back to the car.

▣ Upper Canyon Area

This area comprises the headwaters of Pine Creek, including the massive terrain in Four Gables and the amazing Royce Lakes/Granite Park area. The scenery here epitomizes the High Sierra splendor and should be on every backcountry enthusiast's list of places to visit before they die. Summer or winter, this high-alpine basin, surrounded by large, clean, granite peaks, is an amazing setting for whatever your intended activity may be.

△ FOUR GABLES *12,808'*

Clearly visible from Highway 395 as you gaze up into Pine Creek, Four Gables looms at the upper portion of the canyon and is comprised of a series of hanging gullies separated by steep, pronounced ridgelines. This terrain is often overlooked, as it is not the easiest (or quickest) to access, but it does provide a good bang for your buck, with a ton of quality line choices.

↘ TUNGSTAR BOWLS — Four Gables

Aspect | Consequence/Exposure: 3 | Slope: 35°, 40°

Summit Elevation	11,500'
Descent Vertical	4,000'
Total Vertical	4,000'
Hiking Distance	2 ½ miles
Terrain	Bowls, chutes
Trailhead	37. Pine Creek Trailhead
USGS Quad Maps	Mt. Tom, Mt. Hilgard, Rovana, Tungsten Hills
GPS	37.339 / -118.713193

From the end of Pine Creek Road, the terrain immediately above you to the south is littered with an abundance of predominately north-facing chutes and bowls known as the Tungstar Bowls

The center bowl is the most popular, as it has the easiest access to numerous options. Climbing into any of these drainages during periods of low snow can be a challenge. The nice thing is that it doesn't take very long to reach the higher elevations, and subsequently deeper snowpack.

Approach: With a deep snowpack, it is best to head south directly into one of two canyons above the road from Pine Creek Trailhead (#37). If there is not much snow, it is often better to hike the summer trail for a distance, utilizing its switchbacks to access the mouth of the gullies (the slopes are littered with shrubs, which make skinning miserable in a shallow snowpack). Once in the canyons, the terrain will be obvious and clearly visible—choose your line and climb to its top.

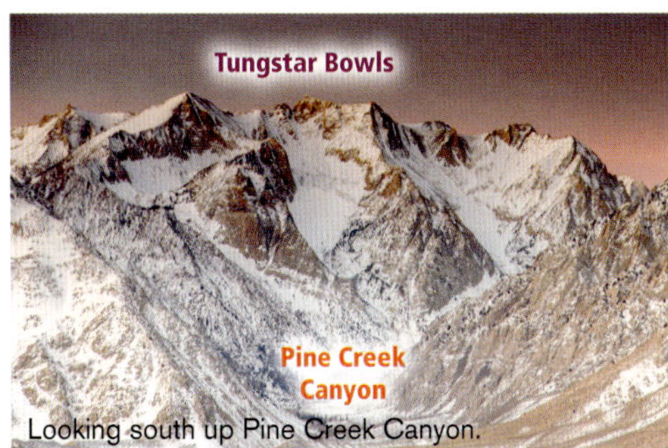

Looking south up Pine Creek Canyon.

Looking west across Pine Creek Canyon from Mt. Tom.

↘ GABLE LAKES BOWLS

Four Gables

Aspect	Consequence/Exposure	Slope
—	3	35°

Summit Elevation	12,500'
Descent Vertical	2,500'
Total Vertical	5,000'
Hiking Distance	4 ½ miles
Terrain	Bowls, chutes
Trailhead	37. Pine Creek Trailhead
USGS Quad Maps	Mt. Tom, Mt. Hilgard, Rovana, Tungsten Hills
GPS	37.307 / -118.70933K

As with the Tungstar Bowls, this zone is comprised of several small cirques that are accessible via one major drainage. These rocky ridgelines contain an abundance of chutes, gullies, and wide-open bowls.

Approach: From Pine Creek Trailhead (#37), climb south directly up the major drainage below Mt. Tom's west face. It is best to try to follow the location of the summer trail through the lower sections of this climb and avoid dropping back into the Gable Lakes Drainage until you are roughly 1,000' feet above the Pine Creek Canyon floor. An extensive amount of mining

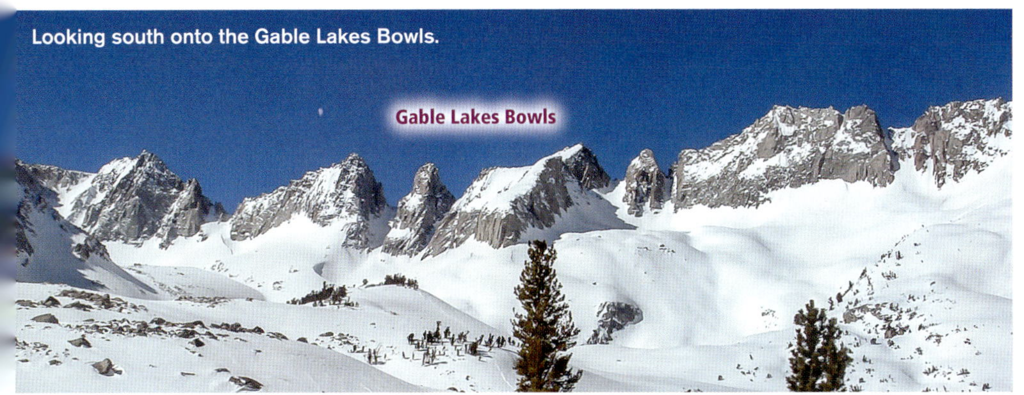

Looking south onto the Gable Lakes Bowls.

equipment and an old gondola system that once ran down the west flanks of Mt. Tom remain in this area. As the terrain levels out, curve around to the west and head toward Gable Lakes. The rocky ridge will be looming above you the entire time, and you should have ample opportunities to scout your line and your approach.

Exit: Retrace your track back to the car.

↘ NORTH COULOIR

Four Gables

Aspect	Consequence/Exposure	Slope
N	3	40°

Summit Elevation	12,808'
Descent Vertical	1,800'
Total Vertical	5,308'
Hiking Distance	4 ½ miles
Terrain	Chute
Trailhead	37. Pine Creek Trailhead
USGS Quad Maps	Mt. Tom, Mt. Hilgard, Rovana, Tungsten Hills
GPS	37.312 / -118.692219

The major attraction in this area is the giant North Couloir on Four Gables Peak. The North Couloir is actually separate from what some maps label as Four Gables Peak, dropping from a prominent point along the undulating ridgeline.

Approach: Follow the approach described above for Gable Lakes Bowls into the Gable Lakes basin. Once at the lakes, head left into the southern drainage, which leads you to the base of the North Couloir. Boot the line to the top.

Chelsea Morgan in the Gable Lakes Drainage.

Trevor Anthes beneath the North Couloir on Four Gables.

△ FEATHER PEAK 13,240'

Feather Peak is the northern of the three prominent peaks in the Royce Lakes/Granite Park Basin—with Royce Peak and Merriam Peak to the south. This small range is exceptionally beautiful, and in a stellar setting.

↘ NORTH COULOIR

Feather Peak

Aspect	Consequence/Exposure	Slope
	4	40°

Summit Elevation	13,240'
Descent Vertical	1,200'
Total Vertical	5,740'
Hiking Distance	6 ½ miles
Terrain	Chute
Trailhead	37. Pine Creek Trailhead
USGS Quad Maps	Mt. Tom, Mt. Hilgard
GPS	37.325 / -118.778535

The North Couloir on Feather Peak is one of the most classic ski descents and ice climbs in the Eastern Sierra. The couloir is somewhat hidden from the eastern view, and it is not until you are directly below it or gazing south at it from the Rock Creek Drainage that you can truly appreciate its grandeur.

Approach: From Pine Creek Trailhead (#37) follow the general alignment of the summer trail up the south side of the canyon toward its head. As you climb higher, the canyon pinches down, and travel can be a bit treacherous as you traverse the north-facing slope above the creek. After passing through this choke point, however, the canyon gets wider again and eventually leads to a gentle, treed bench at Pine Lake.

Continue southwest past Upper Pine and Honeymoon Lakes, ultimately working up through a small pass to Royce Lakes. At this point, Merriam, Royce, and Feather Peaks will be in front of you, with Feather Peak on the right. As you head northwest toward the peak, the North Couloir will come into view. Climb the couloir to the notch below the summit block. If you want to summit, leave your skis here and a scramble up a short, exposed Class 3 section.

In addition to the main North Couloir, there are two other smaller chutes to the east that don't reach the summit.

11 Bishop Creek

Basin Mountain and the Buttermilks.

11. Bishop Creek

BISHOP REGION:

- ▣ Buttermilks Area:
  - △ MT. TOM
  - △ BASIN MOUNTAIN
  - △ MT. HUMPHREYS
  - △ PEAKLET
  - △ PEAK 13,121'
  - △ MT. LOCKE
  - △ MT. EMERSON
- ▣ Aspendell Area:
  - △ PIUTE CRAGS
  - △ TABLE MOUNTAIN
- ▣ Lake Sabrina Area:
  - △ PIUTE PASS
  - △ MT. GOETHE
  - △ MT. LAMARCK
  - △ MT. MENDEL
  - △ MT. DARWIN
  - △ PICTURE PEAK
  - △ POINT POWELL
  - △ GEORGE LAKE RIDGE
- ▣ South Lake Area:
  - △ MT. THOMPSON
  - △ MT. GILBERT
  - △ MT. JOHNSON
  - △ HURD PEAK

Bishop is best known for mules, bouldering, and as a winter escape for those living in Mammoth or other snow-laden communities in Mono County. Sitting at an elevation of 4,000', this high-desert town rarely sees much snow. But Bishop certainly doesn't lack skiing opportunities, and in spring a short drive west into the hills provides easy access to them.

An impressive lineup of peaks, almost all of which are above 13,000', grace the Bishop skyline and tower above the valley below. In the foreground are the Buttermilks, the world-famous bouldering mecca that draws climbers year-round (see *Bishop Bouldering*, www.wolverinepublishing.com). East of town are the White Mountains, at the base of which is the Owens River. In terms of stellar access to amazing outdoor recreation, Bishop really has it all. This town is a desert oasis during the winter and exemplifies the California mountain lifestyle. It is quite possible to ski powder on tall peaks in the morning, and be climbing in shorts and a T-shirt in the afternoon.

With the exception of the terrain in the Aspendell Area, much of the skiing in this region requires a lengthy approach during the winter since the access roads are either dirt or not maintained during the snow season. Though many of these descents are done all winter long, Bishop tends to be a hot spot for the spring-skiing crowd, as the access to great corn on world-class terrain is plentiful. The skiing listed in this chapter is all in the Sierra located west of town, though there is also lots of skiing in the White Mountains to the east.

Getting There & Getting Going

From Mammoth Lakes, head south on Highway 395 for 45 miles. All of the skiing listed in this chapter is accessed off West Line Street (Highway 168), which is the last stoplight on the south end of town. If coming from Mammoth, it is also possible to reach Highway 168 via Ed Powers Road, which avoids downtown Bishop. Ed Powers Road turns off Hightway 395 33 miles south of Mammoth Lakes and intersects West Line Street a couple miles outside of Bishop in the foothills of Bishop Creek.

The quality and quantity of skiing around Bishop can be overwhelming at first. This chapter is divided into four areas, all of which drain into Bishop Creek. These areas vary greatly in terms of elevation and terrain. In addition to that, there are numerous different trailheads (listed below) that can vary with snow depth and season.

40. Buttermilks (Generally Year-Round) *6,100'*

From downtown Bishop, follow Highway 395 to the south end of town and turn right at the last stoplight onto West Line Street/Highway 168. Follow this road west and out of town for roughly six miles, then turn right

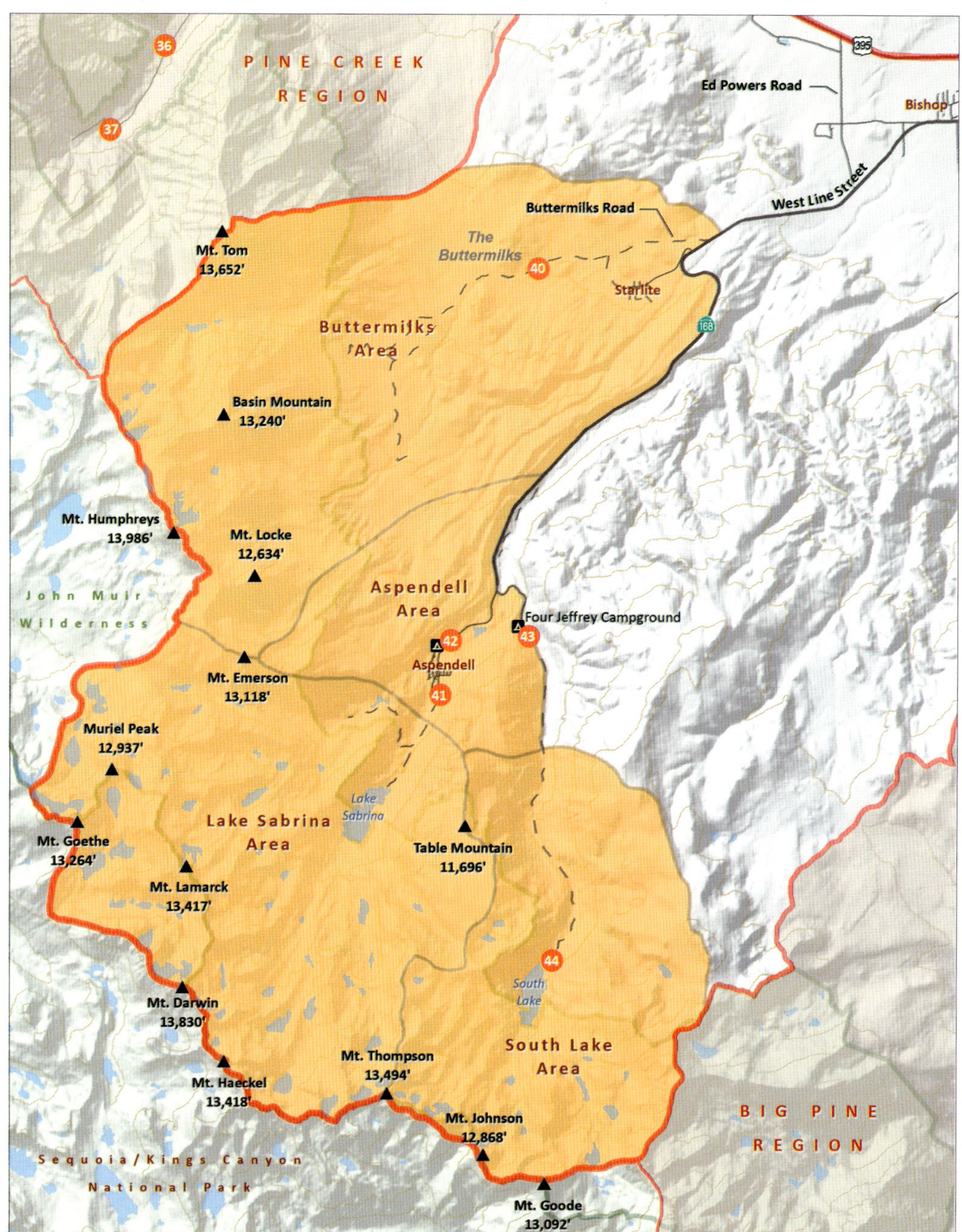

onto Buttermilk Road. This is a dirt road and is not plowed at all, but it is heavily traveled throughout the year, as it is used to access the Buttermilk bouldering area.

The trailhead location and elevation referred to here is the upper climbers' parking lot, just beyond the cattle guard, located approximately three miles from West Line Street. Depending on the time of year and snow line, however, it may be possible to drive farther up this road and decrease the approach. Beware that the road is rather rough and a high-clearance 4WD vehicle is recommended.

Region Trailheads

40. Buttermilks

41. Aspendell

42. Bishop Park Campground

43. Four Jeffreys Campground

44. South Lake Dam

Looking west at the Bishop skyline from across the Owens Valley.

A short distance beyond this parking lot the road splits. The right branch provides access to the summertime trailhead for Horton Creek. This location is referenced later in approaches for Basin Mountain and the South Face of Mt. Tom. To reach the trailhead, bear right at the branch in Buttermilk Road about ½ mile beyond the cattle guard. There should be a small sign that refers to the trailhead. Beware that the upper portion of this road has steep switchbacks that make turning around difficult.

The left-hand branch of this road heads south past McGee Creek toward the road end at a small reservoir below Mt. Humphreys. To reach this point, stay left at the turnoff for the Horton Creek trailhead, following the more heavily traveled road southwest. Eventually this road winds down and crosses McGee Creek, which flows out from between Mt. Humphreys and Basin Mountain. It is quite common for snow to remain on the short, shaded portion on the south side of the creek, but if you get lucky, you can continue farther up this road. About ¾ mile after the creek, the road splits again. Take the right branch uphill, where you pass a couple of short sections of bad road, before the road eventually ends at a small creek where a couple of nice campsites sit high up on the plateau beneath Mt. Humphreys. Just beyond this point is a small reservoir, which is referenced in approach descriptions later in this chapter.

41. Aspendell (Year-Round) *8,500'*

From its intersection with Highway 395 in downtown Bishop, follow West Line Street/Highway 168 for 17½ miles to the small mountain community of Aspendell. Drive past the small collection of homes to the gate that marks the point of winter closure of Highway 168. There is typically ample parking here, but please be sure to park off the road and not block the gate.

42. Bishop Park Campground (Year-Round) *8,300'*

From its intersection with Highway 395 in downtown Bishop, follow West Line Street/Highway 168 for 17 miles to the small mountain community of Aspendell. Just before the lower edge of the community, look for the right-hand turn for Bishop Creek Camp Road. Park here, off the highway.

43. Four Jeffreys Campground (Year-Round) *8,100'*

From its intersection with Highway 395 in downtown Bishop, follow West Line Street/Highway 168 for 15 miles to South Lake Road. Turn left onto South Lake Road and follow it for about one mile, where it ends at a plowed parking area near Four Jeffreys Campground. Park in the plowed lot on the east side of the road.

Note that in the winter months, this is the parking area for the South Lake Area descents as well, since it is not possible to access Trailhead #44.

44. South Lake Dam (Spring Only) *9,700'*

Follow the directions provided for Four Jeffreys Campground (Trailhead #43), but continue up South Lake Road for approximately seven miles to its end point at South Lake.

During the winter months, access to this location is only possible via Trailhead #43, adding about six miles and 1,500' of climbing onto the approach descriptions provided in that section.

Eats, Digs, Services, & Supplies

Finding what you need for your tour should not be a problem in downtown Bishop. Most of the amenities are situated along Main Street (Highway 395) as it passes through town, but if you are new to the area or looking for information on lodging or other recreational opportunities, stop by the White Mountain Ranger Station and Visitor Center located at 798 North Main Street.

Bishop offers many options for eating, shopping, and lodging, and there's no shortage of things to do on rest days. In the spring, the temperature in this lower-elevation town can be perfect for climbing, bouldering, lounging, or wandering around.

Pick up missing gear essentials at Mammoth Mountaineering's Gear Exchange or Wilson's Eastside Sports, both located on Main Street half a block north of Line Street. Get your groceries at Vons, Joseph's Bi-Rite, or Manor Market on West Line. Be sure to hit the Great Basin Bakery on Lagoon Street for fresh bagels and baked goods. Black Sheep Espresso Bar serves excellent coffee. For lunch visit Raymond's Deli or Schat's Bakery on Main Street. Good dinner options include Amigos and Las Palmas for Mexican food, Yamatani for some apres-ski sushi, and Thai Thai (located at the Bishop Airport). And if you haven't been, it is well worth a visit to Galen Rowell's Mountain Light Gallery for visual inspiration.

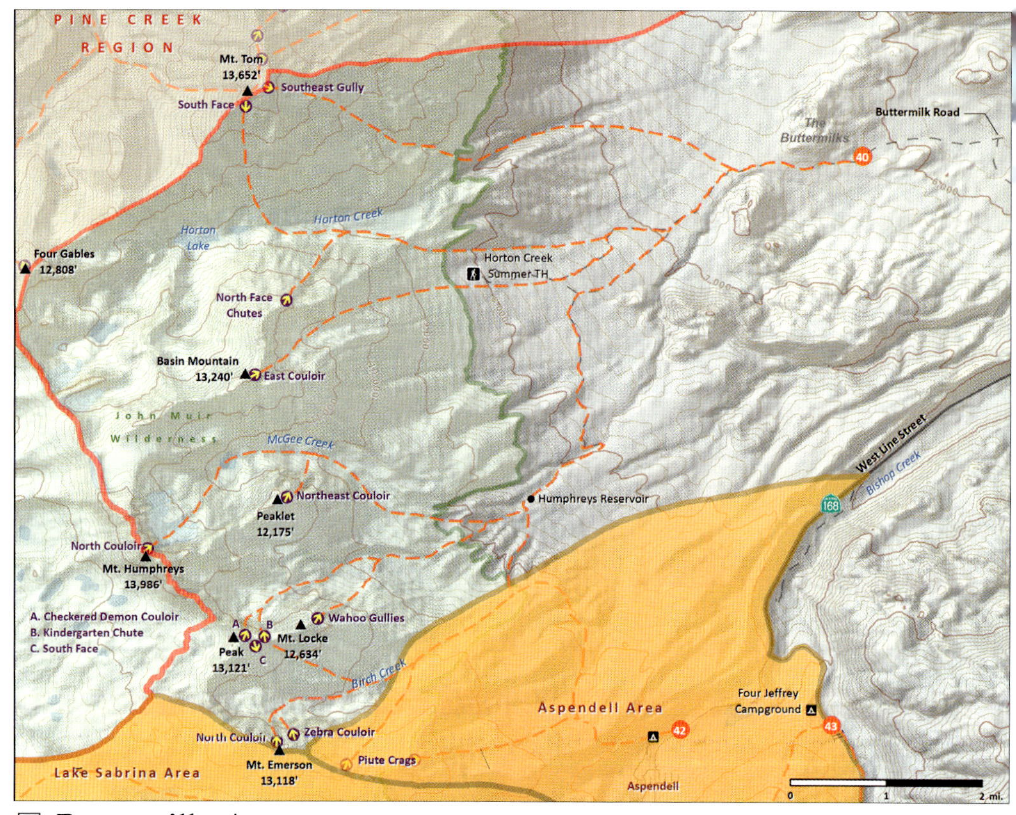

▣ Buttermilks Area

The peaks of the Buttermilks Area comprise the majority of the Bishop skyline. Though the skiing accessed from North and South Lakes is incredible, the Buttermilks Area descents are true Eastside classics. This region is highly visible from Highway 395, making it difficult to keep your eyes on the road as you gaze upon the impressive row of peaks and couloirs while driving up the grade.

With so many descents stacked right next to each other, linking up multiple lines in a day is as easy as your fitness allows. That said, many of the peaks can be difficult to reach and involve long days depending on the time of year and elevation of the snowline. But by no means is this a "spring-only" area, as the approach road sits at a fairly low elevation and gets plenty of sun, helping it melt out relatively quickly after storms.

Δ MT. TOM *13,652'*

When most backcountry enthusiasts speak of Mt. Tom, they typically refer to the classic descents that grace its East Face—such as Elderberry Canyon. Though often overlooked, the South Face of Mt. Tom offers some equally high-quality terrain, much of which drops right from the true summit of the peak.

↘ SOUTH FACE

Mt. Tom

Aspect	Consequence/Exposure	Slope
	3	35°

Summit Elevation	13,000'
Descent Vertical	3,500'
Total Vertical	6,900'
Hiking Distance	6 ¼ miles
Terrain	Gully
Trailhead	40. Buttermilks
USGS Quad Maps	Mt. Tom, Tungsten Hills
GPS	37.3362 / -118.65872

This line drops from Mt. Tom's summit ridge through a series of technical faces, into a large bowl that fans out into the head of the Horton Creek Drainage. Though the upper portion of the face does require some route finding and higher-consequence skiing, it is possible to ski only the lower sections for a beautiful long corn run. All the while, the impressive North Face of Basin Mountain looms over you to the south, and there are stellar views of the terrain in the Upper Horton Lake area.

Approach: From the Buttermilks Trailhead (#40), continue west along the Buttermilk Road to the Horton Creek summer trailhead. From here, skin the short, steep slope directly above the trailhead into a small chute. This ultimately leads to a bench on the northeast ridge of Basin Mountain.

Continue west along this bench into Horton Creek. As the terrain steepens, drop into the drainage then continue west beneath the South Face of Mt. Tom. As you approach the upper reach of the drainage, the South Face will come into view, appearing as a large bowl. Skin and boot your way to the top.

Exit: Reverse the approach. It is better to avoid the lower portion of Horton Creek, and ski back past the Horton Creek trailhead instead.

↘ SOUTHEAST GULLY

Mt. Tom

Aspect	Consequence/Exposure	Slope
	3	40°

Summit Elevation	13,652'
Descent Vertical	5,400'
Total Vertical	7,552'
Hiking Distance	6 ¼ miles
Terrain	Gully
Trailhead	40. Buttermilks
USGS Quad Maps	Mt. Tom, Tungsten Hills
GPS	37.3389 / -118.6553

This line drops from Mt. Tom's true summit via a technical headwall that leads into a gully with some tricky route-finding. Though the skiing as a whole is not overly challenging, it is possible to get cliffed out or find yourself in a less-than-ideal location if you are not thoughtful about your line.

Approach: From the Buttermilks Trailhead (#40), follow the directions to the Horton Creek summer trailhead. From the trailhead, climb a short, steep chute to a bench on the northeast ridge of Basin Mountain, then drop directly into the mouth of Horton Creek. The Southeast Gully will be directly above you at this point. Skin and boot your way to the summit.

Exit: It is advisable to follow your bootpack on this descent to ensure staying on route.

△ BASIN MOUNTAIN *13,240'*

Basin Mountain is the middle of the three large peaks that define the Bishop skyline—with Mt. Tom to its north and Mt. Humphreys to the south. Basin is an impressive peak, dominated by its East Couloir..

Looking west from the Buttermilks.

NORTH FACE CHUTES

Basin Mountain

Aspect	Consequence/Exposure	Slope
	3	40°

Summit Elevation	12,700'
Descent Vertical	3,500'
Total Vertical	6,600'
Hiking Distance	6 miles
Terrain	Chute
Trailhead	40. Buttermilks
USGS Quad Maps	Mt. Tom, Tungsten Hills
GPS	37.3078 / -118.6525

Hidden from view from the Owens Valley, the north face of Basin Mountain hosts some large, impressive terrain. Comprised of a series of interconnected chutes, these lines drop a couple thousand feet from the north summit of Basin into Horton Creek and offer those looking for a little adventure and some steep technical skiing a great day out.

Approach: Follow the approach description for the South Face of Mt. Tom into Horton Creek. As you skin west into the drainage, keep as high a line as possible along the North face of Basin Mountain until you are forced to drop into the creek. After a short distance, you will arrive at the mouth of the gully that marks the exit of the North Face Chutes. Skin and boot your line of choice.

Exit: Reverse your approach.

EAST COULOIR

Basin Mountain

Aspect	Consequence/Exposure	Slope
	2	35°

Summit Elevation	13,000'
Descent Vertical	6,240'
Total Vertical	7,140'
Hiking Distance	6 miles
Terrain	Chute
Trailhead	40. Buttermilks
USGS Quad Maps	Mt. Tom, Tungsten Hills
GPS	37.2969 / -118.6573

Basin Mountain's giant East Couloir is the most striking feature of the Buttermilk Area and is clearly visible from downtown Bishop. As you get closer to it (which takes a while) and begin climbing the flank of the peak, you will begin to realize the scale of the terrain. This couloir is, in essence, a giant bowl, and is one of the classic moderate descents of the Eastside. The top of

Eric Ongerth skiing Basin Mountain.

the couloir provides amazing views of Mt. Humphreys and the Checkered Demon Couloir to the south, as well as the Owens Valley and White Mountains to the east.

Approach: From the Buttermilks Trailhead (#40), follow the directions to the Horton Creek summer trailhead. As you traverse north toward the trailhead, the approach up Basin's east face should be pretty obvious: It climbs the slope to the looker's right of a small, rocky knob before gaining a bench and climbing into the valley at the base of the couloir. As you climb the couloir, you will pass underneath an enormous rock wall that has a handful of narrow chutes that fill in on good snow years.

△ MT. HUMPHREYS *13,986'*

Missing the 14,000' distinction by only a few feet, the unique summit block of Mt. Humphreys is an easily recognizable part of the Bishop skyline. The large granite buttress that extends east from the summit offers sfine high-elevation climbing that is sought after by alpine enthusiasts. The views from this peak into the Humphreys Basin and of Mt. Goethe beyond are unsurpassed.

Humphreys' large summit block forms the southern wall of the spectacular North Couloir. Similar to the Bloody Couloir in prominence and technical difficulty, this is a highly sought-after descent that is clearly visible from downtown Bishop.

↘ NORTH COULOIR — Mt. Humphreys

Aspect	Consequence/Exposure	Slope
NE	3	45°

Summit Elevation	13,200'
Descent Vertical	3,000'
Total Vertical	7,886'
Hiking Distance	9 miles
Terrain	Chute
Trailhead	40. Buttermilks
USGS Quad Maps	Mt. Tom, Tungsten Hills
GPS	37.2715 / -118.6734

Approach: From the Buttermilks Trailhead (#40) continue up Buttermilk Road past McGee Creek to the small reservoir below Mt. Humphreys (see Trailhead #40 description). From this point, walk the road past the reservoir, then begin heading northwest, aiming for a large, rocky buttress at the eastern end of the Mt. Humphreys ridge, known as Peaklet. Continue around the north side of this formation into the McGee Creek Drainage between Basin and Humphreys.

Once below Mt. Humphreys, the North Couloir will be in sight and only a couple thousand feet above you. Reaching the summit from the top of the couloir is complicated and intimidating. If you are planning on going to the summit in winter conditions, a rope is recommended.

Looking southwest at Mt. Humphreys from Peaklet.

△ PEAKLET *12,175'*

Peaklet is the small, rocky subpeak that lies just east of Mt. Humphreys, and is connected by the east ridge. Though a couple thousand feet lower than Humphreys, Peaklet is an impressive feature with a craggy and formidable-looking north face.

↘ NORTHEAST COULOIR — Peaklet

Aspect	Consequence/Exposure	Slope
	3	40°

Summit Elevation	12,175'
Descent Vertical	2,000'
Total Vertical	6,075'
Hiking Distance	7 miles
Terrain	Chute
Trailhead	40. Buttermilks
USGS Quad Maps	Mt. Tom, Tungsten Hills
GPS	37.2790 / -118.6523

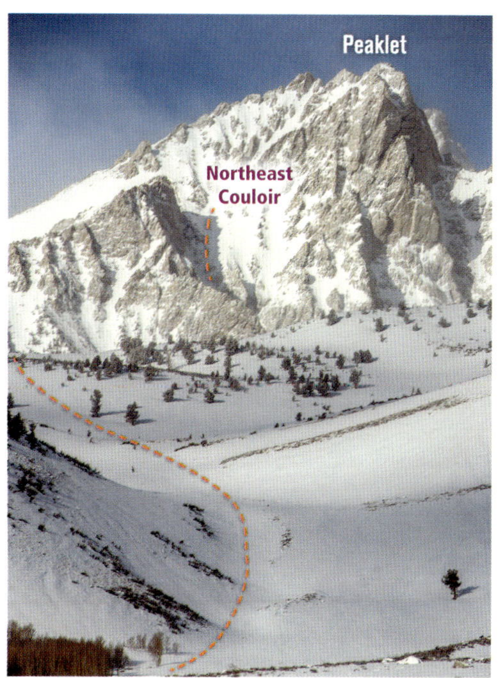

Looking southwest onto Peaklet.

A fine line that is in plain sight from downtown Bishop, the Northeast Couloir on Peaklet is a true gem. This 12,000' peak is dwarfed by the size and notoriety of its neighbors, but with a slightly shorter approach, makes for an excellent ski. From the top, the view of Mt Humphreys is exceptional.

Approach: Follow the approach described for Mt. Humphreys into the McGee Creek Drainage between Basin and Humphreys.

As you enter the drainage, Peaklet will be directly above you to the south. Continue up-canyon to the large bowl on the northwest side of Peaklet. Climb the bowl to the ridge where a short, steep section leads through some rocks and on to the upper chute. Near the top, this chute splits, with both ways leading to the summit ridge.

Exit: After skiing the chute, reverse your approach.

△ PEAK 13,121 *13,121'*

Situated along the looker's left side of the Bishop skyline, this non-distinct peak is really only known because of the two couloirs that drop off its steep north face: Kindergarten Chute and the Checkered Demon Couloir.

↘ CHECKERED DEMON COULOIR — Peak 13,121

Aspect	Consequence/Exposure	Slope
	4	45°

Summit Elevation	12,750
Descent Vertical	1,200'
Total Vertical	6,650'
Hiking Distance	8 miles
Terrain	Chute
Trailhead	40. Buttermilks
USGS Quad Maps	Mt. Tom, Tungsten Hills
GPS	37.2588 / -118.6587

The Checkered Demon Couloir reeks of intimidation—and rightly so. The couloir top is one of the most challenging runs in this book—it's steep and narrow, becoming slightly off-camber as you descend. However, the crux section is short-lived, and the main part of the chute is considerably wider.

Approach: From the Buttermilks Trailhead (#40) continue up Buttermilk Road past McGee Creek to the small reservoir below Mt. Humphreys (see Trailhead #40 description). From here continue west up the main drainage to a bench that flanks the north face of Mt. Locke. Continue west along this bench higher into the

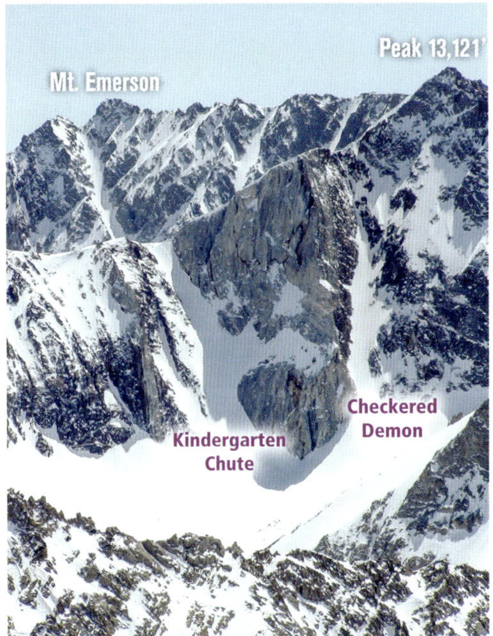

canyon. As you reach the base of Peak 13,121' Kindergarten Chute will come into view—appearing as a broad gully leading to a plateau above.

The most common way to reach Checkered Demon is to climb Kindergarten Chute. Once atop the ridge, continue west along the South Face to the entrance to the chute, located a few hundred feet uphill from the top of Kindergarten. It is also possible to reach this location from Aspendell via the South Face of Peak 13,121'.

Peak 13,121' Exits: This is the only peak in the area where the descent can be a bit tricky. Making the wrong choice could result in a very miserable experience at the end of an otherwise great day.

Though easy to discern on the way up, finding the right drainage on the way out from this terrain can be challenging, especially if there is no snow around to show your up-track. As you finish skiing the line, you will find yourself on a relatively large bench or plateau that trends generally to the east. The gut reaction is to ski fall-line along this bench toward the east and the valley. The best way out, however, is to head north across the flats, before dropping off the east side of the plateau and into the main drainage, which is the way you came up. While the other smaller drainages do go through, they are steep walled and filled with dense vegetation, making hiking with skis or boards unpleasant.

↘ KINDERGARTEN CHUTE

Peak 13,121

Aspect	Consequence/Exposure	Slope
	3	35°

Summit Elevation	12,400'
Descent Vertical	1,100'
Total Vertical	6,300'
Hiking Distance	8 miles
Terrain	Chute
Trailhead	40. Buttermilks
USGS Quad Maps	Mt. Tom, Tungsten Hills
GPS	37.2586 / -118.6557

Kindergarten Chute is the mellower "little brother" of the two chutes on Peak 13,121', and the first one that you reach when approaching from the Buttermilks. It is still a very aesthetic line and a great warm-up for the Checkered Demon.

Approach: Follow the approach for Checkered Demon described at left. It is also possible to reach the top of Kindergarten Chute via the South Face (see next approach description).

Exit: See the Peak 13,121' exit description provided for Checkered Demon Couloir.

Looking north from the Bishop Bowl area.

↘ SOUTH FACE

Peak 13,121

Aspect	Consequence/Exposure	Slope
S	2	30°

Summit Elevation	12,750'
Descent Vertical	1,000'
Total Vertical	6,650'
Hiking Distance	7 ½ miles
Terrain	Face
Trailhead	40. Buttermilks
USGS Quad Maps	Mt. Tom, Tungsten Hills
GPS	37.2572 / -118.6571

On the back side of Peak 13,121' from Checkered Demon and Kindergarten Chute lies the moderate South Face. This is an excellent early spring corn run that catches a lot of sun. Despite its aspect, this face holds snow surprisingly well, and has many different options along its flanks. From here, the views of Mt. Emerson are as good as it gets.

Approach: The South Face drops into the Birch Creek Drainage, which is used to access Mt. Emerson. Follow the approach described for driving to the Mt. Humphreys trailhead, but roughly ¾ mile after climbing out of the McGee Creek crossing, bear left and continue contouring south along the toe of the slope (rather than taking the right-hand fork that climbs west into the Locke-Humphreys Drainage). After a short distance, leave the road and cross Birch Creek before climbing a small knoll to its south. Continue west up the south side of the drainage, beneath the Piute Crags. Before you reach Mt. Emerson, climb the broad south face to your right to the summit of Peak 13,121'.

It is also possible (and relatively common during winter months) to approach this area from the community of Aspendell via Bishop Bowl (see approach described in the Aspendell Area for more information), as well as via Kindergarten Chute.

Exit: See the Peak 13,121 exit description provided for Checkered Demon Couloir.

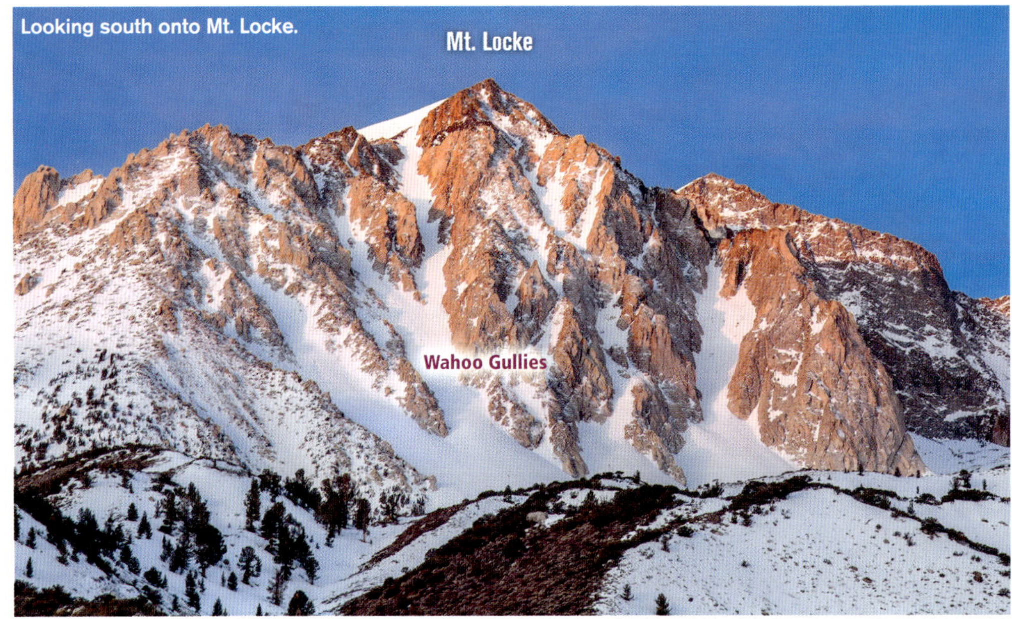

Looking south onto Mt. Locke.

△ MT. LOCKE *12,634'*

From downtown Bishop, the north face of Mt. Locke is clearly recognizable—divided by the Wahoo Gullies and separating the Mt. Emerson/Piute Crags ridgeline from Mt. Humphreys.

↘ WAHOO GULLIES

Mt. Locke

Aspect	Consequence/Exposure	Slope
	2	40°

Summit Elevation	12,634'
Descent Vertical	2,500'
Total Vertical	6,534'
Hiking Distance	7 miles
Terrain	Chutes
Trailhead	40. Buttermilks
USGS Quad Maps	Mt. Tom, Tungsten Hills
GPS	37.2613 / -118.6476

Mt. Locke, named by locals after late Bishop climber Bob Locke, is known less by this name than by the name of the descents on its flanks—the Wahoo Gullies. From a distance, the five Wahoo Gullies resemble the fingers of an open hand placed on the northeast face of Mt. Locke. The gullies are the quintessential spring ski of the Eastern Sierra and are probably the most popular descent in this entire region. The main gully is the center of the five and is the longest and most plumb, though all of them are relatively similar in character.

Approach: From the Buttermilks Trailhead (#40), follow the approach described for Checkered Demon Couloir into the mouth of McGee Creek. As you enter the drainage, a bench to the northeast of Mt. Locke appears. From the bench, the five gullies will be in plain view, as will the best approach to reach them.

Exit: See the exit description provided for Checkered Demon Couloir.

△ MT. EMERSON *13,118'*

From Bishop, the descents on Mt. Emerson lie just out of view in a small cirque behind Mt. Locke and west of the Piute Crags. These descents are two giant couloirs that split the diagonal rocky ledges on Mt. Emerson's North Face and are some of the most picturesque couloirs in the range.

General Emerson Approach: Follow the same approach described for the South Face of Peak 13,121' to reach the base of Mt. Emerson from the Buttermilks Trailhead (#40). It is also possible to access this location from Aspendell (see the approach description for Piute Crags).

Once in Birch Creek, continue up-canyon, staying either on the bench on the left (south side) or the canyon bottom.

Emerson Exits: Reverse your approach.

Dave Mingori beneath Kindergarten Chute.

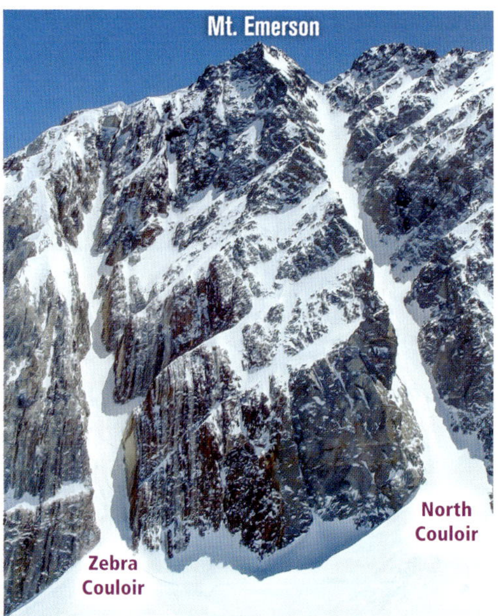

↘ NORTH COULOIR

Mt. Emerson

Aspect | Consequence/Exposure: 3 | Slope: 45°

Summit Elevation	12,500'
Descent Vertical	1,500'
Total Vertical	6,400'
Hiking Distance	9 miles
Terrain	Chute
Trailhead	40. Buttermilks
USGS Quad Maps	Mt. Tom, Tungsten Hills, Mt. Darwin
GPS	37.2433 / -118.6538

Hidden from the Buttermilks, the North Couloir is the second of the two descents gracing the North Face of Mt. Emerson and isn't visible until you are directly below it. The top of the couloir can be tricky, as the rocks don't always fill in with snow, but typically a short, steep scramble is all that is required to reach the ridge. From there, the summit lies just a short distance to the (climber's) right. The top of Emerson provides excellent views of Lamarck, Darwin, and the Pine Creek and Rock Creek areas.

Approach: Refer to the General Emerson Approach on the previous page. As you continue up Birch Creek beneath the base of Mt. Emerson, pass Zebra Couloir (the first chute) to the base of North Couloir (the second chute) then boot to the summit.

Ryan Copenhagen skiing Emerson's North Couloir.

↘ ZEBRA COULOIR

Mt. Emerson

Aspect | Consequence/Exposure: 4 | Slope: 40°

Summit Elevation	12,300'
Descent Vertical	1,800'
Total Vertical	7,018'
Hiking Distance	8 ¾ miles
Terrain	Chute
Trailhead	40. Buttermilks
USGS Quad Maps	Mt. Tom, Tungsten Hills, Mt. Darwin
GPS	37.2443 / -118.6513

The Zebra Couloir gets its name from the colorful stripes in the rock walls on either side of the couloir. Steep, narrow, and striking, the Zebra's only drawback is that it doesn't go all the way to the ridge.

Approach: Refer to the General Emerson Approach on the previous page. As you continue up Birch Creek beneath the base of Mt. Emerson, Zebra Couloir is the first chute you reach. Boot to the top of the couloir, but beware that it ends in a rock headwall and offers very little in the way of a spot to relax and put your skis on.

Forest Becket atop Mt. Emerson's North Couloir.

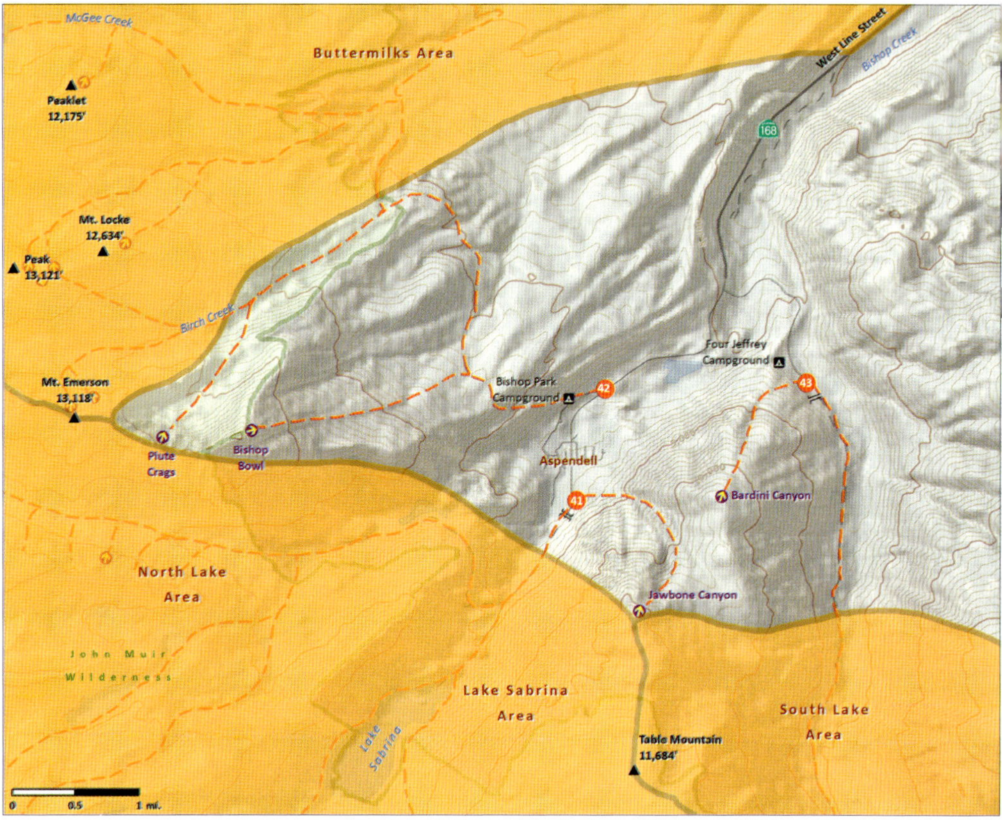

McGee Creek
Buttermilks Area
West Line Street
Bishop Creek
Peaklet
12,175'
168
Mt. Locke
12,634'
Peak
13,121'
Birch Creek
Four Jeffrey
Campground
Mt. Emerson
13,118'
Bishop Park
Campground
42
43
Piute
Crags
Bishop
Bowl
Aspendell
41
Bardini Canyon
North Lake
Area
Jawbone Canyon
John Muir
Wilderness
Lake Sabrina
Area
South Lake
Area
Lake
Sabrina
Table Mountain
11,684'
0 0.5 1 mi.

Laura Beardsley shredding Table Mountain.

Aspendell Area

The quaint community of Aspendell is nestled high in the mountains above Bishop in a small alpine valley beneath the flanks of Table Mountain.

△ PIUTE CRAGS *12,000'*

The Piute Crags are the beautifully colored set of rocky spires that form the ridgeline just east of Mt. Emerson, separating the Buttermilks Area from Aspendell.

↘ PIUTE CRAGS — Piute Crags

Aspect	Consequence/Exposure	Slope
	3	40°

Summit Elevation	12,000'
Descent Vertical	1,500'
Total Vertical	3,700'
Hiking Distance	5 ¼ miles
Terrain	Chutes
Trailhead	42. Bishop Park Campground
USGS Quad Maps	Mt. Tom, Tungsten Hills, Mt. Darwin
GPS	37.2399 / -118.643

There are several chutes in between each of the individual spires that form the Piute Crags, all of which are great descents.

Approach: Although accessible from Trailhead #40, the most common approach is via Bishop Park Campground (Trailhead #42). From this location, ski along the campground road, then climb the south-facing slope on your right to a bench beneath the broad east face of Bishop Bowl above you (see next descent). Continue north beneath this face, contouring around a series of ridgelines into the mouth of Birch Creek. Once in the drainage, continue west up it until you are beneath the crags. Boot the line of choice.

↘ BISHOP BOWL

Piute Crags

Aspect	Consequence/Exposure	Slope
	2	35°

Summit Elevation	12,000'
Descent Vertical	2,700'
Total Vertical	3,700'
Hiking Distance	2 ½ miles
Terrain	Face
Trailhead	42. Bishop Park Campground
USGS Quad Maps	Mt. Tom, Tungsten Hills, Mt. Darwin
GPS	37.2406 / -118.6331

This is one of the few roadside options in the Bishop area, with a small peak offering a few gullies and tree runs on its east face. The summit provides excellent views of the Piute Crags as well as the North Lake area.

Keep in mind that a few feet of snow at the lower elevations is required to really make this a viable destination. It also melts out early in the spring, making Bishop Bowl more of a midwinter spot. While it does see a bit of traffic, the lower section deters many people, as the short south-facing hillside above Aspendell gets hammered by the sun and wind.

Approach: From Bishop Park Campground (Trailhead #42) ski along the campground road, then climb the south-facing slope on your right. Once on top of the slope, you will find yourself on the bench beneath a broad east face that comprises Bishop Bowl. Skin this face to the summit.

Exit: Reverse your approach.

Δ TABLE MOUNTAIN *11,684'*

Table Mountain divides the Aspendell and Lake Sabrina Basin from the South Lake Drainage, and is a popular destination for locals looking for a quick ski tour. There is a tremendous amount of terrain on Table Mountain, but the two most popular descents are Jawbone Canyon, on its Northwest Face, and Bardini Canyon, off its North Ridge.

Looking south at Table Mountain from Bishop Bowl.

Table Mountain
Jawbone Canyon
168 Winter Closure
Aspendell

Alexandra Riddell skiing Table Mountain.

↘ JAWBONE CANYON

Table Mountain

Aspect	Consequence/Exposure	Slope
	2	30°

Summit Elevation	11,286'
Descent Vertical	2,500'
Total Vertical	2,786'
Hiking Distance	1 ½ miles
Terrain	Gully
Trailhead	41. Aspendell
USGS Quad Maps	Mt. Thompson
GPS	37.2207 / -118.5894

Jawbone Canyon is the obvious large canyon that sits above the community of Aspendell on the northwest side of Table Mountain. It is a major avalanche path, and during large storm cycles slides from this canyon threaten some of the homes in the community. Nonetheless, the terrain in this area provides for some great skiing with quick and easy access. The canyon itself is a bit of a terrain trap, with certain sections being worse than others. An alternative is the treed ridge on the (climber's) right.

Glen Holbrook riding Bishop Bowl.

Approach: From Aspendell (Trailhead #41), the entrance to Jawbone Canyon will be directly above you to the east. Choose the safest route up the canyon, which branches slightly at the top.

↘ BARDINI CANYON

Table Mountain

Aspect	Consequence/Exposure	Slope
	2	35°

Summit Elevation	10,600'
Descent Vertical	2,500'
Total Vertical	2,500'
Hiking Distance	1 mile
Terrain	Gully
Trailhead	43. Four Jeffreys Campground
USGS Quad Maps	Mt. Thompson
GPS	37.2334 / -118.5801

Bardini Canyon is a small cleft on the north ridge of Table Mountain, the lower reaches of which are clearly visible and are directly above the Four Jeffreys Campground. This canyon offers some great lower-angled and sheltered terrain, which is perfect for a short tour or storm days.

Beware that the lower slopes of Bardini Canyon are notorious for early season avalanches. The bushes and rocks rarely get covered very well with snow, creating endless hollow spots and inconsistencies in the snowpack. Be extremely careful on the steep slope just above the parking area, as there have been many close calls there over the years.

Approach: From Four Jeffreys Campground (Trailhead #43), skin up the north flank of Table Mountain. After the first 1,000' of climbing, you will reach a small bench, from which the rest of the canyon will be in view above you. Continue up this canyon to the upper reaches of the ridgeline.

Looking south onto Table Mountain from Highway 168.

▣ Lake Sabrina Area

Tucked away high up in Bishop Creek, the Sabrina Basin and North Lake Area offers an incredible amount of terrain that rarely gets skied due to its distance from the trailhead. Those who venture here will find a multitude of steep, technical lines mixed in with a healthy supply of bowls and faces. This area is also one of the best starting points for longer tours to the west side of the Sierra Crest, as both Piute Pass and Lamarck Col are quite moderate by Sierra standards, and take you beyond the realm of the Eastside.

North Lake is perched in a small alpine canyon hidden behind the Mt. Emerson/Piute Crags ridgeline. This terrain is accessed via the North Lake Road, which is exposed to both sun and wind, causing sections of it to melt out quickly after storms (even in the middle of winter). Though these sections are generally short, be prepared to do a small amount of walking. Despite the distance required to reach the lake, the road is frequented by snowmachines, which help pack it down and expedite travel.

Lake Sabrina is quite large and sits at a relatively low elevation, and as a result, can remain unfrozen well into the winter (some winters it may not freeze at all). This can create challenging conditions to gain access to the upper basin, with the long traverse around the lake being a bit of a battle.

North Lake Approach: The following terrain is accessed via North Lake. Each descent references this jumping-off point, along with more detailed descriptions.

To reach North Lake, continue up West Line Street/ Highway 168 from the Aspendell Trailhead (#41) (past the gate) for approximately one mile to the intersection with North Lake Road. Head north across the drainage on this road, and continue along it as it traverses into the drainage above you. After 1¼ miles you will reach North Lake, with the end of the road another ¾ mile beyond it.

△ PIUTE PASS *11,423'*

At 11,423', Piute Pass simultaneously guards and provides access to the high country within the John Muir Wilderness, most notably Humphrey's Basin, the Glacier Divide, and ultimately the Evolution Valley.

↘ PIUTE PASS RIDGE

Piute Pass

Aspect	Consequence/Exposure	Slope
	2	35°

Summit Elevation	12,000'
Descent Vertical	1,800'
Total Vertical	3,500'
Hiking Distance	4 miles
Terrain	Chutes
Trailhead	41. Aspendell
USGS Quad Maps	Mt. Thompson, Mt. Darwin
GPS	37.2266 / -118.6498

This is the north-facing terrain nestled into the prominent ridgeline that forms the south side of Bishop Creek (to your left on the way to the pass). From North Lake, the first view you get of this zone is comprised of a rocky headwall and ridgeline. The ski descents are hidden from view, and this ridge appears to be little more than a wind-scoured face. But as you climb toward the pass, the chutes will come into view.

Jon Crowley above Piute Pass.

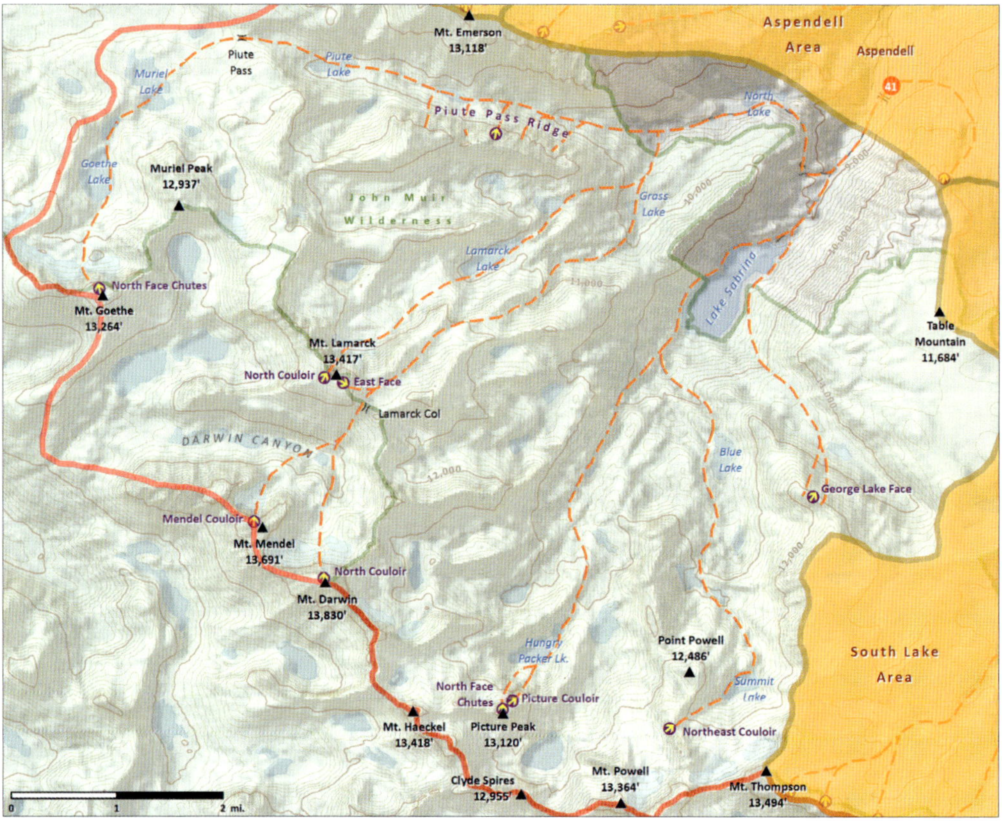

Mt. Emerson 13,118'
Aspendell Area
Aspendell
41
Piute Pass
Piute Lake
Muriel Lake
Piute Pass Ridge
North Lake
Goethe Lake
Muriel Peak 12,937'
John Muir Wilderness
Grass Lake
Lamarck Lake
Lake Sabrina
North Face Chutes
Mt. Goethe 13,264'
Table Mountain 11,684'
Mt. Lamarck 13,417'
North Couloir
East Face
Lamarck Col
DARWIN CANYON
Blue Lake
George Lake Face
Mendel Couloir
Mt. Mendel 13,691'
North Couloir
Mt. Darwin 13,830'
Hungry Packer Lk.
Point Powell 12,486'
South Lake Area
North Face Chutes
Picture Couloir
Summit Lake
Mt. Haeckel 13,418'
Picture Peak 13,120'
Northeast Couloir
Clyde Spires 12,955'
Mt. Powell 13,364'
Mt. Thompson 13,494'
0 1 2 mi.

Jason Templeton atop Mt. Goethe.

Approach: Follow the North Lake Approach directions provided earlier in this section from the Aspendell Trailhead (#41), continuing beyond the lake to the end of the road. From here, continue west up the drainage through North Lake Campground toward Piute Pass. As you begin to climb above the campground, the first of the chutes will come into view, with even more options farther up the canyon beyond Loch Leven Lake.

△ MT. GOETHE *13,264'*

Mt. Goethe (pronounced *GU(R)-tuh*) is quite far from most points in the region. Though Goethe is visible from the top of Mt. Humphreys, its ski descents are barely recognizable from this great distance.

Goethe's notoriety comes from its proximity to one of the most popular tours in the range. Known as the Alpine Col Tour, this classic loop goes over Piute Pass, Alpine Col, and Lamarck Col, and is a favorite in both the summer and winter.

When viewed from the north, Goethe appears to have two summits. The one on the left (east) is the true high point, but the one on the right (west) will have greater appeal to skiers. In between these two peaks is a saddle that is only a few hundred feet lower than the two

Basecamp at Goethe Lake.

summits. Travel along this ridge is quite moderate, so it is easy enough to bag the summit and then continue on to the other peak for the better skiing.

↘ NORTH FACE CHUTES — Mt. Goethe

Aspect	Consequence/Exposure	Slope
N	3	40°

Summit Elevation	13,264'
Descent Vertical	4,764'
Total Vertical	2,700'
Hiking Distance	9 miles
Terrain	Chutes
Trailhead	41. Aspendell
USGS Quad Maps	Mt. Thompson, Mt. Darwin
GPS	37.2064 / -118.7031

The broad north face of Mt. Goethe is split by a number of chutes, the most prominent of which lies to the west of the summit. While there are a few very steep and narrow chutes that drop from the true summit and may fill in on big snow years, most people focus on the chutes to the west of the peak.

Approach: Follow the approach for the Piute Pass Ridge from the Aspendell Trailhead (#41), continuing beyond Piute Lake to the pass itself. From the top of the pass, contour around to the south, dropping down to Muriel Lake and on to Goethe Lake. Skirt the south side of the lake into the upper basin, at which point the peak will be directly above you to the south.

While climbing the bowl between the two summits may seem like the easiest route to the ridge, the top of this (as well as the rest of the ridge) has a tendency to form extremely large cornices. The better option is to boot your line of choice directly from below.

Exit: Retrace your steps to Piute Pass then enjoy a long glide back to the trailhead.

△ MT. LAMARCK *13,417'*

Mt. Lamarck is the primary attraction within the North Lake Drainage, with excellent views into Darwin Canyon from the summit plateau.

While the North Couloir on Mt. Lamarck may be the most prominent descent, do not overlook the many other chutes tucked away in the rocky ridge to the north. Beyond the couloir, the long ridge continues on toward Piute Pass, forming a giant cirque where a massive glacier once sat. Though much of this ridge is a rock headwall, there are a few chutes along the way, and on big snow years, even more will present themselves. In addition, there are other skiable options on the two smaller

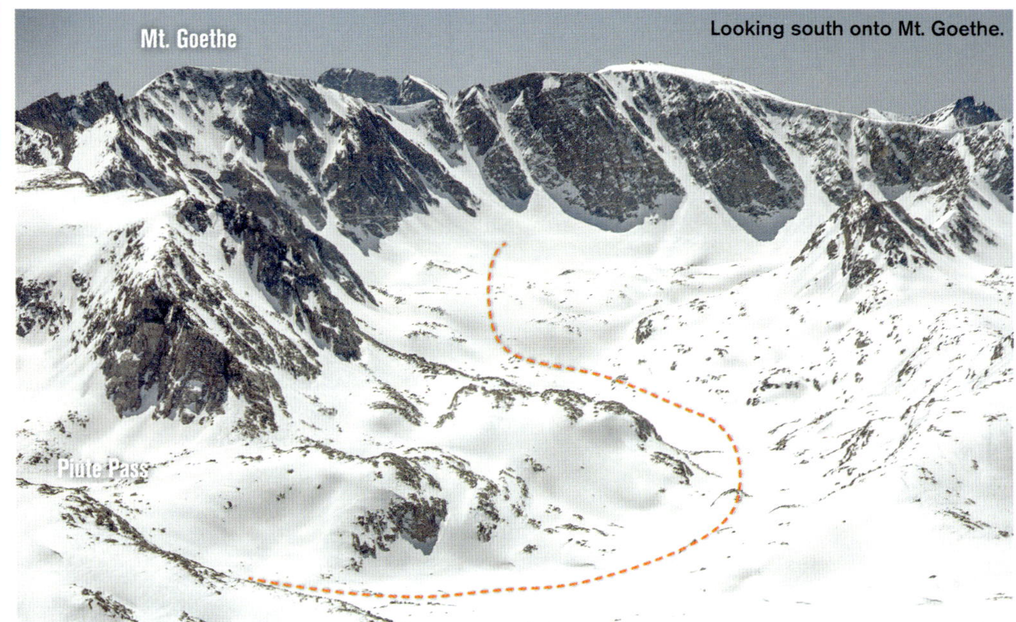

ridges that divide this drainage. All in all, this is an excellent spot to spend a few days, with more than enough skiing to keep you busy.

NORTH COULOIR

Mt. Lamarck

Aspect	Consequence/Exposure	Slope
	3	40°

Summit Elevation	13,400'
Descent Vertical	1,600'
Total Vertical	4,900'
Hiking Distance	6 ½ miles
Terrain	Chutes
Trailhead	41. Aspendell
USGS Quad Maps	Mt. Thompson, Mt. Darwin
GPS	37.1945 / -118.6728

Mt. Lamarck and its dominating North Couloir are barely visible from downtown Bishop, and are obscured from view from just about everywhere else in the area until you are directly beneath them.

The upper section of the couloir tends to get scoured by the wind. If approaching from the top of Lamarck Col, do not be too discouraged by the field of rocks—the heart of the couloir is just out of sight, and is bigger and more protected than it appears from the top.

Approach: Follow the approach description to North Lake from the Aspendell Trailhead (#41) (provided earlier in this section). Skin through the North Lake Campground, then continue across the bridge, and follow the drainage toward Grass and Upper Lamarck lakes, roughly following the location of the summer trail. From Upper Lamarck Lake, climb the moraine to the west to the base of the couloir, then boot it to the summit plateau. From here, a Class 2 walk brings you to the summit.

EAST FACE

Mt. Lamarck

Aspect	Consequence/Exposure	Slope
	2	30°

Summit Elevation	13,417'
Descent Vertical	900'
Total Vertical	4,917'
Hiking Distance	6 ½ miles
Terrain	Face
Trailhead	41. Aspendell
USGS Quad Maps	Mt. Thompson, Mt. Darwin
GPS	37.1938 / -118.6703

The East Face of Mt. Lamarck is quite exposed to the wind, but when filled in provides relatively moderate skiing from a high-elevation summit. Even if it is scoured, continuing on to the summit on foot is easy, considering the elevation. The summit ridge also affords great views of the north faces of Mendel and Darwin.

Jason Templeton beneath Mt. Lamarck.

Looking down the Mendel Couloir.

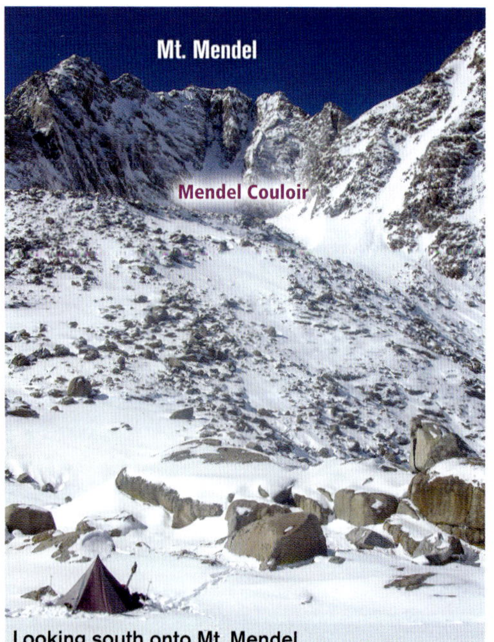

Looking south onto Mt. Mendel.

Approach: The basin above North Lake is roughly divided into three mini-drainages, all of which take you toward Mt. Lamarck. The best way to reach the col is to follow the left-hand drainage. From North Lake, climb the treed slope to Grass Lake, then continue up the left (south) drainage, skirting a rocky ridge to the south and following the most logical route and path of least resistance. The short, steep sections are mixed with moderate slopes as you slowly ascend to a sort of high-elevation plateau.

As you reach the upper portion of the canyon below Lamarck Col, the East Face will appear to your north. Skin to the top.

△ MT. MENDEL *13,691'*

Coming in just a few hundred feet shy of 14,000', Mt. Mendel sits prominently along a ridgeline just north of Mt. Darwin. Mendel is home to the popular summer ice climb known as Ice Nine Couloir.

↘ MENDEL COULOIR

Mt. Mendel

Aspect	Consequence/Exposure	Slope
	5	55°

Summit Elevation	13,600'
Descent Vertical	2,000'
Total Vertical	5,100'
Hiking Distance	7 ½ miles
Terrain	Chute
Trailhead	41. Aspendell
USGS Quad Maps	Mt. Thompson, Mt. Darwin
GPS	37.1756 / -118.6824

The Right Couloir on Mt. Mendel has long held its status as a "testpiece" of sorts. While it will certainly test your skiing ability, the real test is one of patience. This couloir has only seen a handful of descents over the years, as finding skiable conditions in this steep, narrow slot is a once-in-a-lifetime opportunity. There are numerous rock and ice bulges that only get covered under exceptional snowfall, and its incredibly steep pitch will shed snow frequently. Add to that its remote location, and Mt. Mendel will maintain its elusive nature forever.

Assessing conditions prior to heading out is challenging, though the couloir is visible from Mt. Lamarck. Beware: If you do find skiable conditions, make sure your abilities are up to par—this is, by far, the most challenging descent listed in this book. A rope and technical rock and ice gear are recommended for this line.

Looking south from Mt. Lamarck.

Approach: To reach the base of Mt. Mendel, follow the directions to Lamarck Col (see the East Face of Mt. Lamarck). Head over the col and descend the west side into Darwin Canyon. This face is a bit steeper than the east side of the col, and is much more exposed to both the sun and wind. As such, you will most likely have to carry your skis down (and back up) for a short distance. There is also a trail on the south side, but it is a little difficult to find in the intermittent snow.

From Darwin Canyon head west, then climb the moraine below the peak, and up the steep north face to the base of the couloir. The pitch changes significantly as you enter the couloir, and it only gets steeper from there.

Jason Templeton riding Mt. Darwin.

△ MT. DARWIN *13,830'*

This flat-topped peak splits the Evolution Valley from Darwin Canyon and is a gorgeous sight. Another big Eastside classic, Mt. Darwin is known for its elevation, fall ice, and tricky summit block.

↘ NORTH COULOIR

Mt. Darwin

Aspect	Consequence/Exposure	Slope
N	3	35°

Summit Elevation	13,800'
Descent Vertical	2,000'
Total Vertical	5,300'
Hiking Distance	8 miles
Terrain	Chute
Trailhead	41. Aspendell
USGS Quad Maps	Mt. Thompson, Mt. Darwin
GPS	37.1682 / -118.6729

This moderate north face is capped by a slightly more challenging upper chute. Though not incredibly steep, the upper line can be difficult if it has been hammered by the wind.

Approach: Follow the directions to Mt. Mendel over Lamarck Col. From Darwin Canyon, follow the drainage south to the base of Darwin's north face. The narrow chute leads to the summit ridge, and may involve climbing through a short tunnel to reach the giant summit plateau.

Looking southwest onto Picture Peak.

Sabrina Basin Approach: The following terrain described is part of the Sabrina Basin, and is generally accessed via the southwest end of the lake. To reach this point, continue up the road from the Aspendell Trailhead (#41) past the gate for approximately 1¾ miles until you reach the outlet of the lake.

While the summer trail goes around the southeast side of the lake, this route is typically not the best option during winter months. Instead, there is a good fisherman's trail that goes around the other side and can be easier, depending on conditions. The easiest access to the Sabrina Basin is in the spring when the road is open to the lake. Unfortunately, by the time this happens access can be a little difficult: The many gullies and drainages that feed the lake begin melting out and flowing heavily with water. At times like this it is best to follow the main hiking trail around the southeast side of the lake. This goes to Blue Lake, where you will then traverse into the main drainage if headed toward Picture, Clyde Spires, etc.

Δ PICTURE PEAK *13,120'*

The aptly named Picture Peak is one of the most eye-catching and photogenic features in the Sabrina Basin. This peak bears a resemblance to Bear Creek Spire, as both peaks have big couloirs just to the right of their clean rock buttresses.

↘ PICTURE COULOIR — Picture Peak

Aspect	Consequence/Exposure	Slope
	3	40°

Summit Elevation	12,500'
Descent Vertical	2,500'
Total Vertical	4,000'
Hiking Distance	6 ½ miles
Terrain	Chute
Trailhead	41. Aspendell
USGS Quad Maps	Mt. Thompson, Mt. Darwin
GPS	37.1510 / -118.648

Though not as narrow as it looks from afar, the upper section of this line can pose a bit of a challenge. Thankfully, it isn't very steep.

Picture Approach: From Lake Sabrina, climb the slope at the far west end of the lake contouring uphill to the northwest. Continue up the drainage to Hungry Packer Lake, which sits at the base of Picture Peak. From this point, you can either climb directly up the line or up the slope on the north side of the peak. Above the couloir are a number of complicated and challenging chutes taking you closer to the summit.

Looking south across Lake Sabrina.

Picture Exit: On the way out, it is tempting to simply follow the drainage back to Sabrina, but that really isn't a good idea. It's best to make a short climb to the northeast to access Blue Lake, then retrace your steps. Throw your skis on your back, follow the hiking trail, and save yourself a *lot* of frustration.

↘ NORTH FACE CHUTES

Picture Peak

Aspect	Consequence/Exposure	Slope
	4	35°

Summit Elevation	13,000'
Descent Vertical	3,000'
Total Vertical	4,500'
Hiking Distance	6 ½ miles
Terrain	Chutes
Trailhead	41. Aspendell
USGS Quad Maps	Mt. Thompson, Mt. Darwin
GPS	37.1521 /-118.6475

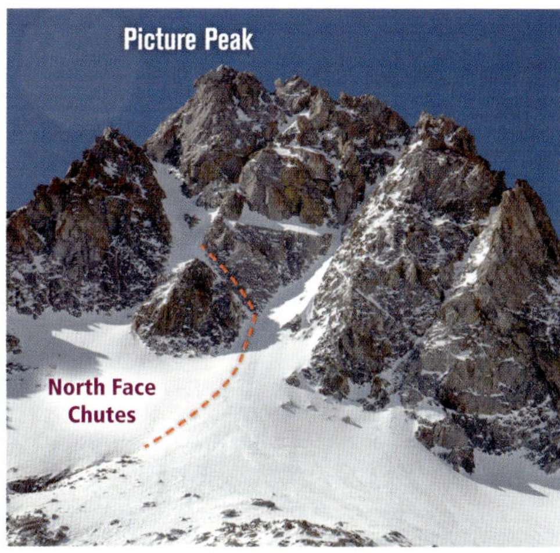

Looking south at Picture Peak from below the North Face.

In addition to the Picture Couloir, there are a handful of steep chutes on the face above the Picture Couloir. On big snow years, many of these will become skiable. The two difficulty ratings on this peak apply to these chutes, and depend on how far up you decide to go.

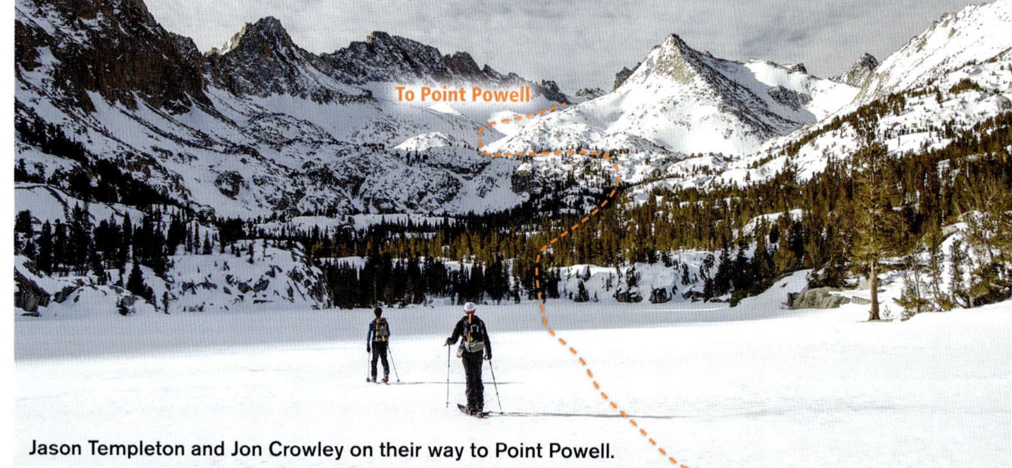

Jason Templeton and Jon Crowley on their way to Point Powell.

△ POINT POWELL *12,486'*

A fairly obscure peak, Point Powell sits on a ridgeline to the north of Mt. Powell and Mt. Thompson.

Almost as obscure as the peak itself, this fantastic line, Point Powell Couloir, sits in a remote drainage above Blue Lake.

↘ NORTHEAST COULOIR — Point Powell

Aspect	Consequence/Exposure	Slope
	3	35°

Summit Elevation	12,300'
Descent Vertical	1,000'
Total Vertical	3,800'
Hiking Distance	7 miles
Terrain	Chute
Trailhead	41. Aspendell
USGS Quad Maps	Mt. Thompson, Mt. Darwin
GPS	37.1485 / -118.6264

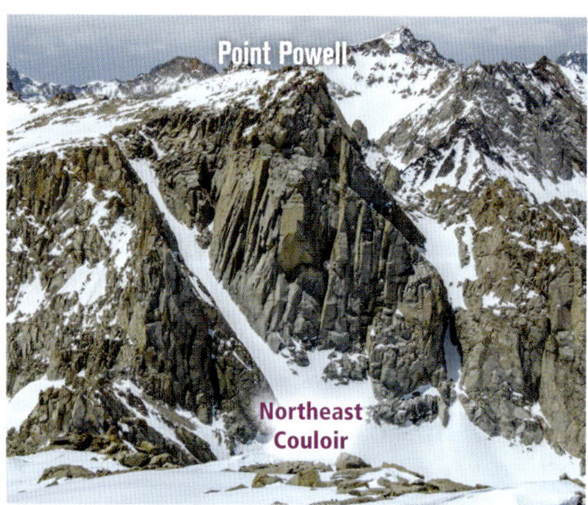

Looking west at Point Powell from Mt. Thompson.

Approach: From the west end of Lake Sabrina, climb the slope to the south into the Blue LakeDrainage. Continue up this drainage, contouring to the left, to Sunset Lake. From here, the couloir will be in view. Climb the couloir to the summit ridge, where a short walk will bring you to the top of Point Powell.

△ GEORGE LAKE RIDGE *12,000'*

Above George Lake is a ridge with a series of chutes and bowls. This ridge continues on to Tyee Lakes, and ultimately the South Lake Road. The stuff just before and above the lake is ideal for a moderate day. It is a much shorter alternative to the rest of the descents in the Lake Sabrina Area.

The top of this ridge provides excellent views of the Sabrina Basin.

↘ GEORGE LAKE FACE — George Lake Ridge

Aspect	Consequence/Exposure	Slope
	3	35°

Summit Elevation	12,000'
Descent Vertical	1,300'
Total Vertical	3,500'
Hiking Distance	4 ¼ miles
Terrain	Chutes & Bowls
Trailhead	41. Aspendell
USGS Quad Maps	Mt. Thompson
GPS	37.1789 / -118.6071

Approach: Follow the south shore of Lake Sabrina toward its western end. Just before this point, turn south and climb the drainage that leads to George Lake.

Jason Templeton beneath Mt. Gilbert.

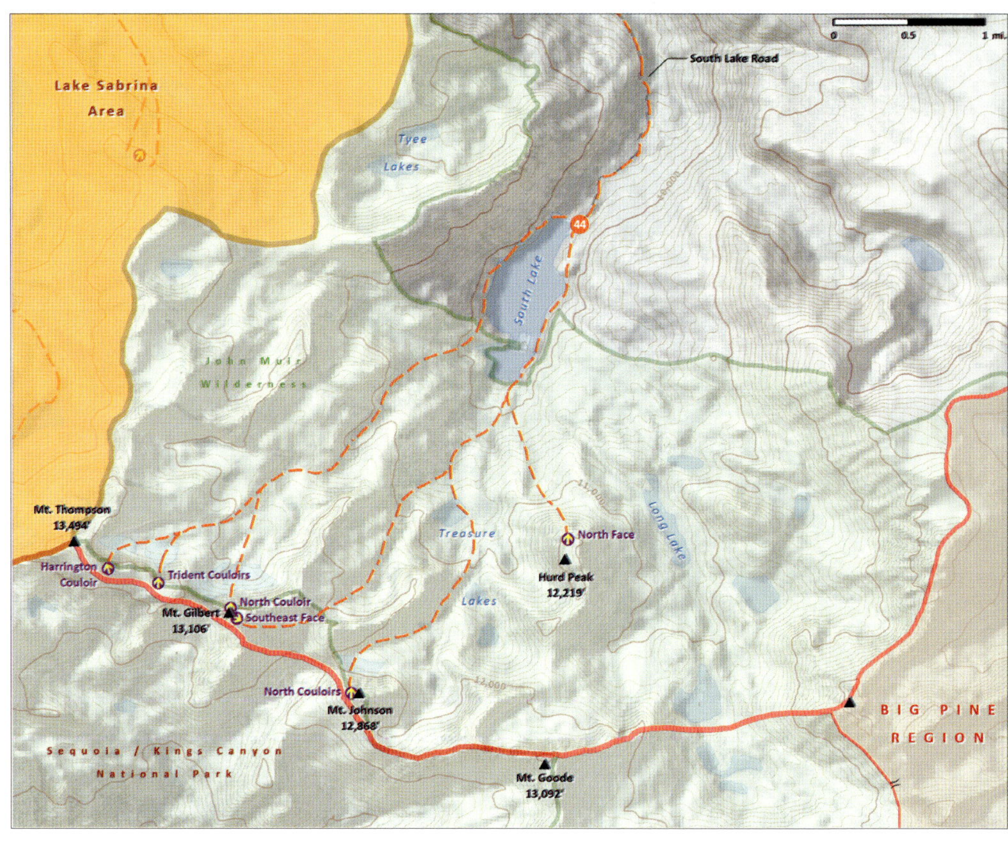

▣ South Lake Area

In the summertime, the South Lake Area is inundated with fishermen and hikers exploring the many lakes and waterways that fill this narrow canyon. During the winter, the road to South Lake is only plowed to Four Jeffreys Campground, from which point it is approximately five miles to South Lake. As a result, few people other than snowmobilers venture into this basin until the road is plowed in spring. When this occurs, though, backcountry skiers descend on the South Lake Area, as most of the terrain mentioned is relatively close to the road and well worth the wait.

△ MT. THOMPSON *13,494'*

Mt. Thompson sits at the head of the South Lake Drainage and is the tallest peak along the ridgeline. There is an abundance of terrain in the area along the Thompson Ridge, as well as in the bowls between Mt. Thompson and Mt. Gilbert, which is where the popular north-facing couloirs of the Thompson Cirque reside.

The cirque immediately south of Mt. Thompson hosts two prominent couloirs—the most well known is the Moynier Couloir. Located at the far western end of the North Face of Mt. Thompson, this is one of the range's more challenging fall ice climbs, with a large chockstone lodged in the center. Unfortunately, the chockstone, along with the ice, keeps the Moynier from being skiable.

↘ NON-MOYNIER COULOIR — Mt. Thompson

Aspect	Consequence/Exposure	Slope
	4	45°

Summit Elevation	13,300'
Descent Vertical	1,000'
Total Vertical	3,600'
Hiking Distance	3 ½ miles
Terrain	Chute
Trailhead	44. South Lake
USGS Quad Maps	Mt. Thompson
GPS	37.1403 / -118.6102

Just a short distance to the looker's left of the Moynier Couloir is another chute, which, for the purposes of this book, we have called the "Non-Moynier Couloir." We

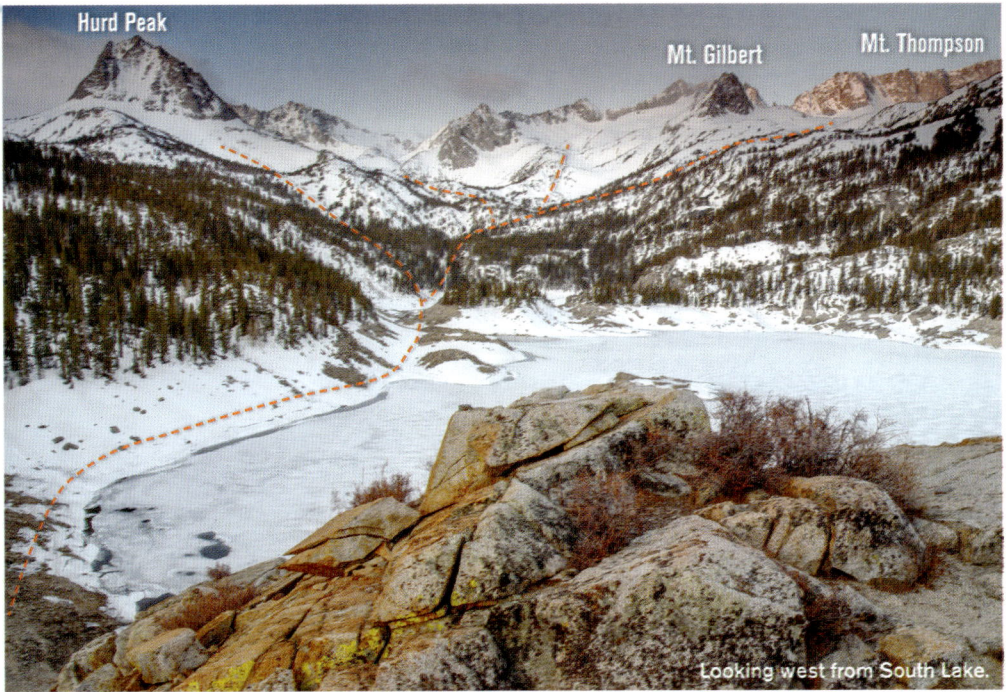

Looking west from South Lake.

were unable to determine the true name, if it even has one. Reports of people skiing the Moynier Couloir have most likely been this chute, as it is incredibly close. This chute does get scoured by the wind, as it sits out on a rock buttress, and has the tendency to form a large cornice on its top.

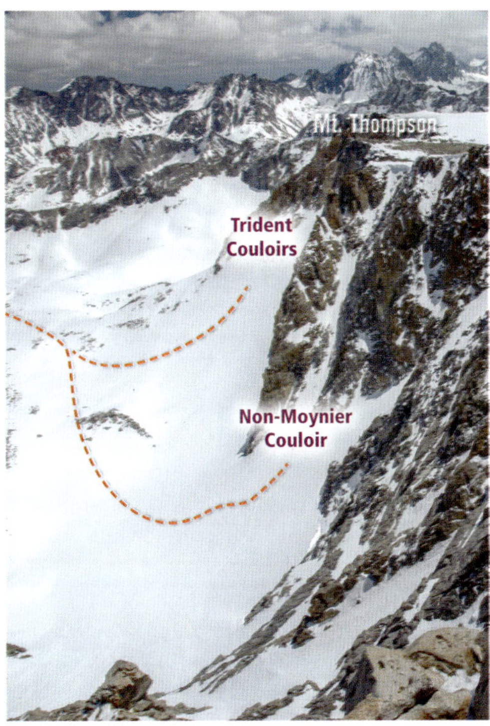

Looking south across Mt Thompson's east face.

Approach: From South Lake Dam (Trailhead #44), travel around the north side of the lake to the small peninsula on its southwest side. From here, head west, climbing into the first drainage northwest of Treasure Lakes. Above some moderately treed gullies you reach the bench at the base of Mt. Gilbert. Curve around to the right (northwest), climbing a morraine to the base of Mt. Thompson. At this point, the Trident Couloirs will be directly above you to the west.

Continue past these to the north where you will find two more steep, narrow chutes tucked away in the cirque. The couloir on the right with the large chockstone in it is the Moynier Couloir; the line to the left is the Non-Moynier Couloir. Boot the line to the top.

Though the summit of Mt. Thompson is closer from the top of this chute than the Tridents, it is still a bit of a walk along the ridge. Luckily, travel along the ridge is incredibly easy, and the views into the Sabrina Basin from the true summit of Thompson are well worth the effort.

Exit: Reverse the approach.

↘ TRIDENT COULOIRS

Mt. Thompson

Aspect | Consequence/Exposure: 3 | Slope: 35°

Summit Elevation	13,200'
Descent Vertical	1,000'
Total Vertical	3,500'
Hiking Distance	3 ½ miles
Terrain	Chutes
Trailhead	44. South Lake
USGS Quad Maps	Mt. Thompson
GPS	37.1390 / -118.6053

These are the three obvious couloirs that are visible from the South Lake parking lot, and are all quite similar in pitch and difficulty. From the top of the couloirs, the summit of Mt. Thompson is still quite far away, though requires little elevation gain—and travel along the ridge is incredibly easy.

Approach: Follow the directions for the Non-Moynier Couloir to the base of the Tridents, and boot your line of choice to the top.

Exit: Reverse the approach.

Δ MT. GILBERT *13,106'*

At 13,106', Mt. Gilbert is the second peak along the ridgeline above South Lake.

↘ NORTH COULOIR

Mt. Gilbert

Aspect | Consequence/Exposure: 4 | Slope: 50°

Summit Elevation	13,106'
Descent Vertical	1,500'
Total Vertical	3,406'
Hiking Distance	3 ½ miles
Terrain	Chute
Trailhead	44. South Lake
USGS Quad Maps	Mt. Thompson
GPS	37.1366 / -118.5983

Similar to neighboring Mt Thompson, Mt Gilbert's North Couloir is more commonly known as an alpine ice climb. This 65 degree WI3 couloir is a High Sierra classic. But in the winter months, it offers a fine steep ski descent through the beautiful surrounding alpine granite. The line is only visible for a brief time as you approach South Lake, then not again until you are almost directly underneath it. It drops through the large, rocky buttress that forms the summit block into the basin between Mt. Thompson and Mt. Gilbert.

Approach: Follow the approach described for the Harrington Couloir into the basin below the Northeast Face of Mt. Gilbert. From this point, break left (southwest) and climb the glacier to the base of the couloir. After booting the couloir, an exposed Class 3 scramble provides access to the actual summit of Mt. Gilbert.

↘ SOUTHEAST FACE

Mt. Gilbert

Aspect | Consequence/Exposure: 2 | Slope: 30°

Summit Elevation	13,106'
Descent Vertical	2,000'
Total Vertical	3,406'
Hiking Distance	3 ½ miles
Terrain	Chute
Trailhead	44. South Lake
USGS Quad Maps	Mt. Thompson
GPS	37.1357 / -118.5977

The Southeast Face of Mt. Gilbert is without a doubt the easier way to access the summit of Mt. Gilbert, and offers a fine moderate descent down into the Treasure Lakes Basin.

Jon Crowley nearing the ridge on Mt. Thompson.

Chris Gallardo beneath Mt. Gilbert.

Looking west from atop Hurd Peak.

Approach: From South Lake Dam (Trailhead #44), skin around the south side of South Lake to its southeast corner, then continue southwest into the large cirque directly above you. This drainage ultimately leads to the Treasure Lakes Basin. Where the drainages split, climb into the northern drainage (rather than to Treasure Lakes) using the west–east-running ridgeline as your guide. At the head of this drainage is a cirque, where a short, steep chute on the north side provides access to the base of the Southeast Face. Climb the face to the summit.

Exit: Reverse your approach back to the car.

∆ MT. JOHNSON *12,871'*

Farther south along the skyline above South Lake is the slightly smaller Mt. Johnson. This peak is somewhat separated from the dominating peaks to the north by the large ridgeline that emanates east from Mt. Gilbert.

Though somewhat obscured from view from South Lake, the North Face of Mt. Johnson is graced with a series of moderately pitched chutes. While there is a great deal of terrain in this drainage, the North Couloirs are the most attractive and sought-after lines.

↘ NORTH COULOIRS

Mt. Johnson

Aspect	Consequence/Exposure	Slope
	4	40°

Summit Elevation	12,871'
Descent Vertical	1,500'
Total Vertical	3,171'
Hiking Distance	5 ½ miles
Terrain	Chutes
Trailhead	44. South Lake
USGS Quad Maps	Mt. Thompson
GPS	37.1287 / -118.5867

Approach: From South Lake Dam (Trailhead #44), skin around the south side of South Lake to its southeast corner, then continue southwest into the large cirque directly above you. This drainage ultimately leads to a stand of trees below the rocky west face of Hurd Peak, and on to Treasure Lakes. From the lakes, continue up the valley, at which point the North Couloirs of Mt. Johnson will come into view. The couloir on the right leads to the ridge just below the summit. If the face above the couloir is covered in snow, it is possible to ski directly from the summit. Be aware, however, that this slope is very exposed and slightly convex.

Exit: Reverse the approach.

Chris Gallardo dropping off the summit of Mt. Johnson.

△ HURD PEAK *12,219'*

Perched directly above South Lake, Hurd Peak becomes a popular spot in the spring when the road opens. The steep, rocky face has one main line that snakes down the center, and on big years other options open up.

The North Face of Hurd Peak is very exposed to the wind and may not hold much snow, depending on the year or time of the season. This moderate descent is well worth the trip, though, as the summit of Hurd provides a great perspective into the Treasure Lakes area, Bishop Pass, and the Palisades.

Jon Crowley crossing South Lake.

↘ NORTH FACE

Hurd Peak

Aspect	Consequence/Exposure	Slope
	3	35°

Summit Elevation	12,100'
Descent Vertical	2,000'
Total Vertical	2,400'
Hiking Distance	2 ¼ miles
Terrain	Face
Trailhead	44. South Lake
USGS Quad Maps	Mt. Thompson
GPS	37.1431 / -118.5660

Approach: Hurd is the closest peak to South Lake, rising almost directly from its south shore. From South Lake Dam (Trailhead #44), skin around the south side of the lake, then continue due south up the drainage to the base of the peak. Skin and boot to the summit.

It is also possible to reach the base from Long Lake. To go this route, follow the location of the Bishop Pass Trail all the way to the lake, and then continue up the steep slope to the base of the chutes.

Exit: With a clear view of South Lake, you should be able to figure this one out ...

12 Big Pine

Jason Templeton pauses for a siesta below the Palisade Glacier.

12. Big Pine

BIG PINE REGION:

- ▣ The Palisades:
  - ◎ NORTH FORK
  - △ THUNDERBOLT PEAK
  - △ POLEMONIUM PEAK
  - △ MT. SILL
  - ◎ SOUTH FORK
  - △ KIDD MOUNTAIN
  - △ SLIDE MTN. / MT. ALICE
  - △ MT. SILL
  - △ NORMAN CLYDE PEAK
  - △ MIDDLE PALISADE
- ▣ McMurray Meadows:
  - △ THE THUMB
  - △ BIRCH MOUNTAIN
  - △ MT. TINEMAHA
  - △ SPLIT MOUNTAIN
  - △ CARDINAL MOUNTAIN

As Highway 395 heads south from Bishop, the character of the Sierra remains dramatic; however, the amount of people and overall backcountry traffic rapidly decline. To many travelers, Big Pine is just another small town that stands in the way between Mammoth and Southern California. But to those seeking big backcountry lines, the Big Pine Region hosts an impressive set of peaks that will keep the adventurous skier busy for a long time.

Without a doubt, the major draw around Big Pine is the Palisade Crest, with its jagged, high-altitude ridge attracting mountaineers from all over the world. In the midwinter, the peaks at the front of the range are just as appealing to backcountry enthusiasts, with huge descents sitting adjacent to the Highway 395 corridor.

Getting There & Getting Going

From downtown Bishop, head south on Highway 395 for 15 miles to Big Pine. All the trailheads mentioned below are accessed off the Glacier Lodge Road, which heads west into the mountains from the center of town.

The Glacier Lodge Road is plowed year-round, providing easier access to the trailhead, but beware that this road is not a high priority for road crews and can remain closed for a day or two after big storms. In recent years the road has only been plowed to Sage Flat Campground, which is 1¾ miles from the Glacier LodgeTrailhead.

45. Glacier Lodge Trailhead (Year-Round) — 7,770'

From downtown Big Pine, head west on Crocker Avenue (which turns into Glacier Lodge Road after a short distance) for 10½ miles, to where the road ends at the Big Pine Creek Trailhead. Park in the large, obvious plowed parking area just before the gate.

46. McMurray Meadows/Birch Creek Trailhead (Spring Only) — 6,100'

This is an unmaintained dirt road, with no snow removal. The first section of the road (closest to Glacier Lodge Road) is lower in elevation and can melt out fairly quickly after storms and in the spring. As the road winds its way south and approaches Birch Mountain, however, it climbs higher and weaves through some shaded spots that can hold snow, rendering the road impassable.

Be forewarned that while most of the road to McMurray Meadows can be passable *without* a high-clearance vehicle, one is strongly recommended. The road is slow going, and requires much longer to travel than most people realize.

From downtown Big Pine, head west on Crocker Avenue (which turns into Glacier Lodge Road) for 2½ miles to the dirt turnoff for McMurray Meadows Road (9S03). Turn left (south) onto this dirt road, then make an immediate right to stay on the more prominent roadway. Follow this south through rolling hills past the first left intersection approximately 3¾ miles

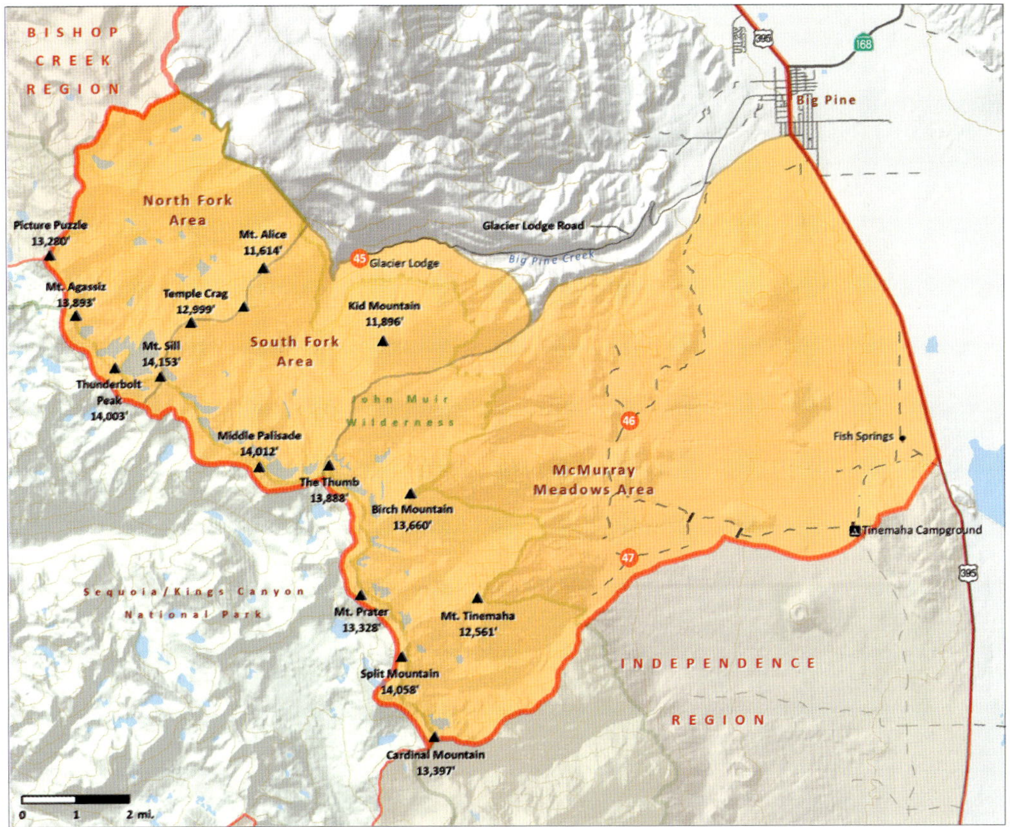

from the beginning of the dirt road. Stay straight, continuing on the main road to the south. The road starts to climb to the southwest until it reaches the junction with 9S03A (which branches off to the right) at approximately 4¼ miles. Stay left on the main road, climbing more to the west, after which the road turns back south and eventually drops you into Birch Creek at a three-way intersection with ample parking.

If there is snow, this is the best place to park and start your skin. But if it is late in the season or you are welcomed by a high snowline, you can continue west across the creek a bit farther. Beware that this section definitely requires high clearance and 4WD.

47. Red Lake Trailhead (Spring Only) *6,600'*

Beware that to reach this trailhead you need a high-clearance 4WD vehicle. The best way to reach the Red Lake Trailhead is to follow the description provided above to reach McMurray Meadows/Birch Creek Trailhead (#46). From the three-way junction at Birch Creek, head west and cross the creek, continuing along Forest Road 9S03 south to Fuller Creek. Continue east along the main road down the Fuller Creek drainage for approximately three miles. At this point, turn right and head south along a road that crosses Tinemaha Creek and after a short distance intersects Tinemaha Creek Road (FS 10S01). Turn right here and head west up this road for another mile or so, passing several small spur roads until the main road ends at the Red Lake Trailhead.

Region Trailheads

45. Glacier Lodge Trailhead

46. McMurray Meadows/Birch Creek Trailhead

47. Red Lake Trailhead

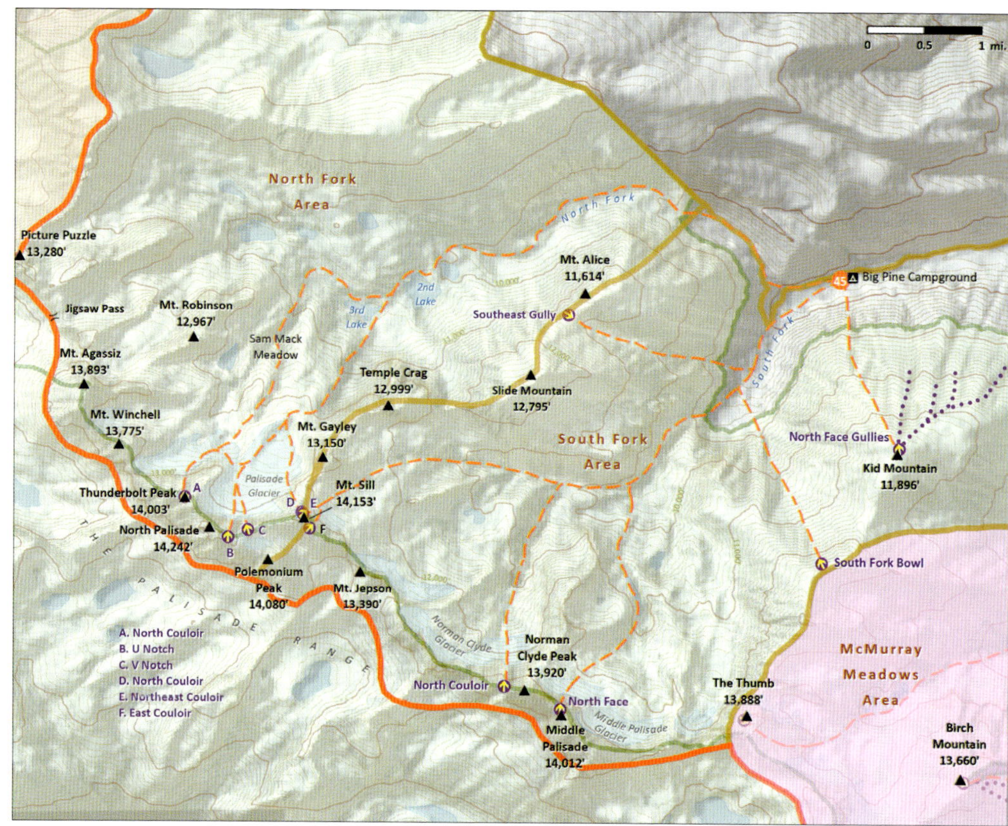

Note that it may also be possible to reach the trailhead from the Tinemaha Campground by using a combination of Fish Springs Road, Fuller Creek Road, and Tinemaha Road. This route does cross through some private property, however, and access can change from year to year and season to season. Please respect private-property rights in this area.

Eats, Digs, Services, & Supplies

The town of Big Pine is rather small but offers the basic necessities, including fuel, restaurants, a grocery store, and bar. For home-style cooking check out the Country Kitchen, and for some of the best burritos around visit the takeout restaurant in the Chevron on Main Street.

▣ The Palisades

The Palisade Region is one of the most rugged sections of the Sierra, and contains the highest concentration of 14,000' peaks in the state, making it the ultimate destination for ski mountaineering in California. With so many sought-after summits, the Palisade drainages see more traffic than other regions south of Bishop. Though it's not nearly as popular as the Mount Whitney zone, be prepared to encounter other parties, particularly in the North Fork Drainage.

As a result of the craggy nature of this range, the skiing is limited to just a handful of chutes that split the ridgeline. The majority of the ski descents are quite steep, and reaching any of the peaks requires mountaineering skills, including glacier travel, comfort on steep snow and ice, and often some rock climbing. Most of the chutes don't terminate anywhere near a summit, so be prepared for a lot of scrambling if the summit is your objective.

The Palisades are split between two drainages—the North and South forks of Big Pine Creek. These two areas are separated by the long ridge that connects Mt. Alice, Temple Crag, and Mt Sill. For descents along the actual crest, the North Fork has a few more options

than the South Fork. These are fantastic areas to set up a winter basecamp, as access is a bit longer and the skiing options are so abundant. If steep couloirs aren't your cup of tea, this is still an excellent place to tour and view the scenery, as there are a number of moderate bowls just below the peaks.

High elevation and high exposure combine in this region, resulting in this area being notorious for high winds. Finding powder in any of the chutes is rare, and wind-packed snow should be considered the norm. Crampons and ice axes are essential for this region, at any time of year, and reaching most of these summits will often require a rope.

Despite the technical difficulty in the ascents/descents, getting to the Palisades is actually quite easy compared to many other regions in this book. In addition to the Glacier Lodge Road being plowed to the trailhead, well-maintained summer hiking trails provide easy access to the snow during the early and late parts of the season.

◎ NORTH FORK

The North Fork Drainage provides access to the base of the main portion of the Palisade range. Despite the relatively gentle grade in the lower reaches of the drainage, there is not always ample snow coverage. Be prepared to carry all your equipment on your back for at least a little while in all but midwinter. During most of the approach the peaks and chutes of the crest are obscured from view, until you reach Temple Crag. At this point the climb steepens as you gain the terminal moraine at the base of the glacier, and the range opens up before you.

At the head of the drainage lies the Palisade Glacier, which requires basic glacier-travel skills to cross and catches some people off-guard. The glacier is much bigger than most people realize, and on low snow years or in the shoulder season when the crevasses and bergschrunds begin to open, it can become quite serious.

Note that the most sheltered camping is found around the lakes at the base of Temple Crag or in Sam Mack Meadow.

North Fork Access: From the Glacier Lodge Trailhead (#45), follow the summer hiking trail across a large bridge and up into the North Fork Drainage. This trail follows the Big Pine Creek Drainage, ultimately switchbacking up to the first bench. As you gain the first bench, look for another large bridge to cross the creek again. From here the hiking trail climbs to the left and traverses the south-facing hillside above. This is one of the few cases where the best route is not on the hiking trail, as the trail faces south and melts out very early in the year. Instead, continue along the canyon floor beneath Mt. Alice, following an old road along the creek. At the head of the lower canyon a short, steep climb will bring you back to the trail and onto the next bench. Continue through the rolling hills, following the drainage past First, Second, and Third lakes to the base of the moraine below Temple Crag. This point is further referenced in each of the detailed approach descriptions that follow.

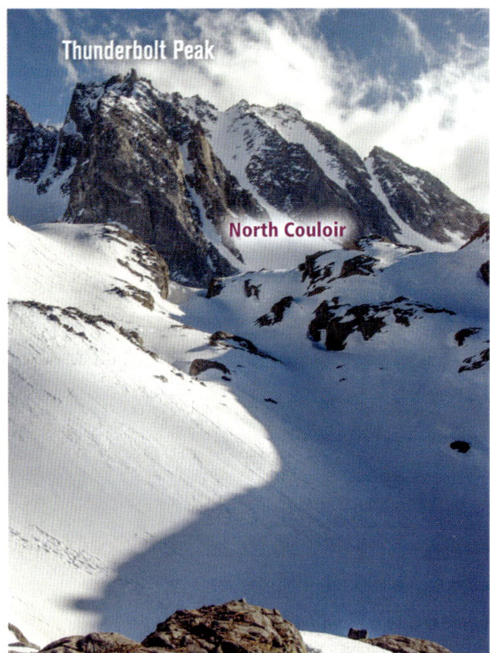

△ THUNDERBOLT PEAK *14,003'*

Marking the beginning of the 14,000' peaks that comprise the Palisade ridge, Thunderbolt is also one of most well known. Reaching the summit of this beautiful peak is no simple feat, with a 5.9 rock face guarding the highest point.

↘ NORTH COULOIR — Thunderbolt Peak

Aspect | Consequence/Exposure: 3 | Slope: 40°

Summit Elevation	14,003'
Descent Vertical	1,500'
Total Vertical	6,300'
Hiking Distance	7 miles
Terrain	Chute
Trailhead	45. Glacier Lodge
USGS Quad Maps	Coyote Flat, Mt. Thompson, North Palisade, Split Mountain
GPS	37.0981 / -118.5176

The giant North Couloir drops steeply from Thunderbolt's 14,003' summit and is a true Eastside classic.

Approach: Follow the North Fork description provided earlier to Third Lake/Temple Crag. From Third Lake continue west up the drainage a short distance then climb south to Sam Mack Meadow. From here, continue up the gullies to the base of the couloir, then climb the couloir to the summit ridge. Near the top, the couloir splits, with the climber's-left branch going closer to the summit. Reaching the summit is complicated, however, with the final section requiring some 5.9 climbing.

Exit: Follow your approach route back to the trailhead.

△ POLEMONIUM PEAK *14,080'*

Surrounded by the neighboring 14,000' peaks of Mt. Sill and North Palisade, Polemonium Peak appears at first glance to be the least impressive on the ridge. What it lacks in scale is made up for in quality, with two of the most highly sought-after lines gracing its north face—U Notch and V Notch.

Sitting side by side, these two lines are better known for ice climbing than backcountry skiing. Alpine ice forms in these gullies during spring and summer months, and on some years (especially low-snow years) may linger throughout the ski season. Anticipate mixed conditions, and be prepared to alter your plan should you arrive to find less-than-optimal skiing conditions.

The bergschrunds at the base of the U and V notches can also be problematic as the season progresses. Do not underestimate the terrain above these and the hazard they present, as they are quite different from anything else in the range. It is often worth bringing a rope to add some safety while crossing the "schrunds", which if you continue on to the summits of Polemonium or North Pal will be necessary anyway.

↘ U NOTCH — Polemonium Peak

Aspect | Consequence/Exposure: 3 | Slope: 40°

Summit Elevation	13,900'
Descent Vertical	1,500'
Total Vertical	6,200'
Hiking Distance	6 ¾ miles
Terrain	Chute
Trailhead	45. Glacier Lodge
USGS Quad Maps	Coyote Flat, Mt. Thompson, North Palisade, Split Mountain
GPS	37.0932 / -118.5121

U Notch is the looker's right and the less steep of the two couloirs. It also provides the easiest and most direct way to the summit of Polemonium Peak.

Jason Templeton below the U Notch.

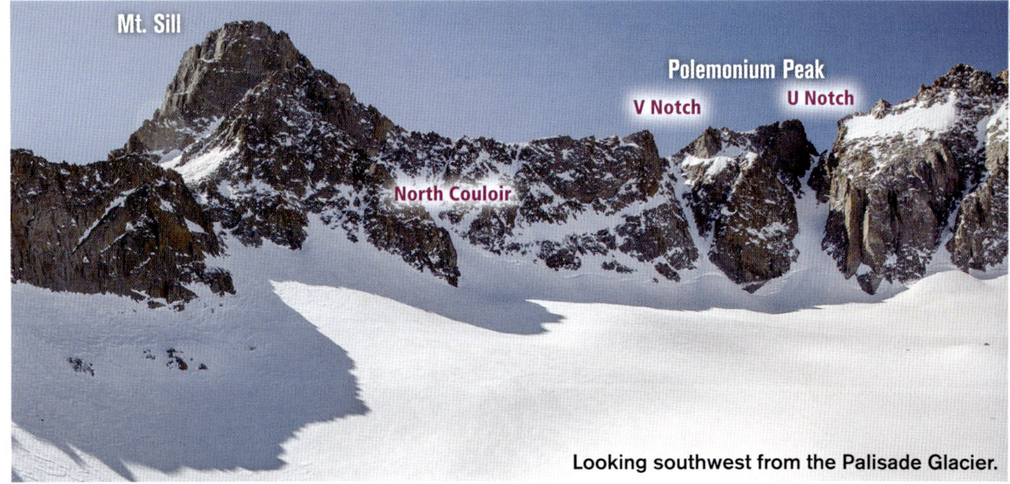

Looking southwest from the Palisade Glacier.

Approach: Follow the North Fork description provided earlier to Third Lake/Temple Crag. From Third Lake head south below Temple Crag and up past Mt. Gayley onto the Palisade Glacier. As you continue south and climb the glacier, U Notch will be above you. Climb the chute to the top of the ridge.

The summit of Polemonium Peak is fairly accessible from here, lying a relatively short distance to the southeast.

Exit: Follow your approach route back to the trailhead.

↘ V NOTCH

Polemonium Peak

Aspect | Consequence/Exposure 4 | Slope 50°

Summit Elevation	13,900'
Descent Vertical	1,500'
Total Vertical	6,200'
Hiking Distance	6 ¾ miles
Terrain	Chute
Trailhead	45. Glacier Lodge
USGS Quad Maps	Coyote Flat, Mt. Thompson, North Palisade, Split Mountain
GPS	37.0941 / -118.5095

The V Notch is slightly steeper than U Notch, and maintains its pitch for the entire length. This is an intimidating and demanding line that should not be taken lightly.

Approach: Refer to the approach for U Notch to reach the base of the couloirs. Some people choose to climb V Notch directly, while just as many choose to utilize U Notch to reach the top. Obviously, if linking up these two lines in a day, it is most desirable to put the bootpack into U Notch and reuse it on the second lap.

From the top of V Notch the summit of Polemonium appears to be an easy Class 2 walkup. While the majority of it is, the last few hundred feet get quite complicated, and should only be attempted by seasoned mountaineers.

Exit: Follow your approach route back to the trailhead.

△ MT. SILL *14,153'*

As you view the Palisade Crest from downtown Big Pine and various points along Highway 395, Mt. Sill dominates the skyline. From a distance nothing appears even remotely skiable on it, but closer inspection reveals a few couloirs tucked away in its large granite walls.

Mt. Sill separates the North and South Fork drainages of Big Pine Creek. Referenced below is the North Couloir, which drops into North Fork. On the east side of the peak are two additional chutes, which are referenced in the South Fork Area later in this chapter.

Hidden from view until you are on the Palisade Glacier, the moderate North Couloir of Mt. Sill cuts through the prominent North Ridge, beginning just below the final headwall that leads to the summit.

↘ NORTH COULOIR

Mt. Sill

Aspect	Consequence/Exposure	Slope
N	3	40°

Summit Elevation	13,800'
Descent Vertical	1,200'
Total Vertical	6,100'
Hiking Distance	6 ¾ miles
Terrain	Chute
Trailhead	45. Glacier Lodge
USGS Quad Maps	Coyote Flat, Mt. Thompson, North Palisade, Split Mountain
GPS	37.0963 / -118.5026

Approach: Follow the approach described earlier for U Notch. As you climb onto the Palisade Glacier, head south and slightly west toward the right-hand side of the large, rocky North Ridge of Mt. Sill. As you approach the peak, the North Couloir will present itself. Though the couloir ends in a rock headwall, there is a nice spot to relax at the top and put on your skis or board.

From the top of the North Couloir, reaching the summit of Mt. Sill is unfortunately quite complicated. Above you is a significant amount of steep granite that requires Class 5 climbing. If the summit really is your objective, the easier option is to climb V Notch then continue east along the large, moderate ridge to the summit.

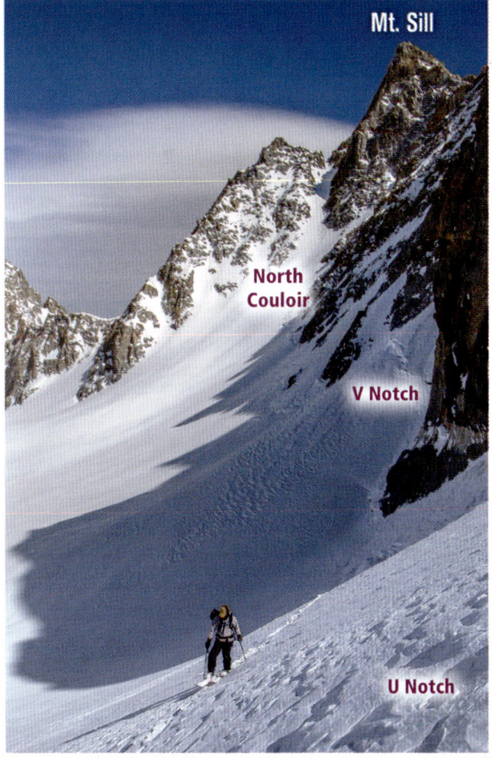

(Top) Basecamp beneath the Palisades.
(Bottom) Jason Templeton climbing the U Notch.

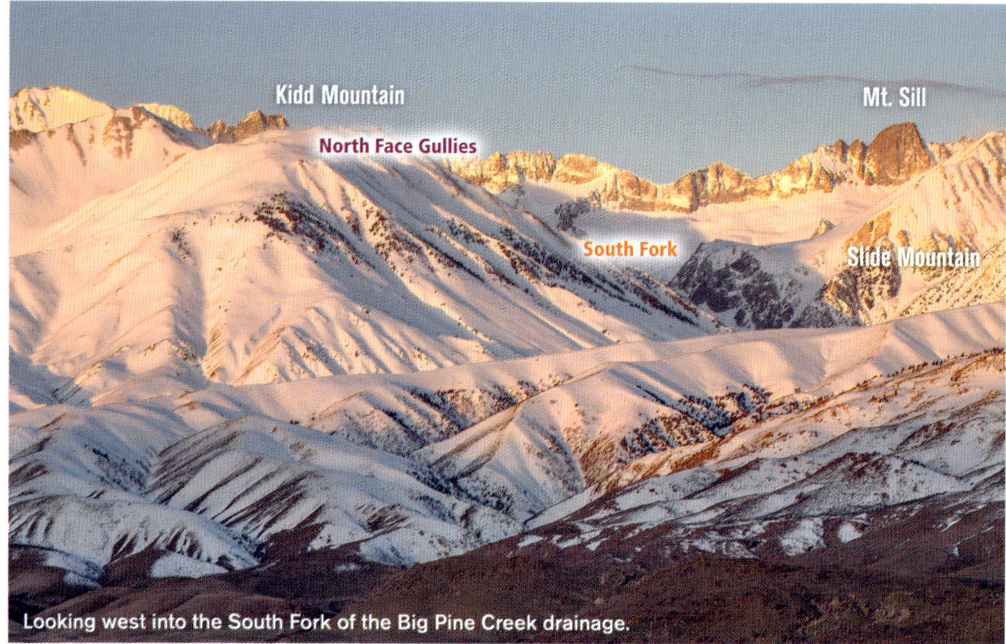

Looking west into the South Fork of the Big Pine Creek drainage.

SOUTH FORK

The South Fork Drainage provides a different point of access and a very different view of the Palisades. In addition to the big terrain of the Palisades at the head of the drainage, several other prominent descents are accessible in the lower reaches of the South Fork.

The terrain in this area is also a bit easier and quicker to get into than that of the North Fork Drainage. The biggest challenge is getting across the South Fork of Big Pine Creek, but once frozen over, the path to the peaks is direct and relatively straightforward.

Δ KIDD MOUNTAIN *11,896'*

Kidd Mountain rises to the south above the Glacier Lodge Trailhead, providing incredibly convenient roadside access to some relatively large terrain. Unfortunately, its location also seems to prevent it from getting the same volume of snow as its neighbors, since it is blocked from the westerly flow and its north slopes are very exposed to the wind that rips through the upper canyon. When the snow is plentiful, however, Kidd Mountain truly delivers and is well worth the trip.

Sitting directly above the Glacier Lodge Road, the North Face of Kidd Mountain is lined with numerous chutes and bowls. Access couldn't be easier—just park, cross the river, and start climbing.

↘ NORTH FACE GULLIES — Kidd Mountain

Aspect	Consequence/Exposure	Slope
	2	35°

Summit Elevation	11,896'
Descent Vertical	4,100'
Total Vertical	4,200'
Hiking Distance	1 ½ miles
Terrain	Gullies
Trailhead	45. Glacier Lodge
USGS Quad Maps	Coyote Flat, Split Mountain
GPS	37.1045 / -118.4270

Approach: This is the one descent in the Palisade Area that does not necessarily start from the Glacier Lodge Trailhead (#45) at the road end. Given the nature of the terrain, you can instead park and start from many points along this road, though parking is not always easy if there is a large snowbank. The best place to cross the river is through Sage Flat or Big Pine campgrounds.

From the road, cross the river and climb whichever gully looks the most appealing.

Exit: Ski the line of choice directly back to the road.

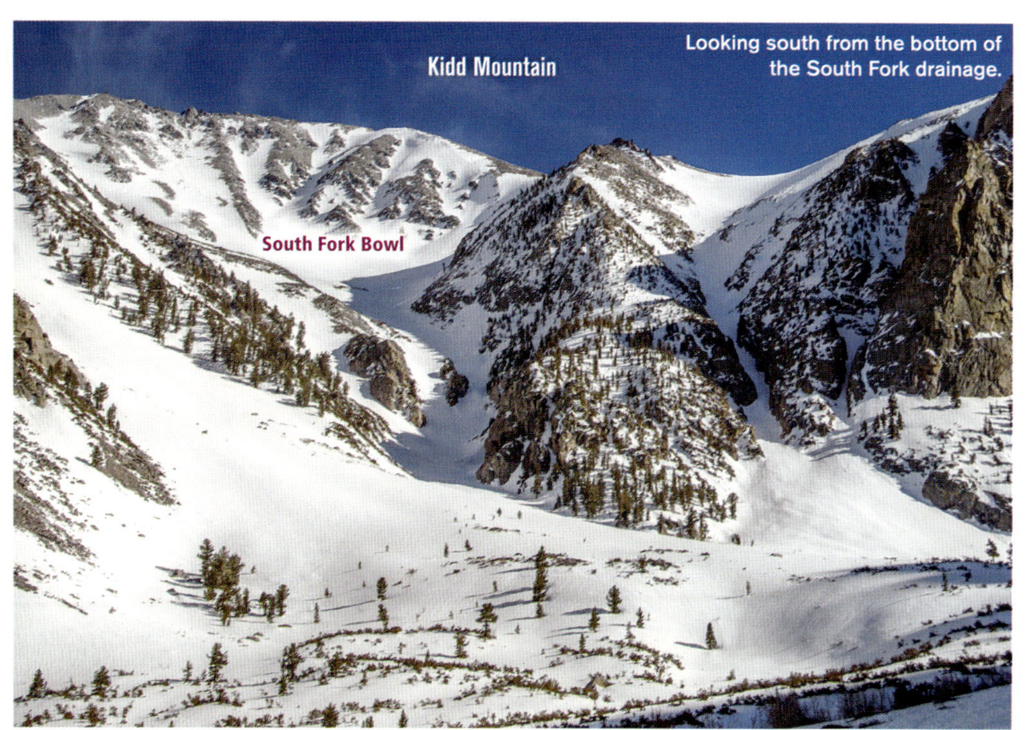
Kidd Mountain
Looking south from the bottom of the South Fork drainage.
South Fork Bowl

➘ SOUTH FORK BOWL

Kidd Mountain

Aspect | Consequence/Exposure | Slope

2 | 35°

Summit Elevation	12,300'
Descent Vertical	4,000'
Total Vertical	4,600'
Hiking Distance	2 miles
Terrain	Bowl
Trailhead	45. Glacier Lodge
USGS Quad Maps	Fish Springs, Split Mountain
GPS	37.0904 / -118.4368

Located along the ridge between Kidd Mountain and The Thumb is a small zone packed with a selection of chutes and open bowls to choose from. The view of Middle Palisade from the top of this terrain is top-notch.

Approach: From Glacier Lodge Trailhead (#45), follow the South Fork hiking trail across the bridge and into the drainage. After a very short distance, the bowl will be visible directly above you to the south. Continue along the trail to the base of the bowl, and then up your line of choice.

Exit: Simply reverse the approach back to the trailhead.

△ SLIDE MOUNTAIN/MT. ALICE *12,800'*

Mt. Alice (and its sister peak, Slide Mountain) are perched above the South Fork Drainage in a spectacular location that divides it from the North Fork. It is separate from the Palisade Crest and has a very different feel to it, with its large, moderate slopes a stark contrast to the rocky faces that are so prominent elsewhere in this section. The views from Slide Mountain are also outstanding, making it one of the most spectacular places to ski in the range.

➘ SOUTHEAST GULLY

Slide Mtn./Mt. Alice

Aspect | Consequence/Exposure | Slope

2 | 35°

Summit Elevation	12,800' (Slide) | 11,600' (Alice)
Descent Vertical	3,500'
Total Vertical	4,100'
Hiking Distance	2 ½ miles
Terrain	Gully
Trailhead	45. Glacier Lodge
USGS Quad Maps	Coyote Flat, Split Mountain
GPS	37.1209 / -118.4689

Though seemingly innocuous, this line is larger than it looks, dropping several thousand feet into the mouth of

South Fork. As with any large sun-exposed line in the range, an early start is key to catch the best conditions. Also be prepared for a little work at the bottom of this run, as it tends to melt out rather quickly.

Approach: From Glacier Lodge Trailhead (#45), follow the South Fork hiking trail across the bridge and into the drainage. Just before climbing out of the lower canyon, a gully will appear on your right. Follow this up to the base of two small bowls where you can either head left to a small ridge or straight up the higher bowl. Both options top out on a large bench that climbs gradually up the face toward the summit.

△ MT. SILL *14,153'*

Mt. Sill is the prominent peak that splits the North and South Fork drainages, and is clearly visible from various points down-canyon, and from Highway 395. The most sought-after line on this peak is the North Couloir, which is accessed from the North Fork Drainage. The South Fork Drainage provides access to the East Face of Mt. Sill, which includes the Northeast and East Couloirs.

The Northeast Couloir tops out at the exact same spot as the North Couloir (listed in the North Fork Section). For a fantastic loop of the Palisade drainages, you can climb the South Fork/Northeast Couloir, and descend the North Couloir/North Fork (or vice versa).

↘ NORTHEAST COULOIR

Mt. Sill

Aspect	Consequence/Exposure	Slope
	3	35°

Summit Elevation	13,800'
Descent Vertical	1,500'
Total Vertical	6,100'
Hiking Distance	5 miles
Terrain	Chute
Trailhead	45. Glacier Lodge
USGS Quad Maps	Coyote Flat, Mt. Thompson, North Palisade, Split Mountain
[illegible]	[illegible]

Approach: From the Glacier Lodge Trailhead (#45), follow the summer trail across the creek and into the South Fork Drainage. Pass Willow Lake and continue to the north (right) up the drainage beneath the southeast faces of Temple Crag and Mt. Gayley, beyond which you will find yourself at the base of Mt. Sill's East Face.

Above you to the right is the Northeast Couloir (and to the left, the East Couloir). Climb the line to the top where a small staging area provides enough room to change over and get ready for the run.

Exit: Follow your approach back to the car. Note that it is also very easy to link this line up with the North Couloir of Mt. Sill, which would drop you into the North Fork Drainage.

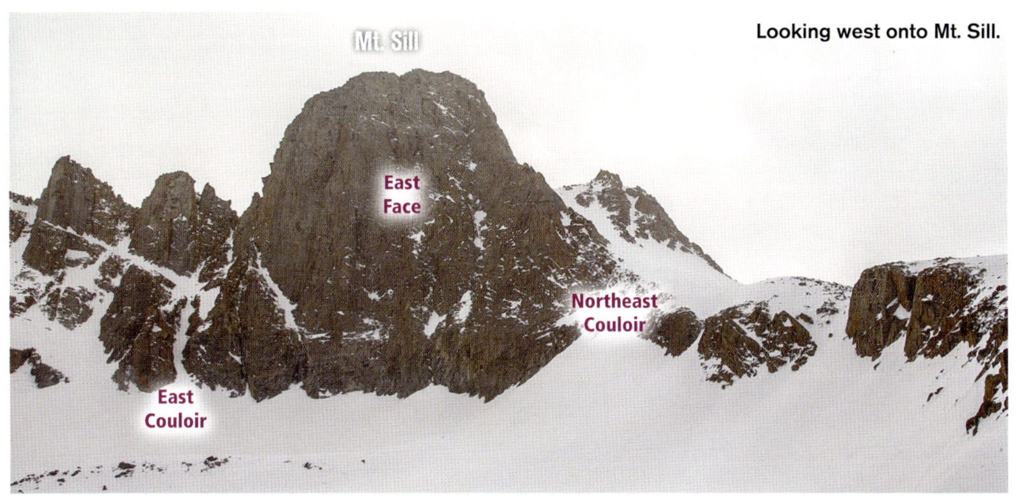

Looking west onto Mt. Sill.

↘ EAST COULOIR

Mt. Sill

Aspect | Consequence/Exposure 4 | Slope 50°

Summit Elevation	13,500'
Descent Vertical	1,000'
Total Vertical	5,800'
Hiking Distance	5 miles
Terrain	Chute
Trailhead	45. Glacier Lodge
USGS Quad Maps	Coyote Flat, North Palisade, Split Mountain
GPS	37.0943 / -118.5016

The East Face of Mt. Sill is an imposing feature, with the large rock buttress almost seeming to overhang as you climb underneath it. Just to the left of this face lies a small sliver of snow. From below, it doesn't look like much, but this line climbs fairly high on the ridge and creates one of the more technical descents on this peak. The crux is a short distance from the top, where a section of the chute is incredibly steep and narrow.

This chute is only visible from a few locations, including from directly beneath it. It is steep and rocky, and doesn't always hold snow. So be prepared to walk a long way for a chute that may not be skiable.

Approach: Follow the approach described for the Northeast Couloir of Mt. Sill. The East Couloir is the left-hand of the two lines on Mt. Sill's East Face. Boot the chute to the top.

Exit: Retrace your steps back to the trailhead.

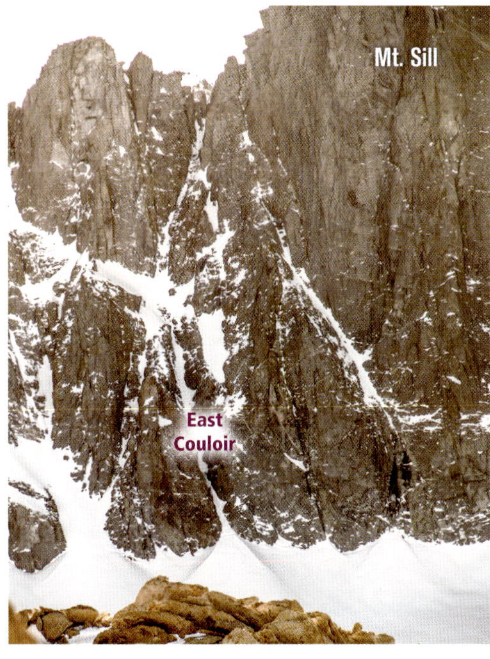

△ NORMAN CLYDE PEAK *13,920'*

Located next to Middle Palisade along the Palisade Crest, this 13,920' peak is named after the great Sierra mountaineer Norman Clyde and is easily recognized by its large north and east rock faces.

The North Couloir on Norman Clyde is one of the few consistently skiable lines along this portion of the Palisade Crest. A long and aesthetic run, the North Couloir is tucked away from view in a slightly obscure drainage between Middle Palisade and Mt. Sill. From the top of the couloir, the route to the summit is supposedly Class 3, though the rock walls on either side suggest otherwise.

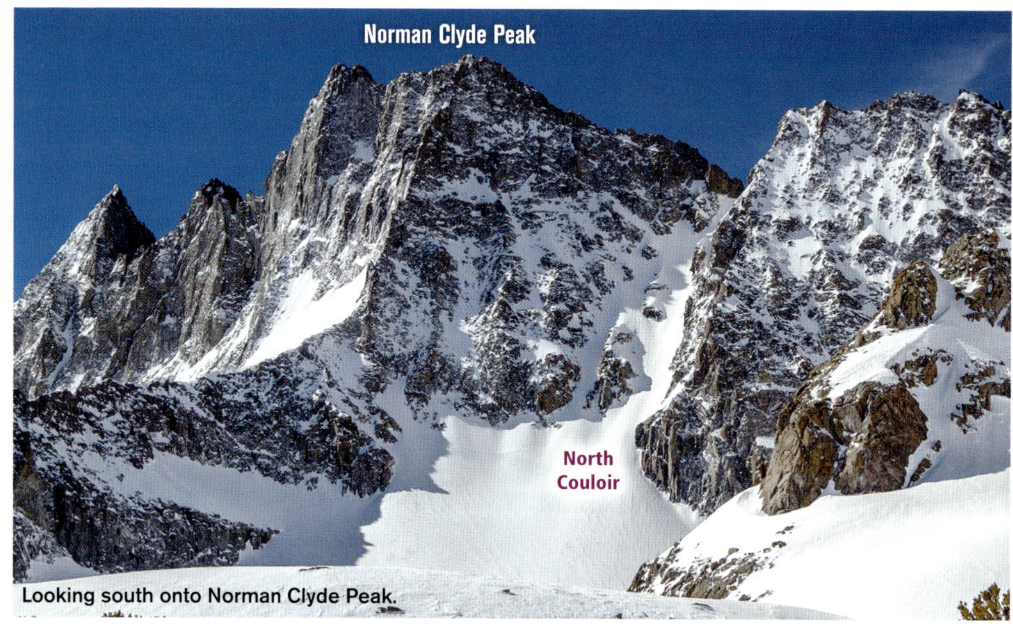

Looking south onto Norman Clyde Peak.

↘ NORTH COULOIR — Norman Clyde Peak

Aspect | Consequence/Exposure: 3 | Slope: 40°

Summit Elevation	13,500'
Descent Vertical	1,800'
Total Vertical	5,800'
Hiking Distance	4 ½ miles
Terrain	Chute
Trailhead	45. Glacier Lodge
USGS Quad Maps	Coyote Flat, Split Mountain
GPS	37.0749 / -118.4768

Approach: Follow the approach for Mt. Sill up the South Fork Drainage. As the drainage turns west toward Mt. Sill, continue south onto the Norman Clyde Glacier, directly below the striking north face of Norman Clyde Peak. At this point, the couloir will be in sight. Continue to the base and climb it to the top.

Exit: Retrace your steps back to the trailhead.

△ MIDDLE PALISADE *14,012'*

Ranking as the 12th highest peak in California, the 14,012' summit of Middle Palisade lies in the center of the Palisade ridgeline. Though the summit itself is fairly well known, it is not skied very often, mostly because the high elevation and steep rock face seem to rarely hold enough snow for it to even be possible.

↘ NORTH FACE — Middle Palisade

Aspect | Consequence/Exposure: 4 | Slope: 50°

Summit Elevation	14,012'
Descent Vertical	2,000'
Total Vertical	6,300'
Hiking Distance	4 ½ miles
Terrain	Face, Chutes
Trailhead	45. Glacier Lodge
USGS Quad Maps	Coyote Flat, Split Mountain
GPS	37.0721 / -118.4697

Visible from both Birch Mountain and The Thumb (as well as the upper section from Westguard Pass, with powerful binoculars), this line is essentially the shallow gully that cuts just east of the summit of Middle Pal. Often referred to by climbers and mountaineers as the Main Chute, this line is highly exposed to the wind, and any snow that does stick to it certainly doesn't do so for very long. Finding enough snow to ski this line involves an immense amount of patience. Big winters and/or heavy snowfall are no indication of what the coverage may be like on this face—it is just as likely to fill in on a low-snow year. It requires a series of storms with very moderate winds, and calm periods in between. This is a rarity around here, but it does happen.

As challenging as it can be to find the line with enough coverage, once filled in, its exposure and highly

Jon Crowley climbing Middle Palisade.

technical terrain pose the real challenge. The face is steep and gets steeper as you climb. The cruxes are narrow and numerous, and later in the year sections of water ice begin to develop beneath the shallow snowpack. This is a high-consequence and very high-exposure line that is not to be taken lightly — do not add it to your list simply because it's a 14er — expert climbing and skiing skills are a must.

Approach: Follow the approach for Mt. Sill into the South Fork Drainage. As the drainage turns west, turn south and continue toward the base of Middle Palisade. The prominent North Ridge of Norman Clyde Peak should be on your right. Continue up this drainage to the Middle Palisade Glacier at the base of the East Face. As you reach the base of the peak, the line will finally come into view (the gullies seen from Willow Lake are not the ones you will be skiing).

If conditions look good, continue up the avalanche cone and directly up the face. Crampons and ice tools are essential on this one, and a rope may also be a nice addition to your equipment list.

Exit: Relieved that you have completed this mission, retrace your steps.

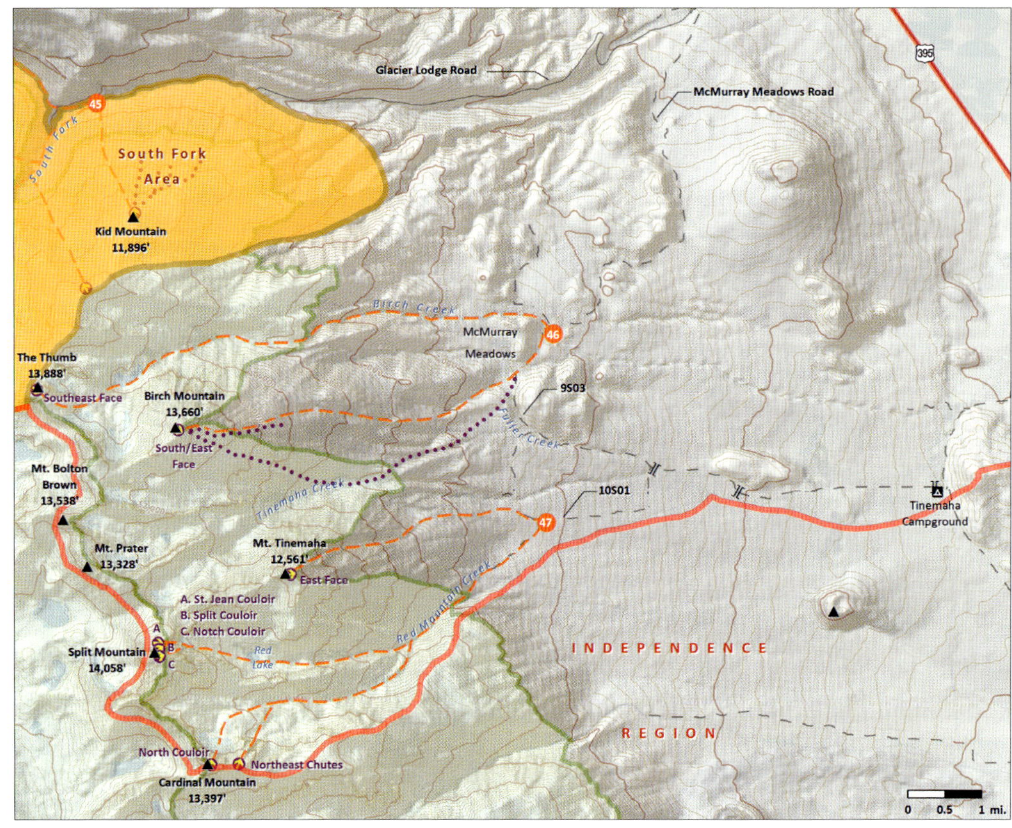

▣ McMurray Meadows Area

Though the Palisade Area clearly dominates the Big Pine Region in terms of density, the peaks to the south of the Big Pine Creek Drainage are equally impressive and offer large, steep, and technical descents.

The entirety of this area is contained within the five miles of ridgeline that extend south from The Thumb to Taboose Pass. The gems here are also some of the bigger descents in the range, including Birch Mountain, Mt. Tinemaha, and the impressive and intimidating Split Mountain—the eighth highest peak in the state.

All of this terrain is accessed from the McMurray Meadows Road or from several small spur roads that leave from it. While this road affords reasonably good access to the lower reaches of the peaks, it is an unmaintained dirt road, which makes winter access difficult and travel during dry periods slow.

This is some of the most wild and engaging terrain in the Sierra, and the quantity and quality of lines here is enough to supply a lifetime of adventure in itself.

△ THE THUMB *13,888'*

The Thumb is one of the several 13,000' subpeaks of the greater Palisades range, perched between its 14,000' neighbors—Split Mountain and Middle Palisade. With straightforward access and unparalleled views of Middle Palisade, The Thumb offers moderate skiing paired with a big-mountain feeling and a very big day.

↘ SOUTHEAST FACE — The Thumb

Aspect	Consequence/Exposure	Slope
SE	2	30°

Summit Elevation	13,500'
Descent Vertical	2,500'
Total Vertical	7,400'
Hiking Distance	6 ¼ miles
Terrain	Face
Trailhead	46. McMurray Meadows
USGS Quad Maps	Fish Springs, Split Mountain
GPS	37.0710 / -118.4464

This is one of the more moderate ski descents in the Big Pine Region, though by no means should it be considered an "introductory peak," as the distance and elevation gain required to summit are sizable. That said, the Southeast Face offers low-angle, low-consequence

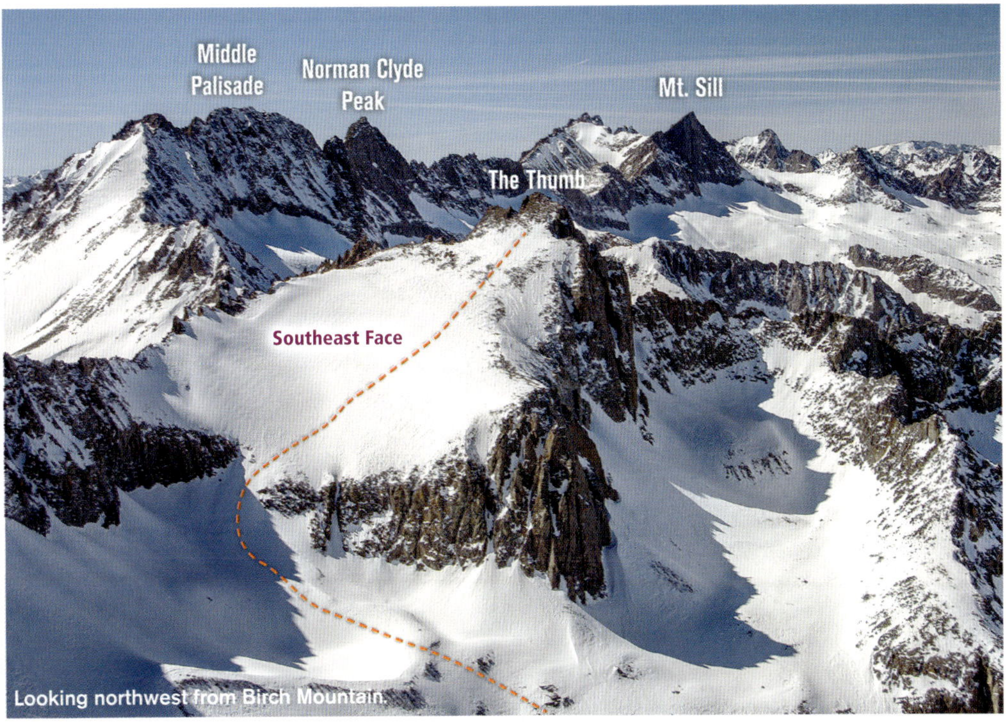

Looking northwest from Birch Mountain.

terrain situated in a beautiful alpine position and is well worth the journey.

Approach: From the McMurray Meadows/Birch Creek Trailhead (#46), head west up the Birch Creek Drainage, passing over a series of benches until you are below the north face of Birch Mountain. Once in the upper drainage, trend left (south) around the rocky ridgeline that forms the east face of The Thumb. As you turn the corner at the southern end of this ridge, the Southeast Face will be directly above you. Skin up this gradual face to the summit.

Δ BIRCH MOUNTAIN *13,660'*

Birch Mountain is one of the giants of the Eastside. Perched along the edge of the range, its 13,600' summit looms over the Owens Valley, and offers stellar views of the Palisade Crest and many other peaks throughout the range. If conditions are good and your timing is right, Birch offers a descent of over 7,000' from summit to trailhead. Unfortunately, the summit of Birch tends to get hammered by the wind, so it is not uncommon for the upper portions to be wind stripped or generally unskiable. It is also a lot larger than most people realize, and more than one party has been caught off-guard by changing conditions due to refreezing or unexpected warming of the large slopes.

Looking west up the Birch Creek drainage.

↘ SOUTH/EAST FACE — Birch Mountain

Aspect	Consequence/Exposure	Slope
	2	35°

Summit Elevation	13,660'
Descent Vertical	7,200'
Total Vertical	7,560'
Hiking Distance	4 ¾ miles
Terrain	Face, Gullies
Trailhead	46. McMurray Meadows
USGS Quad Maps	Fish Springs, Split Mountain
GPS	37.0633 / -118.4185

Looking west across the valley at Birch Mountain.

The most common way to ski Birch Mountain is off the summit via the South Face, then to turn and drop off the ridgeline down the East Face through one of several different gullies. If you are not interested in summiting, skiing from the top of the East Face still affords almost 6,000' of vertical. It is also possible to continue down the South Face toward Tinemaha Creek, through a series of small, steep chutes.

Approach: From the McMurray Meadows Trailhead (#46), follow the McMurray Meadows Road through the Birch Creek Drainage and south for a short distance until you are directly below the gullies of the East Face.

Skin up the face, following one of the gullies or the ridgelines between them to the top of this face. If the summit is your objective, continue up the South Face, but bear in mind that the top is still a good distance away and takes a lot longer than most people expect. As you approach the upper reaches of the South Face, traverse west to a rocky ridge, then climb the final distance to the summit.

Exit: The exit will depend on the line you choose to ski. If you intend to ski down the East Face gullies, you can essentially retrace your approach back to the trailhead. If you intend to ski the South Face all the way into Tinemaha Creek, the actual exit can be a bit more complicated. After skiing the South Face itself, access to the upper portion of the creek is afforded through a handful of small, steep chutes, some of which are steep, and others rocky and exposed. Once in the creek, it is generally best to hug the skier's left-hand side (south face) and hold a high traverse line until you can regain the East Face and follow this back to the trailhead.

△ MT. TINEMAHA *12,561'*

Another front-range giant, Mt. Tinemaha is fairly reminiscent of Mt. Tom, rising straight out of the valley, with its summit towering several thousand feet over the slopes below. This beautiful and iconic peak is sought after by locals and visitors alike, and provides excellent summit views of the north face of Split Mountain and Cardinal Mountain.

The main gully on the East Face of Mt. Tinemaha bears a resemblance to Elderberry Canyon on Mt. Tom. The deeply cut gully drops steeply from the summit ridge all the way to the valley below. In contrast to Mt. Tom's Elderberry Canyon, however, Mt. Tinemaha has a slightly bigger approach and is considerably steeper.

Melissa Buehler atop Birch Mountain.

Looking west from Highway 395.

↘ EAST FACE

Mt. Tinemaha

Aspect | Consequence/Exposure: 3 | Slope: 35°

Summit Elevation	12500'
Descent Vertical	6,000'
Total Vertical	6,400'
Hiking Distance	3 miles
Terrain	Chutes, Face
Trailhead	47. Red Lake Trailhead
USGS Quad Maps	Fish Springs, Split Mountain
GPS	37.0359 / -118.3963

Approach: Follow the driving directions to the Red Lake Trailhead (#47). Just before reaching the main summer trailhead, a small road will branch off to the right (north). Follow this to the end and park. From here continue on foot to the base of Mt. Tinemaha, up the moraine, and into the canyon that splits the East Face.

At the bottom of this canyon is a small cliff that must be negotiated. While the cliff is not incredibly large, the amount of snow present can make this complicated and challenging. Above this you are presented with the option of either continuing straight up the gully or climbing a short, steep chute to the left, which eventually provides access to a larger, hanging canyon above. Both routes converge just below the summit.

Exit: Ski this line right back to the car.

△ SPLIT MOUNTAIN *14,058'*

Split Mountain is truly one of the iconic peaks of the Eastern Sierra. Both beautiful and intimidating, this summit beckons serious ski mountaineers from all over the world. The impressive Split Couloir was named in the book *50 Classic Ski Descents of North America* (www.wolverinepublishing.com), and the terrain that surrounds it is nothing to take lightly either.

Red Lake Approach: From the Red Lake Trailhead (#47) continue up the left branch of the road to the summer trailhead. From here, continue up the Red Mountain Creek Drainage, generally following the route of the summer trail beneath the south face of Mt. Tinemaha to Red Lake.

↘ ST. JEAN COULOIR

Split Mountain

Aspect | Consequence/Exposure: 4 | Slope: 45°

Summit Elevation	13,500'
Descent Vertical	2,500'
Total Vertical	7,400'
Hiking Distance	5 miles
Terrain	Chute
Trailhead	47. Red Lake Trailhead
USGS Quad Maps	Fish Springs, Split Mountain
GPS	37.0228 / -118.4225

Dropping from the northern ridgeline of Split Mountain, the St. Jean Couloir is a steep and demanding line that is clearly visible from Highway 395. The St. Jean gets morning sun and then quickly goes into the shade, which can make timing a bit tricky and conditions a bit challenging.

The north face of Mt. Tinemaha, as seen from the approach to The Thumb.

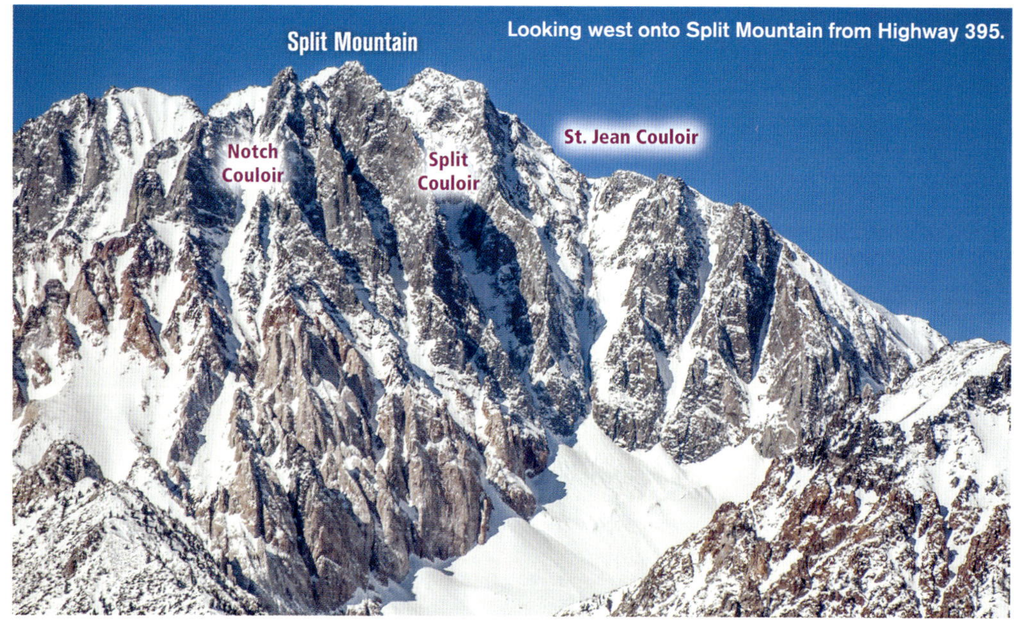

Looking west onto Split Mountain from Highway 395.

Approach: Follow the Red Lake Approach description above to Red Lake. From the lake, the St. Jean Couloir will be directly above the basin to the west, cutting through the east face from the notch on the ridge. Boot the line to the ridgeline.

Exit: Follow your approach back to the trailhead.

↘ SPLIT COULOIR

Split Mountain

Aspect	Consequence/Exposure	Slope
	5	55°

Summit Elevation	14,058'
Descent Vertical	3,000'
Total Vertical	7,958'
Hiking Distance	5 miles
Terrain	Chute
Trailhead	47. Red Lake Trailhead
USGS Quad Maps	Fish Springs, Split Mountain
GPS	37.0216 / -118.4224

Named as one of the 50 Classic Ski Descents of North America, this is the prominent and demanding line that gives Split Mountain its name. This line is technically demanding both because of the difficulty of skiing and the mandatory requirement of a rappel, and is not to be taken lightly. This is very much no-fall terrain, where an un-arrested fall would result in tumbling over a series of cliffs low in the chute. In fact, the Split Couloir claimed the lives of two very competent ski mountaineers in 2011, when an avalanche swept them over the cliffs at the bottom of the chute.

Approach: Getting to the top of the Split Couloir can be accomplished through either climbing it directly or by walking the North Ridge from the top of the St. Jean. Most people choose to climb the chute, as it gives them the opportunity to evaluate conditions and build anchors that are necessary for rappelling on the way down. Climbing the chute definitely requires ice skills and equipment, as there are a couple of mandatory sections of ice that have to be negotiated.

To reach the base of the Split Couloir, follow the approach description provided earlier for the St. Jean Couloir. From Red Lake, the Split Couloir will be directly above you to the south, dropping prominently from the cleft between the two summits.

Looking southwest from Mt Tinemaha.

NOTCH/EAST COULOIR

Split Mountain

Aspect	Consequence/Exposure	Slope
	5	45°

Summit Elevation	13,750'
Descent Vertical	2,500'
Total Vertical	7,650'
Hiking Distance	5 miles
Terrain	Chute
Trailhead	47. Red Lake Trailhead
USGS Quad Maps	Fish Springs, Split Mountain
GPS	37.0203 / -118.4223

Dropping uncharacteristically off the east side of Split Mountain, this line rarely holds enough snow to be skiable. From a distance, it looks like a prominent descent that drops cleanly from the notch to the left of Split's southern summit. As you climb the line, however, it becomes apparent that not only do its upper and lower portions not connect, but that the consequences of falling in the upper portion would be *very* serious—ending in a several-hundred-foot-high cliff that would surely be fatal if fallen over. Luckily the rest of the line is just technical and steep enough to keep you on your toes, which is exactly what you need to be.

Approach: Follow the approach described earlier for the St. Jean Couloir to Red Lake. Once at the lake, a large white-and-red-streaked rock buttress is above you to the south. At the eastern end of this buttress is the bottom portion of the couloir. Boot up the couloir for approximately 1,500', at which point you reach the top of the white rock and the chute cliffs out. Here look for a break in the ridge, which provides a way to downclimb a hundred feet or so and access the upper portion of the chute. Once in the upper chute, boot to the summit notch where there is just enough room to put your skis on.

Josh Feinberg and Nate Greenberg downclimbing the connector between the lower and upper sections of the Notch Couloir. *Photo: Jim Barnes.*

Exit: After skiing the upper portion of the chute, take your skis off and boot back up the hundred-plus feet to access the lower portion. It is critical that you recognize (or mark) the bottom of the downclimb for the way down. If you were to ski beyond or fall at this point, you would tumble over several hundred feet of cliff.

△ CARDINAL MOUNTAIN *13,397'*

Cardinal Mountain is another peak where the quality lines are obscured from view and overshadowed by the prominent neighboring peaks. In contrast to Split Mountain, Cardinal sees few ski descents, though the options are more than worth the effort.

NORTH COULOIR

Cardinal Mountain

Aspect	Consequence/Exposure	Slope
	4	45°

Summit Elevation	13,000'
Descent Vertical	1,800'
Total Vertical	6,900'
Hiking Distance	5 miles
Terrain	Chute
Trailhead	47. Red Lake Trailhead
USGS Quad Maps	Fish Springs, Split Mountain
GPS	36.9996 / -118.4120

Jon Crowley climbing Cardinal Mountain.

The steep and rocky north face of Cardinal Mountain is home to a handful of chutes and couloirs, some of which link through and some of which do not. The North Couloir may not go through on low-snow years, but when it does connect it is instantly attractive, and the most direct line to the summit.

The crux section is near the top of the couloir and comprises a short section of rock slab that doesn't always fill in enough to pass through. At this point, the chute goes around a corner, making it nearly impossible to see from anywhere other than one of the neighboring peaks. As you near the bottom of the couloir, and even as you climb it, it will appear as if the chute just ends in a rock wall beneath the summit. This section is also not visible from the ridge above, so climbing up the back side and dropping in blindly is a risky choice. The only real way to know if the chute links through is to climb it from the bottom and see firsthand.

The top part of this line is an incredibly steep drop off the ridge. While the angle mellows after the first few turns, this is not a place you want to make a mistake. Straight down the fall line will bring you to a cliff band, so extreme caution should be taken here.

Approach: Follow the approach mentioned earlier for the St. Jean Couloir toward Red Lake. As you climb up the drainage below the South Face of Mt. Tinemaha, head left into the southern branch of the drainage. After a short while this will lead you below the north face of Cardinal Mountain.

The first set of chutes you see will be the Northeast Face Chutes. Continue past these to the base of the North Couloir. Boot this line to the top of the couloir from where the summit is an easy Class 3 scramble up the ridge.

↘ NORTHEAST FACE CHUTES

Cardinal Mountain

Aspect	Consequence/Exposure	Slope
	3	40°

Summit Elevation	12,800'
Descent Vertical	2,000'
Total Vertical	6,700'
Hiking Distance	5 miles
Terrain	Chutes
Trailhead	47. Red Lake Trailhead
USGS Quad Maps	Fish Springs, Split Mountain
GPS	36.9998 / -118.406571

The Northeast Face Chutes are the most prominent lines on this peak—clearly visible from the highway and almost always filled with snow. Unfortunately, the summit is quite a bit away from the top of the chutes, so if that is your objective this is probably not the best approach.

Approach: Follow the approach mentioned earlier for the North Couloir of Cardinal Mountain. As you approach Cardinal Mountain, the first set of chutes you see are the Northeast Face Chutes. Choose your line and climb it to the top.

13 Independence

Brooks Goodnight dropping into Deerhorn Mountain.

13. Independence

INDEPENDENCE REGION:

- ▣ Onion Valley Area:
  - △ BLACK MOUNTAIN
  - △ KEARSARGE PEAK
  - △ MT. GOULD
  - △ UNIVERSITY PEAK
  - △ INDEPENDENCE PEAK
  - △ DEERHORN MOUNTAIN
- ▣ Foothill Road Area:
  - △ MT. BRADLEY
  - △ MT. TYNDALL
  - △ MT. WILLIAMSON

Region Trailheads

48. Seven Pines Campground
49. Onion Valley Trailhead
50. Shepherd Pass Trailhead
51. Bairs Creek Trailhead

Wedged between two very popular areas (Whitney and Palisades), Independence epitomizes Southern Sierra skiing: big mountains, fantastic ski terrain, and zero traffic. Seeing another backcountry skier in the winter is rare, and is only slightly more likely in the spring after the road is plowed all the way to Onion Valley Trailhead.

This chapter focuses on a select set of peaks and descents that offer a basic introduction to the Southern Sierra. This is just a fraction of the potential. With a little imagination and a desire for adventure, the opportunities here are nearly limitless.

Getting There & Getting Going

From Bishop, follow Highway 395 south for 41 miles to the town of Independence. All trailheads are accessed from Onion Valley Road, which leaves heading west from the center of town and is further referenced in the specific trailhead descriptions that follow.

48. Seven Pines Campground (Year-Round) *6,200'*

From Highway 395 in downtown Independence, turn west onto Market Street. A short distance after leaving town, the road turns into Onion Valley Road. Follow this road for six miles (from Highway 395) to the point of winter closure, which is typically at Seven Pines Campground. Though the road is not usually plowed beyond this point during winter months, the road will occasionally be snow free, allowing you to drive a bit farther.

49. Onion Valley Trailhead (Spring Only) *9,200'*

The Onion Valley Trailhead is 14 miles from Highway 395, and approximately 7½ miles from Seven Pines Campground, at the end of the Onion Valley Road. To access the trailhead, follow the description to Seven Pines Campground, then continue to the end of the road.

50. Shepherd Pass Trailhead (Spring Only) *5,700'*

From Highway 395 in downtown Independence, turn west onto Market Street. A short distance after leaving town, the road turns into Onion Valley Road. Follow this road for approximately four miles to the intersection with Foothill Road. Turn left and head south on Foothill Road for approximately 2½ miles, passing two left-hand intersections along the way. The trailhead is located where Foothill Road meets Symmes Creek.

51. Bairs Creek Trailhead (Spring Only) *6,100'*

Follow the directions referenced earlier to reach Shepherd Pass Trailhead. Continue beyond the trailhead along Foothill Road for approximately 2¼ miles to the junction with Shepherd Pass Road (FS 14S01). Turn right at the junction and continue south along Foothill Road for another two miles to its intersection with Bairs Creek Road (FS 14S02). Turn right at this junction and head west and slightly south along this road to its end, approximately ¾ mile from the last junction and approximately eight miles from the intersection of Foothill Road and Onion Valley Road.

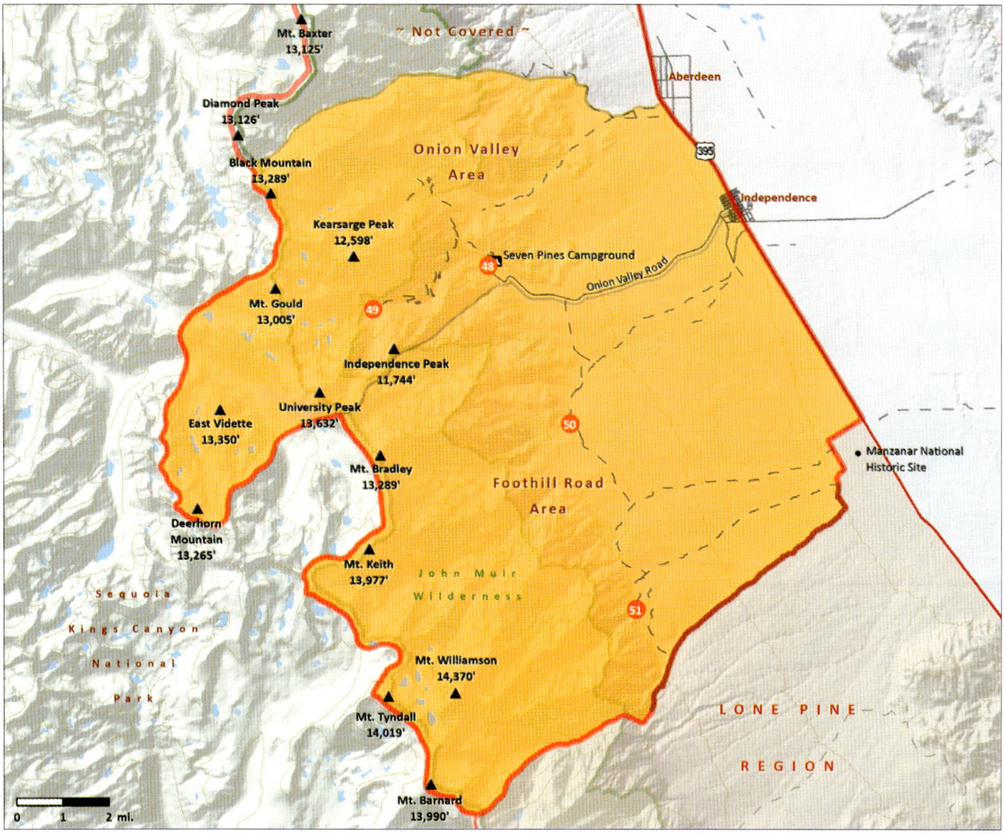

Note that it is also possible to reach this location via a combination of Symmes Creek Road, Shepherd Creek Road, and Bairs Creek Road.

Eats, Digs, Services, & Supplies

Services are quite limited in Independence. The Still Life Café is located here, however, and is one of the best-kept secrets in the Eastern Sierra. There are also a couple of gas stations with convenience stores. If you are looking for anything other than the most basic staples, we recommend stocking up in Big Pine (25 miles north) or Lone Pine (15 miles south).

Scott Coutoure skiing Independence Peak.

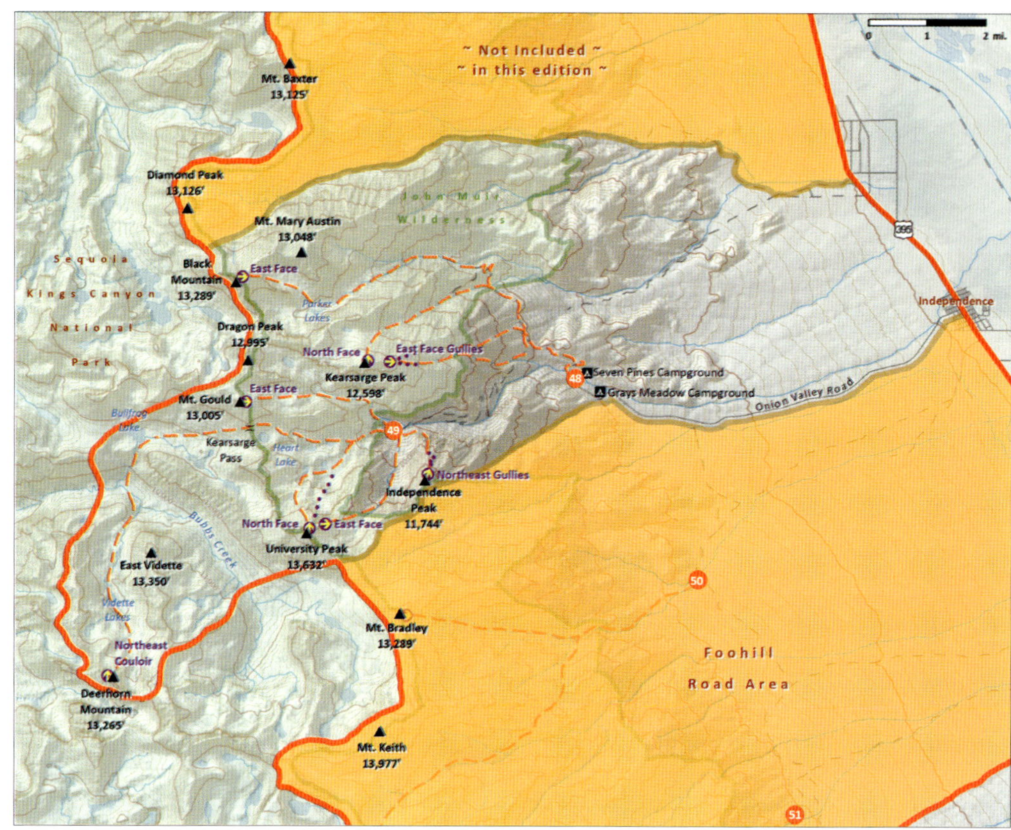

▣ Onion Valley Area

As you leave the high desert and climb into Onion Valley, the winding road and big surrounding peaks will make you question whether you are in California or Europe. Steep and exposed, the Onion Valley Road is one of those engineering marvels that you are thankful for around here—providing great springtime access to some exceptional terrain.

There are a number of descents immediately surrounding the Onion Valley Trailhead, and endless options for longer tours. Kearsarge and Independence peaks are both reasonable day tours, and Kearsarge Pass provides access to Kings Canyon National Park, which seems a world apart from the rest of the Eastside.

△ BLACK MOUNTAIN *13,289'*

An obscure and somewhat remote peak, Black Mountain is tucked away behind the neighboring Mt. Mary Austin, and is just barely visible from Highway 395. This peak is remote, and defines the northern extent of the Onion Valley Area. Dropping off the north side of the peak will put you into the North Fork of Oak Creek, which is a completely separate drainage system. The summit offers great views of the North Face of Dragon Peak to the south, and the Rae Lakes area to the west.

↘ EAST FACE — Black Mountain

Aspect	Consequence/Exposure	Slope
	2	35°

Summit Elevation	13,289'
Descent Vertical	2,400'
Total Vertical	7,089'
Hiking Distance	7 ¼ miles
Terrain	Chutes, bowls
Trailhead	48. Seven Pines Campground
USGS Quad Maps	Kearsarge Peak, Mt. Clarence King
GPS	36.8097 / -118.3777

The East Face of Black Mountain is a jumble of rock that results in a lot of complex terrain features. Sweeping gracefully through all of it, though, is a prominent, aesthetic couloir that drops right from the summit down into the Parker Lakes Basin below.

Looking west onto Black Mountain from Kearsarge Peak.

Approach: From Seven Pines Campground (Trailhead #48), continue up along Onion Valley Road for approximately 2¼ miles to the turnoff for Sardine Canyon. The intersection is marked by a small dirt parking area at the first major switchback on the Onion Valley Road below Kearsarge Peak. Park here, and continue north along the Sardine Canyon Road, which crosses the creek after a short distance and climbs the opposing hillside. After a couple of switchbacks, the road ultimately continues to the west here, climbing high into Sardine Canyon. Instead of following it, continue north over a small ridge into the South Fork of Oak Creek Drainage and continue climbing west toward Parker Lakes.

As you reach the head of this drainage and Parker Lakes, Black Mountain will be evident above you to the northwest. A large, prominent ridge extends southeast from the summit, splitting the East and Northeast Faces. To reach the East Face, continue up the drainage past Parker Lakes, then skin and boot to the top.

Exit: Retrace your steps back to the trailhead.

△ KEARSARGE PEAK *12,598'*

Kearsarge Peak is an Eastern Sierra classic, sitting at the center of Onion Valley and towering above the road. Kearsarge is best skied during the winter months when there is still plenty of snow in the high country. By the time the Onion Valley Road starts to melt out, so do the flanks of this peak.

↘ NORTH FACE

Kearsarge Peak

Aspect	Consequence/Exposure	Slope
	2	30°

Summit Elevation	12,598'
Descent Vertical	2,000'
Total Vertical	6,398'
Hiking Distance	4 ¾ miles
Terrain	Face
Trailhead	48. Seven Pines Campground
USGS Quad Maps	Kearsarge Peak
GPS	36.7894 / -118.3466

Clearly visible from Highway 395 and downtown Independence, this line is heavily sought after by backcountry aficionados. The view of the North Face from afar can be deceiving, with the face often appearing to have a fair bit of rock showing. Though this area does get hammered by wind, the gullies on the North Face are fairly wide and deep, and can hold snow that is not visible until you are below them.

Approach: From Seven Pines Campground (Trailhead #48), continue up along Onion Valley Road for approximately 2¼ miles to the turnoff for Sardine Canyon. The intersection is marked by a small dirt parking area at the first major switchback on the Onion Valley Road below Kearsarge Peak. Continue north along the road into

Ben Kahn and Melissa Buehler atop Kearsarge Peak.

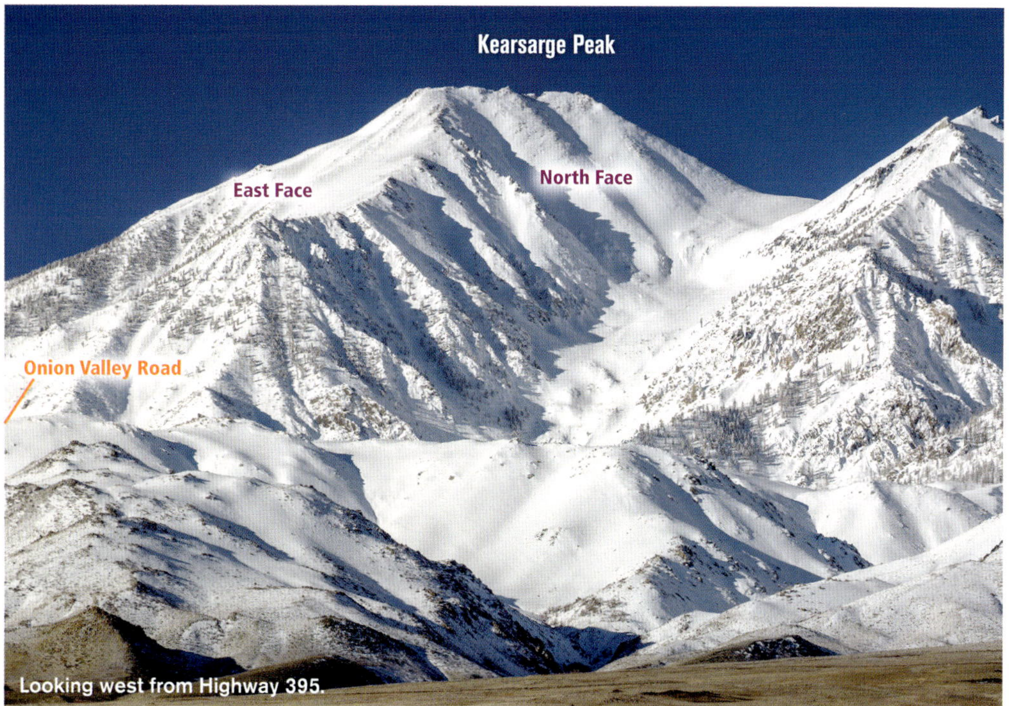

Sardine Canyon, then climb west up the canyon, passing a few benches until you are below the North Face. Pick one of the gullies and make your way to the top.

Exit: Retrace your steps back to the car.

↘ EAST FACE

Kearsarge Peak

Aspect	Consequence/Exposure	Slope
	3	35°

Summit Elevation	12,598'
Descent Vertical	5,000'
Total Vertical	6,398'
Hiking Distance	4 miles
Terrain	Bowls, Chutes
Trailhead	48. Seven Pines Campground
USGS Quad Maps	Kearsarge Peak
GPS	36.7892 / -118.3411

The East Face of Kearsarge Peak has two prominent gullies that funnel down into a narrow canyon below. Though this terrain is highly visible from the road and has fairly easy access, it rarely gets skied. The lower section of this face goes through a narrow slot that is lined with cliff bands. Though not incredibly steep, this section can be technical, and is a major terrain trap.

Approach: From the Seven Pines Campground (Trailhead #48), follow the Onion Valley Road past the first major switchback for approximately ½ mile to the base of a prominent gully. Climb this gully to the terrain above, spending as little time in this area as possible. Once through this choke, the terrain above you opens up and you can choose from one of the two gullies above and climb directly to the summit.

It is also possible to reach the upper slopes of the East Face by climbing the east ridge, which climbs to the summit from the first major switchback on Onion Valley Road.

Exit: Ski back down to the road, then on to your car.

△ MT. GOULD *13,005'*

Mt. Gould comprises the north side of Kearsarge Pass, located at the head of Onion Valley and forming the border of Sequoia/Kings Canyon National Park. As with many of the peaks in this area, the views from the summit of Mt. Gould are truly remarkable in every direction.

Dropping from the summit ridge, the East Face is a fantastic moderate descent, often holding great corn snow in the spring. There are also a few chutes on the North Face of Mt. Gould that can be accessed via the same approach listed below.

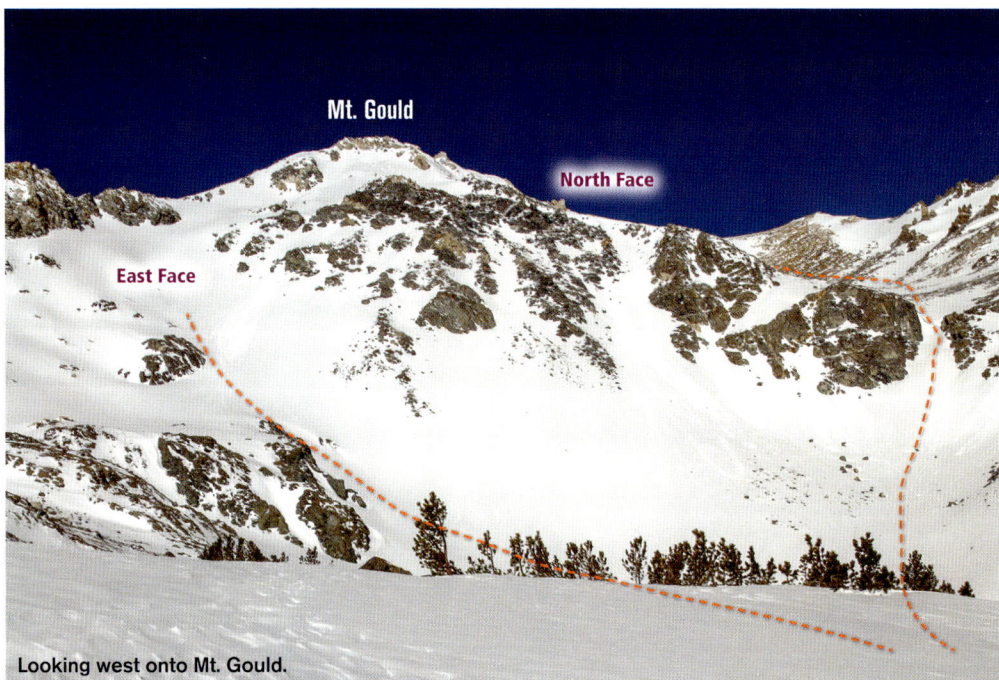

Looking west onto Mt. Gould.

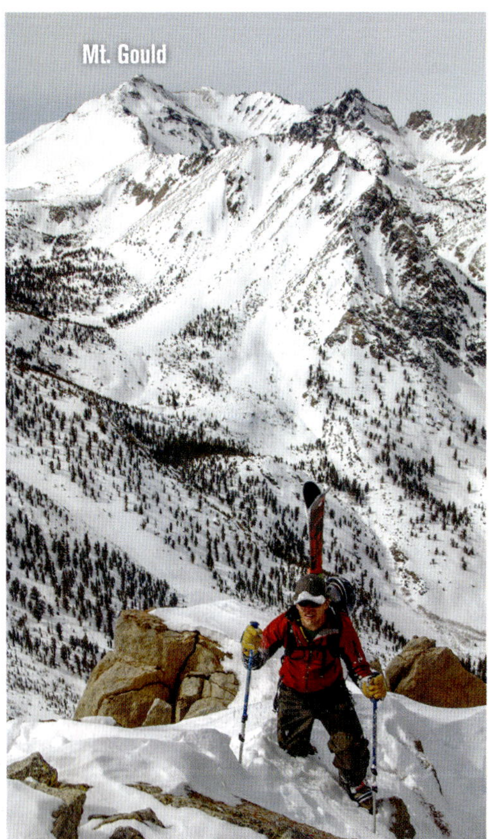

Scott Coutoure atop Independence Peak.

↘ EAST FACE

Mt. Gould

Aspect	Consequence/Exposure	Slope
E	2	35°

Summit Elevation	13,000'
Descent Vertical	3,500'
Total Vertical	3,800'
Hiking Distance	2 ¼ miles
Terrain	Face
Trailhead	49. Onion Valley Trailhead
USGS Quad Maps	Kearsarge Peak, Mt. Clarence King
GPS	36.7795 / -118.3767

Approach: From the Onion Valley Trailhead (#49) climb the steep hillside to the northwest of the parking lot into the mouth of the Golden Trout Lakes Drainage. It is not uncommon for this slope to be melted out by the time the road is open to the trailhead, so be prepared to carry your skis for a short distance. Continue up the drainage toward Golden Trout Lake, which sits below the East Face of Mt. Gould. Weave your way to the summit.

Exit: Reverse your approach back to the car.

△ UNIVERSITY PEAK *13,632'*

First climbed by Sierra pioneer Joseph LeConte and his cohorts in 1896, University Peak is said to have been given its name in commemoration of California's university system. The peak is the first high point south of Kearsarge Pass on the skyline above Onion Valley.

↘ NORTH FACE

University Peak

Aspect	Consequence/Exposure	Slope
	3	35°

Summit Elevation	13,000'
Descent Vertical	2,500'
Total Vertical	3,800'
Hiking Distance	2 ½ miles
Terrain	Chute, Face
Trailhead	49. Onion Valley Trailhead
USGS Quad Maps	Kearsarge Peak, Mt. Williamson
GPS	36.7490 / -118.3608

The North Face of University Peak is comprised of a handful of chutes that feed into a large, open face below. Unfortunately, this face tends to get hammered by the wind and consequently does not hold much snow, forcing you to navigate through a series of "strips" to the rolling terrain below.

In addition to the obvious chutes above the North Face, there are a few other chutes that become evident on the approach. Though these do not provide access to the summit, they are worthwhile lines with fun terrain.

Approach: From Onion Valley Trailhead (#49), head west up the drainage toward Kearsarge Pass, roughly following the alignment of the summer trail. Atop the first bench, turn slightly south at Little Pothole Lake heading toward Slim and Matlock lakes. Continue west up to Bench Lake, which provides access to the large North Face.

Reaching the summit requires climbing this face and exiting out onto the ridge on its eastern edge, with the most direct line gaining the ridge fairly close to the summit. Due to the exposure, the terrain at the ridge's upper end rarely holds snow and is comprised of a bunch of blocky talus, which requires some Class 3 climbing to navigate. As you get higher, more moderate terrain appears to the southeast on the final stretch to the summit.

Exit: Ski one of the chutes off the North Face, then retrace your approach back to the trailhead.

Looking southwest at University Peak.

↘ EAST FACE

University Peak

Aspect	Consequence/Exposure	Slope
	2	35°

Summit Elevation	13,000'
Descent Vertical	2,300'
Total Vertical	3,800'
Hiking Distance	1 ¾ miles
Terrain	Face
Trailhead	49. Onion Valley Trailhead
USGS Quad Maps	Kearsarge Peak, Mt. Williamson
GPS	36.7500 / -118.3570

The East Face of University is one of the ultimate spring corn runs in the Eastern Sierra. Once the Onion Valley Road is open all the way to the trailhead, access to this face becomes a breeze. Be sure to get an early start, though, as the face heats up very quickly in the spring sun, creating perfect conditions for wet slides.

Approach: From the Onion Valley Trailhead (#49), head south across Independence Creek and climb into the treed gully above the parking lot. A short, steep section leads to a series of benches and more moderate terrain on the way to Robinson Lake. Continue past the lake and into the cirque. Directly above you to the north is the East Face with a small chute at the top.

The summit is a little ways west from the top of the East Face, and accessing it requires an exposed Class 3 scramble/traverse.

Exit: Retrace your steps back to the car.

△ INDEPENDENCE PEAK *11,744'*

Directly opposing Kearsarge Peak to the south of Onion Valley is the ever-impressive Independence Peak. Though slightly smaller than its surrounding neighbors, this peak was named after the town below and is certainly a deserving namesake.

The aesthetic lines of the Northeast Gullies sit directly above the Onion Valley Road, with the gully immediately above the roadside being the most popular. On some years it is possible to ski these lines right from the summit via a small chute on the northeast side.

The majority of the main gully is quite moderate, but does steepen gradually as you climb higher. The gully branches near the top, providing two different options—the left line exits onto the east ridge and goes a little higher, with a steeper section near the top. The two difficulty ratings correspond to these options.

Scott Coutoure climbing Independence Peak.

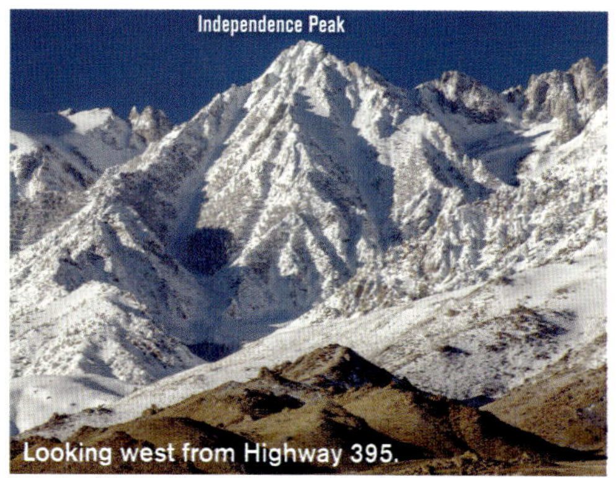

Looking west from Highway 395.

↘ NORTHEAST GULLIES — Independence Peak

Aspect	Consequence/Exposure	Slope
NE	2	30°

Summit Elevation	11,700'
Descent Vertical	2,500'
Total Vertical	2,500'
Hiking Distance	1 ¼ miles
Terrain	Face, Chute
Trailhead	49. Onion Valley Trailhead
USGS Quad Maps	Kearsarge Peak
GPS	36.7621 / -118.3317

Approach: Follow the approach to the Onion Valley Trailhead (#49). After the first set of switchbacks, you will be directly beneath the main gully. From here, head south across Independence Creek, then traverse east below the Northeast Face. Pick your gully and climb it to the top.

Δ DEERHORN MOUNTAIN *13,265'*

Located over the crest of the Sierra in Sequoia/Kings Canyon National Park, Deerhorn Mountain is one of the more remote peaks referenced in this book. Far from any trailhead, access is long and complicated, and is definitely a multi-day affair. Its distance also makes it elusive and visible from only a few locations in the region. Once you lay eyes on it, though, you will never forget.

The Northeast Couloir is a backcountry skier's dream, ranking as one of the most attractive couloirs around, along with Emerson and Red Slate. The line is just steep and sustained enough to keep you on your toes, and makes a proud addition to any tick list.

↘ NORTHEAST COULOIR — Deerhorn Mountain

Aspect	Consequence/Exposure	Slope
NE	3	40°

Summit Elevation	12,800'
Descent Vertical	2,000'
Total Vertical	6,200'
Hiking Distance	7 ¾ miles
Terrain	Chute
Trailhead	49. Onion Valley Trailhead
USGS Quad Maps	Kearsarge Peak, Mt. Clarence King, Mt. Brewer
GPS	36.7133 / -118.4113

Approach: Reaching Deerhorn requires entering Kings Canyon National Park via Kearsarge Pass. From the Onion Valley Trailhead (#49), follow the general alignment of the summer trail over generally moderate terrain to Pothole Lake, then up to the notch of the pass. Descend the west side (which has a tendency to be scoured by the wind) down to Bullfrog Lake. Descend from the outlet of Bullfrog into Bubbs Creek and Vidette Meadow. This slope also melts out quickly in the spring, and getting through this section and across Bubbs Creek can be challenging.

Once across, follow Vidette Creek into the drainage that leads to the base of the North Face of Deerhorn. Climb the couloir to the notch between the two "horns." The true summit is the left (east), though the false summit often holds snow to a much higher point and is therefore equally attractive. Though not technical-looking from below, the climb to the summit can become quite complicated, with snow and cornice challenges to contend with. The route roughly meanders through big talus blocks directly above the couloir and requires more time to navigate than most people realize.

Deerhorn Mountain, as seen from the outlet of Bullfrog Lake.

Foothill Road Area

The Foothill Road Area encompasses the terrain between University Peak and Mt. Williamson, and is named for the dirt road that traverses the toe of the slope, providing access to the terrain above. Two main trailheads are referenced in this area—Shepherd Pass and Bairs Creek (with driving directions provided in the chapter intro)—though there are clearly a number of possible places to leave the road and gain access to the peaks above.

△ MT. BRADLEY *13,289'*

Mt. Bradley is a beautiful alpine summit located directly above the Shepherd Pass Trailhead. Though slightly obscured by its neighbors, the summit offers incredible views of two 14,000' peaks to the south: Mt. Williamson and Mt. Tyndall.

Despite offering over 5,000' of fall-line skiing, the fine East Couloir is rarely skied, mostly due to the challenging approach that is encountered just above Shepherd Pass Trailhead (#50).

EAST COULOIR — Mt. Bradley

Aspect	Consequence/Exposure	Slope
	2	35°

Summit Elevation	13,000'
Descent Vertical	7,000'
Total Vertical	7,300'
Hiking Distance	4 ½ miles
Terrain	Chute
Trailhead	50. Shepherd Pass Trailhead
USGS Quad Maps	Mt. Williamson
GPS	36.7280 / -118.3369

Approach: From the Shepherd Pass Trailhead (#50), follow the summer trail west into the canyon for a little over one mile. At the point where the trail starts to climb the south face of the canyon, cross the creek and slowly begin to climb the northern side of the drainage. As you travel farther up the canyon, you will encounter a waterfall and some complex terrain, which is best negotiated by climbing the hillside to the right (north) onto a bench.

Once on the bench, you'll see two separate drainages that converge at the base of Mt. Bradley—either will

bring you to base of the couloir. At this point, the peak and East Couloir will be in clear view. Follow the canyon to the base, and climb to the top.

△ MT. TYNDALL *14,019'*

Though clearly visible from Highway 395 and various points throughout the range, Mt. Tyndall is probably one of the least popular 14,000' peaks. In contrast to many of the other 14ers in the range, Tyndall offers some moderate terrain options, but requires a bit of effort to reap the rewards.

↘ NORTH FACE — Mt. Tyndall

Aspect	Consequence/Exposure	Slope
N	2	35°

Summit Elevation	14,019'
Descent Vertical	2,000'
Total Vertical	8,319'
Hiking Distance	8 ¼ miles
Terrain	Face
Trailhead	50. Shepherd Pass Trailhead
USGS Quad Maps	Mt. Williamson
GPS	36.6563 / -118.3393

The broad North Face of Mt. Tyndall drops elegantly from the summit all the way to Shepherd Pass, 2,000' below. Its consistent, moderate pitch makes it enticing to backcountry skiers and a worthy addition to any tick list.

Approach: From Shepherd Pass Trailhead (#50), follow the alignment of the summer trail into the Shepherd Creek Drainage and over Shepherd Pass. The terrain along the way is often melted out or stripped of snow, which can make travel difficult, though the presence of the trail makes the route manageable. Once over the pass, continue west a short distance until you are directly below the North Face. Skin to the summit.

△ MT. WILLIAMSON *14,370'*

Checking in at 14,370', Mt. Williamson is the second highest peak in California, and consequently one of the most coveted peaks in the range. Its position along the front range and nearly 10,000' elevation gain make it a quintessential Eastside giant.

For many years, the peak was closed to humans in the spring and summer for bighorn sheep, making it exceptionally difficult to ski. In 2010, however, the regulation was lifted and now the peak is fair game for adventurers throughout the year.

The classic ski descent drops off the East Face of Mt. Williamson into Bairs Creek. The major appeal to this line is its consistent pitch. While many of the peaks in the area require a lot of skiing on flat terrain to reach the base, Bairs Creek offers a descent that is almost completely fall-line for its entirety. In addition to Bairs Creek, there are a handful of technical lines on the north face, including the Giant Steps Couloir. Without firsthand knowledge of these lines, we are unable to include more details.

Looking west from Highway 395.

↘ BAIRS CREEK

Mt. Williamson

Aspect	Consequence/Exposure	Slope
	2	35°

Summit Elevation	14,370'
Descent Vertical	7,000'
Total Vertical	8,170'
Hiking Distance	4 ¾ miles
Terrain	Bowls
Trailhead	51. Bairs Creek Trailhead
USGS Quad Maps	Mt. Williamson
GPS	36.6565 / -118.3090

Bairs Creek is the ultimate Sierra classic — you will be hard-pressed to find another descent of this caliber in the Lower 48. While there are plenty of other 14ers in the country, this is the only one with a continuous ski descent of nearly 8,000 feet.

Approach: Reaching the base of the line is no easy task, and if you do not successfully navigate through the lower section of the drainage, you will be in for a very long day.

The approach begins at Bairs Creek Trailhead (#51) and follows a circuitous route through a rocky ridge before descending back into the drainage. While it may seem odd to add a bunch of unnecessary elevation to your already huge day, it avoids a section of canyon that is practically impossible to get through.

The lower part of this canyon is filled with very dense brush and surrounded by rock walls. Following the river straight up could add six hours to your day. Instead, the best route ascends the ridge on the right (north) side of the canyon. Follow this to a prominent notch where you will be able to see into Bairs Creek. From here, a traversing descent will bring you back to the canyon where you will be able to skin.

The majority of Bairs Creek is incredibly moderate, rarely exceeding 25 degrees. The few steep sections are very short-lived — the worst of it being the hourglass-shaped chute approximately two-thirds of the way up. Above that, a small bench leads to a steeper face and on to the gentle summit plateau.

Exit: Follow your skin track back to the car and a well-deserved cold beer.

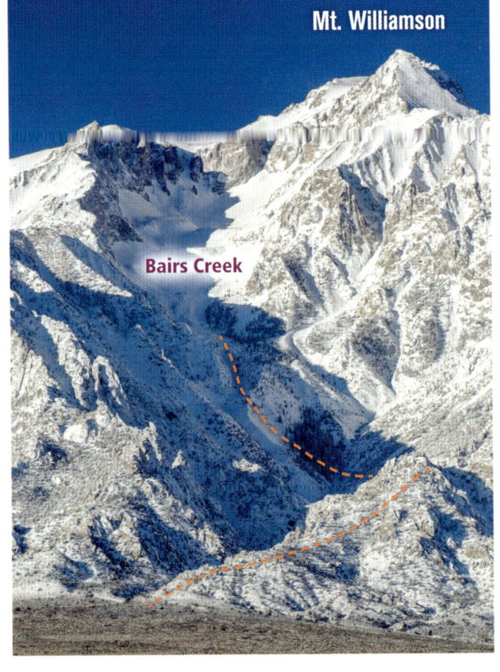

14 Lone Pine

Rich Steel climbing Mt. Langley.

14. Lone Pine

LONE PINE REGION:

- Whitney Portal Area:
  - △ THOR PEAK
  - △ MT. WHITNEY
  - △ MT. RUSSELL
  - △ MT. MUIR
  - △ MT. IRVINE
- Horseshoe Meadows Area:
  - △ LONE PINE PEAK
  - △ MT. LANGLEY

Region Trailheads

52. Whitney Portal Winter Closure
53. Whitney Portal Campground/ Meysan Lake Trailhead
54. Whitney Portal
55. Mt. Langley Trailhead

Marking the southern terminus of the High Sierra is the historic town of Lone Pine. Rich in mountaineering history, the town and adjacent Alabama Hills have been the site of countless western films, and are still frequently used by Hollywood. To most of these visitors, the mountains are simply a backdrop, but to those in the know, this backdrop provides a lifetime of adventure.

The obvious attraction in this drainage is Mt. Whitney—the tallest peak in the Continental US—and what a beauty she is. The jagged ridgeline, compromised of Whitney, Keeler, Day, and Third Needles, dominates the skyline as it spans the distance between the equally impressive 14,000' neighboring peaks of Mt. Russell and Mt. Muir. Though most people focus in on Whitney itself, this zone certainly has a lot more to offer, and for the adventurous spirits, there is a lifetime of fun at your fingertips.

Getting There & Getting Going

The town of Lone Pine is located 60 miles south of Bishop along Highway 395. All of the terrain described in this chapter is accessed off Whitney Portal Road, which departs to the west from the stoplight at the center of town.

52. Whitney Portal Winter Closure (Year-Round) 6,500'

From the stoplight at Highway 395, head west on Whitney Portal Road for 8¼ miles to the point of winter closure. This is approximately one mile beyond Lone Pine Campground and just before the first switchback which starts the climb into the canyon above. This is the actual trailhead for Lone Pine Peak, as well as the winter-time trailhead for the rest of the descents described in the Whitney Portal Area section.

53. Whitney Portal Campground/Meysan Lake Trailhead (Spring Only) 8,000'

From the stoplight at Highway 395, head west on Whitney Portal Road for approximately 11¼ miles. Approximately one mile before the road ends at Whitney Portal is the Whitney Portal Campground on the south side of the road. Park on the side of the Whitney Portal Road, outside the campground.

A small sign within the campground marks the Meysan Lake Trailhead. The actual trail travels south through the campground and then back to the east along a small paved road which provides access to a handful of summer cabins.

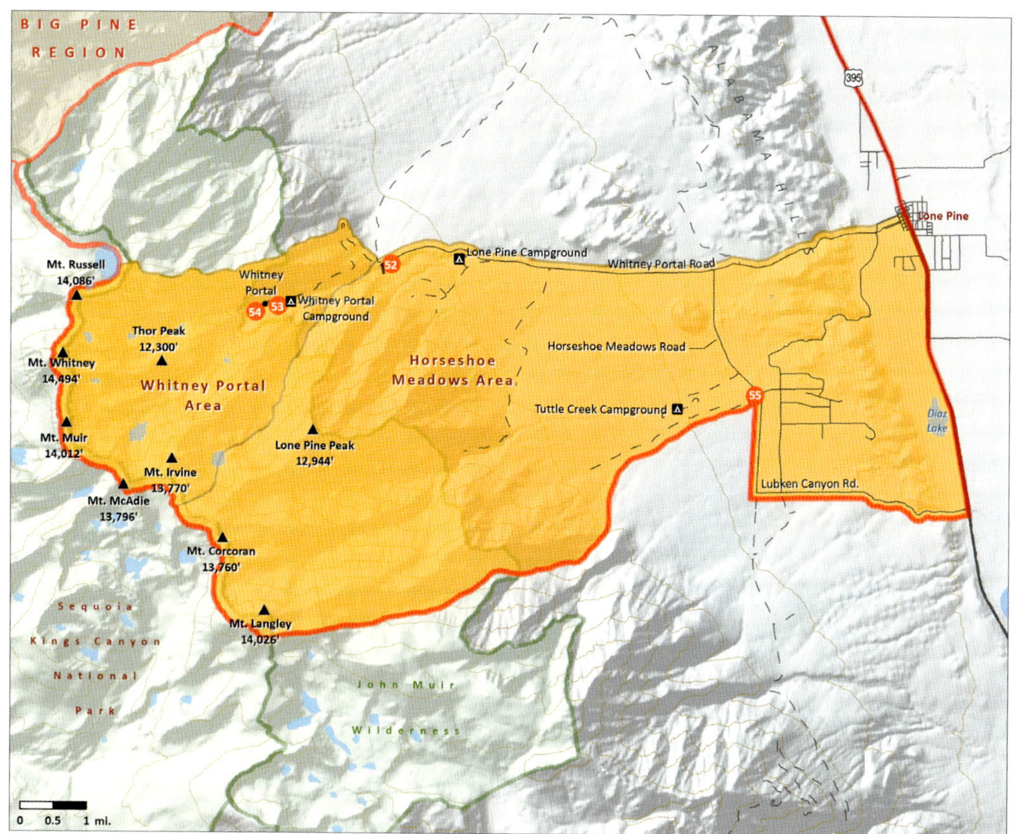

54. Whitney Portal (Spring Only) *8,300'*

From the stoplight at Highway 395, follow Whitney Portal Road for approximately 12 miles to where the road ends at Whitney Portal. A small store is located here along with a small campground.

55. Mt. Langley Trailhead (Year-Round) *4,600'*

From Highway 395, follow Whitney Portal Road for roughly three miles to Horseshoe Meadows Road. Turn left and head south on Horseshoe Meadows Road for two miles to Granite View Drive. Turn right onto Granite View Drive and follow it as far as you can. During the winter, the snowline will prevent you from driving very far beyond the intersection, making for a fairly long approach to Mt. Langley.

Eats, Digs, Services, & Supplies

Though Lone Pine is a pretty small community, the steady flow of travelers passing through allow it to maintain a few more services than many similar-sized towns along the Highway 395 corridor. Joseph's is a small grocery store on Main Street that offers all the essentials. Elevation is a small climbing/mountaineering shop located on the corner of Main Street and Whitney Portal Road. For eats, check out Pizza Factory on Main Street or the Alabama Hills Cafe on West Post Street. If you are seeking out a cheap bed or a quick shower, drop into the Whitney Portal Hostel and Store on Main Street.

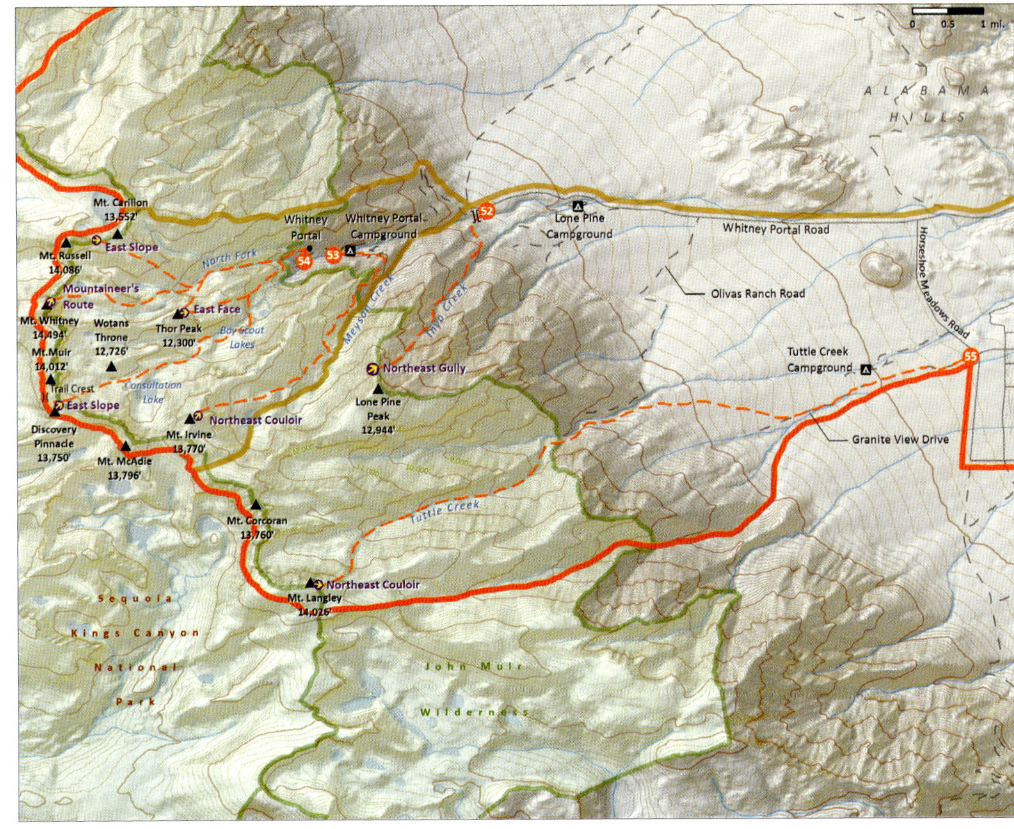

▣ Whitney Portal Area

The Whitney Portal Area comprises the majority of this chapter and contains all of the terrain that is accessible directly from the Whitney Portal Road. The portal road is only plowed about eight miles during the winter months, leaving another four miles to the actual trailhead. As spring approaches, the lower portions of the road will melt out, but snow will linger in the shady switchbacks preventing travel by vehicle. Consider bringing approach shoes, or a bike (though the climb is rather steep).

As spring progresses, the County posts a 'Road Closed' sign at the bottom of the grade. Though it may be possible to drive farther, recognize that you are doing so at your own risk. The road is notorious for springtime rockfall, with some boulders the size of cars often making their way down onto the pavement. It is also possible to return to a towed or ticketed car.

△ THOR PEAK *12,300'*

Pinnacle Ridge extends east from the Mt. Whitney massif, dividing the North and South Forks of Lone Pine Creek. At its eastern terminus is Thor Peak. Thor is a spectacular sight from locations along the Whitney Portal Road, dominating the view as you look up toward Mt. Whitney.

↘ EAST FACE

Thor Peak

Aspect | Consequence/Exposure: 3 | Slope: 40°

Summit Elevation	12,300'
Descent Vertical	2,500'
Total Vertical	4,000'
Hiking Distance	2 miles
Terrain	Face, Chute
Trailhead	54. Whitney Portal
USGS Quad Maps	Mt. Langley, Mt. Whitney
GPS	36.5767 / -118.2650

A fine alpine descent with one of the best views in town, Thor Peak is a great way to experience the Whitney area without experiencing the crowds. The rocky summit is perched directly in front of Mt Muir, Whitney, and everything in between.

The ski descent starts on the broad upper face of Thor Peak, and quickly funnels into the entrance of the two lower chutes. These chutes can be a little cruxy, and add a significant degree of difficulty to this otherwise moderate descent.

Approach: From Whitney Portal (Trailhead #54), follow the alignment of the old summer trail and eventually rejoin the new trail a short distance above the Portal. Continue along the summer trail for roughly another mile until the two chutes of Thor Peak are in view. Climb up the drainage, then choose one of the chutes and follow it to the face above. The broad face above the chutes ends abruptly at a rocky ridge, with the summit just a short distance to the west through easy 3rd Class terrain.

If the chutes on the East Face aren't appealing, it is also possible to reach the summit via the more moderate North Face. To do so, follow the summer trail into the North Fork drainage to Lower Boy Scout Lake, and then turn and climb the bowl on your left (south). This section is very exposed to the wind, and doesn't always hold snow.

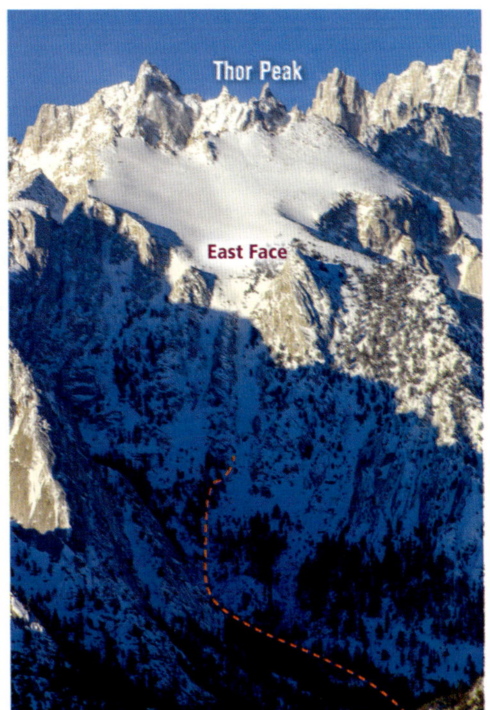

Thor Peak as viewed from the town of Lone Pine.

△ MT. WHITNEY *14,494*

Without question, Mt. Whitney is the most iconic peak in the Lower 48. Even if it weren't the highest point, the beautiful East Face of Mt. Whitney would still be an incredible attraction to mountain lovers. Every morning the rocky face lights up in the sunrise, and is electrified by the alpenglow in the evening. The summit is one of a kind—large and flat enough to host a stone walled summit house surrounded by perfect granite boulders and stellar views. This is an exceptional place to hang out and enjoy yourself before skiing off one of the most coveted summits in the nation.

The steep granite walls and spires of Whitney's south ridgeline host a number of high quality alpine rock climbs, but don't make for the best skiing. Luckily, the North Face of Mt. Whitney is home to the Mountaineer's Route. During non-snowy times of year, this is the standard descent for climbers, and the typical summit route for mountaineers looking for less than 5th Class terrain.

↘ MOUNTAINEER'S ROUTE

Mt. Whitney

Aspect | Consequence/Exposure 3, 4 | Slope 35°, 45°

Summit Elevation	14,494'
Descent Vertical	1,900'
Total Vertical	6,195'
Hiking Distance	4 ½ miles
Terrain	Face, Chutes
Trailhead	54. Whitney Portal
USGS Quad Maps	Mt. Langley, Mt. Whitney
GPS	36.5785 / -118.2930

The lower section of the line is a classic Sierra couloir, which climbs nearly 1,500' from Iceberg Lake to a notch below the North Face. Though the couloir itself is not that steep, the terrain above is considerably steeper and of higher consequence as it climbs the final 500' or so to the summit plateau. What makes matters worse is that the terrain on the North Face below the notch is comprised of large cliffs that if fallen over would most likely be fatal. This makes the upper portion of this line a no-fall zone and something that should not be taken lightly.

Kevin Smith riding the Mountaineer's Route.

The Alabama Hills, Thor Peak, and Mt. Whitney, as seen from Highway 395.

Bear in mind that the Mountaineer's Route is popular year-round and frequented by skiers and mountaineers alike during the winter months. Some of these visitors are savvy backcountry travelers with skis or boards; others are just out to climb the peak by any means necessary. This often translates to the approach being in rough shape, with wall-to-wall snowshoe tracks and boot packs that can often make the skinning unpleasant. Another aspect of the high traffic volume is the exposure you have to people above you, or the risk you pose to those below you. Avalanche danger is a significant concern in this area, and given the high consequences of the terrain and exposure, it is important that you are mindful of your surroundings, including other parties.

Regardless of the conditions or the crowd, this is a mega-classic and a must do for anyone interested in ski mountaineering or skiing the highest and most beautiful peaks in the world.

Note: The two different C/E ratings and slope ratings are due to the variable nature of the slope above the notch in contrast with the couloir below. Given the exposure to the wind, this could be snow covered and in great condition making the 40° slope feel comfortable, or wind packed and frozen making it terrifying. Luckily there are a number of rappel stations along the sides of this face which can increase the safety if descending (or climbing) in difficult conditions. If you are concerned about conditions, we recommend bringing a rope, harness, and a small selection of rock gear to protect this section.

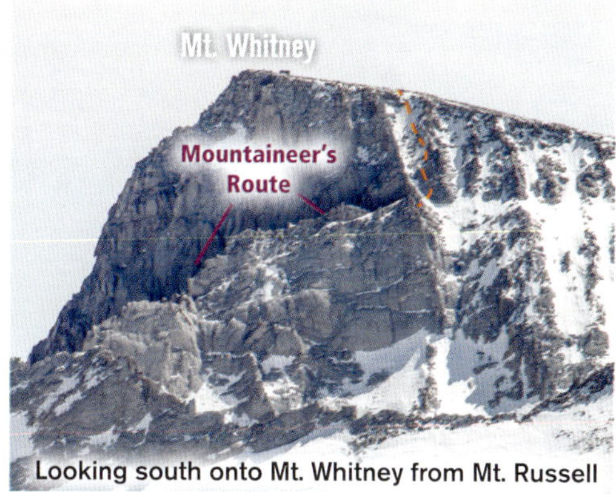

Looking south onto Mt. Whitney from Mt. Russell

Approach: From Whitney Portal (Trailhead #54) head west up the drainage following either the main or old summer trails from the parking lot for approximately one mile into the mouth of the North Fork of Lone Pine Creek drainage. At this point a smaller climber's trail breaks off and heads west into the North Fork drainage, with the main trail continuing south. Head into North Fork, staying on the right (north) side of the creek and climb through some trees and steep pinch points higher up into the drainage. Depending on the amount of

The North Fork drainage, as seen from atop Thor Peak

snow, this section can potentially be quite challenging, as the canyon is filled with brush making for hollow spots as the snow melts out.

As you climb higher into the drainage, veer left before reaching Upper Boy Scout Lake, choosing the canyon that is immediately north of Pinnacle Ridge. Continue up this canyon for another ½ mile until the slope to your north lessens. Climb this slope to access Iceberg Lake and the bench beneath the lower couloir of the Mountaineer's Route.

Climb the couloir to a small notch, which provides access to the North Face above. Directly above the notch, the slope becomes significantly steeper and you are immediately exposed to the terrain below the notch, making this section very intimidating. Luckily, the crux is right above the notch and relatively short lived. Once through it, the rest of the slope above weaves its way through a shallow gully that is filled with a series of small benches and lined with rock ridges on either side. As you climb higher in the gully, the pitch lessens and the exposure becomes less daunting until it reaches the dramatic summit plateau. Once atop the plateau, the actual summit of Whitney lies a short distance to the southeast and is marked by a stone summit house.

Exit: Reverse your approach taking care to not ski below the notch on the North Face.

△ MT. RUSSELL *14,086'*

Neighboring Mt. Whitney to the north is the 14,086' peak of Mt. Russell. The South and West faces of Russell are comprised of steep granite faces and ridges, which are a climbers paradise. Unfortunately, they don't afford very simple access to the summit, and consequently don't offer very good skiing. Luckily, the East Face of Russell offers a great line from the ridge of another beautiful 14er located right next door to Whitney with exceptional views of the surrounding terrain.

↘ EAST SLOPE — Mt. Russell

Aspect	Consequence/Exposure	Slope
E	2	35°

Summit Elevation	13,400'
Descent Vertical	2,750'
Total Vertical	5,100'
Hiking Distance	4 miles
Terrain	Face
Trailhead	54. Whitney Portal
USGS Quad Maps	Mt. Langley, Mt. Whitney
GPS	36.5911 / -118.2825

The East Slope of Mt. Russell descends a long broad face from the eastern ridgeline that connects Russell and Mt. Carillon. The slope sees an incredible amount of sun, making it a great spring corn run, but can also be a fun ski during the more wintery months.

For this book, we have chosen to only include the East Slope. Though there are a few other lines on Mt Russell that have been skied, without firsthand knowledge we are unable to provide details.

Approach: Follow the approach for the Mountaineer's Route on Mt. Whitney to Lower Boy Scout Lake. Just beyond the lake, the lower portion of the East Slope will appear above you to the north. Climb a short steep section to a bench which provides access to the exit of the shallow gully that is the lower portion of this line. Climb the gully to the upper reaches of the slope where

Looking into the South Fork drainage from atop Thor Peak.

it meets the Russell/Carillon ridgeline. At this point, the snow will likely run out and give way to rock. Unfortunately the summit is still a good distance away to the west, and the ridge somewhat exposed. If you are planning on going to the summit, a rope is recommended to manage some of the exposed sections.

△ MT. MUIR *14,012'*

Few people even know where Mt. Muir is, as it is surrounded by a handful of prominent peaks that form the Mt. Whitney ridgeline to the north. But this 14,000' peak shouldn't be overlooked, or underestimated, as it marks the northern side of Trail Crest and offers some spectacular ski mountaineering terrain.

The two couloirs that cut through the steep North Face of Mt. Muir and are the most direct lines to the summit. They are also some of the most technical lines covered in this book, and are rarely in good enough shape to be skied. The more prominent of the two was likely skied for the first time in 2010 by Chris Davenport, Christian Pondella, and Ryan Boyer. Without first hand knowledge of these descents, we chose to not include them in this edition.

The more moderate descent off Mt. Muir is via the East Slope, which is the location of the 99 switchbacks that comprise the summer trail and provide access to Trail Crest. While this slope does not descend directly from the summit, the summit is a short distance away and relatively easy to access from Trail Crest and the top of this line.

↘ EAST SLOPE / 99 SWITCHBACKS — Mt. Muir

Aspect	Consequence/Exposure	Slope
	2	35°

Summit Elevation	13,700'
Descent Vertical	1,700'
Total Vertical	5,400'
Hiking Distance	8 ¼ miles
Terrain	Face
Trailhead	54. Whitney Portal
USGS Quad Maps	Mt. Langley, Mt. Whitney
GPS	36.5591 / -118.2914

Approach: From the Whitney Portal (Trailhead #54), follow the alignment of the summer trail into the South Fork of Lone Pine Creek drainage, as though you were going to Thor Peak. Continue up the drainage to Consultation Lake, where the East Slope will come into view to the west. Climb the broad face to its summit, which is known as Trail Crest. If the summit is your objective, continue north along the west side of the ridge until you are below the summit, then climb to the obvious summit block.

△ MT. IRVINE *13,770'*

Mt. Irvine is a less known peak that checks in just under the 14,000' mark to the south of Mt. Whitney. The peak forms the beginning of the ridgeline that separates the Lone Pine Creek drainages from the Meysan Lake area and consists of dramatic and complex terrain on its north and east aspects.

Looking west at Mt. Irvine from Lone Pine Peak.

↘ NORTHEAST COULOIR

Mt. Irvine

Aspect | Consequence/Exposure: 3 | Slope: 40°

Summit Elevation	13,600'
Descent Vertical	2,000'
Total Vertical	5,600'
Hiking Distance	5 miles
Terrain	Chute
Trailhead	53. Meysan Lake Trailhead
USGS Quad Maps	Mt. Langley, Mt. Whitney
GPS	36.5563 / -118.2629

This fine ski descent is well off the beaten path, providing a pleasant and uncrowded escape in one of the most popular drainages in the range. The Northeast Face of Irvine is relatively difficult to reach, located high in the Meysan Lakes drainage. Luckily a hiking trail provides access into the drainage, making this a great option for late winter or early spring.

Approach: The Meysan Lakes Trailhead (#53) originates from the Whitney Portal Campground, which is approximately one mile before the end of the Whitney Portal Road. Walk south through the campground, following a handful of small wooden signs that guide you along the Meysan Lake trail. This trail weaves through a collection of small paved roads that provide access to summer cabins at the back of the campground.

Follow the alignment of the [illegible] trail as it contours beneath a treed ridge to the east into the mouth of the Meysan Creek drainage. Once in the drainage, work the right (western) side as best you can, climbing up toward the Meysan Lakes. As you reach the upper portion of the canyon, Mt. Irvine will appear. Cutting through the rocky East Face is a striking couloir, with the Northeast Couloir located just to the looker's right of the rocky rib. Climb the line to the summit ridge, from which point the summit is just a short 3rd Class scramble to the south.

It is also possible to reach the summit of Mt. Irvine via the large funnel-shaped bowl that lies between Irvine and Mt. Mallory.

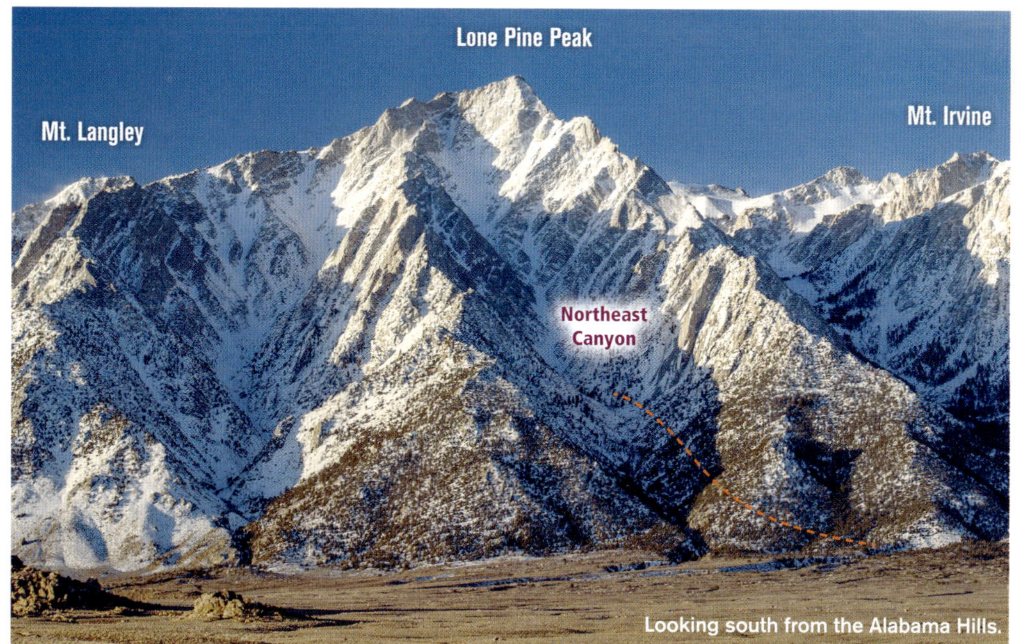

Looking south from the Alabama Hills.

▣ Horseshoe Meadows Area

The Horseshoe Meadows Area comprises the terrain to the south of Whitney Portal and the drainages that feed into Lone Pine Creek. Two main trailheads serve as the jumping off points for the terrain referenced in the pages that follow. Though these trailheads are accessible by car during the winter, it is important to recognize that they are low in elevation and far away from the peaks, making for big days. In other words, this is remote terrain that is difficult to access, comprised of complex approaches, with significant vertical relief.

△ LONE PINE PEAK *12,944'*

Though hordes of people flock to this region for Mt. Whitney, Lone Pine Peak is an equally justified destination. Perched along the front of the range, the arching canyons and rocky ridgelines provide the backdrop for the Alabama Hills. Lone Pine Peak is a coveted Sierra classic, regardless of the time of year. Countless high quality alpine rock climbs ascend nearly every section of rock on this peak, and nestled right in between it all is an equally outstanding ski descent.

The Northeast Canyon of Lone Pine Peak is unlike many of the canyons on the Eastside. Rock slabs replace the talus we are accustomed to, and create a unique geography and feel. They simultaneously create complex terrain riddled with terrain traps that require great care and navigation skills during the winter time.

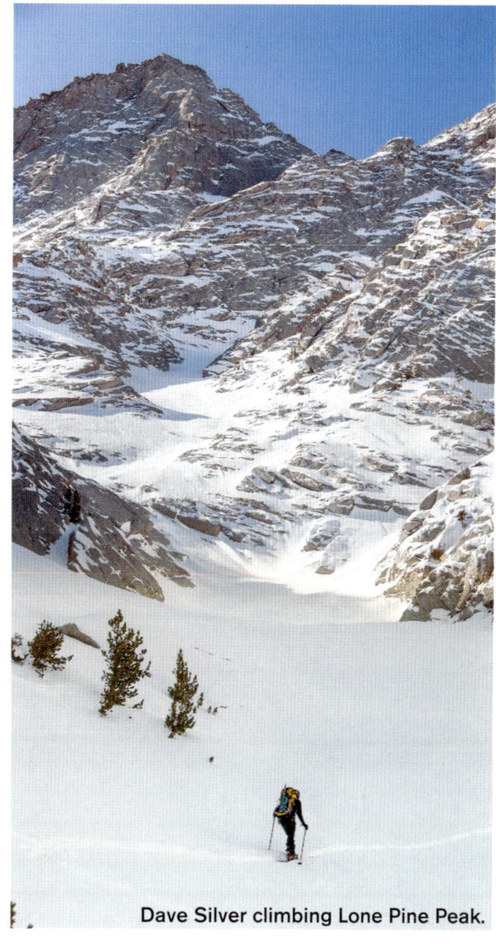
Dave Silver climbing Lone Pine Peak.

Looking west across Lone Pine Peak, at the hidden upper chute of the Northeast Canyon.

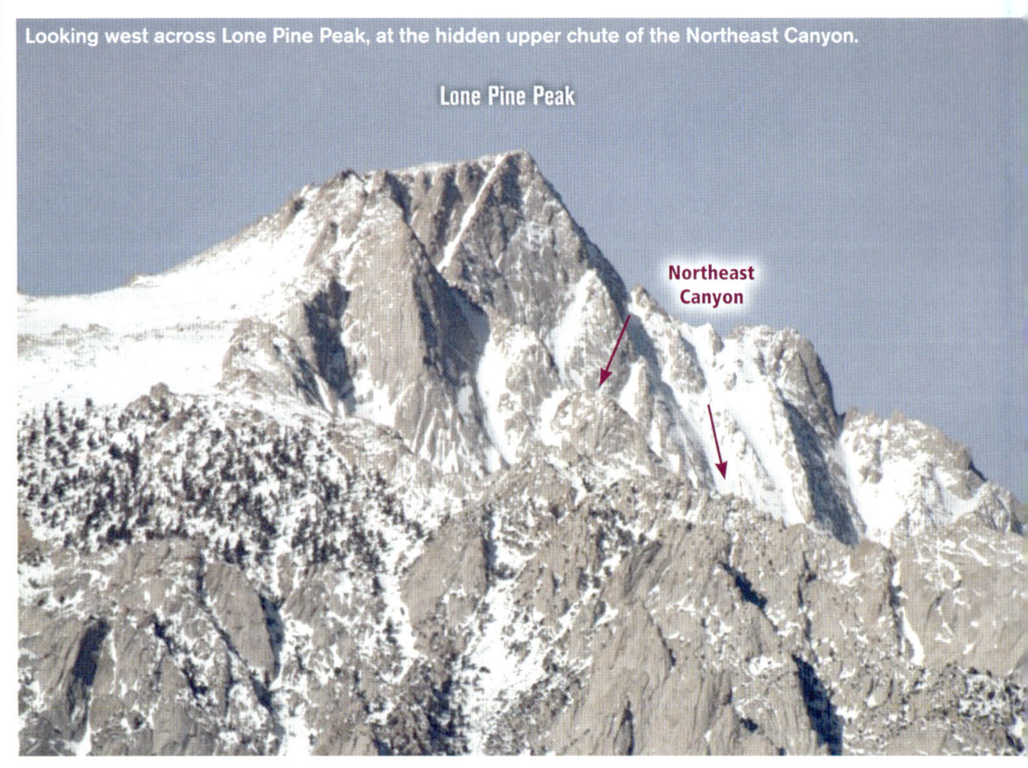

↘ NORTHEAST CANYON

Lone Pine Peak

Aspect	Consequence/Exposure	Slope
	3	40°

Summit Elevation	12,800'
Descent Vertical	4,500'
Total Vertical	5,600'
Hiking Distance	3 miles
Terrain	Gully
Trailhead	52. Whitney Portal Winter Closure
USGS Quad Maps	Mt. Langley
GPS	36.5653 / -118.2262

This large, open canyon is capped by a rock headwall, where just a sliver of snow cuts through to the summit ridge. This upper chute is hidden from view from almost everywhere, and is only barely visible from Highway 395 just to the south of town. As you climb the canyon, most of your day will be spent staring up at the rocky headwall above, causing you to wonder whether you are in the right place or not. But a little faith goes a long way, as the mysterious line that appears steep and narrow from afar reveals itself to be a great little ski descent well off the beaten path.

Approach: From the point of winter closure along Whitney Portal Road (Trailhead #54), continue south along a small dirt road that drops down to the creek. Cross the bridge, then continue along the road for a short distance as it rounds the corner and heads into Inyo Creek. Begin climbing onto the treed slope above you to the west, and as the terrain allows, traverse into the canyon.

Though the canyon walls are steep and often difficult to navigate cleanly, they are far superior to the terrain in the canyon bottom below. It is best to hold a high traverse along the lower section of the canyon, sticking to the west side of the drainage. This is quite possibly one of the more challenging approaches listed in this book, and it is important to allow plenty of time for getting through this section on the way in and out.

Once in the main part of the drainage, travel becomes infinitely easier. Continue up the gradually steepening gully to the base of two chutes that appear in the ridgeline to your right (north). Follow the climber's right of the two to the plateau above, where a short scramble over mellow terrain will deliver you to the summit.

Chris Gallardo riding Mt. Langley.

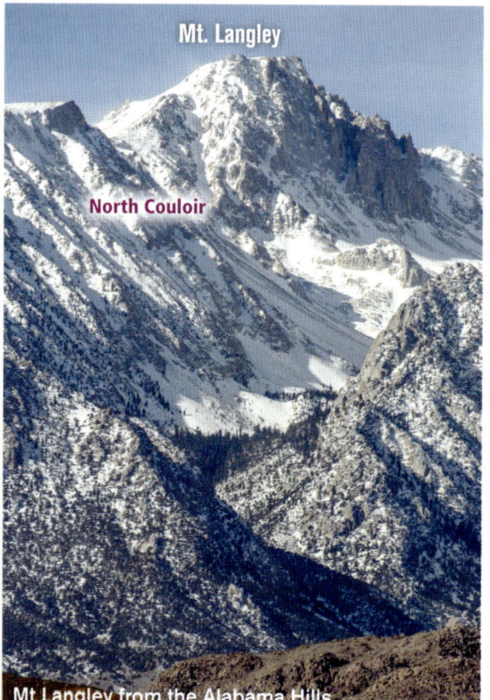

Mt Langley from the Alabama Hills.

△ MT. LANGLEY *14,026*

Marking the unofficial end to the High Sierra, Mt. Langley is the southernmost 14er in the range, and the last of the big peaks around. As you near the top, the view to the south reveals a dramatic difference in terrain. The mountains seem to taper off just past this 14,026' summit. While there are still plenty of peaks and valleys out there, the dramatic summits and ridges that define the range to the north end here.

Langley is also one of the less popular 14ers in the region, and doesn't see nearly the amount of traffic that Whitney's neighboring peaks do. But being one of the more moderate of its class, it does attract winter adventurers, and is certainly a worthy objective.

Chris Gallardo rescues a six pack on his way down from Mt. Langley.

↘ NORTH COULOIR

Mt. Langley

Aspect	Consequence/Exposure	Slope
	3	35°

Summit Elevation	14,026'
Descent Vertical	3,500'
Total Vertical	9,426'
Hiking Distance	9 miles
Terrain	Face, Chute
Trailhead	55. Mt. Langley Trailhead
USGS Quad Maps	Mt. Langley
GPS	36.5229 / -118.2382

The North Couloir of Mt. Langley is an incredible line on a beautiful peak, and is clearly visible from various points along Highway 395 and the Whitney Portal Road. As an added benefit, this line can be skied from almost right off the summit, providing roughly 3,500' of fall line skiing back into Tuttle Creek.

Approach: From the winter location of the Mt. Langley Trailhead (#55), continue west up Granite View Drive past the summer trailhead along an old road. After a short distance, begin to contour and climb to the northwest toward the mouth of Tuttle Creek. As the drainage comes into view, stay high and left (west) on the toe of the slope, and then drop into the drainage when possible. The lower sections of the drainage are quite dense, and are best avoided.

Once in the drainage, continue climbing west past a few benches that eventually give way to the base of the peak where the couloir will come into view above you to the southwest. Climb the couloir, which eventually exits onto the East Ridge. With sufficient coverage, there is another ribbon of snow that continues to the summit.

Exit: Retrace your steps back down Tuttle Creek, taking care to stay out of the bottom of the drainage as you did on the way in.

Index

Nate Greenberg grew up in the mountains, backpacking and skiing throughout the Sierra from a very young age. By the time he graduated college from UC Davis, Nate's was determined to create a life in Mammoth—with the goal of playing as much as possible. Since 2000, Nate has called the Eastern Sierra home, and is committed to building community and helping this region grow. In 2005, along with a group of dedicated individuals, Nate helped form the Eastern Sierra Avalanche Center with the goal of providing winter backcountry users the information they need to make informed decisions and stay safe in avalanche terrain. Today he serves as the Director of Information Technology/GIS Coordinator for Mono County and the Town of Mammoth Lakes, and stays true to his original goal of playing as much as possible in the Eastern Sierra.

Dan Mingori moved to Mammoth in 1999, after 20 years of honing his snowboard skills on the East Coast. It didn't take long for him to determine that the Sierra Nevada possessed the stuff dreams are made of, and he quickly made it home. Married to his snowboard, he spent most of his time at Mammoth Mountain. As he progressed in age, that focus remained the same, but his energy shifted from the chairlifts to the backcountry.

Surrounded by an endless playground of mountains, Dan developed a handful of other hobbies, including a renewed interest in photography. Spending time in the backcountry created ample opportunities to refine his camera skills. He has slowly built a business on that photography, which is what allows him to justify all of the time he "wasted" over the years.

Dan is currently on hiatus away from the Eastern Sierra, and is instead focusing on his wife, child, and cat. But he vows to return soon!